EAVESDROPPING ON TRIAL

EAVESDROPPING ON TRIAL

EDITH J. LAPIDUS, LL.B., Ph.D.

MEMBER, NEW YORK BAR

Political Science Department, Queens College
City University of New York

HAYDEN BOOK COMPANY, INC.

Rochelle Park, New Jersey

Library of Congress Cataloging in Publication Data

Lapidus, Edith J
  Eavesdropping on trial.

  Includes bibliographical references.
  1. Eavesdropping—United States. 2. Wire-tapping
—United States. I. Title.
KF9670.L37   345'.73'052   73-17207

Printed in the United States of America

1   2   3   4   5   6   7   8   9   PRINTING

74 75 76 77 78 79 80 81 82   YEAR

Editorial Helen L. Garfinkle
Design A. Victor Schwarz

Foreword

The history of American liberty has been a continuing struggle between the desire for security and the human striving for personal freedom. Too often it appears that the choice is easy — for example, that the issue of law and order is one of balancing the rights of society against the rights of criminals. But the choice is never as easy as that deceptive formulation suggests. The great challenge of our constitutional system is the continuing reconciliation of these two strong and competing interests. Without law there can be no true liberty, but a constant and exclusive preoccupation with security is the death of human liberty. This was recognized by American patriots as long ago as 1775: "Those who would give up essential Liberty, to purchase a little temporary Safety, deserve neither Liberty nor Safety."

The citizen who truly honors liberty knows that there are no easy choices. The public leader who is true to his obligation to inform and educate the citizenry recognizes that he must shun emotional appeals. It is a great disservice to the public to succumb to the temptation to make issues of crime and liberty a political football. Unfortunately, politicians forever fall victim to the temptation, especially in recent years.

Of the issues of crime and liberty that have arisen in the past decade, one of the most difficult has been the question of wiretapping. It is, in the words of Justice Holmes, "dirty business." To eavesdrop on the private communications of others offends the sensibilities of all but the most callous. Yet a strong case exists for the use of electronic interception in crime fighting and in national security. However distasteful one might find it, the prevailing opinion seems to be that eavesdropping is necessary in law enforcement; it will be conducted legally if possible, but even illegally if necessary. The task, then, for both legislator and citizen is to decide whether to prohibit wiretapping entirely and drive it underground, as it was for so many decades, or to authorize it under specific circumstances and subject it to strict controls.

Whether to authorize wiretapping at all was bitterly fought out in the courts and Congress for decades, and the decision reluctantly reached was that some wiretapping should be legalized. Strong feelings existed then and still persist over that decision. But difficult as that decision was, a far more difficult task remained to define the limits and circumstances of legalized eavesdropping. That process culminated in Title III of the Omnibus Crime Control and Safe Streets Act of 1968.

The mere fact of passing a law never resolves a controversy as fierce as this one. The enactment of the eavesdropping legislation was only a watershed in the continuing debate, reconsideration, and revision. It remains for courts, educators, and others to test the legislation, its strength and weak points, and to keep in the public eye the decisions made and the compromises reached in passage of Title III.

This book is designed to facilitate public understanding of wiretapping and electronic surveillance by describing the legal and practical issues in an objective and factual manner. These issues are too important to be left to the "expert" — be he lawyer, legislator, judge, or prosecutor. While the issues are complex, this is no arcane subject which the private citizen may safely leave to others. Few people are neutral about issues such as eavesdropping, but the public is not well served by rhetoric. As difficult as it may be to address the subject fairly, openly, and accurately, to do so is necessary if the public is to be well served. Certainly, it is necessary to view critically the weaknesses as well as strengths in existing governmental policy. This, Dr. Lapidus has done exceedingly well. While she, like all of us, has strong views on the subject, this book does not seek to impose them on the reader. It is not a brief for prosecutor or civil libertarian. Rather, it seeks to help the reader to understand the issues and to come to a better understanding about them for himself in a readable, nonlegalistic, impartial, and scholarly manner. It is no common achievement for such a complex and controversial subject.

SENATOR SAM J. ERVIN, JR.
Chairman, Subcommittee on Constitutional Rights
Senate Committee on the Judiciary

Preface

This book has a broad and bold objective—to discuss the controversial and technical subject of eavesdropping in language that laymen as well as professionals can understand. It is based on a study of a newly authorized technique in law enforcement to combat crime, and its impact on the right of privacy and freedom in the United States. Specifically, the text examines and evaluates the practical operation of Title III of the Omnibus Crime Control and Safe Streets Act of 1968 in which Congress, for the first time in the history of the United States, authorized wiretapping and electronic surveillance by law enforcement officials.

Legalization of eavesdropping is an innovation in national policy of great interest to students of politics, law, criminology, and the social order, and to law enforcement officials, lawyers, and judges. It should also be a matter of deep concern for every member of American society. The startling revelations of wiretapping, bugging, and break-ins in the Watergate affair have brought a new awareness of intrusions into individual privacy to a large segment of the public. An effort must now be made by every intelligent citizen to understand why eavesdropping received official sanction and how it is working out in practice.

The primary aim of this report on eavesdropping under Title III of the Omnibus Act of 1968 is to stimulate objective appraisal of an important subject that has suffered from professional partisanship and, at least before Watergate, from public indifference. The material has been deliberately designed for a wide audience since eavesdropping—legal or illegal—affects all of us and can be controlled only with full knowledge of what it is all about. We must know what the law says, what it does not say, how government officials have understood their duties and are fulfilling them, how the courts are dealing with legal and practical problems of eavesdropping, and what effect wiretapping and electronic surveillance may have on the quality of life in the United States.

Title III is an attempt to balance the conflict between the individual's right to privacy and society's need for effective law enforcement in the face of rising crime. Achievement of a reasonable equilibrium obviously depends on the clarity of the law, the existence and observance by law enforcement officials of proper standards and guidelines, and scrupulous adherence to the safeguards sought by Title III. It is the thesis of this book that such a balance also requires continuing vigilance by the general public, as well as the experts, as to the operation of the 1968 law. If ambiguities in the law are tolerated, if standards and guidelines are lacking, if Government fails to exercise restraint in eavesdropping, then the "free society" that Americans take for granted may really be in danger, as critics of the 1968 law claim.

To the non-lawyer, legislative history and citations of court decisions can be disturbing interruptions in a fast-moving narrative that tells the story of government eavesdropping in practice. Development of the law, however, must be discussed in a work that aims at full understanding of the subject. Law, as well as practice, has responded to political, social, and technological change.

For some laymen, this book may be an initial encounter with a thorny and tangled subject, requiring patience and effort in understanding the intricacies of official wiretapping and electronic surveillance. If Chapters 1 and 2, which provide the legislative and legal background of eavesdropping, seem formidable and make the going rough, turn to Chapter 4 on organized crime, or to Chapter 6 covering the battle over eavesdropping without court order on political dissidents. Read on to the end, and then return to earlier chapters. They will fall into place and be as readily understood by the intelligent layman as by the lawyer or political scientist. Each chapter can stand on its own.

Consecutive reading of the text is preferable for the professional and for the student of politics, law, and the social aspects of government eavesdropping. Taking Chapters 1 through 10 in chronological order may be more arduous than browsing, but for most readers it will be worth the added effort. The book has been planned to present to the general public a coherent, logical analysis of eavesdropping—in practice and under law—from the invention of the telephone to the discovery of the laser beam, and from an ineffective ban on wiretapping to Congressional sanction of electronic surveillance by Federal and State officials. The results may satisfy neither the opponents nor the adherents of eavesdropping under law, but it is hoped that they may throw some much-needed light on a murky, emotionally charged subject, and help the public to decide whether eavesdropping in practice is an indispensable tool of law enforcement or a grave threat to American society.

This book on government wiretapping and electronic surveillance should be approached with an open mind. No one can afford to be neutral on the subject, but the attempt must be made to be fair and unbiased, to weigh the difficult choices, and to reconcile conflicting interests as far as possible.

EDITH J. LAPIDUS

New York, N.Y.

Acknowledgments

How is one to thank the many friends and acquaintances who transformed a blank and seemingly impenetrable wall into an open door? Attempts at piercing the veil of secrecy that surrounds official eavesdropping can be expected to meet with initial resistance, but even the seasoned researcher is unprepared for the fierce defensiveness of law enforcement officials in shielding from public view the day-to-day process of wiretapping and electronic surveillance. Continued polarization of opinion on government eavesdropping has made cautious individuals wary and suspicious. Patience, persistence, and the kind intercession of others are needed to convince officials that an unbiased approach to the problem is possible, and that eavesdropping in law enforcement must have public understanding and support if it is to survive as a technique to combat crime.

The names of those who gave much time, thought, and information for this project are listed below in alphabetical order to provide a measure of anonymity. Most officials are reluctant to be saddled with public expressions of opinion on specific aspects of government eavesdropping. Some of those who made invaluable contributions must remain unnamed, for they are in the storm center of the controversy over eavesdropping under law.

To the many individuals, named and unnamed, who contributed to this book, the author is greatly indebted and expresses sincere appreciation.

Anderson, Robert L., District Attorney, Plymouth District, Massachusetts.
Ascione, Alfred M., Justice of Supreme Court of the State of New York.
Baer, Harold, Jr., United States Attorney, Southern District of New York.
Blakey, G. Robert, Chief Counsel, Subcommittee on Criminal Laws and Procedures, Senate Committee on the Judiciary.
Bolton, Arthur K., Attorney General of Georgia.
Cahn, William, District Attorney, Nassau County, New York.
Caming, H. W. William, Counsel, American Telephone and Telegraph Co., New York.
Campbell, Donald, United States Attorney, District of Columbia.
Celler, Emanuel, (Dem., N.Y.) House of Representatives, Washington, D.C.
Danziger, Martin B., Law Enforcement Assistance Administration (L.E.A.A.), Organized Crime Unit, Washington, D.C.
DeCastole, Peter, Police Department, New York, N.Y.

Dillon, Denis E., Strike Force, Eastern District of New York, U.S. Department of Justice.

Engler, Robert, Professor, Political Science Department, Graduate Center of the City University of New York.

Fields, Howard, Police Department, New York, N.Y.

Flug, James, Legal Assistant to Senator Edward M. Kennedy, Chairman, Subcommittee on Administrative Practice and Procedure, Senate Committee on the Judiciary.

Gleason, Raymond M., Lieutenant, Police Department, New York, N.Y.

Gold, Eugene, District Attorney, Kings County, New York.

Golden, Elliott, Chief Assistant District Attorney, Kings County, New York.

Greenfield, Aaron, Law Assistant, New York Supreme Court.

Gualtieri, Frank A., District Attorney, Onondaga County, New York.

Halloran, Norbert A., Administrative Office of the United States Courts, Washington, D.C.

Heath, Theresa, Police Department, New York, N.Y.

Hogan, Frank S., District Attorney, New York County, New York.

Holcombe, Jon K., Senior Assistant District Attorney, Onondaga County, New York.

Hollman, Daniel P., Joint Strike Force, Southern District of New York, U.S. Department of Justice.

Jensen, William, Federal Communications Commission, Law and Enforcement Division, Washington, D.C.

Johnson, Russell, Police Department, New York, N.Y.

Juviler, Michael R., Assistant District Attorney, Appeals Bureau, New York County, N.Y.

Kasanof, Robert, Attorney, New York, N.Y.

Kelley, James M., Assistant Attorney General, Minnesota.

Konefsky, Samuel J., (deceased) Professor of Constitutional Law, Brooklyn College of the City University of New York.

Krieger, Albert J., Attorney, New York, N.Y.

Landau, Jack C., (former) Director of Public Information, U.S. Department of Justice, Washington, D.C.

Landynski, Jacob W., New School for Social Research, New York, N.Y.

Levine, George, Assistant District Attorney, Nassau County, New York.

Levy, Norman, Chief of Rackets Bureau, District Attorney, Nassau County, New York.

Mackell, Thomas J., (former) District Attorney, Queens County, New York.

Maltz, Michael, National Institute of Law Enforcement and Criminal Justice, Washington, D.C.

McKenna, William H., Chief of Rackets Bureau, District Attorney, Westchester County, New York.

Modjeska, Lee M., Attorney, Washington, D.C.

Murphy, Tim, Judge of the Court of Special Sessions, District of Columbia, Washington, D.C.

Phillips, James, United States Attorney, U.S. Department of Justice, Washington, D.C.

Reid, Inez, Professor, Political Science Department, Brooklyn College of the City University of New York.

Roberts, Burton B., (former) District Attorney, Bronx County, New York.

Robertson, James, Assistant District Attorney, Queens County, New York.

Robinson, James, United States Attorney, U.S. Department of Justice, General Crimes Section, Criminal Division, Washington, D.C.

Rosenblatt, Albert M., District Attorney, Dutchess County, New York.

Rosenthal, Benjamin S., (Dem., N.Y.) House of Representatives, Washington, D.C.

Rotker, Seymour, Assistant District Attorney, Bronx County, New York.

Ruff, Charles, United States Attorney, U.S. Department of Justice, Washington, D.C.

Saraniero, Anthony, Police Department, New York, N.Y.

Schweitzer, Mitchell D., (retired) Justice of Supreme Court of State of New York.

Scotti, Alfred J., Chief Assistant District Attorney, New York County, New York.

Speiser, Lawrence, American Civil Liberties Union, Washington, D.C.

Spinnato, Joseph E., Assistant District Attorney, Nassau County, New York.

Umin, Steven M., attorney in office of Edward Bennett Williams, Washington, D.C

Uviller, Richard, Professor, Columbia University School of Law, New York, N.Y.

Vergari, Carl, District Attorney, Westchester County, New York.

Vitrano, Paul, Chief of Detective Squad, Police Department, New York, N.Y.

Wulf, Melvin L., Legal Director, American Civil Liberties Union, New York, N.Y.

Zuckerman, Roger E., United States Attorney, U.S. Department of Justice, Washington, D.C.

Contents

EAVESDROPPING ON TRIAL

1

Conflict and Controversy in Eavesdropping

In June 1968, for the first time in the history of the United States, Congress sanctioned wiretapping and electronic surveillance by law enforcement officials. By an overwhelming vote in the Senate (72 to 4) and in the House of Representatives (368 to 17), it enacted the Omnibus Crime Control and Safe Streets Act, including Title III authorizing government eavesdropping. One of the avowed purposes of this novel law was to combat organized crime. Federal and state officials were empowered to intercept wire and oral communications under specified conditions, with safeguards designed to protect the right of privacy. Eavesdropping by private individuals was banned. "Law and order" was to be restored to balance with liberty.

Title III is a complex and controversial law on which the opinion among both professionals and laymen continues to be sharply divided. Proponents of government eavesdropping insist that it is essential if law enforcement officials are to deal effectively with organized crime and serious offenses. Critics charge that it is an unconstitutional invasion of privacy, a threat to liberty, and ineffective in law enforcement; that the law has been applied in a discriminatory manner and diverted to political purposes, and that it is leading the nation into a police state. Others complain that the safeguards sought to be provided by Title III are inadequate; that many of its terms and clauses are ambiguous; that State and Federal officials are misinterpreting some provisions and failing to carry out others.

Time has sharpened the controversy over eavesdropping, not dulled it. Emotions run high on the subject and rhetoric often displaces reason. The public, confused by conflicting contentions, is uncertain and uneasy. Whose wires are being tapped? By whom and for what purpose, and how often? Does the average, law-abiding citizen who minds his own business have any cause for concern that his private conversations may be overheard? Is government eavesdropping necessary and is it tolerable in a free, democratic society?

Widespread fear of crime induced Congress to legalize official eavesdropping in the interest of "law and order." The resulting threat to privacy impelled the legislators to impose limitations and prescribe detailed procedures. The 1968 Act sought to balance the need of society for law enforcement and safety against the right of the individual to his constitutional liberties. Could a balance be achieved? Is it being achieved? Are law enforcement officials complying with the safeguards provided by Title III, or is the law so complex and ambiguous that compliance with its requirements is impossible?

There is a feeling afoot in the United States today that official eavesdropping may be getting out of hand. Public uneasiness has been heightened by disclosures of wiretapping and bugging that resulted in dismissal of the Pentagon Papers trial of Russo and Ellsberg and in Congressional investigation of the Watergate affair. "Big Brother" is listening and George Orwell may have been more prophetic than imaginative when he envisaged pervasive surveillance by 1984. The average individual jokes about wiretapping when he hears a click on his telephone, but his laugh is getting nervous.

This study of legalized wiretapping and electronic surveillance examines the politics of "law and order" and the fear of crime in the shadow of which the eavesdropping statute was enacted in 1968, and sifts through the technical verbiage of the law. It describes how the provisions of Title III have been interpreted in practice, and gives an account in plain language of the day-to-day procedures developed at the Federal and State level. Its general theme can be stated simply, although the implications may be vast and thorny: that ambiguities in the law encourage varied interpretations and prevent uniform and sound exercise of a governmental power that has great potential for abuse; that public understanding and support must be enlisted to urge clarification by Congress or the courts and to press for greater care and restraint in use of official wiretapping and electronic surveillance. Title III is not merely a law enforcement measure; it is a political judgment that cannot stand unless it is shared by the three branches of government and accepted by the people of the United States.

The practical operation of Title III since 1968 must serve as a focus in any evaluation of government eavesdropping under law, for this is what will determine whether or not it is an intolerable threat to the fabric of American society. However, law and procedure are so interwoven in problems of wiretapping and electronic surveillance and their conflict with the right to privacy, that a look at legislative, executive, and judicial action on the subject is also needed, to understand what is going on and why. Practical problems were scarcely considered by Congress in enacting Title III, for many of them could not be foreseen. They have been exposed gradually as key clauses are put into effect by Federal and State officials.

Title III, in theory and practice, has raised troubling problems for the Government and the people, as well as for its intended targets. The facts of eavesdropping under law, as presented here, are drawn largely from official documents, reported cases, extensive interviews, and questionnaires. Law enforcement officials of various persuasions were selected by the author for questioning—those who favored eavesdropping strongly and used it extensively; those who disliked it and employed it moderately and reluctantly; and those who felt that Title III was so restrictive that it was hardly serviceable. Judges, lawyers, and others consulted also differed in their personal attitudes toward government eavesdropping. All were aware, in varying degrees, of the many problems presented by Title III and were groping for solutions. This is a starting point in providing some practical answers.

The Meaning of Eavesdropping

The late Supreme Court Justice Hugo L. Black, who saw no reason why eavesdropping should not be used as a law enforcement technique, observed philosophically that the practice has undoubtedly gone on since the beginning of human society. He defined eavesdropping as:

> Listening secretly and sometimes "snoopily" to conversations and discussions believed to be private by those who engage in them.[1]

Surreptitious overhearing of conversations is an old pastime with a purpose. In the eighteenth century the great English jurist and legal commentator, Sir William Blackstone, characterized eavesdroppers as:

> Such as listen under walls or windows, or the eaves of a house, to hearken after discourse, and thereupon to frame slanderous and mischievous tales.[2]

Today, eavesdropping is done in more sophisticated fashion with the aid of electronics, and an intent to slander is usually not its primary aim.

In common parlance, the term "eavesdropping" includes both wiretapping and electronic surveillance (popularly known as "bugging"). Wiretapping is the interception of telephone calls and normally involves a physical entry into a telephone circuit. It has been going on since the telephone was invented in the late nineteenth century. "Bugging"—the listening in on conversations in a given area by means of electronic devices without penetrating into a wire—is of more recent origin. Both types of surveillance have become highly developed with the advance of technology since World War II, and increasingly hard to detect. Modern techniques of eavesdropping sometimes make it difficult to tell where wiretapping leaves off and electronic surveillance begins. As one expert explained it:

All telephones have wires; some miniature listening devices too. In both wiretapping and bugging the intercepted dialogue is usually recorded on magnetic tape . . . the technique of the one is sometimes performed by the instruments of the other . . . a telephone may be made to function as a clandestine listening device . . . portions of the telephone system may be used to transmit face-to-face dialogue . . . bugs can be concealed within telephone instruments.[3]

Sophisticated electronic devices can intercept any wire or oral communication, under proper conditions. This is a far cry from listening under windows with the naked ear, according to Justice William O. Douglas of the Supreme Court, a critic of government eavesdropping:

What the ancients knew as "eavesdropping" we now 'call "electronic surveillance"; but to equate the two is to treat man's first gunpowder on the same level as the nuclear bomb.[4]

Another Supreme Court Justice, William A. Brennan, likewise noted that electronic aids add a wholly new dimension to eavesdropping:

They make it more penetrating, more indiscriminate, more truly obnoxious to a free society.[5]

New dimensions in electronic eavesdropping can be expected. Video tape has already made its appearance; at least two court orders authorizing eavesdropping provided for the use of this device. Sophisticated listening instruments are now being developed that can tap a television set with installation of two-way cable television. Experts warn that cabletapping can become as great a threat as wiretapping:

Without your knowledge they could listen to and record the programs you watch, your transactions with department stores and banks, and even your living room conversations.[6]

Title III of the Omnibus Crime Control and Safe Streets Act of 1968 does not use the term "eavesdropping" nor does it legalize wiretapping and electronic surveillance directly. It *prohibits* "interception of wire and oral communications" *with certain exceptions,* and defines such communications. The exceptions include designated Federal and State officials who are authorized to intercept wire and oral communications in certain cases if they comply with procedures detailed in the law. The heart of this procedure is the obtaining of a *court order* authorizing the eavesdropping, similar to a warrant for search and seizure. In some instances, eavesdropping is permitted *without* court order.

Congress employed the words "wire and oral communication" in Title III to cover both wiretapping and bugging without fusing the two forms of surveillance. The distinction between them may, however, assume some importance in determining the power of Congress to regulate under the "commerce clause" of the United States Constitution.[7] Federal control of wiretapping under national authority over interstate commerce is clear, but some forms of electronic surveillance may conceivably elude national supervision.[8] If the electronic device uses the telephone, although it is not a wiretap, the "commerce clause" would seem to give the Federal government power to regulate, for the telephone communication network crosses state lines. Similarly, if a wireless radio transmitter is used, it may fall within the power of Congress to regulate. A homemade bugging device, however, such as a microphone, nontelephone wire, or tape recorder that operates locally, may involve a purely *intra*state activity that is outside the scope of Federal restrictions.

Court-Ordered Eavesdropping

The safeguards to individual privacy sought to be provided by Title III consist of requiring a court order before a government official may intercept a wire or oral communication. A judge is to decide whether or not an order shall be issued, and the interception is subject to supervision by him. Title III lists a wide variety of offenses for which a court order may be obtained, the Federal officers who may apply for a court order, the judges to whom applications must be presented, and the necessary findings by the judge of "probable cause" on which orders are to be based. State officials may also apply for court orders to eavesdrop provided the particular State enacts a law conforming to Title III.

An order may be granted for a period not exceeding thirty days, with an indefinite number of renewals. Notice of the interception must be given to the persons named in the order or application, and to others in the discretion of the judge, within ninety days after termination. Judges and prosecuting officials are required to file reports on each order with the Administrative Office of the United States Courts in Washington, D.C., and this agency, in turn, must file an annual report with Congress.

Heavy penalties are provided for violations of Title III: imprisonment up to five years and a fine of $10,000 or both. Civil damages are also recoverable—actual damages but not less than liquidated damages computed at the rate of $100 a day for each day of violation, or $1,000, whichever is higher; punitive damages and counsel fees and other litigation costs are also recoverable. Conversations intercepted unlawfully are barred from introduction in evidence.

These seemingly simple provisions for court-ordered eavesdropping by government officials have raised some difficult questions and generated much heated discussion. Does Title III actually permit eavesdropping in investigating *any* offense, without limitation as to the nature of the crime? Is the group of officials who may apply for an order too broad for safety? Can applicants go "judge-shopping?" Is the period for interception too long? How is it possible to avoid overhearing many innocent conversations or privileged communications, such as those between doctor and patient, lawyer and client? Is notice required to be given only to the person named in an order or application, regardless of whose conversations were overheard? What purposes are the reports intended to serve and do they fulfill their function? Each of these questions must be considered in detail to determine whether it is true, as some critics claim, that Title III allows "too many people to listen in on too many conversations for too long a time in too many types of cases." [9]

Eavesdropping without Court Order

In addition to court-ordered eavesdropping, the Federal law permits wiretapping and electronic surveillance by government officials *without* court order in two broad types of cases: (1) during a forty-eight-hour emergency, and (2) to protect national security, under authority of the President.

Emergency situations are described as involving two types of conspiratorial activity: (1) threatening national security, and (2) characteristic of organized crime. Emergency eavesdropping may be carried on for forty-eight hours by "any investigative or law enforcement officer" who may be specially designated by the Attorney General of the United States, or by the chief prosecuting attorney of any State or subdivision acting under a State statute. All conditions necessary for issuance of a court order must be present before emergency surveillance begins, and application may be made for *subsequent* judicial approval. If no application is made or if an application for a court order is denied, the eavesdropping is considered to be in violation of Title III. The District of Columbia and the State of New Jersey have provided for forty-eight-hour emergency eavesdropping. In New York, it was proposed but rejected.

The emergency clause has been widely attacked as vague, open to abuse, and unconstitutional. The term "national security" is not defined, and the law does not indicate what offenses are "characteristic of organized crime." No report is required to be filed of an emergency surveillance without court order, and there is no way for the public to know how much of it has been going on.

In addition to the emergency clause, exemption from court-order requirements is provided for national security related eavesdropping undertaken "by authority of the President." Title III declares that nothing in the Act shall limit the constitutional power of the President to take measures that he deems necessary:

1. To protect the Nation against actual or potential attack or other hostile acts of a foreign power;

2. To obtain foreign intelligence information deemed essential to the security of the United States; or

3. To protect national security information against foreign intelligence activities.

Nor is any limitation to be placed on the constitutional power of the President to protect the United States against: (1) overthrow of the government by force or other unlawful means, or (2) any other clear and present danger to the structure or existence of the Government. Interception without court order must, however, be "reasonable," if the communications seized are to be received in evidence in any trial, hearing, or other proceeding.

Eavesdropping without court order in "national security" cases under presidential authority raised a storm of protest that has not yet fully subsided. Many who were ready to accept official wiretapping and electronic surveillance to combat crime if an order was first obtained found the provision dispensing with judicial sanction highly ambiguous and unconstitutional. Denunciations increased in bitterness when the Attorney General of the United States, John N. Mitchell, declared that "national security" may involve threats from *domestic* groups, as well as from foreign powers, and it was revealed that Federal agencies had tapped the phones of political dissidents without court order. President Nixon characterized the reaction of the public as "hysteria" and "political demagoguery," and Lewis F. Powell, Jr., before his appointment to the United States Supreme Court, called it "a tempest in a teapot." [10] On June 19, 1972, however, the United States Supreme Court rejected the Government's claim by a vote of 8 to 0. [11] The opinion of the Court, written by Justice Powell, declared that presidential authority to protect the nation does not give the Government power to tap without court order the wires of domestic radicals who have "no significant connection with a foreign power, its agents, or agencies." This landmark Supreme Court decision, its limitations, and the impact it may have on policy and practice are discussed in Chapter 6.

Privacy and Freedom

One of the avowed purposes of Title III of the Omnibus Act of 1968 was to protect the privacy of individuals by banning eavesdropping other than by duly authorized law enforcement officers who complied with the safeguards provided by the law. Much has been written in recent years about the nature of privacy and its function in a democratic system. Privacy is a cornerstone of the American ideal of liberty and a vital element in a "free society." The American system limits governmental power and presumably places a high value on the privacy of the individual.

Privacy has been defined as "the claim of individuals, groups, or institutions to determine for themselves when, how, and to what extent information about them is communicated to others." Put more simply, privacy is "control over knowledge about oneself." In relation to official eavesdropping, privacy is "the right to be left alone by government."[12] Some governmental intrusion into private lives is inevitable in wiretapping and electronic surveillance. The question is: Does Title III in actual practice provide adequate safeguards against *undue* invasion of privacy, that is, beyond the limits tolerable in a "free" society.

Critics of Title III claim that the protections provided are inadequate and that legalized eavesdropping jeopardizes privacy and freedom as we have known it for 200 years. The danger is aggravated, they say, because information gathered by the Government is fed into computers. Congressional hearings conducted under the leadership of Senator Sam J. Ervin, Jr. have revealed that vast amounts of data about individuals, some of it inaccurate and highly personal, find their way into "data banks" which are open to misuse and present a grave threat to freedom. Besides, the sanctioning of eavesdropping in some instances encourages illegal wiretapping and electronic surveillance.

Freedom in the United States is rooted in the protection of basic rights guaranteed by the Constitution. Most important among these are the right to be secure against unreasonable search and seizure under the Fourth Amendment, and the right to freedom of speech and association under the First Amendment. Opponents of government eavesdropping charge that interception of conversations by wiretapping and electronic surveillance violates the strictures of the Fourth Amendment, and that it has a "chilling effect" on freedom of thought and expression under the First Amendment.

These objections raise serious constitutional issues with subtle social and political overtones that call for wide public discussion. Some constitutional experts fear that our freedoms under the Bill of Rights are in jeopardy and that the American people have "lost some of the vigilance that we have traditionally exercised in defending our sacred rights."[13] If individual privacy and freedom are to be saved without undermining the safety of society, laymen as well as the professionals must take the time and exert the effort to understand government eavesdropping under law and make certain that it is kept within bounds.

Organized Crime

Best-selling novels, prize-winning movies, and sundry TV programs have made "organized crime" a household word in the United States, and perhaps even endeared it to a large segment of the American population.

There is something appealing about the hood who makes good, and in the game of cops and robbers the traditional "good guys" are not always depicted as lily-white. In law enforcement, however, organized crime is an overwhelming problem on which justification for government eavesdropping may ultimately depend. The rationale for official wiretapping under Title III was and still is claimed to be the need to combat "organized crime." This persistent phenomenon in American life must, therefore, be stripped of sentimentality and scrutinized coldly.

What is organized crime? Does it actually exist? What are its roots, ethnic composition, activities, structure, effect on the economy? Does it have its own code of ethics, a formal mode of operation? Is it true that organized crime has ties with legitimate business and inevitably corrupts public officials? These questions will be considered later in detail, but the general premise is accepted that organized crime does exist, that it is not confined to any one ethnic group, that it engages in any activity that promises to yield substantial profits. It can also be conceded that organized crime tends to corrupt public officials, and that it poses an enormously troublesome task in law enforcement.

Organized crime is not defined in Title III of the Omnibus Crime Control and Safe Streets Act of 1968. Title I of the Act [Part F, Sec. 601(b)], however, states that:

> "Organized crime" means the unlawful activities of the members of a highly organized, disciplined association engaged in supplying illegal goods and services, including but not limited to gambling, prostitution, loan sharking, narcotics, labor racketeering, and other unlawful activities of members of such organizations.

This is a descriptive or functional definition, rather than a legal one. No accepted legal definition of organized crime has as yet been formulated. A descriptive definition that is often quoted is that adopted in New York State by the Oyster Bay Conference on Combating Crime at its May 1965 meeting:

> The product of a self-perpetuating criminal conspiracy to wring exorbitant profits from our society by any means—fair and foul, legal and illegal. . . . It survives on fear and corruption . . . obtains a high degree of immunity from the law . . . is totalitarian in its organization . . . imposes rigid discipline on underlings who do the dirty work while the top men of organized crime are generally insulated from the criminal act and the consequent danger of prosecution.[14]

A detailed description of organized crime and its activities also appears in the Report of the President's Commission on Law Enforcement and Administration of Justice issued in 1967.[15] An eminent sociologist and expert on organized crime, Donald R. Cressey, has offered the following organizational definition reflecting concern with the corrupting influence and violence characteristic of organized crime:

> An organized crime is any crime committed by a person occupying, in an established division of labor, a position designed for the commission of crime, providing that such division of labor also includes at least one position for a corrupter, one position for a corruptee, and one position for an enforcer.[16]

Legislators have been urged to enlist the aid of organization specialists and systems analysts to formulate a workable definition of organized crime. A Canadian critic of American efforts to deal with organized crime defines it simply as "the application of corporate principles to the business of crime."[17] This is a damnatory definition, accepting what others have intimated, that there is much similarity between organized crime and legitimate business.

One of the most frequent complaints regarding official eavesdropping under Title III is that the law has been diverted from the pursuit of organized crime; that it is used largely against petty gamblers and small-time narcotics peddlers; that in any event no amount of wiretapping can catch the "big-shots" of organized crime. This strikes at the heart of the conflict and controversy over government eavesdropping, for if the law is not fulfilling its avowed purpose, then official intrusion into privacy cannot and will not be tolerated by the American public.

2
Four Decades of
Indecision: 1928–1968

Legislative and Executive Proposals

Advances in technology since World War II have increased the ease with which private conversations can be overheard by wiretapping and electronic surveillance, and encouraged eavesdropping by public officials and private individuals. Legislators have been responding to public concern over these invasions of privacy for some time. Over the past few decades Congressional committees have conducted investigations periodically on eavesdropping and invasion of privacy. Between 1934 and 1967 at least sixteen sets of Congressional hearings were held, aimed largely at filling the gaps and blocking loopholes in existing Federal law *banning* eavesdropping.[1]

Until passage of the Omnibus Crime Control and Safe Streets Act of 1968, the only Federal statute on the subject was Section 605 of the Federal Communications Act of 1934. This section, prohibiting interception *and* divulgence of conversations, dealt only with wiretapping, and the ban had proved largely ineffective. The United States Department of Justice had construed Sec. 605 to mean that a violation occurred only if the intercepted conversation was divulged to outsiders, and the issue was never decided by the United States Supreme Court. No Federal law regulating electronic surveillance existed prior to 1968, although surreptitious listening was widely frowned upon as an invasion of privacy and often labeled "dirty business."

Until the 1960s, Congress seemed more inclined to *ban* eavesdropping entirely, rather than to permit it even under limited conditions. It repeatedly rejected proposals initiated by the Executive to legalize wiretapping and electronic surveillance by Federal agencies. In 1954 under the Eisenhower Administration, Attorney General Herbert Brownell proposed a bill to permit wiretapping in national security prosecutions, and to make the evidence obtained admissible in court. The bill was directed against subversives, not organized crime. It passed the House of Representatives, but was defeated in the Senate.[2]

Eavesdropping to combat organized crime was urged for the first time in 1961 when the Kennedy Administration endorsed a proposal to authorize Federal agencies to wiretap in cases of national security, organized crime, and other serious crimes. Highly publicized hearings had been begun in 1961 before the Permanent Subcommittee on Investigations headed by Senator John L. McClellan (Democrat of Arkansas), of the Senate Committee on Government Operations. Congress took no action on the 1961 proposal, and the following year the Kennedy Administration sent another bill to Congress authorizing Federal wiretapping in cases of national security, organized crime, and other serious crimes. Congress again took no action. The Administration bill was reintroduced in the Senate in 1963, but it died in the Senate Committee on the Judiciary. This was the year of the televised hearings before the Subcommittee on Investigations in which an underworld informant, Joseph Valachi, described to a nationwide audience the operations of a crime syndicate. In its report on the Valachi hearings in 1965, the Senate Government Operations Committee asked for legislation to authorize wiretapping.[3]

Despite repeated refusals of Congress to legalize eavesdropping, over sixty executive agencies were reported to have extensive electronic monitoring hardware which they used in investigations. The Internal Revenue Service of the Treasury Department conducted a seven-week course for agents in electronic eavesdropping, installing microphones, and monitoring calls.[4] The Department of Justice in 1962 created an Organized Crime Division and authorized investigations to be made by use of electronic equipment.

Pressure on Congress to authorize eavesdropping increased in the 1960s for various reasons: (1) growth of the crime problem; (2) reaction to judicial and legislative efforts to curtail unlawful police practices; and (3) technological advances that made eavesdropping less expensive as a law enforcement tool.[5] In 1967 hearings were held before the Subcommittee on Criminal Laws and Procedures, Senate Committee on the Judiciary, on "Controlling Crime Through More Effective Law Enforcement," under the chairmanship of Senator McClellan. A bill was introduced by the Senator, designated S 675, permitting eavesdropping pursuant to presidential order for national security purposes, and where authorized by court order in investigation or prosecution of certain crimes. In the House of Representatives, the Committee on the Judiciary and its Subcommittee No. 5 considered a similar bill, H.R. 10037. This was introduced by Representative William McCulloch (Republican of Ohio), ranking minority member of the House Judiciary Committee. H.R. 10037, like S 675, permitted the use of wiretap and electronic surveillance by law enforcement agencies of Federal and State governments in specific categories of criminal cases under court control. A bill identical with the McCulloch Bill was introduced in the

Senate as S 2050 by Senator Roman L. Hruska (Republican of Nebraska) on June 29, 1967.

While Congress was being urged to *authorize* eavesdropping in order to combat crime, counterpressures to *ban* it in order to protect privacy continued. Congressional concern with invasions of privacy grew in the 1960s with revelations of widespread tapping and bugging by private and public eavesdroppers. Between 1964 and 1967 hearings on invasion of privacy were held before the Subcommittee on Administrative Practice and Procedure of the Senate Judiciary Committee under the chairmanship of Senator Edward V. Long (Democrat of Missouri). A huge record was amassed by the Committee containing examples of electronic surveillance, wiretapping, and other forms of intrusion.[6] Hearings in a Special Inquiry on Invasion of Privacy were also held in 1965 before a subcommittee of the House Committee on Government Operations under Representative Cornelius E. Gallagher (Democrat of New Jersey).

The outcome of these extensive hearings on invasion of privacy was a bill entitled "The Right of Privacy Act of 1967" introduced in the Senate by Senator Long as S 928 and referred to the Committee on the Judiciary. A similar bill, H.R. 5386, was presented in the House of Representatives by Representative Emanuel Celler (Democrat of New York), Chairman of the House Committee on the Judiciary and its Subcommittee No. 5. In these twin proposals, use of eavesdropping devices without the consent of at least one of the parties to the conversation was *prohibited* except in national security cases. The proposed ban on eavesdropping was approved by the Johnson Administration. The President, in his State of the Union Message of 1967, had said:

> We should protect what Justice Brandeis called the "right most valued [by] civilized men"—the right to privacy. We should outlaw all wiretapping, public and private . . . except when the security of the nation itself is at stake and only then with the strictest safeguards. We should exercise the full reach of our constitution[al] powers to outlaw electronic "bugging" and "snooping."[7]

His Attorney General, Ramsey Clark, publicly endorsed the prohibition against eavesdropping on the ground that it was "neither effective nor highly productive."[8] With respect to wiretapping, the 1967 Right of Privacy bills went far beyond the restrictions then contained in Sec. 605 of the Federal Communications Act of 1934. As to electronic surveillance, the proposed law sought Federal prohibition through legislation for the first time in the history of the United States.

While Congress and the Executive grappled with the problem of whether to ban or to authorize limited eavesdropping, pressures on the Executive to meet the problem of rising crime continued. An Executive

Order issued on July 23, 1965 created a President's Commission on Law Enforcement and Administration of Justice to examine "every facet of crime and law enforcement in America" and to make recommendations to the President on ways to combat crime. This Commission issued its general report, "The Challenge of Crime in a Free Society," in February 1967. Included in the report was a special Task Force Report on Organized Crime in which a divided commission took a position on eavesdropping contrary to that of the President and the Attorney General: A majority of the members recommended legislation *permitting* eavesdropping by law enforcement officers. Pending in the United States Supreme Court at the time the Commission's report was released was the case of *Berger v. New York* involving the constitutionality of the New York law authorizing court-ordered eavesdropping.[9] Since 1938, the Constitution of the State of New York has permitted interception of wire communications under court order, and orders are obtainable under procedures outlined in the New York Code of Criminal Procedure. The President's Commission acknowledged that the decision of the United States Supreme Court on the New York eavesdropping law would be controlling:

> A majority of the members of the Commission believe that legislation should be enacted granting carefully circumscribed authority for electronic surveillance to law enforcement officers . . . consistent with the decision of the Supreme Court in *Berger v. New York*. . . . The other members . . . have serious doubts about the desirability of such authority and believe that there is insufficient basis to strike this balance against the interests of privacy.[10]

Minority members of the Commission denounced official eavesdropping and charged that the majority had made its decision to recommend it on ideological rather than factual grounds.

Four months after the President's Commission made its Report, the United States Supreme Court handed down its decision in *Berger*, declaring the New York eavesdropping law to be unconstitutional on its face. The opinion of the majority was delivered by Justice Tom C. Clark, father of Attorney General Ramsey Clark who favored enactment of the "Right of Privacy Act of 1967" banning eavesdropping and later opposed passage of Title III of the Omnibus Act of 1968 permitting eavesdropping by law enforcement officials. Dissenting in *Berger*, Justice White prophesied:

> Our decision can be expected to have a substantial impact on current legislative consideration of these issues.[11]

After the *Berger* decision, hearings continued before the Subcommittee on Criminal Laws and Procedures under Senator McClellan on "Controlling Crime Through Effective Law Enforcement." Those who opposed government eavesdropping interpreted the Supreme Court's opinion in *Berger* as a declaration that all wiretapping and electronic surveillance are constitutionally impermissible. Others who favored eavesdropping as a law enforcement technique read *Berger* as an invitation to Congress to fashion a law permitting wiretapping and electronic surveillance, with safeguards to protect constitutional liberties. Under consideration by the Senate Subcommittee were various proposals to authorize eavesdropping, including S 675 introduced by Senator McClellan and S 2050 proposed by Senator Hruska. These two bills formed the basis for Title III of the Omnibus Crime Control and Safe Streets Act of 1968 sanctioning government eavesdropping under specified conditions. Congress had come to a decision after decades of wavering and contentious wrangling.

The Supreme Court and Eavesdropping

Two landmark decisions on eavesdropping were rendered by the United States Supreme Court in 1967. One was *Berger v. New York*, already mentioned, and the other was *Katz v. United States*.[12] In *Berger*, the Court held that the New York law permitting court-ordered eavesdropping was unconstitutional on its face because it was too broad in its sweep and violated the Fourth and Fourteenth Amendments to the United States Constitution. In *Katz*, eavesdropping was declared to be a "search and seizure," subject to the restrictions contained in the Fourth Amendment. These two cases were the culmination of a slow and tortuous development during the past four decades of constitutional law on wiretapping, electronic surveillance, search and seizure, and the right of privacy. *Katz* involved only electronic surveillance, not wiretapping, but in this case the Court made no distinction between the two types of eavesdropping. Before *Katz*, the Court treated wiretapping and bugging separately, not for technological reasons but because the only Federal law on the subject (Sec. 605 of the Federal Communications Act of 1934) prohibited only wiretapping.[13] Bugging had been outlawed by decisions of the Supreme Court (discussed later in this chapter) prior to *Katz* only if there was a physical intrusion into a constitutionally protected area. In *Berger*, the Supreme Court used the term "eavesdropping," following the New York statute under consideration.

The Supreme Court is now being asked to decide whether all or any part of Title III is unconstitutional; whether the safeguards provided by Title III and put into practice by law enforcement officials are adequate to protect privacy and freedom from unreasonable search and seizure under the Fourth Amendment; whether wiretapping and electronic surveillance by government officials have a "chilling effect" on freedom of expression as guaranteed by the First Amendment. These questions are being raised in State and Federal courts, and litigants are pressing for answers.

To put into focus the constitutional and practical problems created by Title III and form some basis for predicting how the Supreme Court may deal with them, it is necessary to consider separately the leading decisions of the Court since 1928 on wiretapping, electronic surveillance, search and seizure, and privacy. Some of these pronouncements of the Court will have to be taken into account in current litigation attacking the validity of Title III. *Berger* and *Katz* merit detailed analysis, for they are of great significance in determining the constitutionality of Title III and the acceptability of eavesdropping practices and procedures developed under the law. In sanctioning government eavesdropping, Congress indicated that it was complying with Supreme Court decisions in *Berger* and *Katz*. Critics of the law claim that compliance has not been achieved.

The Wiretapping Cases

The Prohibition Era brought the first case on wiretapping to the United States Supreme Court in *Olmstead v. United States*, decided in 1928.[14] Federal agents tapped the telephone of Roy Olmstead, suspected head of a large bootlegging operation in the State of Washington. Olmstead had been a lieutenant in the Police Department of Seattle, but lost his job after pleading guilty to a charge of smuggling liquor. Thereafter he devoted himself to developing an elaborate organization that supplied liquor illegally to the best hotels and restaurants in Seattle, with the alleged cooperation of the mayor and the police. Several Seattle policemen were indicted with Olmstead for conspiring to violate the Federal liquor and tariff laws, and tried in the United States District Court. A statute of the State of Washington made it a crime to intercept a message over a telephone or telegraph line, but the trial court ruled that the wiretap evidence of Olmstead's bootlegging operations was admissible. The jury brought in a verdict of guilty, and the conviction was affirmed by the United States Court of Appeals.

The United States Supreme Court, by a vote of 5 to 4, upheld Olmstead's conviction. The majority opinion was written by Chief Justice Taft, reputed to be a teetotaler. Wiretapping, said the Court, did *not* amount to a search and seizure within the meaning of the Fourth Amendment; no *physical* intrusion had occurred:

> The Amendment [Fourth] does not forbid what was done here. There was no searching. There was no seizure. The evidence was secured by the use of the sense of hearing and that only. There was no entry of the houses or offices of the defendants.[15]

Justice Brandeis wrote a strong dissenting opinion. He argued that the protection guaranteed by the Fourth Amendment was much broader in scope than the majority claimed, and made an eloquent plea in behalf of the right of privacy that has become a classic statement of the relation between government and the individual:

> The makers of our Constitution . . . sought . . . to protect Americans in their beliefs, their thoughts, their emotions and their sensations. They conferred, as against the government, the right to be let alone . . . the most comprehensive of rights and the right most valued by civilized men. To protect that right, every unjustifiable intrusion by the government upon the privacy of the individual, whatever the means employed, must be deemed a violation of the Fourth Amendment. And the use, as evidence in a criminal proceeding, of facts ascertained by such intrusion must be deemed a violation of the Fifth.[16]

Justice Holmes, also dissenting in *Olmstead*, called wiretapping "dirty business" and expressed the view that it is "a less evil that some criminals should escape than that the government should play an ignoble part." [17]

The majority of the Court in *Olmstead* recognized the fact that Congress could protect the secrecy of telephone messages by making them, if intercepted, inadmissible in Federal criminal trials, but no such Federal law existed at the time. Six years after the decision, Congress passed the Federal Communications Act of 1934, Sec. 605 of which provided that "no person not being authorized by the sender shall intercept any communication and divulge or publish the existence, contents, substance, purport, effect or meaning of such intercepted communications to any person." [18] The statute was enacted merely to codify existing regulations covering radio broadcasting, but the United States Supreme Court construed Sec. 605 to prohibit wiretapping. In *Nardone v. United States* decided in 1937, the Court ruled, by a vote of 7 to 2, that evidence obtained by wiretapping without the consent of the sender, in violation of Sec. 605, could not be introduced in evidence in a Federal court.[19] The two dissenters were Justice Sutherland and Justice McReynolds who had voted with the majority in upholding the conviction of Roy Olmstead. Without overruling *Olmstead*, the Supreme Court began a slow process of eroding the principle laid down in that case which encouraged wiretapping by placing it outside the restrictions of the Fourth Amendment. That process of erosion was completed in 1967 in *Katz v. United States.*

After Nardone's conviction was reversed by the Supreme Court, he was retried and convicted a second time. In the second Nardone case decided in 1939, the Court went a step further to undo its decision in *Olmstead* and to curtail eavesdropping;[20] it ruled that under Sec. 605 evidence was barred not only if obtained directly by wiretapping, but also through use of "leads" obtained in the course of the wiretap, a doctrine known as "fruit of the poisonous tree." In the same year the Court decided that Sec. 605 applied to interception and divulgence of *intra*state telephone calls, not only *inter*state (*Weiss v. United States*).[21]

While the Supreme Court was deciding whether information obtained in violation of Sec. 605 was admissible in evidence, Federal and State agencies were construing the wording of Sec. 605—"no person shall intercept and divulge." Interception, they declared, was prohibited only if the conversation or information was also divulged to someone outside the government agency. The Supreme Court never passed on this question, but it has now become obsolete. Section 605 was amended by the Omnibus Crime Control and Safe Streets Act of 1968; the new section is directed at the conduct of communications personnel, rather than wiretapping in general.

The rule that evidence obtained by wiretapping in violation of Sec. 605 would be excluded in a *Federal* court was settled by the Nardone cases, but the Supreme Court had still to decide whether or not such evidence was admissible in *State* courts. In 1952 the Court held that under Sec. 605 it was a Federal crime for State officers to divulge information obtained through wiretapping, but that such evidence was admissible in a State court (*Schwartz v. Texas*).[22] An opposite conclusion was reached by the Court sixteen years later in *Lee v. Florida;* the Court decided that tape recordings of defendant's telephone conversations by State police having a telephone connected to a party line without defendant's knowledge were *not* admissible in State criminal prosecutions.[23] Section 605 was now applicable to the States. Justices Black, Harlan, and White dissented, arguing that the Court should follow *Schwartz v. Texas* and that any change should be made by Congress, not by the Court. To prevent overturning of State convictions obtained in good-faith reliance on *Schwartz*, the Court gave *Lee* only prospective application; the exclusionary rule was to be applied only to trials in which evidence was sought to be introduced after the date of the decision in *Lee* (*Fuller v. Alaska*).[24]

The Supreme Court has also had to deal with the problem of wiretapping by State officers where State law permitted the practice and Federal law prohibited it. In 1957, the Supreme Court ruled that wiretapping by State officers conducted under color of State law violated Sec. 605 if divulged, and evidence so obtained was not admissible in a Federal Court (*Benanti v. United States*).[25]

The "Bugging" Cases

Since Sec. 605 of the Federal Communications Act prohibited only wiretapping, the Supreme Court treated this form of surveillance separately from "bugging," in considering issues raised by eavesdropping. However, the physical intrusion or trespass theory on which *Olmstead* was based was also applied in development of the law on electronic surveillance. The first case to reach the Supreme Court involving bugging was *Goldman v. United States*, decided in 1942.[26] The Court ruled that evidence obtained by electronic eavesdropping is inadmissible only where a *physical* invasion of the premises occurred. Evidence had been obtained through use of a detectophone placed against a partition wall. The device had a receiver which picked up sound waves in an office on the other side of the wall. Federal agents overheard conversations in the office and a stenographer transcribed them. They also overheard conversations over the office telephone. Since there was no physical invasion in use of the detectaphone, said the Court, no violation of the Fourth Amendment had occurred and the evidence was admissible. The agents had, in fact, resorted to the detectaphone after a listening apparatus installed in an aperture of the partition wall failed to work. The prior trespass in installing the listening apparatus did not make illegal what was heard over the detectaphone.

In 1961, almost twenty years after its decision in *Goldman*, the Supreme Court had another opportunity to consider the "physical intrusion" theory formulated in *Olmstead*. This time the evidence was obtained by inserting a foot-long spike with microphone attached under a baseboard into a party wall, making contact with a heating duct to pick up conversations in another part of the building. The Court ruled that the evidence was *not* admissible. Since there was physical penetration, it constituted an intrusion into a protected area and violated the Fourth Amendment (*Silverman v. United States*).[27] In another six years, however, in *Katz v. United States*, the Court rejected the physical intrusion or trespass theory.

Supreme Court Decisions in Berger and Katz

A fundamental change in constitutional principles governing wiretapping and electronic surveillance was effected by the 1967 decisions of the Supreme Court in *Berger v. New York* and *Katz v. United States*.[28] These two cases are of the utmost importance in considering the constitutionality of Title III and procedures developed under the law. Title III purports to comply with the requirements of the Supreme Court in the 1967 decisions, and law enforcement officials claim that their practices follow the mandates of the Court.

Berger, which struck down as unconstitutional the New York law permitting court-ordered eavesdropping, was decided after the President's Commission on Law Enforcement and Administration of Justice made its report in which a majority of the Commission members recommended legislation authorizing official eavesdropping. In *Katz*, the Supreme Court held for the first time that electronic surveillance constitutes a "search and seizure" subject to the protections and limitations of the Fourth

Amendment to the Constitution. The Court did not overrule *Olmstead* in which a contrary conclusion had been reached in 1928; it merely recognized that the doctrine of *Olmstead* had been "eroded."

The *Katz* decision was widely interpreted as an invitation to Congress to enact a law authorizing eavesdropping by law enforcement officials, with certain safeguards. The views expressed by individual Justices in *Berger* and *Katz*, especially those still on the bench, must be taken into account in any prognostication as to how the Court will approach Title III problems. The facts in each case, the circumstances under which eavesdropping was conducted, and the basis of majority, concurring, and dissenting opinions, illuminate the questions later raised by legislative action in Title III of the Omnibus Crime Control and Safe Streets Act of 1968.

Berger v. New York

Ralph Berger, a Chicago public relations man, was convicted after a jury trial in the New York Supreme Court of conspiracy to bribe the Chairman of the New York State Liquor Authority, a public agency that controls issuance of liquor licenses. The evidence against Berger consisted of tape recordings of conversations intercepted over a sixty-day period by means of electronic devices installed pursuant to a court order obtained under the New York law. The trial court upheld the validity of the New York eavesdropping statute; the Appellate Division affirmed without opinion, and the New York Court of Appeals, the highest court in the State, likewise affirmed but by a divided vote. The United States Supreme Court reversed the conviction of Berger by a vote of 6 to 3 on the ground that the New York statute was "too broad in its sweep," resulting in a "trespassory intrusion into a constitutionally protected area," and therefore violated the Fourth and Fourteenth Amendments to the Constitution.[29] The Court ruled that the New York statute *on its face* failed to meet certain standards that were constitutionally mandatory. *Berger* involved electronic surveillance, but the Court used the term "eavesdropping" as in the New York statute and did not distinguish between wiretapping and "bugging."

While the Berger case involved only two court orders for electronic surveillance, forty-two orders were obtained in the course of the investigation, twenty-three for wiretaps and nineteen for bugging. More than seventeen people were indicted, among them the Chairman of the New York State Republican Committee, the Chairman of the New York State Liquor Authority, a judge of the New York State Court of Claims, various employees of the New York State Liquor Authority, several attorneys, and Ralph Berger![30]

The opinion of the Supreme Court in *Berger v. New York* was written by Justice Tom C. Clark. Concurring opinions were written by Justices

Douglas and Stewart. Dissenting opinions were handed down by Justices Black, Harlan, and White, reflecting deep division in the Court. The views expressed by each must be examined closely, for although the decision was rendered in 1967, they relate to questions that raise serious problems under Title III.

Justice Clark's opinion traces the development of eavesdropping from the days of Blackstone in the eighteenth century to the modern era of advanced electronic technology; the law has not kept pace with advances in scientific knowledge, "though jealous of individual privacy." The history of the right of privacy and the concept that intrusions into it are "subversive of all the comforts of society" date back to 1765. Analysis of the New York eavesdropping statute in the light of decisions from *Olmstead* in 1928 led the Court to conclude that the New York law did not provide adequate judicial supervision or protective procedures, and was deficient in the following respects:

1. *Particularity:* It laid down no requirement for particularity in the warrant as to what specific crime has been or is being committed, nor the place to be searched or persons or things to be seized, as required by the Fourth Amendment.
2. *Time period:* Eavesdropping for a two-month period is equivalent to a series of intrusions, searches, and seizures pursuant to a single showing of probable cause. The New York statute failed to require *present probable cause* for a two-month extension.
3. *Termination of interception:* The statute placed no termination date on the eavesdrop once the conversation sought is seized, leaving it entirely in the discretion of the officer listening to the conversations.
4. *Notice or exigent circumstances:* No notice was required by the New York statute, nor was this lack overcome by requiring some showing of special facts or exigent circumstances to avoid notice.
5. *Return:* The New York law did not provide for a return on the warrant, leaving full discretion in the officer as to use of seized conversations of innocent parties, as well as guilty ones.

The Court, said Justice Clark, has found "no empirical statistics on the use of electronic devices (bugging) in the fight against organized crime" to support the fervent claim that eavesdropping is a most important technique of law enforcement and that outlawing it would severely cripple crime detection, particularly organized crime; indeed there are figures on wiretapping "which indicate to the contrary." Concluding, Justice Clark said:

> Few threats to liberty exist which are greater than that posed by the use of eavesdropping devices. . . . The Fourth Amendment . . . prescribe(s) a constitutional standard that must be met before official invasion is permissible.[31]

In a concurring opinion, Justice Douglas called wiretapping and bugging "the greatest of all invasions of privacy." He could not see how an electronic surveillance that collects evidence or provides leads to evidence is or can be constitutional under the Fourth or Fifth Amendments. The opinion of the Court, said Justice Douglas, brings wiretapping and other electronic eavesdropping fully within the privilege of the Fourth Amendment. We could, added Justice Douglas, amend the Constitution and authorize eavesdropping—a step that would take us closer to a totalitarian regime.[32]

Justice Stewart concurred in the result reached by the majority, but agreed with the dissenters that the New York law was entirely constitutional. The real issue was this: Was the particular search and seizure *reasonable* or not? In *Berger* the eavesdrop order was not justified, according to Justice Stewart, for the affidavits on which it was based did not show "probable cause." Electronic eavesdropping for a sixty-day period involves a broad invasion of a constitutionally protected area. "Only the most precise and rigorous standard of probable cause should justify an intrusion of the scope and duration permitted in this case."[33]

To Justice Black in dissent, it seemed that the holding of the majority "makes it completely impossible for the State or the Federal Government ever to have a valid eavesdropping statute," despite faint intimations to the contrary. He attributed the decision, in part, to the Court's hostility to eavesdropping as "ignoble" and "dirty business," and to fear that science and technology are making eavesdropping more effective. In his opinion eavesdropping was *not* forbidden by the Constitution, nor should it be deemed inadvisable by legislative policy. Justice Black accused the majority of the Court of rewriting the Fourth Amendment as barring invasions of "privacy" rather than prohibiting unreasonable searches and seizures:

> Use of "privacy" as the keyword in the Fourth Amendment simply gives this Court a useful new tool . . . to usurp the policy making power of the Congress and to hold more state and federal laws unconstitutional when the Court entertains a sufficient hostility to them.[34]

Like Justice Stewart, Justice Black believed that the question in *Berger* should have been: Was the particular search and seizure *reasonable*. The Fourth Amendment relates to tangible things, not conversations, argued Justice Black; it does not apply to eavesdropping. To him it seemed that the New York statute contained more safeguards than the Fourth Amendment.

The dissenting opinion of Justice Harlan, like that of Justice Black points an accusing finger at the majority. The Court is establishing "newly contrived constitutional rights . . . without any apparent concern for the empirical process that goes with legislative reform"; it is disregarding construction of a State statute by the State's own courts. A "distaste for eavesdropping" is blamed for the Court's haste in disregarding established principles. Electronic eavesdropping as such, or as permitted by the New York law, is *not* an unreasonable search and seizure. The time period, said Justice Harlan, should be considered on a case-by-case basis.[35]

Justice White joined the other two dissenters in accusing the Court of seeming to be "irresistibly determined to strike down the New York statute" and to be "intent upon creating out of whole cloth new constitutionally mandated warrant procedures carefully tailored to make eavesdrop warrants unobtainable." That, declared Justice White, is not a judicial function.

> Regardless of how the Court would like eavesdropping legislation to read, our function ends in a State case with the determination of these questions [whether *this* case complied with Fourth Amendment standards].[36]

Justice White examined the claim that the eavesdropping violated Berger's right against self-incrimination under the Fifth Amendment to the Constitution, and rejected it on the ground that the conversations were "not the product of any official compulsion."

The three dissenters were convinced that the majority opinion made it impossible to fashion any eavesdropping statute that would meet constitutional requirements. Some commentators interpreted *Berger* as a veiled prohibition against eavesdropping. Others viewed it as a sanction for more carefully drawn statutes with adequate safeguards. G. Robert Blakey, Chief Counsel to the Subcommittee on Criminal Laws and Procedures who took a leading part in drafting Title III, read the *Berger* opinion as "laying down a constitutional blueprint for electronic surveillance . . . an invitation by the Court to Congress to get down to the difficult business of drafting a fair, effective, and comprehensive electronic surveillance statute."[37]

Katz v. United States

Charles Katz was convicted in the United States District Court in California of transmitting wagering information by telephone from Los Angeles to Miami and Boston, in violation of a Federal statute. At the trial, the Government was permitted to introduce evidence of telephone conversations by Katz overheard by F.B.I. agents. An electronic listening and recording device had been attached by the agents to the outside of the public telephone booth from which Katz placed his calls. Based on previous visual observations, the agents knew he would use the booth for several minutes at about the same time each morning.

Surveillance of Katz was confined to brief periods during which he used the telephone; six recordings, averaging about three minutes each, were obtained and admitted in evidence. They related only to Katz's end of conversations concerning the placing of bets and receipt of wagering information. On one occasion when statements of another person were inadvertently intercepted, the agents refrained from listening to them. There was no physical penetration of the telephone booth, part of which was made of glass through which Katz was clearly visible.

On appeal, Katz's conviction was affirmed by the United States Court of Appeals for the Ninth Circuit; the appellate court decided that no violation of the Fourth Amendment had occurred because there was no *physical* entrance into the area occupied by Katz. The United States Supreme Court, however, reversed the conviction by a 7 to 1 vote.[38] The sole dissenter was Justice Black. Consistent with the position taken by him in *Berger,* Justice Black insisted that electronic eavesdropping did not constitute a search and seizure within the meaning of the Fourth Amendment. Justice Marshall did not participate.

The opinion of the Supreme Court in *Katz v. United States* was delivered by Justice Stewart. Three separate concurring opinions were written, one by Justice White, another by Justice Douglas in which Justice Brennan joined, and a third by Justice Harlan, indicating that the members of the Court arrived at the decision by different routes. The majority ruled that the electronic listening and recording constituted a search and seizure within the meaning of the Fourth Amendment, and that it violated the privacy on which Katz relied while using the telephone booth.

Justice Stewart, writing for the majority, rejected the view that eavesdropping constituted a "search and seizure" subject to the safeguards of the Fourth Amendment only if the telephone booth was a "constitutionally protected area":

> The Fourth Amendment protects people, not places. What a person knowingly exposes to the public, even in his own home or office, is not a subject of Fourth Amendment protection. . . . But what he seeks to preserve as private, even in an area accessible to the public, may be constitutionally protected.[39]

What Katz sought to exclude when he entered the booth was "the uninvited ear." The reach of the Fourth Amendment, said Justice Stewart, no longer turns on presence or absence of physical intrusion into a given enclosure.

> The underpinnings of *Olmstead* and *Goldman* have been so eroded by our subsequent decisions that the "trespass" doctrine there enunciated can no longer be regarded as controlling.[40]

Justice Stewart made it clear that the Fourth Amendment could not be translated into a general constitutional right of privacy. The Fourth Amendment protects individual privacy against certain kinds of governmental intrusion, but its protections go further and often have nothing to do with privacy at all. Other provisions of the Constitution—such as the First, Third, and Fifth Amendments—protect personal privacy from other forms of governmental invasion. While the particular search and seizure did not comply with constitutional standards in the Katz case, it might have done so. A judicial order *could have* accommodated the legitimate needs of law enforcement, but the Court refused to validate the conduct of the F.B.I. agents retroactively. The Court listed the safeguards that were lacking in the surveillance of Katz:

1. Showing "probable cause" for scrutiny by a neutral magistrate before the search.
2. Observing precise limits during the search, fixed in advance by a court order.
3. Notifying the judge of what had been seized, after the search was completed.

In a footnote, Justice Stewart observed that the case did not present the question of whether prior authorization was necessary in "national security" cases. A more positive stand on dispensing with a court order in such cases was taken by Justice White in his concurring opinion: the warrant procedure should not be required if the President or the Attorney General has considered national security requirements and authorized electronic surveillance as reasonable. This view was sharply rejected by Justice Douglas who called it:

> [A] wholly unwarranted green light for the Executive Branch to resort to electronic eavesdropping without a warrant in cases which the Executive Branch itself labels "national security" matters.[41]

Under the separation of powers, said Justice Douglas, the Executive Branch is not supposed to be neutral and disinterested. Justice Douglas anticipated the problem that later developed under Title III in interpreting the meaning of "national security" and eavesdropping without court order on domestic radicals. Prior to June 1972 when the Supreme Court ruled on the issue, extensive wiretapping and electronic surveillance of political dissidents were conducted by Federal agencies without judicial authorization. (The decision of the Supreme Court limiting warrantless eavesdropping in domestic security cases is discussed in Chapter 7.)

Justice Harlan's concurring opinion in *Katz* emphasized as critical the fact that the subject of the surveillance had an actual *expectation of privacy* and that the expectation was reasonable.[42]

Justice Black's dissent relied on *Olmstead* and *Goldman* which, he insisted, had *not* been "eroded" as the majority claimed. As in his *Berger* dissent, he accused the Court of distortion, language-stretching, and rewriting the Constitution. Had the Framers of the Constitution desired to outlaw or restrict use of eavesdrop evidence they would have done so in the Fourth Amendment by appropriate language. Eavesdropping was known to the Framers, and wiretapping is simply eavesdropping by telephone. Substituting the Court's language designed to protect privacy for the Constitution's language, designed to guard against unreasonable searches and seizures, was "clever word juggling." Justice Black derided "broad policy discussions and philosophical discourses on such nebulous subjects as privacy." He pinpointed one of the great dilemmas that now face law enforcement officials and judges under Title III. He foresaw that the *particularity* requirement of the Fourth Amendment would be difficult if not impossible to meet in obtaining an eavesdrop order. Under the Fourth Amendment, the warrant must "particularly" describe the things to be seized. Justice Black demanded:

> How can one "describe" a future conversation, and if one cannot, how can a magistrate issue a warrant to eavesdrop one in the future?[43]

The Katz case appeared to be a clean break with the past. The Court was aware of its far-reaching effect; in an effort not to upset the applecart too violently, the Court gave Katz prospective application. In *Desist v. United States*, decided in 1969, the Court ruled that *Katz* was to be applied only to cases in which the prosecution seeks to introduce the fruits of electronic surveillance conducted after December 18, 1967.[44]

Search and Seizure under the Fourth Amendment

The decisions of the Supreme Court in both *Berger* and *Katz* rested primarily on the Fourth Amendment prohibiting unreasonable searches and seizures. It had taken the Court thirty-nine years to reject the rule laid down in *Olmstead* in 1928 that the Fourth Amendment relates only to tangible things, not to conversations. Now in deciding eavesdropping cases the Court will have to take into account its "search and seizure" rulings, and the task will not be easy. The Court has been struggling with interpretation of the restrictions in the Fourth Amendment since the latter part of the nineteenth century. The amendment, adopted in 1791 as part of the Bill of Rights, provides:

> The right of the people to be secure in their persons, houses, papers and effects against unreasonable searches and seizures shall not be violated, and no warrants shall issue, but upon probable cause, sup-

ported by oath or affirmation, and particularly describing the place to be searched, and the person or things to be seized.

This amendment was a direct repudiation of the general warrant, the "fishing expedition" which so enraged the American colonists against imperial England in its program for economic exploitation of its overseas possessions. Blanket orders were issued to search for contraband, and opposition to this method of apprehending violators was so strong that it has been claimed that the American Revolution began with the speech in February 1771 attacking the general warrant.

At the core of the Fourth Amendment is the right to be secure against arbitrary intrusion by the police, a protection basic to a free society. The emphasis of the Fourth Amendment is on *unreasonable* searches and seizures. To obtain a warrant, justification for a proposed search and seizure must be shown to the proper judicial officer, and it must be based on "probable cause." The place to be searched, the person or things to be seized, are required to be described with *particularity*.

What is "unreasonable?" What is "probable cause?" How can the description meet the particularity requirement? Does the prohibition apply against the States as well as against the Federal government, and what may or may not be seized? Since the decision of the Supreme Court in *Katz v. United States* holding that eavesdropping falls within the protections and limitations of the Fourth Amendment, a new question has been raised: Should the same criteria of reasonableness, probable cause, and particularity be applied to wiretapping and electronic surveillance as to the ordinary search and seizure of tangible objects? Proponents of Title III can see no difference between eavesdropping and normal search and seizure. Critics of Title III disagree. They believe that eavesdropping involves a far more serious intrusion on privacy and requires greater safeguards.

Before 1949, the Fourth Amendment ban on unreasonable search and seizure was held to apply exclusively to Federal law enforcement and could not be invoked against the States. This rule was modified in *Wolf v. Colorado* decided in that year.[45] The case involved conspiracy to commit abortion. Officers seized a physician's appointment book and a conviction was obtained based on this evidence. The Supreme Court decided unanimously that protection against unreasonable search and seizure under the Fourth Amendment was part of the fundamental protection which the "due process" clause of the Fourteenth Amendment extended to individuals in relation to their State and local government. But the majority of the Court refused to reverse the conviction. Most of the States, said the Court, do not have an exclusionary rule barring from criminal trials evidence obtained in violation of the prohibition against unreasonable search and seizure, and the evidence obtained should therefore *not* be excluded; the Supreme Court should not impose the exclusionary rule on the States. The conclusion reached by the Court was paradoxical, but its decision in *Wolf v. Colorado* was important in development of the law relating to search and seizure.

For more than a decade after *Wolf,* Federal agencies were permitted to introduce illegally seized evidence provided it had been obtained by *State* officials, not Federal. The evidence was handed to Federal prosecutors on a "silver platter." The "silver platter" doctrine was finally repudiated in 1960 in *Elkins v. United States;* in a 5 to 4 decision the Supreme Court ruled that Federal agents could not properly use such evidence.[46] The following year the Court overruled *Wolf v. Colorado;* it held that tainted evidence must be excluded, and the exclusionary rule applies to the States as well as to the Federal government (*Mapp v. Ohio*).[47] This was the basis for reversal of the conviction in *Berger v. New York;* the evidence obtained under eavesdrop orders issued pursuant to an unconstitutional State statute should not have been admitted at the trial in the State court.

Consent Eavesdropping

A question left unsettled by the Supreme Court in *Katz* and *Berger* was whether consent by one of the parties to a conversation to listening by a third person or to recording the conversation removes it from the prohibition of the Fourth Amendment against unreasonable search and seizure. The problem has been presented to the Supreme Court in various forms over a period of two decades, and the Court has generally sanctioned eavesdropping without a warrant if one of the parties to the conversation gave his consent to the interception.

In 1953 the Court upheld the right to wire an informant for sound in order to transmit statements of the suspect to police officers listening at a receiver outside the building (*On Lee v. United States*).[48] In this case, government agents enlisted the services of Chin Poy, a former friend of Lee who was suspected of engaging in illegal narcotics traffic. Poy was equipped with a "minifon" transmitting device which enabled outside government agents to monitor Poy's conversations with Lee. In the privacy of his laundry, Lee made damaging admissions to Poy which were overheard by the agents and later related at trial. Poy did not testify. Justice Jackson, writing for five members of the Court, declared that the testimony was admissible; in the absence of a trespass, no constitutional violation had occurred.

Four years later the Supreme Court handed down an opinion that no unlawful interception occurred where police officers listened in on a telephone conversation through an extension and one of the parties to the conversation had given his consent to the eavesdropping (*Rathbun v. United States*).[49] A more troublesome problem was presented to the Court in 1963. The operator of a cabaret was convicted in a Federal District Court of attempting to bribe an Internal Revenue Agent investigating evasion of excise taxes. The agent was equipped with a pocket wire recorder which recorded conversations of the cabaret operator offering $420 to the agent to help him conceal cabaret tax liability. The meetings took place in the operator's office. The Supreme Court decided that the evidence obtained through the recording device was properly admitted; there was no unlawful invasion of the office, for the agent was in the office with the operator's consent. The recording device was used only to obtain the most reliable evidence possible of a conversation in which the agent participated. The conviction was affirmed (*Lopez v. United States*).[50]

The traditional principle on which the validity of consent eavesdropping rests is that a party to a conversation takes his chances that the other participant may increase his present or future audience. Justice Brennan, dissenting in *Lopez*, protested that "in a free society people ought not to have to watch their every word so carefully." Some doubts as to the implications of *On Lee* and *Lopez* were raised by the decision of the Supreme Court in 1966 in *Osborn v. United States*.[51] In this case, one of James R. Hoffa's attorneys hired a man named Vick to make background investigations of people listed on a jury panel. He did not know that Vick had agreed to report to Federal agents. At a meeting on November 7, 1963, the attorney discussed with Vick the possibility of bribing one of the prospective jurors who was Vick's cousin. On the basis of an affidavit by Vick as to this conversation, two judges authorized concealing a recording device on Vick's person for a meeting on November 11. The recording of a conversation on the 11th was played to the jury, and on this evidence the attorney was convicted for attempting to bribe a member of the Federal jury panel.

The Supreme Court affirmed Osborn's conviction on the ground that the recording was properly admitted as evidence at the trial. *Osborn* left unclear whether a conversation recorded by a party to the conversation could be introduced in evidence only if prior judicial authorization had been secured. *On Lee* and *Lopez* appeared to have established that a record of conversations taken by a party to the conversation was not constitutionally objectionable under the Fourth Amendment even *without* court authorization.

The issue of consent eavesdropping now appears to be settled, at least until the Supreme Court agrees to reconsider the question. In *United States v. White*, decided in 1971, the Court ruled that the Fourth Amendment is not violated by governmental electronic eavesdropping effected by wiring an informant for sound, having him talk to the suspect, and then having agents to whom the conversation is transmitted repeat the communications at the suspect's trial.[52] This exception of consent eavesdropping from court order requirements is reflected in Title III of the Omnibus Act of 1968.

Section 2511(2)(c) declares that it is *not* unlawful for a law enforcement officer to intercept a wire or oral communication if he is a party to the communication or if one of the parties gave prior consent to the interception.

Deep cleavages in the Supreme Court on the subject of consent eavesdropping were revealed by the opinions of the Justices in *United States v. White*. The Supreme Court reversed the judgment of the Court of Appeals and upheld White's conviction by a vote of 5 to 4, but no agreement could be reached on a majority opinion. The plurality view, expressed by Justice White, led to the irresistible quip of labeling the case "White on White." The White case is worth a close look, for eavesdropping without a court order but with the consent of informants (many of whom are rather shady characters) is used extensively in law enforcement.

United States v. White

The White case involved illegal transactions in narcotics amounting to about $5,000. James White was convicted in 1966 and sentenced in a United States District Court, as a second offender, to imprisonment for twenty-five years and fined $35,000. The evidence against him consisted of conversations regarding narcotics sales with an informant, Harvey Jackson. Agents of the Bureau of Narcotics and Dangerous Drugs overheard the conversations by monitoring the frequency of a radio transmitter concealed on Jackson's body. Some of the meetings occurred in Jackson's home and in his car; one took place in White's home. The informant Jackson disappeared, but the agent who conducted the electronic surveillance testified to the conversations.

White's conviction was reversed by the United States Court of Appeals on the ground that the Supreme Court decision in *Katz* in 1967 had rendered inadmissible the agent's testimony concerning conversations which Jackson broadcast to him without a warrant. The Supreme Court disagreed; *Katz* did not indicate in any way that "a defendant has a justifiable and constitutionally protected expectation that a person with whom he is conversing will not then or later reveal the conversation to the police."[53]

The plurality opinion of the Supreme Court written by Justice White was joined by Chief Justice Burger and Justices Stewart and Blackmun. Justice Black concurred only in the judgment for the reasons set forth in his dissent in *Katz*—that electronic surveillance was not a search and seizure subject to the Fourth Amendment. Justice Brennan filed a separate opinion concurring in the result on the ground that *Katz* was not retroactive. Strong dissenting opinions were filed by Justices Douglas, Harlan, and Marshall.

The question to be decided was this, according to the plurality opinion: What expectations of privacy are constitutionally "justifiable"—

what expectations will the Fourth Amendment protect in the absence of a warrant? A police agent who conceals his identity may write down his conversations with a defendant and testify concerning them without a warrant. No different result, said the Court, is required if the agent records the conversations with electronic equipment carried on his person (as in *Lopez*), or carries radio equipment which transmits the conversations to recording equipment located elsewhere or to agents monitoring the transmitting frequency (as in *On Lee* and in *White*).

Sharp differences of opinion were provoked by the White case outside the judiciary as well as within it. The dissenters came under attack by commentators. One critic complained:

> A sordid, petty transaction became the subject of emotional dissertations on privacy by Justices Harlan and Douglas. . . . Justices Douglas, Harlan, Brennan, and Marshall have swallowed the pig and choked on its tail.[54]

The four dissenters had objected to equipping agents with eavesdropping devices in the absence of a court order, but had approved of use of informants without judicial supervision. It was suggested that "a far greater danger to our free society is presented by the prospect that friends and associates may be employed as government spies" than by equipping informants with electronic transmitting devices.

The lengthy dissenting opinions of Justices Harlan and Douglas were a head-on confrontation with a broad philosophical question. The issue, as Justice Harlan saw it, was whether "uncontrolled consensual surveillance in an electronic age is a tolerable technique of law enforcement, given the values and goals of our political system." Justice Harlan considered the issue one of great magnitude because the technique was used so extensively by the police. He cited the observation of Professor Alan Westin that "participant recording, in which one participant in a conversation or meeting, either a police officer or a cooperating party, wears a concealed device that records or broadcasts to others nearby . . . is used tens of thousands of times each year."[55]

Justice Harlan made a distinction between third-party monitoring and other undercover techniques such as single-party informer bugging. He rejected the assumption that there is no greater invasion of privacy in the third-party situation. The critical question for him was "whether under our system of government, as reflected in the Constitution, we should impose on our citizens the risks of the electronic listener or observer without at least the protection of a warrant requirement."[56] The impact of the practice of third-party bugging seemed to Justice Harlan to undermine that confidence and sense of security in dealing with one another that is characteristic of individual relations between citizens in a free society.

Third-party electronic monitoring, subject only to the self-restraint of law enforcement officials, has no place in our society. . . . The burden of guarding privacy in a free society should not be on its citizens; it is the Government that must justify its need to electronically eavesdrop. [57]

The dissent of Justice Douglas in *White* was even sharper than that of Justice Harlan. Justice Douglas could see no excuse for not seeking a warrant in the White case. He based his dissent not only on the Fourth Amendment ban on unreasonable search and seizure, but also on freedom of speech guaranteed by the First Amendment:

Monitoring, if prevalent, certainly kills free discourse and spontaneous utterances. Free discourse—a First Amendment value—may be frivolous or serious, humble or defiant, reactionary or revolutionary, profane or in good taste; but it is not free if there is surveillance. . . . Free discourse liberates the spirit, though it may produce only froth. [58]

Must everyone live in fear that every word he speaks may be transmitted or recorded, demanded Justice Douglas. He could imagine nothing that has a more chilling effect on people speaking their minds and expressing their views on important matters.

Supreme Court Decisions on Privacy

In litigation attacking the constitutionality of eavesdropping under Title III, counsel for defendants rely heavily on the claim to a right of privacy under Amendment IV, and also under Amendments I, III, V, and IX. Individual privacy, they say, is a constitutional privilege entitled to protection against governmental intrusion. The difficulty with this argument is that no such right appears in *any* amendment of the Constitution. Where then does it come from, and where is the Court to look for guidance in cases claiming the right of privacy?

In the United States, the claim to privacy is traced back most clearly to 1890. In a seminal article published that year in the *Harvard Law Review*, Samuel D. Warren and Louis D. Brandeis (later a Justice of the Supreme Court) pointed out that the right of privacy was recognized at common law—the law arising from customs and created by judges. The two young lawyers urged that a legal remedy be provided for the invasion of individual privacy. The common law, they said, secures to each individual the right of determining "to what extent his thoughts, sentiments, and emotions shall be communicated to others."

That the individual shall have full protection in person and in property is a principle as old as the common law; but it has been found necessary from time to time to define anew the exact nature and extent of such protection.[59]

As civilization advanced, they argued, an individual's feelings and intellect, as well as his physical being, came within the scope of the legal "right to be let alone." Warren and Brandeis concluded that existing law provided a principle that could be invoked to protect one's personality, as well as ordinary property rights. The common law recognized a man's house as his castle; one's house now included the inner self.

In 1890 Warren and Brandeis were concerned, not with eavesdropping, but with intrusions on privacy by the press and unauthorized circulation of portraits. This is the type of invasion of privacy that the Court rejected in the case of Jacqueline Kennedy Onassis. In July 1972, the United States District Court in New York enjoined the photographer, Ronald E. Galella, from approaching Mrs. Onassis and her children within a fixed distance to take their photographs, and from using them for advertising or trade purposes without her consent. His actions, said the judge, relentlessly invaded her "right to be left alone." Galella's "endless snooping," said the Court, "constitutes tortious invasion of privacy."[60]

Supreme Court decisions acknowledging the right to privacy give some indication of the weight that the Court may accord to it in balancing the individual's interest against the public need. This delicate task of weighing competing values has been complicated by the fact that the right of privacy has always been a controversial concept, and the Court has responded cautiously and sometimes ambiguously to opposing views. Opinions involving Amendments I and V have referred to the right of privacy almost casually, as though one could take it for granted that in a free society an individual has private rights, free from government interference. Amendment IX was cited as a basis for a claim to privacy for the first time in 1965, and then only by a minority of the Court. The right of privacy rests most securely on Amendment IV prohibiting unreasonable searches and seizures and requiring a warrant, but early Supreme Court decisions involving Amendment IV did not stress the right of privacy.

Amendment I of the Constitution provides that Congress shall make no law abridging "the freedom of speech . . . or the right of the people peaceably to assemble and to petition the Government for a redress of grievances." In *N.A.A.C.P. v. Alabama* (1958), the Supreme Court recognized the "close nexus between the freedoms of speech and assembly," and their relation to liberty:

> It is beyond debate that freedom to engage in association for the advancement of beliefs and ideas is an inseparable aspect of the "liberty" assured by the Due Process Clause of the Fourteenth Amendment, which embraces freedom of speech.[61]

The Court saw a "vital relationship between freedom to associate and privacy in one's associations." It decided that a State could not compel the National Association for the Advancement of Colored People (N.A.A.C.P.) to reveal the names and addresses of its Alabama members and agents. Disclosure of identity would expose them to economic reprisals and physical harm. Immunity from State scrutiny of the membership list was related to the right to pursue "lawful private interests privately."

Associational privacy has also been protected by the Supreme Court against Congressional investigation. In *Watkins v. United States* (1957), a witness before a Subcommittee of the Committee on Un-American Activities of the House of Representatives refused to make certain disclosures regarding the political affiliations of others on the ground that the Committee had no power to compel him to give such testimony. While admitting the power of Congress to conduct investigations as part of its legislative function, the Supreme Court considered the limitation on the investigating power when First Amendment rights were threatened. The Court declared that Watkins's conviction was invalid as a violation of the "due process" clause of the Fifth Amendment, and indirectly asserted a right of privacy:

> The public is entitled to be informed concerning the workings of its government. That cannot be inflated into a general power to expose where the predominant result can only be an invasion of the private rights of individuals.[62]

The Court made it clear that there was no general authority to expose the private affairs of individuals without justification, nor could a legislative committee indulge in "broad-scale intrusion into the lives and affairs of private citizens."

When a vague or overbroad law forces citizens to hesitate in exercising their constitutional rights, or deters them entirely because of uncertainty, it is said to have a "chilling effect." The claim that government eavesdropping has a chilling effect on freedom of speech and assembly in violation of Amendment I has been presented to the Supreme Court in various cases, but the Court has not ruled on this issue. In the 1972 decision limiting warrantless surveillance in domestic security cases discussed in Chapter 6, Justice Powell recognized the effect of unauthorized government eavesdropping on free discussion, and Justice Douglas expressed his concern that eavesdropping gave the government power to intimidate its critics.

Amendment III of the Constitution provides that "No soldier shall, in time of peace be quartered in any house, without the consent of the Owner, nor in time of war, but in a manner to be prescribed by law." The quartering of soldiers in private homes without the owner's consent had been one of the flagrant violations of the individual's right to privacy by the colonial government. The purpose of the Third Amendment was:

> To secure the perfect enjoyment of that great right of the common law that a man's house shall be his own castle, privileged against all civil and military intrusion.[63]

This amendment is generally cited in eavesdropping cases to support the claim to privacy.

Amendment V provides that "no person . . . shall be compelled in any criminal case to be a witness against himself." In *Miranda v. Arizona* (1966) the Supreme Court ruled that in prosecution of a person accused of crime, statements made by the accused during custodial interrogation could not be used against him in the absence of procedural safeguards securing the privilege against self-incrimination.[64] Modern in-custody interrogation, observed the Court, was psychologically oriented and exacted "a heavy toll on individual liberty." It was as destructive of human dignity as physical intimidation. The privilege against self-incrimination is part of an individual's substantive right, a "right to a private enclave where he may lead a private life." The Constitution guarantees that a person has a right to remain silent. Justice Stewart, speaking for the majority in another 1966 case (*Tehan v. United States* ex rel. *Shott*) said:

> The Fifth Amendment's privilege against self-incrimination is not an adjunct to the ascertainment of truth. That privilege, like the guarantees of the Fourth Amendment, stands as a protection of quite different constitutional values—values reflecting the concern of our society for the right of each individual to be let alone.[65]

The ruling of the Supreme Court in *Miranda v. Arizona* has been weakened by Title II of the Omnibus Crime Control and Safe Streets Act of 1968 permitting introduction in evidence of voluntary confessions even if procedural safeguards have not been followed, but the Fifth Amendment still stands as protection of the "right to be let alone."

To substantiate the claim that a right of privacy is guaranteed by the Constitution, Amendments I, III, IV, V, and IX, as well as Amendment XIV were cited in *Griswold v. Connecticut*, decided by the Supreme Court in 1965.[66] The case merits detailed analysis, for members of the Court were deeply divided as to the basis for claiming a constitutional right of privacy, as well as to the existence of the right itself.

In *Griswold*, the Executive Director of the Planned Parenthood League of Connecticut and its Medical Director were convicted in the Circuit Court in New Haven as accessories for violating a State statute prohibiting the giving of information, instruction, and advice to married

persons as to means of preventing conception. The conviction was affirmed
in the State appellate courts, but on appeal the United States Supreme
Court reversed by a vote of 7 to 2. The Connecticut law, said a majority of
the Justices, was an invasion of the right of privacy of married persons and
was unconstitutional.

Justice Douglas expressed the views of five members of the Court. The
First Amendment, he said, includes peripheral as well as specific rights, and
"has a penumbra where privacy is protected from governmental intrusion"
a zone of privacy is, in fact, created by several fundamental constitutional
guarantees:

> The right of association contained in the penumbra of the First
> Amendment is one . . . the Third Amendment . . . is another facet of
> that privacy. The Fourth Amendment explicitly affirms the "right of
> people to be secure in their persons, houses, papers, and effects against
> unreasonable searches and seizures." The Fifth Amendment in its
> Self-Incrimination Clause enables the citizen to create a zone of
> privacy which government may not force him to surrender to his
> detriment. The Ninth Amendment provides: "The enumeration in the
> Constitution of certain rights, shall not be construed to deny or
> disparage others retained by the people."[67]

A separate concurring opinion by Justice Goldberg, in which Chief
Justice Warren and Justice Brennan joined, relied heavily on the Ninth
Amendment:

> The language and history of the Ninth Amendment reveal that
> the Framers of the Constitution believed that there are additional
> fundamental rights protected from governmental infringement,
> which exist alongside those fundamental rights specifically mentioned
> in the first eight constitutional amendments.[68]

Justice Goldberg denied hotly that the holding of the majority
interfered with any regulation that a State could properly make. No State,
he said, had power to experiment with fundamental liberties. In
determining what rights are fundamental and protected against the States
by the "due process" clause of the Fourteenth Amendment, judges must
look to the traditions and "conscience of our people."

Justice Harlan, while concurring in the conclusion of the majority that
the Connecticut law was unconstitutional, objected to basing the decision
on "some right assured by the letter or penumbra of the Bill of Rights." To
him, the question seemed to be whether the State law violated basic values
"implicit in the concept of ordered liberty."[68] Justice White, concurring in a
separate opinion, argued that the Connecticut law deprived marital couples

of "liberty" without due process of law as guaranteed by the Fourteenth Amendment.[68]

The two dissenters in *Griswold*, Justices Black and Stewart, could see no violation of any constitutional provision. Most emphatically, Justice Black denied the existence of a constitutional right of privacy, and accused the majority of "stretching" the First Amendment:

> The court talks about a constitutional "right of privacy" as though there is some constitutional provision . . . forbidding any law ever to be passed which might abridge the "privacy" of individuals. But there is not. There are, of course, guarantees in certain specific constitutional provisions which are designed in part to protect privacy at certain times and places with respect to certain activities. Such, for example, is the Fourth Amendment's guarantee against "unreasonable searches and seizures."[69]

Justice Black warned against substituting words in a constitutional guarantee:

> "Privacy" is a broad, abstract and ambiguous concept which can easily be shrunken in meaning but which can also . . . easily be interpreted as a constitutional ban against many things other than searches and seizures.

Government, he said, has a right to invade privacy unless prohibited by some specific constitutional provision; he could find no such ban in the case of the Connecticut law and accused the Court of claiming power to invalidate any legislative act which the judges found "irrational, unreasonable, or offensive." The power to decide what laws are unwise or unnecessary is a *legislative* one; the Court has no power to sit as "a supervisory agency" to set aside laws they believe to be "unwise, arbitrary, capricious or irrational."[70]

Justice Stewart, in dissent, characterized the Connecticut statute as "an uncommonly silly law" but, like Justice Black, found nothing unconstitutional about it. Which of the six amendments mentioned by the majority is infringed, he asked—the First, Third, Fourth, Fifth, Ninth, Fourteenth? Reliance on the Ninth Amendment was "turning somersaults with history!"

The decision of the Supreme Court in *Griswold* applied only to marital relations and was limited to the Connecticut law.[71] Commentators suggested, however, that the ruling furnished the basis for declaring wiretapping and other eavesdropping unconstitutional. This view has not been borne out by later decisions of the Supreme Court and was put to rest, at least for the present, by enactment of Title III of the Omnibus Crime Control and Safe Streets Act of 1968 authorizing eavesdropping under law.

3

Politics of "Law and Order"

An Australian jurist, addressing the Philadelphia Bar Association a few months before Title III of the Omnibus Act of 1968 went into effect, reminded his American audience of a fact that no one would dispute:

> Any freedom worth having is freedom under the law . . . no individual freedom is secure or lasting except in an ordered society . . . you can't have order without law, justly and firmly administered . . . most freedoms involve abridgement of the freedom of others.[1]

The visiting lecturer criticized people in the United States for setting personal freedom above the need for effective administration of the criminal law, and suggested (softly) that perhaps revision of our Bill of Rights was needed. His listeners were probably shocked regardless of their political affiliations, for Americans revere the Bill of Rights as a precious heritage—in theory at least. The plea in behalf of "law and order," however, must have struck a responsive chord. There is always a tendency to believe that "law and order" is threatened, and in 1968 the phrase had become a powerful political slogan.

Fear of crime and the clamor for "law and order" produced the first Federal law in the history of the nation to legalize eavesdropping.[2] Until 1968 when Title III was passed, every attempt to enact a law authorizing eavesdropping had ended in failure. As shown in Chapter 2, thirty or more years of public debates, Congressional hearings, Executive directives, and Supreme Court decisions produced nothing but confusion, uncertainty, and sharp disagreement. No one would have predicted early in 1967 that Congress could pass a law permitting wiretapping and electronic surveillance and providing a mechanism that would encourage States to adopt similar legislation. Yet Title III and the Omnibus Act of which it was a part passed in both the Senate and in the House of Representatives by an overwhelming vote.

How did near unanimity replace perennial division on such a controversial subject? Rising concern over invasions of privacy in the modern age of electronics seemed to favor *banning* eavesdropping, not legalizing it. The recommendation of the President's Commission on Law Enforcement and Administration of Justice that law enforcement officials be authorized to eavesdrop in order to combat organized crime could not have been decisive in enactment of Title III; the Commission was divided on the matter, and legislators do not feel bound to take the advice of an agency created by the Executive. Nor could the decisions of the Supreme Court in *Berger* and *Katz* account for Title III; the Justices themselves disagreed whether a law authorizing eavesdropping could be drafted to satisfy constitutional requirements. Only the political climate of an election year and the assortment of "crime" measures dumped into a single piece of legislation can explain the vote in favor of the Omnibus Crime Control and Safe Streets Act of 1968. The very title of the Act made it "politically irresistible."[3]

During the debates on the Omnibus Act, leading Republicans proclaimed that "crime" and "law and order" were to be central issues in the presidential election campaign of 1968. Existing laws must be strictly enforced, and additional tools provided to obtain convictions. The courts were blamed for lawlessness in the United States and Richard Nixon declared himself in favor of the eavesdropping provisions of the Omnibus Act. Crime in the District of Columbia was a national disgrace and a complete overhaul of the criminal system of justice in the Federal city was needed. The Supreme Court was accused of "coddling criminals" and "handcuffing the police." President Johnson was charged with failing to recognize fully the problem of crime and responding to its challenge. The way to decrease crime, said the Republicans, was by increasing convictions. At the Republican National Convention, the Platform Committee made the following statement on crime:

> Republicans believe that respect for the law is the cornerstone of a free and well-ordered society.[4]

The call for "law and order" was skillful political strategy. It had powerful appeal even for those who were fully aware that the language of politics is one of exaggeration and excess and who recognized "law and order" as a vote-catching phrase. Some libertarians charged that this clever slogan had racial as well as political overtones; that it veiled an attack on the Supreme court by those who resented the Warren Court's decisions on desegregation of public schools and securing the rights of indigent defendants. Ramsey Clark claimed openly that behind the phrase "law and order" many concealed their opposition to civil rights enforcement and to political dissent. Law and order had lost its true meaning—the protection of everyone's rights against coercion, violence, and repression under uniform laws, evenly enforced.

Democrats as well as Republicans wanted a "crime" bill enacted. President Johnson had sent a message to Congress in February 1967 warning that "fear of crime" had developed into a public malady, and proposing Federal grants to States in aid of law enforcement. This was the origin of Title I of the Omnibus Act of 1968. As finally enacted, the Act contains eleven titles covering a wide range of subjects, some of them only remotely related to crime. Title VI, for example, provides that the Director of the Federal Bureau of Investigation shall be appointed by the President with the consent of the Senate. Title II is a thinly veiled attempt to set aside three decisions of the Supreme Court relating to the admission of testimony in criminal prosecutions: *Miranda v. Arizona, Mallory v. United States*, and *United States v. Wade.*[5]

As indicated in Chapter 2, Title III is a combination of proposals in a bill introduced by Senator McClellan in January 1967 (S 675) and a bill submitted by Senator Hruska (S 2050) after the decisions of the Supreme Court in *Berger* and *Katz*. Senator Hruska's bill purported to comply with safeguards to constitutional liberties as laid down by the Court. Title III contains an outright ban on private eavesdropping, but authorizes interception of wire and oral communications by designated law enforcement officials provided certain procedures are followed. The language of the law and the manner in which it has been interpreted and carried out in practice will determine whether wiretapping and electronic surveillance are tolerable in a democratic society.

A provision for limited control of firearms was added to the Omnibus Act of 1968 as the measure moved through the legislative process. Dr. Martin Luther King, Jr. was assassinated on April 4, 1968 during the debates on the Act, and rioting broke out in various cities of the United States including Washington, D.C. Two months later Robert F. Kennedy was killed in Los Angeles. In the wake of this second tragedy, the House of Representatives passed the Senate version of the Omnibus Act without changes, thus eliminating reconsideration of the bill in conference.

In signing the Omnibus Act of 1968, President Johnson said it "contains more good than bad." As to Title III, he urged Congress to repeal its "unwise" provisions; sanctioning eavesdropping by Federal, State, and local officials, in an almost unlimited variety of situations, could result in producing a nation of snoopers bending to the keyholes of the homes and offices of America, spying on our neighbors.[6] Attorney General Ramsey Clark instructed Federal law enforcers not to exercise their powers under the new law. He considered eavesdropping an invasion of privacy, doubted the constitutionality of Title III, and insisted that effectiveness of eavesdropping in law enforcement had not been proved.[7]

During the presidential election campaign, Richard Nixon criticized Clark's refusal to use eavesdropping under Title III and charged him with being remiss in the fight against organized crime. After his election, President Nixon directed all Federal agencies to cooperate fully with the Department of Justice in its anticrime efforts, and pledged that he would appoint "law and order" advocates to the United States Supreme Court—a promise that he sought to fulfill by the four Justices who joined the bench: Warren E. Burger (as Chief Justice), Harry A. Blackmun, Lewis F. Powell, Jr., and William H. Rehnquist. President Nixon's appointee as Attorney General, John N. Mitchell, told the Senate Committee on the Judiciary, at the hearing on his confirmation, that he intended to use eavesdropping powers under Title III, and he did so during his entire tenure of office.[8]

The Department of Justice has repeatedly called to public attention the fact that the previous administration "refused to use court-authorized wiretapping." The Nixon Administration, in turn, has been charged by its critics with adopting a permissive attitude toward wiretapping, nourishing the fear of crime, and subverting "law and order" by running a highly political Department of Justice.[9] "Law and order" continued to be a political issue in 1970 and again in the 1972 presidential campaign. The cry for "law and order" has taken an ironic turn since seven men were caught on June 17, 1972 in the Watergate break-in and bugging (discussed later in this chapter), implicating the highest government officials, among them former Attorney General John N. Mitchell. His successor, Richard G. Kleindeinst, was forced to resign because of his close association with some of the Watergate suspects. In May 1973 a new Attorney General took office—Elliott D. Richardson, formerly Under Secretary of State and Secretary of Health, Education and Welfare in the Nixon Administration. In the hearing on his confirmation as Attorney General, Richardson assured the Senate Judiciary Committee that he would pursue the Watergate investigation vigorously and would appoint an independent prosecutor. He named as Special Prosecutor Archibald Cox, Professor at Harvard Law School and Solicitor General in the Kennedy and Johnson Administrations.

Has the politics of "law and order" surrounding enactment of Title III of the Omnibus Crime Control and Safe Streets Act of 1968 been carried over to the practical operation of official wiretapping and electronic surveillance, as some have claimed? This is, perhaps, the most vital question raised with respect to eavesdropping under law. If government eavesdropping is politically motivated, then it is an intolerable threat to privacy in a democratic system.

The Ban on Private Eavesdropping

One of the most persuasive and compelling arguments in Congress for enactment of Title III was that it prohibited private eavesdropping. No Senator or member of the House of Representatives, whether Democrat or

Republican, could voice objection to a legislative ban on private intrusions into personal privacy. Protection of privacy is a stated purpose of the law. Title III indicates clearly that it is to serve a dual function:

1. To protect the privacy of individuals by banning eavesdropping other than by duly authorized law enforcement officers, and prohibiting manufacture, sale, possession, or advertising of eavesdropping devices designed primarily for surreptitious interception.

2. To give law enforcement officers an effective tool—wiretapping and electronic surveillance—under specified conditions and with proper safeguards, to combat organized crime and other serious offenses.

The law makes it a Federal offense for private individuals to manufacture, sell, advertise, distribute, transport, or possess wiretapping and electronic devices designed primarily for surreptitious eavesdropping. Violations are punishable by fine up to $10,000 or imprisonment up to five years, or both (Sec. 2512). In the event of violation, the devices are subject to seizure and forfeiture (Sec. 2513). The test of whether a device falls within the ban of Title III is whether its design renders it *primarily* useful for *surreptitious* listening. The obvious difficulty of applying this criterion was recognized by the *Senate Report* on the bill:

> The sort of judgment called for . . . in close cases would warrant the use of expert testimony. . . . The prohibition will be applicable . . . to the martini olive transmitter, the spike mike, the infinity transmitter and the microphone disguised as a wrist watch, picture frame, cuff link, tie clip, fountain pen, stapler or cigarette pack. . . . Size alone is not the criterion.[10]

Is the prohibition against private eavesdropping contained in Title III meaningful? Before its enactment, eavesdropping devices were sold widely to private individuals who used them for a variety of purposes: in divorce cases and other domestic relations suits, business competition, supervision of employees, idle curiosity, and blackmail. Today suppliers claim they sell such equipment only to law enforcement officials. Skeptics ask if the vast private eavesdropping industry has not simply gone underground. A private individual desiring an eavesdropping device need not go to a manufacturer or distributor in the business. He can buy parts more cheaply at an electronics supply house and put them together with a little radio or electronics know-how and experience.

Long-standing laws in various states prohibiting wiretapping, say critics of Title III, did not deter private eavesdropping or result in extensive prosecution. Section 605 of the Federal Communications Act of 1934 banning wiretapping likewise produced few cases against violators; in more than thirty years less than thirty cases were brought against private wiretappers and none against law enforcement officers.

Effectiveness of any statute prohibiting eavesdropping by private individuals must depend largely on receipt of complaints and vigorous enforcement. State law enforcement officials report that few, if any, complaints have been received since passage of Title III.

Detection of unlawful tapping is difficult, and it may be even harder when an electronic device is installed. Some feel that the Federal government has now preempted the field, although it is quite clear from the Senate Report on Title III that no such preemption was intended. The Federal Communications Commission (F.C.C.) has assumed no law enforcement duties or authority under Title III. It interprets the ban on private eavesdropping contained in Sec. 2511 of Title III as evidencing "a Congressional intent to fix the primary jurisdiction over wiretapping and eavesdropping activities with the Department of Justice." This view has been accepted by the Justice Department.[11]

The United States Department of Justice has been more active than the States in dealing with complaints against private eavesdroppers under Title III, but few prosecutions have resulted. Paucity of complaints and prosecutions may be explained, in part, by the comparative ease with which the ban on private eavesdropping can be circumvented. An expert lists "a few distinct possibilities" to manufacturers and sellers of eavesdropping equipment:

1. Change the advertising . . . sell telephone sound augmentation devices for the hard-of-hearing instead of radio wiretapping equipment.

2. Sell separate parts. There are at least 200,000 individuals in the United States who have the expertise to assemble an electronic eavesdropping device.

3. Manufacture and sell *visual* surveillance equipment which is *not* banned by Title III.

4. Set up operations in Canada and fill mail orders.[12]

The victim of eavesdropping is advised not to complain to the authorities, but to use a "scrambler" that changes the words electronically, making them unintelligible except at the receiving end where similar equipment reconverts the conversation into understandable language!

Ineffectiveness of the ban on private eavesdropping may lend support to the claim of critics of Title III that the arguments which swayed members of Congress to vote affirmatively in the name of "law and order" were a political hoax.

Eavesdropping at Watergate

The most notorious charge of private eavesdropping was made in June 1972 against individuals seized with electronic surveillance equipment at headquarters of the Democratic Party in the Watergate Office Building in

Washington, D.C. Indictments were returned by a Federal grand jury against two former White House aides and five men caught at Watergate, charging them with conspiring to commit illegal wiretapping and planting electronic surveillance devices. A civil suit was brought by Lawrence F. O'Brien, former Democratic Party Chairman, against Maurice H. Stans, as Chairman of the Finance Committee to Re-elect the President, and several aides, under Sec. 2520 of Title III of the Omnibus Act of 1968.[13] A Federal judge subsequently stayed the civil proceedings pending trial of the criminal case.

In January 1973 five of the seven defendants caught at Watergate pleaded guilty to charges of conspiracy, second-degree burglary, and wiretapping. One of the remaining defendants, James W. McCord, Jr., was security coordinator for the Committee to Re-elect the President. The other defendant, G. Gordon Liddy, a former White House aide, was counsel to the Finance Committee to Re-elect the President. Both were found guilty on January 30, 1973 by a jury of eight women and four men of attempted wiretapping, attempted bugging and wiretapping, and other offenses.

After the conviction McCord wrote to the trial judge, John J. Sirica, of the United States District Court, Washington, D.C., that he was ready to reveal important details about Watergate. Disclosures implicated high White House officials and members of the Committee for the Re-election of the President in planning the Watergate bugging and in subsequent attempts to cover up illegal acts.[14]

On May 17, 1973, televised hearings began before the seven-member Select Committee on Presidential Campaign Activities, now known as the "Watergate Committee," with Senator Sam J. Ervin, Jr. as chairman. In his opening statement before the Committee, Senator Ervin outlined the assertions that the 1972 presidential campaign had been influenced by illegal activities, including widespread wiretapping of the telephones, political headquarters, and residences of candidates and their campaign staffs and of members of the press; that following the Watergate break-in there had been a massive attempt to cover up the improper activities; that governmental instrumentalities had been used in attempts at political surveillance of candidates in the 1972 campaign. He emphasized that the purpose of Committee hearings was not prosecutorial or judicial, but investigative and informative. If the allegations were true, then those involved in the Watergate affair were seeking to steal "the right to vote in a free election."[15]

Weeks of hearings before the Watergate Committee produced conflicting testimony as to who planned, authorized, paid for, had knowledge of, or covered up illegal wiretapping, bugging, and other intrusions into the privacy of citizens. Some of the testimony implied that President Nixon knew of the cover-up before the 1972 election. The President refused to appear before the Senate Committee or to release White House documents that might throw light on the issue on the ground that disclosure would violate the constitutional principle of "separation of powers" and the doctrine of "executive privilege." The United States Supreme Court has never been called upon to determine the circumstances under which the Executive may refuse to reveal information to Congress, nor do historians agree as to use of "executive privilege" by former Presidents.

The Watergate hearings revealed a "mind-boggling" story of illegal acts, characterized by former Attorney General John N. Mitchell himself as "White House horrors." Besides "extracurricular" eavesdropping, the alleged activities included burglarizing the office of the psychiatrist of Dr. Daniel Ellsberg (who was accused of stealing the "Pentagon Papers"), spiriting out of Washington of Dita D. Beard, lobbyist for the International Telephone and Telegraph Company, falsification of a cable to link President Kennedy with the death of South Vietnam President Ngo Dinh Diem, and a proposal to firebomb the Brookings Institution, a private research organization. At least some of the participants in Watergate and its aftermath appeared to have been guided by the view that *the end justifies the means*.

While the Watergate Committee hearings headed by Senator Ervin were going on, a grand jury in Washington, D.C. was investigating the case. The grand jury went into recess temporarily in order to give the Special Prosecutor Archibald Cox and his staff an opportunity to familiarize themselves with the case. Cox attempted unsuccessfully to have the televised Senate Committee hearings suspended, and the investigations continued simultaneously, one a legislative inquiry and the other judicial.

On July 16, 1973, a former deputy assistant to the President testified under oath before the Senate Watergate Committee that secret tape recordings were made of conversations over the President's telephone and in certain rooms in the White House for the sake of "history." These tapes could shed light on who is telling the truth about Watergate. The President's refusal to release any of the recordings to the Watergate Committee or to the Special Prosecutor under the so-called doctrine of "executive privilege" has created a constitutional crisis that the American people must face in the coming years, as well as the courts and Congress. The legal, political, and social consequences of Watergate and its practical effect on eavesdropping may not be fully apparent for a long time.

Eavesdropping under State Laws

When Title III became law in 1968, only a few States permitted eavesdropping by law enforcement officials under court order: Maryland, Massachusetts, Nevada, New York, and Oregon. Most States, including California, Illinois, and Pennsylvania, had laws *prohibiting* wiretapping, the statutes of which specifically barred wiretapping by law enforcement officials. Louisiana, on the other hand, allowed law enforcement officials to wiretap without a court order. Title III makes State, as well as Federal eavesdropping, possible. It authorizes State law enforcement officers to engage in intercepting wire and oral communications under conditions at least as restrictive as the Federal law, provided two conditions are met:

1. The State enacts a statute for that purpose.
2. The State statute conforms to the requirements of Title III.

The States have been rather slow to take advantage of this encouragement to eavesdrop, and a variety of reasons have been proffered: concern over invasion of privacy, influence of powerful organized crime figures and State officials, or possibly mere apathy. Some of the State laws now permitting court-ordered eavesdropping merely amended existing statutes. A few states enacted completely new laws to conform to Title III, among them Florida, Minnesota, Nebraska, New Jersey, Rhode Island, and South Dakota. New York, which has had court-ordered eavesdropping for over thirty years, enacted a new law in 1969 conforming to Title III, to replace a 1968 law that preceded Title III by two weeks. These new State laws follow the Federal statute in a general way, but they differ from Title III and from one another in various details: who may apply for a court order, covered offenses, and the maximum time period for intercepting communications.

New Jersey permits emergency wiretapping without a court order; a few States provide for reports to State officials (Massachusetts, Minnesota, New Jersey, New York). Several States attempt to deal with "national security" cases (Colorado, Georgia).

Some of the State laws seem to be more restrictive than the Federal law. For example: Florida specifically limits orders in gambling cases to those of an organized nature or involving conspiracy; Georgia sets a maximum period of ten days for warrants, and makes physical destruction of evidence or information obtained mandatory if the eavesdropping does not produce evidence of the specific crime set forth in the warrant; Massachusetts directs the law pointedly against organized crime, and places reports in the public domain; Minnesota, like Georgia, limits orders to a period of ten days and requires recording on wire or tape. New Jersey's "emergency" clause offers added protection against misuse; verbal approval of a judge is required during the emergency period, and if no application is made or an application is denied, the tape recording must be delivered to the court and sealed.

Two changes in the New York law make it less restrictive than it was in 1968: the time period for an order was increased from twenty to thirty days, and a "return" summarizing conversations intercepted is no longer required. The return requirement was eliminated from the New York statute because the Federal law does not include it, but failure of Title III to require a return has been cited as a constitutional deficiency.

Politics may play a considerable part in the ultimate decision of a State to authorize or ban eavesdropping. The "law and order" mood of the country has prompted serious proposals to permit wiretapping even in States which have traditionally been opposed to the practice, such as California and Illinois. If the Federal government continues to step up use of its eavesdropping powers throughout the country, States may have no choice but to enact laws to conform to Title III. Law enforcement is, after all, primarily a matter of local concern, and the States have always guarded their preserves against national encroachment. An advocate of eavesdropping in Illinois warned that failure to change the State law would give its citizens no assurance that their communications were not being intercepted:

> They may be intercepted by Federal agents acting pursuant to valid Federal court order.[16]

Commenting on a proposed bill introduced in the California legislature, one proponent of the law said:

> We are past the point where the question is whether or not we will allow any eavesdropping—passage of the Omnibus Act insures that Federal agents will have this tool. What California can do is to improve on the Federal legislation . . . the way to guard against abuse of this technique is simply to control it.[17]

Proposed laws in the States reflect some of the dissatisfactions with weaknesses in the Federal law and in eavesdropping practices. In the California bill, fewer persons were authorized to apply for orders than the Federal Act permitted, and to facilitate control, a statement of the identity of the police officer who is to carry out the order was required. In Illinois, it was recommended that orders should not be valid for more than fifteen days, and that communications intercepted but not covered by the judicial order should not be permitted to be used for any purpose. In Montana, it was proposed that mandatory training schools be established for local, State, and Federal law enforcement officials to instruct and explain potential advantages and vast responsibilities that accompany electronic surveillance.

In each State, those who argued in favor of the proposed law to legalize official eavesdropping stressed the need to fight organized crime. Those who opposed it were troubled by the difficulty in striking a balance between the problem of organized crime and the preservation of individual freedom. Politics may play a part not only in enacting legislation to permit eavesdropping, but also in the extent to which eavesdropping authority is exercised. Not all states which have laws sanctioning court-ordered wiretapping and electronic surveillance use them. For the calendar year 1970, only twelve of the nineteen States which had such laws were listed in the annual report to Congress by the Administrative Office of the United States Courts as having obtained eavesdrop orders. For 1971, only fourteen of the twenty jurisdictions with power to make applications exercised their authority under State law. In 1972, eighteen of the twenty-one jurisdictions which had laws authorizing courts to issue orders permitting wiretapping or bugging were reported to have used such statutes. New York accounted for 45 percent of all orders signed by State judges in 1972, New Jersey for 36 percent, leaving only 19 percent for all the rest of the States.

The Watergate exposures may cause some States to reconsider passage of any law that encourages eavesdropping, legal or illegal.

4

Organized Crime— Target of Title III

Before passage of Title III in 1968, the reason for legalizing eavesdropping offered most frequently and with greatest fervor was that it was necessary to combat organized crime. Congress acknowledged this need in its introductory findings in the law [Sec. 801(c)]:

> Organized criminals make extensive use of wire and oral communications. . . . The interception of such communications . . . is an indispensable aid to law enforcement and the administration of justice.

Section 2518(7)(a) of Title III provides for forty-eight-hour emergency eavesdropping without court order in case of "conspiratorial activities characteristic of organized crime." No other direct reference to organized crime appears in the statute. Was Title III intended by Congress to be directed primarily against organized crime? Sponsors of the law have not denied that syndicated crime was its prime target, but opponents of government eavesdropping claim that it has been diverted to other purposes—for large-scale arrests of petty gamblers and small-time narcotics dealers to fatten up the statistics of success, and for more direct political purposes. If eavesdropping under Title III is not succeeding in flushing out leaders of organized crime, it may be inferred that this method of surveillance is not very effective for the purpose.

Senator John L. McClellan, chief sponsor of court-ordered eavesdropping, has stated unequivocally that organized crime was a chief target:

> Our major purpose in enacting Title III was to strike at organized crime.[1]

The *Senate Report* on Title III likewise states that "the major purpose of Title III is to combat organized crime." Several pages of the report are devoted to discussion of the growth of modern organized crime with its attendant corruption of political and law enforcement processes, its activities

49

and threat to the democratic system. Explaining the need for electronic surveillance as a weapon against organized crime, the *Senate Report* quotes
from the report of the President's Crime Commission, "The Challenge of
Crime in a Free Society" (1967):

> In organized crime enterprises . . . the possibility of loss or
> seizure of an incriminating document demands a minimum of written
> communication. Because of the varied character of organized crime
> enterprises, the large numbers of persons employed in them, and fre-
> quently the distances separating elements of the organization, the
> telephone remains an essential vehicle for communication.[2]

In the hearings before the Subcommittee on Criminal Laws and
Procedures on the proposed bill authorizing court-ordered eavesdropping,
the following colloquy took place between Senator McClellan and a witness, William Walsh, an attorney from Houston, Texas:

> *Sen. McClellan:* Are we to permit organized crime, the hoodlums,
>   the underworld, to continue to use this technique but not
>   combat it with the same effort, the same instrumentalities?
> *Mr. Walsh:* Senator, organized crime is basically a police problem.
>   You do not have organized crime without the consent and
>   toleration of the police. We do not have organized crime in
>   Houston. . . .
> *Sen. McClellan:* . . . I think *the end justifies the means* [italics added]
>   because of conditions we have in this country today with or-
>   ganized crime increasing. It is definitely entrenched in many lo-
>   calities and wiretapping is one of the most effective ways to get
>   to the top.

The issue was put clearly by the Senator before the Subcommittee as a
choice between combating organized crime or insisting on the right of privacy:

> Is the risk of having an occasional conversation overheard where
> something is said that you would not want anybody else to hear going
> to deter our law enforcement officials from combating organized
> crime, or is that presumed right of privacy more precious to us than
> using this instrumentality to effectively combat organized crime . . .
> that is the issue before us.

Senator McClellan concluded that "if we are unwilling to take this
small risk, then organized crime will continue to flourish."[3] Commenting in
1971 on the effectiveness of authorized eavesdropping, the Senator called
Title III the "culmination of attempts over the past forty years . . . to arm

law enforcement with a sorely needed tool to combat the forces of organized crime."

> If we can at the Federal and State level arm our police with the tools they so sorely need, I am hopeful that we can arrest and reverse the growth of organized crime in the United States.[4]

G. Robert Blakey, one of the chief draftsmen of Title III, testified at the hearings in the Senate that court-ordered eavesdropping was needed because without "effective legal tools" it was impossible to "move against the top people" in organized crime.[5] Similar testimony was presented by Frank S. Hogan, District Attorney of New York County for more than a quarter of a century and one of the staunchest supporters of court-ordered eavesdropping. According to Mr. Hogan, wiretapping is "the single most valuable and effective weapon of law enforcement," and this is true "particularly in the battle against organized crime." In his office, he said, it was "almost exclusively . . . used in the field of organized crime."[6]

The use of eavesdropping to fight organized crime was also stressed by John N. Mitchell, the Nixon Administration's first Attorney General. At the Senate Judiciary Committee hearing on his confirmation as Attorney General, Mr. Mitchell said his administration would be different in the "extent to which electronic surveillance may be used, particularly in the area of organized crime." In July 1970, he declared that investigative wiretapping against organized crime under court order increased 100 percent over the orders obtained in 1969. Later, in an address before the International Association of Police in Atlantic City, New Jersey, Mr. Mitchell reminded the group that the Democrats were opposed to police wiretapping, and said:

> In this period of intensive organized crime activity, we cannot afford to shun a method that is both effective and compatible with constitutional law.

At a convention of the Associated Press Managing Editors Association in Philadelphia late in 1971, Mr. Mitchell reported on the status of the Federal effort against organized crime and the key role of Title III in that effort.[7]

It seems reasonably clear that Title III was intended to deal primarily with organized crime, but whether that intent has been carried out is an open question that must be met in evaluating the law. One must also ask whether catching a few top leaders in organized crime will cripple a syndicate or even ruffle those who get caught. In 1971 a witness before the Senate Permanent Investigations Subcommittee who had turned State's evidence after reduction of a sentence for transportation of stolen securities asked the Senators, to their obvious amusement:

What can you do to the big guy? He's got so much money two years in the can is like a vacation to him.[8]

His comment was no joke, but a blunt statement of fact. Investigation of a county jail in New York by undercover agents was reported to reveal that "some organized crime figures received favored treatment, including liquor, narcotics, and services of women prisoners."[9] A witness suggested that the best solution to the crime problem was to leave the bosses alone and go after the agents on the street. This may be practical advice, but street agents are visible to the police and wiretapping is not needed to expose them.

What Is Organized Crime?

The problem of organized crime is complicated by the fact that no generally accepted definition of the term has ever been formulated. The descriptive and functional definitions presented in Chapter 1 are too vague for use under Title III. The very existence of organized crime is disputed, as well as its ethnic composition, method of operation, internal structure, extent of power and role in American society. Sociologists have been saying for almost two decades that organized crime is a product and reflection of our national culture; that it is interrelated with behavior patterns and social institutions in American life. Like the political machine, crime has a "functional role" in the society; it serves as a means for marginal groups to attain wealth, fame, and power, a shortcut to the great American dream of individual success. The gangster in the crowded slum tries to acquire what is denied to him by the "complex orderings of a stratified society." His goals are normal; he wants what the ordinary citizen strives to attain—independence, social advancement, and prestige.[10]

Two decades ago, Daniel Bell wrote a persuasive article in which he traced the involvement of immigrant groups in marginal business and crime, in their attempt to establish a place for themselves in American life. One after another, the Irish, the Eastern European Jews, and then the Italians tried to climb the ladder of social mobility through the urban rackets, the illicit activity organized for continuing profit. Bell criticized the Kefauver Committee for failing to understand that organized gambling was a function of a mass consumption economy and that crime was a route of social ascent. The Italian community was simply achieving wealth and political influence much later and in a harder way than previous immigrant groups. The foundation of many distinguished older American fortunes was laid by sharp practices and morally reprehensible methods not unlike those currently used.

The early settlers and founding fathers, as well as those who "won the west" and built up cattle, mining, and other fortunes, often did so by shady speculation and a not inconsiderable amount of violence. They ignored, circumvented, or stretched the law when it stood in the way of America's destiny, and their own—or were themselves the law when it served their purposes.[11]

Bell predicted, inaccurately, that the lush profits were passing from gambling and that organized crime would therefore abandon this form of illegal activity. He foresaw that attempts to regulate public morals and discourage gambling by outlawing it would meet with repeated failure.

Sixteen years after Bell's seminal study, another sociologist, Stuart L. Hills, complained that "little attention has been directed to the recognition that organized crime is an integral and vital part of the American way of life." It is impossible, said Hills, to cope with this pattern of syndicated, systematic criminal activity, if it is viewed as a detached social phenomenon—alien to American values and institutions. Increased use of wiretapping and electronic bugging devices may be useful, but the "dangers of abuse may outweigh the benefits." Persistent efforts to curb the human appetite by legislation reflected a puritanical value system that brooked no compromise with an "evil," although the laws were unenforceable. Hills restated the reasons, intimated by Bell, for the difficulties in dealing effectively with large-scale organized crime: criminality was viewed in terms of individual malady rather than a consequence of participation in a social system; activity in which significant segments of the public desired to indulge was made illegal; the society placed a higher value on the rewards of individual success than the means of achievement; and opportunities for these rewards were becoming increasingly limited for various minority groups.[12]

Despite the protests of sociologists that "organized crime" is not the exclusive domain of any one ethnic group and that it is rooted in the American get-rich-quick culture, the term is often used synonymously with the "Mafia" or "La Cosa Nostra," implying that it is composed exclusively or largely of persons of Italian extraction.[13] Since 1957, when eavesdropping revealed the meeting in Apalachin, New York, of about seventy-five alleged leaders of the "Mafia," many law enforcement officers, prosecutors, and Congressional investigators have become convinced that organized crime does exist and that it is controlled by a confederation of persons of Italian extraction.[14] Federal agencies, including the Federal Bureau of Investigation and the Bureau of Narcotics and Dangerous Drugs, say they have identified thousands of members of a highly organized criminal group related by nationality, marriage, and other ties, most of them Italians. The President's Commission on Law Enforcement and Administration of Justice shared this view of the ethnic nature of organized crime. In 1967 the Commission reported:

> Today the core of organized crime in the United States consists of 24 groups operating as criminal cartels in large cities across the Nation. Their membership is exclusively Italian, they are in frequent communication with each other, and their smooth functioning is insured by a national body of overseers. . . . These 24 groups work with and control other racket groups, whose leaders are of various ethnic derivations.[15]

Unlike the sociologists, the Commission attributed failure of efforts to curb the growth of organized crime in the United States to difficulties in obtaining proof, lack of resources and coordination among law enforcement agencies, failure to develop strategic intelligence, leniency of judges, and absence of sustained public commitment. "The public," said the Commission, "does not see or understand the effects of organized crime in society." Former Attorney General Ramsey Clark agrees that the "Mafia" exists in the United States, but believes that monopoly of certain enterprises in organized crime is giving way to Blacks and Spanish-speaking entrepreneurs. He sees organized crime as a minor part of total crime in America. Others say there is an organized crime "industry" of more than 100,000 gangsters who operate with the "Mafia" or independently.

The Nixon Administration, particularly the Criminal Division of the Department of Justice, has been criticized for transferring emphasis from crime in general to investigations of persons of Italian extraction.[16] In protest, an organization of Italian-Americans picketed Federal agencies, charging them with discrimination and harassment.[17] The Italian-American Civil Rights League claimed that 20 million Italian-Americans felt they were being stereotyped in the public eye by the activities of a few underworld figures. The "Mafia," said the League, is a figment of the imagination of the police and the press. But the shooting in July 1972 of Joseph A. Colombo, Sr., head of the League, at a street rally celebrating Italian-American Unity Day in New York City, set off a wave of gangland murders that may never be solved. After a few innocent bystanders were killed in the process, the police were ordered to "dry up the profits of organized crime."[18]

Major activities of organized crime are usually listed as gambling, narcotics, and loan sharking. Organized crime supplies goods and services desired by a large part of the public. Within recent years it has diversified its operations and infiltrated legitimate business. It is also generally undisputed that organized crime can flourish only if there is official corruption. The President's Commission reported:

All available data indicate that organized crime flourishes only where it has corrupted local officials. . . . In different places at different times, organized crime has corrupted police officials, prosecutors, legislators, judges, regulatory agency officials, mayors, councilmen, and other public officials.[19]

The connection between organized crime and official corruption was recognized long ago. The United States has been called a racket-ridden and corrupted society, "a society in pursuit of the meretricious and the unreal," with each man scrambling to grab a piece of the racket for himself according to the business ethic that only profit counts. For specific instances of corruption, one need only glance at the newspapers. In June 1972, the press reported the indictment of the one-hundred thirty-first public official in the State of New Jersey since the beginning of the "crackdown" on corruption in 1969.[20] In September 1972, the Governor of the State of New York, Nelson A. Rockefeller, appointed Maurice H. Nadjari as special Deputy Attorney General to combat corruption among police, prosecutors, and judges in New York City, pursuant to the recommendation of the Knapp Commission. In his first five days in office, it was reported that Nadjari had received hundreds of complaints—and tips![21]

The police disclaim the charge of widespread corruption and say that "the real miracle is that so few police officers will take money." They place the blame elsewhere:

> Gambling, prostitution, narcotics are controlled by big business . . . the police officer is a fall guy for the demand of the press to end corruption.[22]

Police Departments in major cities have been conducting intensive drives to expose corruption among policemen and to eliminate it. Administrative changes have been suggested, but it is doubtful that this would stop police graft. The F.B.I. reported that a man suspected of running a 6 million dollars a year policy racket paid out $1,500 a month for city police protection. The victim's only complaint was that since reorganization of the Police Department he had to pay thirty-two policemen instead of the nineteen formerly on his payroll! One commentator expressed the hopelessness of ending corruption in victimless crimes, particularly gambling:

> As long as a pleasure-loving society paradoxically insists on making several of its chief pleasures illegal, then police corruption will inevitably spring up in the void between the law and reality . . . if consenting adults wish to gamble . . . the government is wasting its money . . . if it tries to stop them.[23]

Table 1. Percentage of Orders According to Nature of Offense

Year	Gambling (%)	Narcotics (%)	Other (%)
1968	11½	40	48½
1969	33⅓	25	41⅔
1970	55	20	25
1971	70	15	15
1972	58	27	15

Data from the annual reports to Congress by the Administrative Office of the United States Courts, Washington, D.C.

The vast majority of eavesdrop orders obtained under Title III during the past few years related to gambling and narcotics, as shown in Table 1.

While the figures indicate a shift in 1972 from gambling cases to narcotics, the combined percentage of the two offenses remained the same, 85 percent in both 1971 and 1972. In view of this emphasis on gambling and narcotics, it may be helpful to examine the various levels at which operations are conducted. If the objective of government eavesdropping is to expose the higher echelons of organized crime which are shielded from investigation and prosecution under normal investigative techniques, then the status within the criminal group of those reached with the aid of Title III is significant in evaluating its operation.

Gambling and Organized Crime

Gambling has been called "the very heartbeat" of organized crime, the largest single producer of income, the treasure chest of the underworld that makes loan sharking and all other rackets possible. It has been estimated that illegal gambling yields a gross income to organized crime of 50 billion dollars annually, but the amount is really unknown.[24] Illegal gambling may take any one of a variety of forms:

1. Bookmaking and poolselling
2. Numbers, policy, bolita, and lotteries
3. Dice games and roulette
4. Card games
5. Coin-operated devices

A *bookmaker* accepts the bets of others on a particular event, fixes the odds, and pays off winners. *Numbers, policy,* or *bolita* are more widespread than any other gambling activity except bookmaking. It can be played for pennies, nickels, dimes, quarters, or higher stakes. Today the play is often $.50, $1, or $10. It is popular with the urban poor, but has also spread to

Wall Street. The player bets that he can guess the three-digit number that will appear on a certain tabulation, such as the total amount bet at a designated race track on a particular day. Money "moves upward from the street" through at least six levels, beginning with the bettor who hands his few cents or dollars to the runner on the street.[25]

A chief target of court orders for wiretapping under Title III has been the person who handles the "layoff," a type of gambling insurance carried on by bookmakers on a neighborhood, regional, or national basis. A bookmaker who has received too large an amount in bets on a particular horse or other event spreads the play with another "bookie" or "layoff man" with fewer bets on that event. The layoff man, in turn, has arrangements with individuals on the next level of the hierarchy. A "bookie" does not look for a gambler; it is the gambler who seeks out the bookie.

It is almost impossible for gambling on a large scale to function without the knowledge of local law enforcement. New York State Supreme Court Justice John M. Murtagh, in sentencing two gamblers, said that the case clearly demonstrated widespread corruption of police by gamblers, and that gambling is accompanied almost inevitably by police corruption. Judge Murtagh made it clear that he disapproved of laws that made gambling illegal:

> I don't believe that gambling is a violation of any moral law. But our society has seen fit to make it illegal.[26]

Traditionally, gambling has been considered a problem for State regulation. Large-scale gambling, however, operates across State lines, as witnesses at Congressional hearings explained to Senators.

> You cannot have professional gambling unless you get the morning line from somewhere, and that is usually out in the West, either in Chicago or Minneapolis. Big gamblers, when they want to lay off any bets, lay them off either in Kentucky, New Orleans, or Miami. . . . They also have a system of . . . sending out the race results within a few minutes after a race . . . will telephone the results . . . to Maryland where they then send it over the entire country.[27]

The Organized Crime Control Act of 1970 prohibits illegal gambling businesses on the theory that it "involves widespread use of, and has an effect upon, interstate commerce." It also establishes a "Commission to Review National Policy toward Gambling," but the report of the Commission's findings will not be submitted until October 1976.[28]

Legalization of gambling has often been suggested to enable the government to reap the profits, rather than organized crime. This intriguing idea is gaining in popularity, and financial pressures are beginning to outweigh moral, political, and practical objections in some States.[29] Instead of increasing State and local taxes to meet rising costs of Government, why not raise revenue by legalizing gambling? Gambling taxes were reported to have netted the State of Nevada almost 55 million dollars in 1972, an increase of 31.7 percent over the previous year.[30] In New Jersey, hearings on widening legalized gambling began in July 1972 upon defeat of a State income tax proposal. All forms of gambling were considered, including the game of jai alai, policy, and betting on sport pools. Lobbying for legalized gambling at the hearing was a group of women whose husbands had been jailed for gambling offenses, wearing tags reading "Ladies in Waiting"![31]

Creation of the Off-Track Betting Corporation in New York and establishment of State lotteries are attempts to drain off some of the money that normally finds its way into illegal gambling. New Hampshire initiated a lottery in 1964, New York in 1967, and New Jersey in 1970. In 1972, Connecticut, Massachusetts, Michigan, and Pennsylvania also succumbed to the lure of this source of income. Some lotteries direct their appeal to poor people in the cities by selling tickets at $.50 and offering many prizes with an occasional tantalizing million-dollar payoff. Opponents of legalized gambling shake their heads in disapproval; organized crime will "muscle in" anyway, they predict.

The entry of State governments into the business of gambling adds weight to the argument that it is sheer hypocrisy to treat gambling as crime, and that costly wiretapping and electronic surveillance should not be used to seek convictions for gambling.

Narcotics and Organized Crime

Narcotics interests appear to be closely related to those of gambling. Profits from illegal betting are reported to be used to finance large-scale heroin importation and distribution.[32] As in gambling, profits in narcotics are said to be enormous—$350 of raw material can assume a value of $500,-000 by the time it is sold as heroin at retail. Until a few years ago, most corruption among police was supposed to involve gambling. More recently, it appears that the single largest graft problem may be narcotics. The illegal sale and distribution by organized crime of narcotics and dangerous drugs move through six levels of personnel, at each of which the drug is diluted and adulterated:

1. Importers of multi-kilo lots—the top level
2. Kilo men who buy from the importer-supplier and obtain delivery through a courier; at least one kilogram of heroin is handled at a time
3. Quarter-kilo men
4. Ounce men
5. Deck men, handling less than an ounce
6. Street dealers who sell in five-grain packets, known as "bags," "packs," or "balloons"

An estimated half-million addicts in the United States consume about six to ten tons of heroin a year, all of which comes from abroad.[33] There is much dispute as to who controls the illegal narcotics industry in the United States. One crime expert claims the "Mafia" decided to retire from narcotics at the end of 1958 and that Spanish-speaking criminals have moved in—Spaniards, Cubans, Puerto Ricans, and South Americans. However, the Bureau of Narcotics and Dangerous Drugs and the Bureau of Customs say that the old leaders continue to run the industry from "on high."

Attempts to stem the flow of narcotics into the United States by checking the growth of opium poppies around the world have not proved very effective. As one source of supply is plugged, another opens up. Formerly, most of the heroin imported illegally into the United States was believed to have originated in the poppy fields of Turkey and to have been processed near Marseilles in southern France. Now much of it is known to be cultivated in the Middle East and Indochina, and laboratories have sprung up in Brussels, Amsterdam, Madrid, and Zurich. A report, "World Opium Survey, 1972," released by the State Department in August 1972, identifies three basic smuggling routes: from Europe direct to the United States or through Canada; from Europe by way of Mexico; or from Europe by way of Latin America and the Caribbean. According to the report, the United States and other countries have succeeded in seizing "only a small fraction of the illegal flow" of heroin.[34] The poor results of law enforcement efforts were attributed to "widely varying national attitudes toward the drug problem." In summarizing the traffic in various countries, the report listed Italy as one of the transit points and stated:

> Some organized groups of Mafiosi remain in close liaison with their Corsican counterparts and the American Mafia in the international traffic in heroin . . . arrests appear to have involved only minor figures.

The report estimated that France was still responsible for 80 percent of the heroin that came into the United States. Early in 1972 a former French intelligence agent, Roger deLouette, pleaded guilty to Federal charges of smuggling into the United States heroin worth 12 million dollars. DeLouette claimed he had been recruited into an international narcotics smuggling ring in France by a top French counterespionage official, Colonel Paul Fournier. The French authorities refused to extradite Fournier but sent their chief examining magistrate, Gabriel Roussel, as a one-man grand jury to interrogate deLouette. In the presence of United States officials, Roussel sought to undermine deLouette's credibility and defend the integrity of French intelligence agencies. Fournier, the alleged "boss," is still in France. DeLouette, the underling who says he took on the narcotics job to support a wife, their five children, a mistress, and an illegitimate child, was sentenced to jail for eighteen months. Despite the evidence, the French Defense Minister insisted that the charges against Colonel Paul Fournier "come from a man with an imagination like a serialized novel."[35]

The American Ambassador to France has denied that the French are dragging their feet and showing lack of vigor in the war on drugs. "The biggest cops-and-robbers game in history is going on around Marseilles," he said.[36] Unfortunately, as anyone knows who has seen the movie, "The French Connection," or read Robin Moore's book, the game does not necessarily land the top man in jail. It is the lower echelon go-between whose wire is tapped and who is likely to get caught.

Wiretapping under Title III of the Omnibus Act of 1968 has been used extensively in narcotics investigations—25 percent of court orders in 1969, 20 percent in 1970, 15 percent in 1971 and 27 percent in 1972. However, the annual report to Congress does not show whether the targets were importers of multi-kilo lots, street dealers, or middle echelon suspects. Administration officials admit that the best they can do is to "make it hard for the professionals," upset supply systems, and persuade some to get out of the business. Critics say that piecemeal programs and eavesdropping on couriers are ineffective and sorry efforts in a drug crisis, like "baling out the Atlantic Ocean with a teaspoon."[37]

Loan Sharking and Organized Crime

Loan sharking is the lending of money at excessive rates, higher than the limit prescribed by law. The rate fixed by the underworld loan shark is what the traffic will bear, reputed to be about 20 percent a week.[38] Next to gambling, loan sharking is said to be the greatest income producer for organized crime, and there is a connection between the two forms of activity. A series of coordinated raids in 1972 by the New York State "Organized Crime Task Force" and county district attorneys indicated that bookmaking and loan sharking operations overlapped. As in gambling, the loan shark does not hunt for a victim. The would-be borrower seeks out the "juice man."

Government competition in lending has been suggested as a way to eliminate loan sharking by organized crime. Marginal businessmen and low-income individuals who are unable to obtain funds through legitimate financial sources often turn to the loan shark. Congress placed loan sharking under Federal control by enacting Title II of the Consumer Credit Protection Act of 1968 (Public Law 90-321, Sec. 201). Extortionate credit transactions, said Congress, though purely intrastate, adversely affect interstate commerce, and there is a sufficient connection between loan sharks and interstate crime to sustain Federal regulation of such activities. The role of loan sharking in organized crime was spelled out in the House debates:

> The loan shark . . . is the indispensable "money mover" of the underworld. He takes "black" money tainted by its derivation from the gambling and narcotics rackets and turns it "white" by funneling it into channels of legitimate trade. In so doing, he exacts usurious interest . . . and . . . by his imposition of impossible penalties, he greases the way for the underworld takeover of entire businesses.[39]

Senator Proxmire, in presenting the Conference Report on the proposed legislation, defended Federal assumption of responsibility for loan sharking:

> Organized crime operates on a national scale. . . . If we are to win the battle against organized crime, we must strike at their source of revenue and give the Justice Department additional tools.[40]

Obviously, the Senator did not think that government eavesdropping was adequate to deal with loan sharks; "additional tools" were needed. Compared with gambling and narcotics, few court orders have been obtained under Title III of the Omnibus Act of 1968 in investigations of loan sharking or usury: in 1969 five orders; in 1970 seven orders; in 1971 five orders. In 1972, the number increased to thirteen, of which seven were Federal orders and only six were State orders, evenly divided between New York and New Jersey. This rise in number represented only .015 percent of all orders issued.

The Federal law against loan sharking was upheld by the United States Supreme Court in 1971 (*Perez v. United States*).[41] The Court recognized loan sharking in its national setting as "one way organized interstate crime holds its guns to the heads of the poor and the rich alike and syphons funds . . . to finance its national operations." In the majority opinion of 8 to 1, Justice Douglas discussed in detail the economic, financial, and social setting of the problem as revealed to Congress:

> The loan shark racket provides organized crime with its second most lucrative source of revenue, exacts millions from the pockets of people, coerces its victims into the commission of crimes against property, and causes the takeover by racketeers of legitimate businesses.[42]

The facts in the case presented to the Supreme Court for review were gruesome, but typical of a loan shark operation. Alcides Perez advanced $1,000 to Miranda, the owner of a new butcher shop, to be repaid in instalments of $105 for fourteen weeks. The terms seemed not unconscionable, considering the prevailing bank interest rate. Soon, however, the transaction took a sinister turn. Justice Douglas tells the sad story in the matter-of-fact language of the courts:

After paying at this rate for six or eight weeks, [Perez] increased the weekly payments to $130. In two months Miranda asked for an additional loan of $2,000 which was made. . . . Miranda was to pay $205 a week. In a few weeks [Perez] increased the weekly payments to $330. When Miranda objected, [Perez] told him about a customer who refused to pay and ended up in a hospital. So Miranda paid. In a few months [Perez] increased his demands to $500 weekly which Miranda paid, only to be advised that at the end of the week petitioner would need $1,000. Miranda made that payment by not paying his suppliers; but, faced with a $1,000 payment the next week, he sold his butcher shop.[43]

Perez pursued Miranda relentlessly, first threatening the butcher's wife and then telling Miranda he could have him castrated. Miranda insisted he could pay no more than $25 a week. He was told to steal or sell drugs if necessary; even going to jail was better than going to a hospital with a broken back or legs. Perez boasted:

I could have sent you to the hospital, you and your family, any moment I want with my people.

A jury found Perez guilty, and his sentence was affirmed by the United States Court of Appeals, with one judge dissenting. The maximum penalty under Federal law was twenty years in prison and a fine of $10,000. Perez was sentenced to jail for eighteen months. The United States Supreme Court affirmed the conviction, rejecting his "impassioned plea" that the Federal statute was unconstitutional. The lone dissenter, Justice Stewart, could see no rational distinction between loan sharking and other local crime. The transaction between Perez and Miranda, he said, was a wholly local activity. It was beyond the power of Congress to enact a law under which a man could be indicted without any proof of interstate movement, of the use of facilities of interstate commerce, or of facts showing that his conduct affected interstate commerce.

It is not enough to say that loan sharking is a national problem, for all crime is a national problem.[44]

Not all victims are as willing as Miranda, the butcher, to risk the wrath of the loan shark. Often they are like the Brooklyn baker who, according to a story told by the head of the Brooklyn Strike Force Against Organized Crime, paid $8,000 on a one-year loan of $5,000 to open his shop and later contradicted information given to the F.B.I., apparently because of fear for his life. This usury victim pleaded guilty to lying to the Federal grand jury. The alleged extortionist was Joseph Gambino, brother of Carlo Gambino, reputed boss of a powerful "Mafia" family in the New York metropolitan area.[45]

Legitimate Business and Organized Crime Compared

There are some striking similarities between organized crime and legitimate business enterprises. Both seek to establish and maintain monopolies, to maximize profits, and to control or influence elected and appointed government officials. Organized crime, like big business, is a bureaucracy; no member is indispensable and the jailing of an individual, whether low or high echelon, may disrupt the organization temporarily while he is being replaced, but his absence leaves it structurally intact.[46] The following list of structural characteristics of organized crime would fit those of the large modern corporation:

1. Hierarchy of authority.
2. Complex division of labor.
3. Departmental specialization.
4. Impersonality.
5. Profit motive.
6. Desire for continuity and survival.
7. Effort to control the market and eliminate competition.[47]

The difference most frequently cited between organized crime and the ordinary large legitimate corporate enterprise is that the former is ready to use a fist, club, or gun to sell its services and maintain its monopolies, while the latter is usually limited to sharp or unfair business practices. However, a perceptive observer notes:

> It is evident from the history of business abuses in the 19th and 20th centuries that "unfair competition" of a drastic sort, including violence, has not been confined to the underworld.[48]

The parallel between the code of ethics of members of organized crime and the ordinary American was deplored by the President's Commission on Law Enforcement and Administration of Justice:

> The leaders of Cosa Nostra and their racketeering allies . . . preach a sermon that all too many Americans heed; the government is for sale; lawlessness is the road to wealth, honesty is a pitfall and morality a trap for suckers.[49]

A member of organized crime was overheard on tape recordings of the F.B.I. expressing a similar view of the prevailing philosophy, but in more colorful language:

> Yeah, if you're a real honest guy, you wind up hunchback and with headaches.[50]

He echoed Al Capone's cynical observation in an earlier time:

Nobody's really on the legit when it comes down to cases.[51]

Criminal activity of legitimate business firms, such as conspiracy in restraint of trade, tax evasion, illegal labor practices, or the marketing of dangerous drugs and harmful foods, are dealt with by regulatory agencies. The same approach in dealing with "black-market" crimes such as gambling and narcotics has been suggested. These are crimes only because a choice has been made to legislate against the service or commodity that they provide. They are "consensual" crimes supplying goods and services that people want. Where the demand is great, law enforcement cannot prevail—with or without eavesdropping.[52]

One respect in which organized crime clearly differs from legitimate business is in its attitude toward communication. No letters are written by organized criminals. Few, if any, records are kept. Conversations over the telephone are guarded, cryptic, and often untranslatable and unintelligible. References to specific individuals are purposely vague to make identification difficult. Nicknames are commonly used, and real names may never be revealed. Conversation is often conducted in code, and top echelon members are insulated from direct participation in crime. The practical difficulties that these modes of communication present in using eavesdrop evidence effectively are highlighted in the cases now moving through the courts to test the constitutionality of eavesdropping under law.

Another striking difference was noted by a long-time student of organized crime after the fifteenth (or some say the twenty-seventh) gangland murder since the shooting of Joseph E. Colombo, Sr., at an outdoor rally in Columbus Circle in New York City:

> When they [the Mafia] want the top jobs they may not be as sophisticated in the way they go after them as the guys at . . . General Motors, but they're a lot more decisive.[53]

Infiltration of Legitimate Business by Organized Crime

Organized crime is believed to have monopoly control over certain types of business enterprises such as garbage collection, jukeboxes, and vending machine distribution. The lever for "muscling in" on these enterprises has been loan sharking. If an owner falls behind on payments to a loan shark, his business may simply be confiscated. An individual who borrows from a loan shark may be forced to place a member of organized crime on the payroll at a high salary, and eventually the company may be taken over by hoodlums. Other methods have been identified by which organized crime obtains control of a wide variety of legitimate businesses:

1. Investment of profits from illegal enterprises, such as gambling and narcotics.

2. Acquisition of business interests in settlement of gambling debts.
3. Foreclosure of mortgages securing usurious loans.
4. Extortion by strong-arm methods or more sophisticated techniques.[54]

All of these devices have been used to infiltrate banks, brokerage houses, real estate syndicates, finance companies, and large public service corporations. The Internal Revenue Service (I.R.S.) says that of 113 top figures in organized crime, 98 have property interests in 159 legitimate businesses.[55] A student of the "Mafia" says that if one were to name every mobster-owned or mobster-infiltrated business, every letter could be filled from A to Z.[56] Conservative Senators like Roman L. Hruska see the infiltration of legitimate business by organized crime as a major threat to the American economic system:

> The proper functioning of a free economy requires that economic decisions be made by persons free to exercise their own judgment. Force or fear limits choice, ultimately reduces quality, and increases prices. When organized crime moves into a business, it brings all the techniques of violence and intimidation which it used in its illegal business. . . . Its effect is even more unwholesome than other monopolies because its position does not rest on economic superiority.[57]

According to the President's Crime Commission, however, "too little is known about the effects on the economy of organized crime entry into the business world." A special study made for the Commission observed that the greatest gambling enterprise in the United States had not been significantly touched by organized crime—the stockmarket! Underworld characters have, however, manipulated some listed stocks on major exchanges, and the method used has been described in detail: a brokerage house is penetrated by obtaining a job for a customer's man with criminal ties. The new man attracts "customers" with substantial funds for investment. Extensive, controlled purchases of stocks in target companies are negotiated. The selling price of the affected stock is run up, rumors are circulated of potential earnings or product development, and mergers and acquisitions are promoted or pretended. When the stock price reaches a high enough level, the underworld manipulators take their profits, leaving management, creditors, and stockholders "holding the bag." This is a familiar technique for manipulating a listed stock and is believed to have been used by so-called respectable members of the business community as well as organized crime.[58]

Legislation designed to prevent infiltration of legitimate business by organized crime has been enacted. In 1967 Senator Hruska introduced a bill (S 2048) making the use of intentionally and deliberately unreported income derived from one line of business in another enterprise a violation of the Antitrust Law. Another bill (S 2049) prohibited investment in legitimate business enterprises of income derived from specified criminal activities, such as gambling, bribery, narcotics, and extortion. Companion bills were introduced in the House of Representatives by Congressman Richard Poff (Republican of Virginia). These proposals are reflected in Title IX of the Organized Crime Control Act of 1970 prohibiting persons who received income from a "pattern of racketeering activity" or through collection of an unlawful debt, to invest it in any enterprise affecting interstate or foreign commerce.[59] The effectiveness and constitutionality of the law are open to attack and testing.

In October 1971 the Senate Commerce Committee chaired by Senator Warren Magnuson opened hearings on infiltration of legitimate business by the underworld. In mid-1973 the hearings had not yet been completed. Hearings on the role of organized crime in thefts of stocks, bonds, and other negotiable instruments from brokerage houses and banks and from the United States mails have also been conducted by the Permanent Subcommittee on Investigations of the Senate Committee on Government Operations, under Senator John L. McClellan. Infiltration of organized crime into sports has been investigated by the House Select Committee on Crime chaired by Congressman Claude Pepper. In July 1972 the Committee listened for ninety-five minutes to an angry Frank Sinatra "bellowing denials . . . that he had ever been a front man for the Mafia." It was reported that a squealing audience laughed and clapped in approval of "The Voice." [60]

Top level members of organized crime are reputed to be multimillionaires, like legitimate business tycoons. They live quietly in the best residential sections, wear Ivy League suits, send their children to select colleges, and sometimes hire public relations firms to bolster their image. They have been called the "robber barons" of the twentieth century, the living proof that crime does pay in America.[61] Has Title III of the Omnibus Act of 1968 been useful in dealing with organized crime and reaching top echelon members? The answer must weigh heavily in evaluating eavesdropping under law. The 1970 Crime Control Act providing law enforcement officers with additional tools and the continuing investigations of Congressional committees would seem to indicate that wiretapping and electronic surveillance have not been very effective in combating organized crime.

The F.B.I. and Organized Crime

Is the F.B.I. doing all it should be doing in the area of organized crime? This is a question that the former Acting Director of the Federal Bureau of Investigation, L. Patrick Gray III, asked himself publicly when he assumed office in May 1972 on the death of J. Edgar Hoover.[62] During forty-eight years of service as Director under sixteen Attorneys General, Hoover was often accused of being slow to recognize the threat of organized crime and hesitant in attacking it.[63] Until 1957 he denied that organized crime existed and denounced wiretapping as a lazy man's tool and an obstacle to the "development of ethical, scientific, and sound investigative techniques." In 1939, Hoover said:

> While I concede that the telephone tap is from time to time of limited value in the criminal investigation, I frankly believe that if a statute of this kind were enacted, the abuses arising therefrom would far outweigh the value which might accrue to law enforcement as a whole.[64]

When the meeting of alleged Mafia chieftains at Apalachin, New York in 1957 was revealed through eavesdropping by a New York investigator, Hoover changed his mind about organized crime and announced dramatically:

> The battle is joined. We have taken up the gauntlet flung down by organized crime. Let us unite in a devastating assault to annihilate this mortal enemy.[65]

The assault on organized crime by Hoover was, in the opinion of his critics, less than devastating. They complained that the Director of the F.B.I. was too preoccupied with spy-thriller intrigues of Communists and other "subversives."

In 1960 the F.B.I. began to provide the Justice Department's Organized Crime and Racketeering Section with intelligence reports on organized crime.[66] Congress gave the F.B.I. jurisdiction to investigate activities of organized crime in the Fall of 1961 under the Travel Act which outlawed interstate shipment of gambling material and made it a Federal crime to travel in interstate commerce for racketeering purposes.[67] From 1961 to 1965 the F.B.I. secretly installed microphones in homes of alleged Mafia chieftains, in offices where they worked, and in bars and restaurants that they frequented, to collect long-term intelligence about organized crime. Transcripts of the surveillance covered thousands of pages, but none of the conversations intercepted could be used in evidence, for the eavesdropping was illegal.[68]

The entire transcript of the recordings made by the F.B.I. was filed in the United States District Court in New Jersey in June 1969, in an action against Samuel Rizzo (Sam the Plumber) DeCavalcante and others, charged with extorting money from gamblers. The attorney for DeCavalcante made a motion to require disclosure of the recorded conversations, apparently in the belief that the Government would rather withdraw the case than release the illegally acquired information. He knew it had been the policy of the

Department of Justice to oppose disclosure of eavesdropping. However, between the time the motion was made and June 12, 1969, the United States Supreme Court had handed down a decision (*Alderman v. United States*)[69] requiring the prosecution to disclose illegal wiretap or bugging evidence to defense counsel, and the Justice Department had changed its policy.

Defendant's counsel failed to ask for a restrictive order making the transcript available only to him and not to the press and public. The United States Attorney, Frederick B. Lacey, Jr. (who later became a Federal judge) thereupon filed the entire transcript of conversations. It exposed intrigues, executions, labor racketeering, extortion, and infiltration of legitimate business by organized crime. The tapes also disclosed wrangling between "families" over jurisdiction in recruiting members and in gambling rackets, and mistrust between partners in the numbers game. Recorded conversations included much "name dropping," implicating high government officials.[70]

When the illegal eavesdropping was revealed by publication of the DeCavalcante recordings, the American Civil Liberties Union of New Jersey asked the United States Attorney to get criminal indictments against F.B.I. agents and officials who had ordered the eavesdropping between 1961 and 1965. No such action was instituted. Hoover insisted that the F.B.I. had not used wiretaps without the authority of the Attorney General, and then only to a limited extent in cases involving the "national security." His dispute with Robert F. Kennedy as to whether such authority had been granted has never been fully resolved. Victor Navasky in his book *Kennedy Justice* seems to divide the blame between Hoover and Kennedy, although he intimates that the F.B.I. Director misled the Attorney General.[71]

The F.B.I. annual report for the past few years has contained a separate section on organized crime, listing a large number of gambling raids and arrests based on information obtained through court-approved eavesdropping. The 1971 report stated that most of the 1,200 arrests under the Organized Crime Control Act were made possible by electronic surveillance. Tom Wicker of the *New York Times* called the F.B.I. annual report "one of Washington's more imaginative documents." He disputed the figures and pointed out that arrests are not convictions; even if organized crime convictions rose by 200 in one year, the record failed to support the claim that the increase was attributable to wiretapping or electronic surveillance.[72]

J. Edgar Hoover was unhappy with the provisions of the Organized Crime Control Act of 1970 charging the F.B.I. with the job of investigating illegal gambling where five or more persons are involved who remain in business thirty days or produce a daily gross of $2,000. "I believe," said Hoover, "this is a function of local law enforcement."[73] The Director of the F.B.I. seemed to be more interested in investigating "subversives." A former agent who served for a year in the F.B.I. claimed that agents were indoctrinated with radical right-wing propaganda and that in training classes "derogatory and obscene remarks were frequently made attacking the motives and integrity of the Supreme Court."[74] A group called "Citizens Commission to Investigate the F.B.I." charged that files lifted from the Bureau's office in Media, Pennsylvania, showed pervasive, illegal surveillance of individuals without evidence of wrongdoing. It was reported that one of the stolen documents consisting of instructions for interviewing applicants for clerical jobs warned:

> Be alert for long hairs, beards, mustaches, pear-shaped heads, truck drivers, etc. . . . . We are not that hard up yet.[75]

In the Fall of 1971, a conference was conducted at Princeton University by a "Committee for Public Justice" to inquire into the role of the F.B.I. in American life. The Committee called the F.B.I. the foremost weapon of government political repression. Friends of the F.B.I. countered by characterizing the conference as a "witchhunt." George S. McGovern, as Senator from South Dakota, urging an investigation of the F.B.I. before Hoover's death, asked:

> Has the F.B.I. outgrown its gang-busting image and preoccupation with spy-thriller intrigues of Communists sufficient to focus attention on real problems of crime regardless of politics?[76]

Hoover defended the record of the F.B.I. He acknowledged the difficulty of dealing with organized crime, but blamed much of it on public apathy.

Since the death of J. Edgar Hoover in May 1972, no clear policy has emerged on F.B.I. dealings with organized crime or use of eavesdropping. On April 27, 1973, the Acting Director of the F.B.I., L. Patrick Gray, III, resigned after disclosure that, at a meeting with White House officials, he had received documents obtained from a key figure in the Watergate bugging and had destroyed the records without examining them.[77] The President then appointed as interim Acting Director William D. Ruckelshaus, formerly Administrator of the Environmental Protection Agency.[78]

On June 26, 1973, the Senate Committee on the Judiciary unanimously approved the nomination of Clarence M. Kelley as Director of the F.B.I. The appointment was confirmed by the Senate, and he took office on July 9, 1973. Kelley, formerly Police Chief of Kansas City, Missouri, had served as an F.B.I. agent under J. Edgar Hoover for more than twenty years. He promised "to serve only justice and to avoid any other force or influence that hurts the cause of justice." Kelley is only the second Director in the entire history of the F.B.I. and the first to take office under the Omnibus Crime Control and Safe Streets Act of 1968, which requires consent of the Senate to the appointment. There is still no limitation on his term of office or compulsory retirement age.

Public Attitude toward Organized Crime

For years, law enforcement officers and Congressional investigators have been trying to convince the public that organized crime exists on a national scale and that it is a grave social problem threatening American society. Public apathy and indifference have been blamed, not only by J. Edgar Hoover but by others, for the inability of law enforcement to deal effectively with organized crime.[79] The public has been interested in the problem intermittently, after each sensational disclosure of the activities of organized crime and the political corruption that supports it. Public pressure for corrective action is exerted for a short while, but soon eases as interest wanes. The public wants the services that organized crime provides, and few can see the connection between gambling and organized crime. People who want to gamble are not dissuaded by the dire warning that a "$2 bet means murder."

In 1967 it was reported that the public was just beginning to confront organized crime. Most Americans did not feel closely threatened by it, although they had "a discomforting awareness of street crime, consumer frauds, and white collar crime." A study of the politics of vice and corruption in a real town, fictitiously called "Wincanton, U.S.A." was made for the President's Commission on Law Enforcement and Administration of Justice. A survey of public attitudes toward gambling and prostitution in the town revealed a general awareness of the existence of these illegal activities, but little perception of payoffs to the police. Information available to the public as to corruption depended on the extent of newspaper coverage. Specific knowledge that a particular official received a kickback to approve a contract became known only after legislative hearings. Residents of the community were tolerant of gambling and intolerant of corruption, but few believed that one produced the other. Warnings of the connection between the two were repeated so often that they made no impact. Only when Federal investigations began to attract national attention did the public respond by voting the ruling party in "Wincanton" out of office and cleaning up the town. The report concluded glumly that "Wincanton" would soon fall back into its old ways unless the voters realized that illegal activities produce corruption.[80]

Today, after much sensational publicity in the press about "Mafia" chieftains and their connection with official corruption, and a popular novel and prize-winning movie whose charming hero becomes a leader of "La Cosa Nostra," organized crime has become a byword. There is, however, no evidence that this has had any effect whatsoever on the demand for the services that organized crime provides, or on the realization by the public that they are both supporters and victims of organized crime. The public turned out in droves for the film "The Godfather," with Marlon Brando playing the role of an aging "Mafia" chieftain.[81] One newspaper writer observed ruefully that the public was already "in midstream of a love affair with the Mafia." Why this fascination with the underworld, he asked, and offered a plausible answer:

> The mystery behind the organization . . . its initiation rites and elaborate code of honor . . . viewing men who can seemingly flaunt the law at will but have precise rules of conduct to live by offers vicarious satisfactions . . . or perhaps it's just nostalgia for the extended family.[82]

Brando's persuasive performance may have unwittingly increased the peculiar affection of the American public for the bold gangster and bolstered its indifference to the impact of organized crime. The "Mafia" Don, as portrayed in the film, is the "amiable, warm-hearted senior citizen," the tragic hero, the family man struggling in order to reach the common goal—a life-style that fits the American dream. After the gangland murder in April 1972 of Joseph Gallo, alleged head of a New York "Mafia" family, as he celebrated his birthday with his bride of a few weeks and her ten-year-old daughter in a public restaurant in Greenwich Village, the *New York Times* delivered a stern rebuke to the public:

> No amount of exaltation in book, film and television can make lovable the overlords of organized crime, men who traffic in the systematic and savage degradation of society, heedless of the wreckage or destruction of life.[83]

How the public feels about organized crime, and whether it is indifferent to it, may influence the general attitude toward government eavesdropping in criminal investigations. Why intrude on personal lives and violate the precious right of privacy by wiretapping and electronic surveillance to control organized crime if it is merely part of the system, or if eavesdropping is ineffective in dealing with the leaders of organized crime?

5

Flaws in Court-Ordered Eavesdropping

The drafting of Title III received distinguished praise in the Supreme Court decision of June 1972 requiring a court order in domestic security cases. Justice Powell, writing for the Court, said that the classes of crime for which an order could be obtained were "carefully specified," offenses were described "with meticulous care and specificity," conditions for use of an order were "carefully circumscribed," and other sections of the Act were drafted with "extraordinary care."[1] However, the law authorizing court-ordered eavesdropping is so detailed and intricate that almost every clause has generated dispute. This cannot be chalked off to poor draftsmanship, as some critics have asserted; it is more justly attributable to the practical necessities of Congressional compromise. Conflicting ideas had to be translated into legislative language that was politically realistic and acceptable, and both intent and attitude differed among those who drafted the law and some of those who voted for it. The common problem of expressing Congressional intent without ambiguity was complicated by the necessity of conforming to the requirements laid down by the Supreme Court in *Berger* and *Katz*, some of which can be described as "slightly fuzzy."

Criticism of court-ordered eavesdropping centers around seven aspects of the procedure mandated by Title III:

1. Offenses for which an order may be obtained are practically unlimited, and are not restricted to those characteristic of organized crime or serious offenses.
2. The provision that the application and order shall describe the *type* of communication sought to be intercepted does not comply with Supreme Court requirements as to particularity.
3. Judge-shopping is possible, and there is opportunity for laxness in supervising interception of conversations.
4. Overhearing of innocent conversations and privileged communications is unavoidable and may be constitutionally impermissible.

5. The thirty-day period allowed for listening in, with an unlimited number of thirty-day extensions, may protract eavesdropping excessively and violate requirements of the Supreme Court.
6. The law is ambiguous as to who is to be notified of the eavesdropping, who may object, and when motions to suppress evidence may be made.
7. Reports required to be filed are inadequate to inform the public and to form the basis for evaluation of operation of Title III.

Both practical and legal problems are involved in these complaints. The day-to-day procedures developed by Federal and State officials and now being tested in the courts are discussed more fully in Chapters 7 and 8. A look at the language of the law is needed first, to fathom the intent of Congress.

Offenses Covered

Government eavesdropping, say its most ardent supporters, is an indispensable tool in fighting organized crime. Its persistent critics retort: the law permits eavesdropping in investigation of many offenses that are not and will not be associated with organized crime. A long list of offenses for which Federal officers may seek a court order appears in Sec. 2516 (1) of Title III:

(a) Offenses relating to espionage, sabotage, treason, riots, and enforcement of the Atomic Energy Act of 1954.
(b) Violation of Federal law restricting payments and loans to labor organizations, or offenses in labor racketeering.
(c) Bribery of public officials and witnesses and sporting contests, unlawful use of explosives, transmission of wagering information . . . obstruction of . . . law enforcement; Presidential assassinations, kidnapping and assault; interference with commerce by threats or violence; interstate and foreign travel or transportation in aid of racketeering; influencing operations of employee benefit plan . . . etc.
(d) Counterfeiting.
(e) Bankruptcy fraud; manufacture, importation, receiving, concealment, buying, selling, or dealing in narcotic drugs, marihuana, or other dangerous drugs.
(f) Extortion, including extortionate credit transactions.
(g) Conspiracy to commit any of the enumerated offenses.

These offenses were selected, according to the *Senate Report* on Title III, because of their seriousness or because they were characteristic of the activities of organized crime.[2] However, eavesdropping in any offense seems to be sanctioned on the theory that organized crime has not limited itself to the commission of any particular offense. The American Bar Association's "Standards Relating to Electronic Surveillance," which follow the *Senate Report* closely, state in conclusion:

> We . . . find that the use of electronic surveillance technique is necessary in the administration of justice in the area of organized crime. . . . The use of these techniques to get evidence of organized crime is not, we feel, the "dirty business" rightly condemned by Mr. Justice Holmes.[3]

The need for eavesdropping in combating organized crime was stressed by witnesses at the Congressional hearings on Title III. Jacob Grumet, then Chairman of the New York State Commission of Investigation, who favored government eavesdropping said:

> In the area of organized crime, there wiretapping is important.

Senator Edward M. Kennedy (Democrat of Massachusetts), who had serious doubts about the wisdom of wiretapping except, perhaps, in homicide cases asked:

> You do not see a relationship between the possibility of wiretapping and solving homicides?

To which Mr. Grumet replied:

> In homicides, no, not too close a relation . . . I was in charge of the Homicide Bureau in New York for many years and handled hundreds of homicides and prosecuted many myself. Wiretapping was not too frequently used if at all, in investigating homicides.[4]

To reach the top men in organized crime, great reliance was placed on the final category of *conspiracy* [Sec. 2516(1) (g)]. Conspiracy has been defined as:

> A combination of two or more persons, by some concerted action, to accomplish some criminal or unlawful purpose, or to accomplish some purpose, not in itself criminal or unlawful, by criminal or unlawful means.[5]

Conspiracy theory has developed as a legal tool against criminal groups who present a special danger to society because they are insulated from normal investigative techniques and have great potential for corrupting government officials. There are Federal and State laws against conspiracy. All members of the group are liable for the conspiracy by association, and leaders are accountable not only for the conspiracy but also for specific offenses committed by other members of the group in furthering the enterprise. The legal concept of conspiracy has been used against political dissidents, including Father Philip E. Berrigan and other antiwar activists, despite the objection that it violates freedom of association guaranteed by the First Amendment to the Constitution.[6] It was intended to be used against organized crime; government eavesdropping would provide direct evidence of the identity of the leaders.

The list of offenses in which State officials may obtain a court order is shorter, but perhaps even broader, than that of the Federal Government [Sec. 2516(2)].[7] The State list appears to be practically unlimited. According to Title III, State statutes may authorize eavesdropping in connection with:

> . . . the offense of murder, kidnapping, gambling, robbery, extortion, or dealing in narcotic drugs, marihuana or other dangerous drugs, or other crime dangerous to life, limb, or property, and punishable by imprisonment for more than one year [or any conspiracy to commit any of these offenses].

Commenting on the phrase "dangerous to life, limb, or property, and punishable by imprisonment for more than one year," the *Senate Report* states:

> This limitation is intended to exclude such offenses as fornication and adultery, which do not involve danger to life, limb, or property. The term "property," however, is not to be read restrictively. For example, the activities of organized crime in "cigarette bootlegging" which pose a substantial threat to the revenue of some cities and States could be made a designated offense if the penalty were made high enough.[8]

The phrase "dangerous to . . . property" has been criticized as highly ambiguous. It is suggested that this means *physically* dangerous to property and should not include importing cigarettes, as the *Senate Report* contends. The wisdom of the open-ended clause "punishable by imprisonment for more than one year" has also been questioned. This gives States tremendous leeway and may not be an accurate way of distinguishing between petty and serious offenses. Use of eavesdropping in petty crimes was never openly championed in the Congressional debates on eavesdropping under law.

G. Robert Blakey, who played a key role in setting up Title III and defending it at Senate hearings, agrees that the statute as enacted contains practically no limitation as to the nature of the offense covered, other than the one-year imprisonment limitation in certain cases. The drafters of Title III, says Blakey, made a judgment—that it was not necessary to limit the nature of the offenses. In the Senate hearings, however, he recognized the potential for abuse inherent in eavesdropping over a wide area:

> The use of electronic surveillance . . . presents a very serious problem and as a society we should not authorize people to use these

techniques except . . . where it is absolutely necessary and a serious criminal problem is presented. . . . If we found that the possibility of abuse was higher in certain areas . . . we could exclude them.[9]

Have court orders been obtained only for offenses characteristic of organized crime or serious offenses? The nature of the offense for each court order granted and a summary of these offenses appear in each annual report to Congress by the Administrative Office of the United States Courts. A few broad categories of crime predominate, as shown in Table 2.

Table 2. Number of Orders According to Nature of Offense

Year	Gambling	Narcotics	Homicide	Robbery	Larceny	Bribery
1968	20	71	21	0	19	5
1969	102	71	19	24	10	12
1970	326	127	20	13	31	16
1971	570	126	18	17	31	16
1972	497	230	35	9	22	9

At both Federal and State level, eavesdropping has been used most extensively in gambling and narcotics cases. Combined, these two offenses accounted for over 50 percent of all court orders in 1968, almost 60 percent in 1969, 75 percent in 1970, and 85 percent in 1971 and 1972. The reports do not reveal whether organized crime was involved or the seriousness of the offense.

Strategic and Tactical Intelligence

An application for a court order must show that a *particular offense* has been, is being, or is about to be committed [Sec. 2518(1) (b) (i)]. This would seem to limit applications to those seeking specific information about a particular crime—that is, tactical, as distinguished from strategic intelligence. Strategic intelligence consists of general information on the criminal activities of an individual that may enable officials to link him to other suspects or to some specific crime. Some experts believe that Title III outlaws the gathering of strategic intelligence.[10] Others insist that two types of court orders are available:

1. Prosecutorial—to get evidence with respect to a specific offense by the person surveilled.
2. Investigative—to link a subordinate suspected of crime with his unknown superiors and to ascertain their identity and activities.

Those who believe Title III permits gathering strategic intelligence argue that the very purpose of the law is to provide Government with an investigative tool against organized crime.[11] An order may be issued only upon a showing that "normal investigative procedures" are inadequate [Sec. 2518(3) (c)]. Members of organized crime, particularly top echelon, are insulated from police detection by the structure, code, and operation of the syndicate. This wall of protection can be pierced only by investigative eavesdropping that falls under the rubric of strategic intelligence.

At the Senate hearings, Professor G. Robert Blakey explained the difference between strategic and tactical surveillance to Senator Hruska, and the need for obtaining strategic information in investigation of organized crime:

> In the investigation of organized crime . . . you have known criminals but unknown crimes . . . it is necessary to subject the known criminals to surveillance . . . to identify their criminal and noncriminal associates . . . their areas of operation, both legal and illegal. Strategic intelligence attempts to paint this broad, overall picture of the criminal's activities.[12]

Blakey acknowledged that "the use of electronic equipment for strategic intelligence purposes is fraught with the possibility for abuse." Senator McClellan suggested that perhaps there should be separate sections to deal with the two types of intelligence, one for longer periods and one for shorter periods. The dilemma, which has not yet been solved, was summed up tersely by Senator Edward M. Kennedy:

> The problems are how you get the big shots . . . if there could be any legitimate reason for wiretapping in organized crime it is . . . to get the big shots. And the problem . . . is how to get probable cause as to the big shots . . . without listening in on an inordinate number of calls of little shots and innocent people.[13]

Eavesdropping for strategic intelligence is further complicated by Sec. 2517(5) which permits interception and use of a communication relating to an offense other than that specified in the order if the judge finds, on *subsequent* application, that the contents of conversations were intercepted as provided by Title III. The United States Court of Appeals for the Tenth Circuit upheld this provision in *United States v. Cox.*[14] In May 1972, the United States Supreme Court refused to hear an appeal, over the objection of Justices Douglas, Brennan, and Marshall (*Cox v. United States*).[15] Justice Douglas wrote a sharp dissenting opinion on denial of the petition for writ of certiorari, reaffirming his view that "Title III offends the Warrant Clause of the Fourth Amendment."

The Cox case illustrates vividly the usefulness of court-ordered eaves dropping—and its limitations. A fitting headline for the Cox story migh have read:

BANK ROBBERY REVEALED BY NARCOTICS TAP

Eddie Cox, together with three others, LaNear, Ford, and Piggie were indicted for robbing a bank in Kansas. Cox was white, the other three were black. Cox was identified through tape recordings of intercepted telephone conversations as the driver of the getaway car. Ford and Piggie pleaded guilty. LaNear, who had made a confession, was tried separately and the trial resulted in a hung jury. Cox was convicted in the United State District Court and appealed to the United States Court of Appeals.

A routine narcotics investigation had led to Cox's arrest in the bank robbery. An order had been obtained from a judge of the United States Dis trict Court authorizing agents of the Bureau of Narcotics and Dangerous Drugs to wiretap the phone of a man named Gene Richardson for narcotic violations. During the monitoring of conversations over Richardson's phone, Federal agents overheard talk relating to robbing a bank. An order was then obtained from a District Court judge pursuant to Sec. 2517(5) o Title III, authorizing use and disclosure of the intercepted communication regarding the bank robbery. Tape recordings of some of these conversation were admitted in evidence at Cox's trial. Cox contended that Sec. 2517(5 was unconstitutional. The issue as the Court of Appeals saw it was this: I *subsequent* judicial scrutiny of unanticipated material obtained incident to a warrant describing other subject matter compliance with Fourth Amendment requirements.

The Court of Appeals answered yes. It ruled that Sec. 2517(5) was constitutional and affirmed Cox's conviction. The very nature of this form of invasion of privacy, said the Court, is conducive to producing unexpected information.

> If wiretapping is to be validated . . . then the interception and use of information which is so related to the original search is not to be excluded. . . . Once the listening commences, it becomes impossible to turn it off when a subject other than one which is authorized is over- heard.

The Court recognized the general unmanageability of electronic sur- veillance and felt that Congress had dealt with the problem as well as could be expected. Suppose, said the Court, that in electronic surveillance of or- ganized criminals involved in gambling, information was intercepted dis- closing a conspiracy to commit murder. It would be demoralizing if officials could not use this information for lack of specific prior authorization.

The tape recordings identifying Cox as the driver of the car were somewhat vague, but they were useful in obtaining a conviction. In one conversation Piggie and LaNear discussed plans for the proposed bank robbery. LaNear asked who would drive the car.

> *Piggie:* Ah, Eddie.
> *LaNear:* Eddie who?
> *Piggie:* You know . . . the white fella.

LaNear complained to Piggie that he did not "trust that white dude. I don't even know him." On the day of the robbery Piggie asked Gene Richardson to call Eddie and tell him it was ready. Richardson then called Eddie Cox.

> *Gene:* Ok, but, uh, Mike just called and told me to tell you he's ready for you, give you call.
> *Eddie:* Who? Mike?
> *Gene:* Yeah.
> *Eddie:* O.K., then I'll stop by there tonight.
> *Gene:* O.K.

This cryptic dialogue is typical of conversations overheard by wiretapping, but in this case there was some corroborating evidence against Eddie Cox; the automobile used in the bank robbery fitted the description of the car owned by Cox and a white man was driving it.

An incident in the Cox case that is not revealed in the appellate court documents was reported in the *Congressional Record* by Senator Mc-Clellan. It reads like a movie scenario. A conversation intercepted under the court order in the narcotics case was believed to relate to a murder plot.

> A helicopter was sent up to cover the intended murder scene, while other police maintained surveillance near the home of the marked victim. At a given signal, the victim's home was surrounded— warning shots were fired and the would-be killers surrendered.[16]

Would the intercepted conversation regarding the proposed murder be admissible in evidence at trial on a charge of intent to kill? Senator Mc-Clellan did not ponder this question or tell the outcome of the story. He merely drew the conclusion that the incident "dramatically illustrates the effectiveness of legally sanctioned wiretapping."

The Supreme Court has noted that different types of surveillance may be needed in different types of cases. For example, in domestic security investigations as distinguished from ordinary crime, the gathering of intelligence is long-range, the exact targets may be hard to identify, and the emphasis may be on prevention of unlawful activity or enhancing preparedness for some future emergency. The Court has suggested that

Congress might wish to consider different standards in such cases.[17] It is quite possible that the Supreme Court may ultimately encourage Congress to make special provision for gathering strategic intelligence to reach the leaders of organized crime, as Senator McClellan suggested at the Senate hearings.

The Particularity Requirement

The *Senate Report* on Title III states categorically that the legislation on wiretapping and electronic surveillance conforms to the constitutional standards set out by the Supreme Court in 1967 in *Berger* and *Katz*. Those who drafted the law were fully aware of the importance of conforming to these two decisions if eavesdropping was to be upheld by the courts. Law enforcement officials also know that practice and law are inextricably interwoven in eavesdropping and that procedure must also conform to Supreme Court requirements.

Title III requires that the application and order shall contain a particular description of the *type* of communication sought to be intercepted (Sec. 2518). In *Berger*, however, the Court made it clear that it was necessary "to describe with particularity the conversations sought," otherwise the officer would be given a roving commission to seize any and all conversations. In litigation attacking the constitutionality of Title III, it is claimed that merely describing the *type* of conversation does not comply with *Berger*. Since it is practically impossible, especially in offenses of a continuing nature such as gambling and bookmaking, to describe a particular conversation sought, the prosecuting official is faced with a real dilemma. To comply fully with *Berger*, the particularity requirement would have to be narrowly construed, and strict enforcement would make Title III unusable in organized crime cases.

Justice Black anticipated the problem of "particularity" in his dissenting opinion in *Katz;* he could not see how one could "describe" a future conversation. In 1972, Justice Douglas was still protesting that:

> It would be extremely difficult to write a search warrant specifically naming the particular conversations to be seized and therefore any such attempt would amount to a general warrant, the very abuse condemned by the Fourth Amendment.[18]

Until the issue of "particularity" is settled by the Supreme Court, the best that prosecuting officials can do is to describe the conversations sought as specifically and as accurately as possible.

Judge-Shopping for Court Orders

A heavy burden is placed on Federal and State judges in court-ordered eavesdropping. They must decide whether or not an order should be issued.

The judge to whom an application is presented has to determine if all the requirements of the law are satisfied. Before signing the order, he must find from the facts set forth in the application that there is *probable cause* for belief that:

1. An individual is committing, has committed, or is about to commit an offense covered by Title III.
2. Particular communications concerning that offense will be obtained through interception.
3. The facilities from which the communications are to be intercepted are being used, or are about to be used, in connection with such offense, or are leased to, listed in the name of, or commonly used by the particular individual.[19]

These findings are intended to link up a specific person, a specific offense, and a specific place. If an extension of an order is requested, the judge must be sure that probable cause has not become stale; *new* probable cause must be shown.

How is a judge to decide if probable cause exists? No guidelines are furnished either by Title III or the *Senate Report*. Former Justice Tom C. Clark of the United States Supreme Court says that reliance must be placed on the impartial judgment of the judicial officer that probable cause clearly exists "in the true tradition of that term."[20] The trouble is that no one knows what the "true tradition" is, and the elusive meaning of probable cause is hard to pin down. In *Berger*, Justice Clark writing for the majority defined probable cause:

> Probable cause under the Fourth Amendment exists where the facts and circumstances within the affiant's knowledge, and of which he has reasonably trustworthy information, are sufficient unto themselves to warrant a man of reasonable caution to believe that an offense has been or is being committed.[21]

Supreme Court decisions in ordinary search and seizure cases will carry much weight in deciding whether probable cause exists for obtaining an eavesdrop order.[22] However, judges may have to fix higher standards in eavesdropping cases. Justice Stewart in his concurring opinion in *Berger* warned that "only the most precise and rigorous standard of probable cause should justify an intrusion of this sort."[23]

In addition to findings of probable cause, the judge must decide if the facts in the application show that *normal investigative procedures* have been tried and failed, or reasonably appear to be unlikely to succeed if tried or to be too dangerous [Sec. 2518(3) (c)]. The purpose of this requirement is to establish that "exigent circumstances" exist to justify search without prior notice, as required in *Berger* and *Katz*. Title III does not define

"normal investigative procedures," but as stated in the *Senate Report* it
would include:

> Standard visual or aural surveillance techniques by law
> enforcement officers, general questioning or interrogation under an
> immunity grant, use of regular search warrants, and the infiltration of
> conspiratorial groups by undercover agents or informants. [24]

Can a judge ever know whether normal investigative procedures are
unlikely to succeed or are too dangerous? He is a magistrate, not an investigator. It is suggested that the "judgment would involve consideration of all
the facts and circumstances" and that it has to "be tested in a practical and
common sense fashion"; the question is one of need and what constitutes
proof of that need. No one denies that the need for wiretapping or
electronic surveillance is hard to show. Some claim that it is impossible to
demonstrate that normal techniques could not produce the same result.

An order may require periodic reports to the judge showing what
progress has been made and the necessity for continued interception. As indicated in Chapter 7, few, if any, State judges have required progress
reports. Failure to make these reports mandatory has been criticized as
seriously undermining judicial supervision of the operator who is listening to
the conversations. Progress reports are intended to serve as a check on the
continuing need to conduct the surveillance and to prevent abuse, as the
Senate Report clearly recognized:

> At any time the judge is convinced the need is no longer es-
> tablished, he may order the surveillance discontinued. [It] will serve
> to insure that extended surveillance is not undertaken lightly. This
> provision will serve to insure that it is not unthinkingly or auto-
> matically continued without due consideration. [25]

The importance of progress reports was underscored by Senator McClellan
at hearings before the Senate Subcommittee on Criminal Laws and
Procedures:

> I want to keep it under absolute control of the court. I am
> willing to go further to strengthen the bill to see to it that they make
> interim reports to the court and permit the court to require them to
> make notes of the progress being made. [26]

Frank S. Hogan, District Attorney of New York County and one of the
strongest proponents of court-ordered eavesdropping, agreed with Senator
McClellan that progress reports were essential:

> I think there should be reporting requirements to the court, the
> court, in effect, should be a monitor, as well as the instrument that au-
> thorizes the interception.

Judges also have responsibility for safeguarding the records. As soon as the time period fixed in the eavesdrop order has expired, the recordings must be made available to the judge who issued the order, and sealed under his direction. Custody of the recordings "shall be wherever the judge orders." The recordings may not be destroyed except on court order and must be kept for ten years. Duplicate recordings may be made for authorized disclosure. The judge's seal must also be placed on applications and orders, and he directs where they shall be kept. The law also gives the judge discretionary power to decide whether certain individuals shall be notified of the eavesdropping and what portions of the recordings shall be made available for inspection.

The onerous duties and responsibilities of the judge in official eavesdropping make it an unattractive job to sign an order, even for those who favor this technique of law enforcement. The officer who wants a warrant to wiretap or use electronic surveillance must find a judge who is willing to issue it and take on all the judicial duties fixed by the law. A wide choice is open to the applicant, for an order may be signed by any judge of competent jurisdiction. This is defined in Sec. 2510(9) as:

(a) A judge of the United States district court or a United States court of appeals; and
(b) A judge of any court of general criminal jurisdiction of a State who is authorized by a statute of that State to enter orders authorizing interceptions of wire or oral communications.

No safeguard against "judge-shopping" is provided by Title III. Practical necessity forces applicants to pick a judge who is known to be receptive to eavesdropping and at least reasonably lenient in signing orders. Selection of a friendly judge is almost always possible, particularly in State practice.

The rationale for court-ordered eavesdropping is that a limited and controlled number of officials may apply to an impartial and detached judge, thus safeguarding against excessive governmental intrusion. Federal authority to apply for an order is restricted to "the Attorney General, or any Assistant Attorney General specially designated by him." State authority is much more widely dispersed. State applicants include "the principal prosecuting attorney of any State, or the principal prosecuting attorney of any political subdivision thereof," provided they are authorized by State statute. Most State applications have been made by District Attorneys or Attorneys General, and in some States their number has been large. In New York, more than twenty-five applicants are listed in the annual report to Congress submitted in April 1973, and this does not include Assistant District Attorneys who may actually prepare the applications and handle the investigations. In New Jersey, the number of applicants for orders reported in 1973

is more than fifteen. State power to use eavesdropping has been left in too
many hands, according to the critics of Title III. No serious charge of abuse
has been leveled as yet against any State official, but wide divergence in attitude and practice exists even within a particular State, as the description of
practice and procedure in Chapter 7 will show.

Overhearing Innocent Conversations

Congress knew that government eavesdropping would inevitably result in intercepting innocent conversations and tried to deal with the
problem. The law requires that "every order and extension . . . shall contain
a provision that [it] shall be conducted in such a way as to minimize the interception" of innocent conversations [Sec. 2518(5)]. How is it to be kept to
a minimum? The law does not say, although the question was raised at the
hearings of the Senate Subcommittee on Criminal Laws and Procedures.
Senator McClellan asked an attorney from Houston, Texas, who had come
to testify in behalf of another bill what he thought about court-ordered
eavesdropping, and was surprised to get the following answer pointing out
the inevitability of overhearing many innocent conversations:

> *Mr. Walsh:* There is no way you could tap a telephone under a court
> order that would satisfy the fourth amendment. If somebody
> wants to tap my telephone they are not only listening to me;
> they are listening to every individual who may choose to call my
> law office . . . that is the essential difference between the search
> warrant contemplated by the fourth amendment.
>
> *Sen. McClellan:* In searching your office would he not see many
> things you would not want him to see besides what he is looking
> for?
>
> *Mr. Walsh:* That may be, but he is not listening to every conversation
> with every client who would call me. If I got a search warrant to
> search Senator McClellan's telephone I would be listening to
> every constituent, every Federal employee who might have an
> occasional call to you. There would be no way to limit it. That
> . . . is the ultimate vice in the wiretapping situation.[27]

Senator Edward Kennedy also raised the question of overhearing innocent conversations in interrogating a District Attorney, who had testified
in favor of Title III, regarding the eavesdropping law of New York State:

> *Sen. Kennedy:* [We] do not know . . . how many innocent conversa-
> tions they listened to to get a certain lead, do we?
>
> *Mr. Cahn:* No Sir. It would be almost impossible to give you those
> figures.

Sen. Kennedy: Does the person listening on the other end make the decision on the spot as to whether a certain conversation is relevant or not?

Mr. Cahn: Yes, it has to be done that way.[28]

Those who opposed wiretapping were concerned that inevitably many innocent conversations would be overheard. Their apprehensions have, unfortunately, materialized in both Federal and State practice. The most practical suggestion made for minimizing such intrusions is to train monitoring agents to recognize innocent conversations as such and stop recording them. Critics of eavesdropping were also worried that privileged communications would be intercepted, such as those between attorney and client, doctor and patient. The American Civil Liberties Union maintained that wiretapping and electronic surveillance are uncontrollable, as far as privileged communications are concerned:

> There is no way to limit the tap to the persons or conversations in which the police officer may have a legitimate interest. . . . Such invasions cannot possibly be avoided once the tap is put in . . . the necessary confidentiality of legally privileged conversations is inescapably destroyed, even if unintended.[29]

An attempt to protect privileged communications was made by Congress in Sec. 2517(b) of Title III which provides that such communications shall not lose their privileged character whether the interception is lawful or unlawful. It is doubtful that this effort has been very successful. As the account of practice and procedures in Chapters 7 and 8 shows, monitoring agents are ill-equipped to decide when to stop listening.

Time Period for Listening In

A court order may allow interception of conversations to continue for a period up to thirty days, with an unlimited number of thirty-day extensions [Sec. 2518(5)]. The time length raises policy as well as constitutional problems.[30] Should it be so long? In *Berger*, the Supreme Court disapproved of surveillance over a two-month period and called it "indiscriminate" seizure. In *Katz*, the Court turned to a case-by-case approach, and the *Senate Report* on Title III also expressed the view that the duration of surveillance would have to be justified on a case-by-case basis:

> What is important is that the facts in the application on a case-by-case basis justify the period of time of the surveillance.[31]

A narrow construction of *Berger* would seem to indicate that interception for an entire thirty-day period constitutes a general search and is therefore unconstitutional. As a matter of policy, if an application asks for a period that is longer than necessary, it may indicate a lack of caution and sloppiness in preparing the application. There should be no greater invasion of privacy than is necessary under the circumstances. A United States District Court judge in Philadelphia ruled in May 1972 that Title III was unconstitutional on its face as a violation of the Fourth Amendment because the law allowed continuous searches for too long a period (*United States v. Whitaker*).

> Title III permits the government to conduct lengthy continuous searches with great discretion in the hands of the executing officers, thus violating the Fourth Amendment's prohibition against general searches.[32]

The judge granted a motion, made by seven defendants in a gambling case, to suppress evidence gathered by electronic surveillance. (Decisions of State and Federal courts upholding the thirty-day provision and the constitutionality of Title III in general are discussed in Chapters 7 and 8.)

Limitation on length of surveillance may be spelled out from provisions of the law other than Sec. 2518(5). Authorization to intercept must be executed "as soon as practicable," and interception must end automatically when the described type of communication has been first obtained, unless the application shows probable cause to believe that additional communications of the same type will occur later [Sec. 2518(1) (d)]. The order must include a statement as to whether or not interception shall terminate automatically when the described conversation has been obtained [Sec. 2518(4) (e)]. One foe of Title III insists that this limitation on length of surveillance is no limitation at all. A continuous series of intrusions, possibly lasting for years, is envisaged as a possibility under Title III.

One of the rules laid down by the Supreme Court in *Berger* was that the order must state that as soon as the conversation sought is recorded, the authorization shall cease. The subject of termination was not discussed in *Katz*. The recording introduced at the trial in *Katz* consisted of only six conversations lasting an average of three minutes each. The opinion does not indicate whether these all took place on the same day or over a period of three days.

If the rule stated in *Berger* is applied rigidly and authorization must terminate as soon as the conversation sought is recorded, the purpose of the order may be thwarted. Recording of one conversation may not furnish adequate evidence for conviction. Suppose, on the other hand, that the officer continues listening after he has obtained a recording of a conversation as specified in the order. Does continuance of surveillance constitute an invasion of privacy that invalidates all the interceptions? These are troublesome problems that will have to be settled by the courts.

In a case in New York, an order was obtained to tap the telephone of a forty-four-year-old elementary school principal who was indicted with one of his former teachers, a woman of twenty-six, for conspiring to cause the death of the principal's wife, the mother of his three children. A rag soaked in chloroform had been placed over the wife's nose and face. The defendant claimed he had found his wife dead in bed beside him in their suburban home. The wiretap order failed to include a provision that the authorization to intercept be executed as soon as practicable and that it be conducted in such a way as to minimize the interception of conversations not subject to the order. Sixty conversations were overheard. Every incoming and outgoing phone call was recorded; the interception was never cut off. Calls were overheard between the school principal's father, his doctors and dentists; between his mother and Medicare; between his children and their friends.

The State Court granted defendant's motion to suppress all the conversations. Tape recordings and transcripts were also barred from evidence. The Court ruled that it was mandatory under New York law to include a provision in the court order for prompt execution and for minimization of interceptions (*People v. Holder*).[33] It followed a decision of the United States District Court in the District of Columbia in which *all* communications were suppressed (*United States v. Scott*)[34] rather than another decision of the District Court in California in which only unauthorized intercepted communications were held to be inadmissible (*United States v. King*). The State court concluded:

> Only by imposing a prophylactic rule can the Court effectively protect itself from becoming an unwilling participant in illegal government activity and protect the privacy of citizens.[35]

Both the principal and the teacher were nevertheless found guilty in the State Supreme Court in New York. Some of the most damaging evidence consisted of telephone conversations intercepted under a later wiretap order, in which the teacher was said to have expressed her love for the principal. This wiretap order, unlike the earlier one, complied fully with the law. The intercepted conversations were accepted in evidence, although they contained no admission of guilt.

Notice of Eavesdropping, Objections, and Disclosure

Serious ambiguities are created by the provisions of Title III requiring notice of eavesdropping and permitting aggrieved persons to object to the use of evidence obtained. Some injured persons may never be given notice, and it is not clear who has "standing" to object or what should be disclosed.

The law requires that individuals named in a court order or application shall be served with an "inventory" which shall include a notice of:

(1) the fact of entry of the order of application.
(2) the date of entry and period of time authorized.
(3) whether conversations were intercepted.

This "inventory" or notice must be given within a reasonable time, but no later than ninety days after termination of interception (or filing of an application which is denied). *In the discretion of the judge*, other parties to intercepted conversations may also be given such notice [Sec. 2518(8) (d)].

The purpose of the notice, called an "inventory," is to give "aggrieved persons" an opportunity to make objections by a motion to suppress evidence. An aggrieved person is defined as anyone "who was a party to any intercepted wire or oral communication or . . . against whom interception was directed" [Sec. 2518(11)]. Under this definition, an individual may be incriminated by an unlawful interception and yet have no "standing" to object. A person may be "aggrieved," yet the judge may decide that no notice shall be given to him. Furthermore, the notice need not state exactly *what* was intercepted; it is left to the judge to determine what portions, if any, of the overheard conversations shall be available for inspection in the interests of justice.

In 1969 the Supreme Court ruled that the owner of premises subject to electronic surveillance, and any person whose conversation was overheard unlawfully, may object to admission of evidence so obtained (*Alderman v. United States*).[36] The Court also held in this case that the Government must make the record of such conversations available to the aggrieved person without prior screening *in camera* by the trial judge, even if the Government claims that the conversations were irrelevant. Later in the year the Court pointed out that it had not addressed itself to the problem of disclosure in cases relating to "foreign intelligence" (*Giordano v. United States*).[37]

The questions of "standing" to object, disclosures to be made, and procedure to determine relevancy were raised again in June 1972 in the case involving publication of the "Pentagon Papers," the secret study on the Vietnam War, in which defendants, Dr. Daniel Ellsberg and Anthony J. Russo, were accused of espionage, conspiracy, and misuse of government property. No court order to wiretap was obtained; the Government claimed that none was needed since it involved a "foreign intelligence" investigation. The Department of Justice admitted that it had picked up a conversation of a defense lawyer or consultant, but refused to reveal which of the ten defense lawyers or five consultants had been overheard. The trial judge examined the transcript privately and ruled that the conversations overheard had nothing to do with the secret study on the Vietnam War, that they did not relate to the confidential attorney-client relationship, and that defendants had no right to see the transcript. On appeal, the Court of Appeals for the Ninth Circuit decided that defendants had no "standing" to object, apparently because the conversations were deemed irrelevant. After a jury had been sworn in, Justice Douglas granted a stay of the trial pending decision by the Supreme Court of this "profoundly important" question (*Russo v. Byrne*).[38] The Supreme Court, however, declined to hear the appeal and the stay was dissolved. Ellsberg, Russo, and their attorneys and consultants then brought suit against Federal officials for damages caused by alleged "illegal eavesdropping."

The trial of Ellsberg and Russo ended abruptly on May 11, 1973 when Judge William Matthew Byrne, Jr. granted defendants' motion to dismiss the case and declared a mistrial "with prejudice." His decision was precipitated by disclosure that one or more conversations of Ellsberg had been intercepted by the Government through electronic surveillance, and that all the records had vanished from the files of the F.B.I. and the Department of Justice (they were reported to have been found shortly thereafter among the files of John D. Ehrlichman, President Nixon's chief domestic adviser who resigned in the wake of the Watergate affair). The totality of the circumstances, said the Judge, offended "a sense of justice and interfered with defendants' constitutional right to a fair and speedy trial with due process of law."

Disclosure of the wiretap was made by the Government a year after the trial judge had ordered that all information on wiretaps be submitted to the court. The judge cited "an extraordinary series of disclosures regarding the conduct of several governmental agencies," including burglarizing the office files of Dr. Ellsberg's former psychiatrist, led by two of the Watergate conspirators who were allegedly operating from the White House. The decision did not mention that during the trial the judge had been approached by high White House officials with an offer of the Directorship of the F.B.I.[39]

Other problems have been created by the provisions of Title III requiring the giving of notice (called an "inventory"). The duty of causing service of the "inventory" is placed on the judge, and he may postpone it indefinitely.[40] The *Senate Report* acknowledges this fact but states that the notice requirements should assure the community that the techniques of eavesdropping are "reasonably" employed; eventually the interceptions must become known to the subject who can then seek redress if he believes his privacy has been invaded illegally. Unfortunately, not all judges have acted "reasonably." In one case, a Federal judge attempted to waive the giving of notice entirely; the result was that the interceptions were barred from evidence (*United States v. Eastman*).[41]

An "aggrieved person" may move to suppress evidence obtained by eavesdropping on one of the following grounds: (1) that the order was insufficient on its face; (2) that the interception was not in conformity with the order; or (3) that the communication was unlawfully intercepted. The law is ambiguous as to *when* such a motion may be made. Section 2518(10)(a) says it must be made "before the trial, hearing or proceeding" unless there was no opportunity to do it or the person was not aware of the grounds of the motion. Is the motion premature if made before arrest and indictment? This issue was raised by the Department of Justice, but the Court of Appeals for the Fifth Circuit declined to make a substantive ruling on the issue and merely held that it had no jurisdiction to entertain the appeal (*Application of United States*).[42] The United States has a right of appeal from an order granting a motion to suppress if the appeal is not taken for the purpose of delay [Sec. 2518(10)(b)]. Few motions to suppress have been granted.

In addition to the ninety-day notice of eavesdropping, the law requires that within ten days before trial, hearing, or proceeding, a copy of the court order and accompanying application be furnished to each party; otherwise the interceptions may not be received in evidence or disclosed in the proceeding [Sec. 2518(9)]. The ten-day notice may be waived by the judge if he finds that it was impossible to furnish the information within the designated time and that delay will not be prejudicial. An attempt to clarify this vague "waiver" clause was made in the *Senate Report:*

> Such a situation might arise . . . when an intercepted communication became relevant only as a result of the character of a defense presented by the defendant. Ordinarily, prejudice would be shown only where it was established that the trial could not be reasonably recessed in order that the motion to suppress could be fully heard or that the granting of a mistrial . . . would be grossly unfair.[43]

It has been suggested that Title III may have deliberately left some matters of notice and disclosure unsettled on the grounds that procedural details should be left to the States. This view is highly questionable. Procedural requirements are the heart of the law, and lack of clarity and uniformity can only jeopardize court-ordered eavesdropping.

Statistical Reports for Evaluation of Eavesdropping under Title III

To assure the public that court-ordered eavesdropping is being properly administered and to provide some basis for evaluating it, three reports are required:

1. Report by the judge issuing or denying an order, within thirty days after expiration of the order or its denial.

2. Report by prosecuting officials in January of each year on each application for an order or extension during the preceding year.
3. Annual report to Congress in April of each year.

The reports by judges and prosecuting officials are made to the Administrative Office of the United States Courts, Washington, D.C. The Administrative Office, in turn, uses the information obtained to make the annual report to Congress. The intent, nature, and effect of these reports were explained officially:

> They are intended to form the basis for a public evaluation of its operation. The reports are not intended to include confidential material. They should be statistical. . . . It will assure the community that the system of court-ordered electronic surveillance . . . is properly administered.[44]

The Administrative Office of the United States Courts has prepared a standard form that is used by prosecuting officers and judges. General opinion seems to support the critics of Title III that the reports are not fully satisfactory. They neither inform the public adequately nor furnish sufficient data for evaluation of eavesdropping under law. The reports of prosecuting officials and judges have not been made available to the general public as a matter of policy, and distribution of the report to Congress has been limited.

The report to Congress has been helpful in itemizing the number of court orders issued, the areas where eavesdropping took place, the names of prosecuting officials who applied for orders and the judges who signed them, the general nature of offenses involved, and the number of arrests and convictions. The statistical nature of the reports has been criticized as a "head count," a simple compilation of figures that tell us something about the operation of Title III, but far from enough. The reports do not show whether the crimes were serious, if targets were involved in organized crime, whether top, middle, or low echelon members were involved. They may, however, tend to inhibit any one judge from granting orders too freely, for his name appears prominently in the report to Congress and it is a simple matter to add up how many orders a judge has signed during a particular year. In the report Congress released at the end of April 1973 for orders signed in 1972, it appeared that more than 115 Federal judges had signed 206 orders. However, in one State (New Jersey) one judge was reported to have signed over 130 orders.

In December 1971 the American Civil Liberties Union, one of the most vocal and persistent opponents of government eavesdropping, issued a paper entitled: "A Report on the Costs and Benefits of Electronic Surveillance." It was prepared by Herman Schwartz, Professor of Law at the State University of New York at Buffalo, a leading academic spokesman against official eavesdropping. Professor Schwartz charges that the figures reported as required by law "raise doubts as to accuracy." With regard to costs of eavesdropping as reported by prosecuting officials, he says:

> We know so little about how well the reporting has been monitored, and the history of self-reporting by police and other enforcement agencies is so poor, that the figures must be taken with skepticism.

The Administrative Office of the United States Courts to whom prosecuting officials and judges report makes no attempt to monitor the reports. The law imposes no obligation upon it to do so. Only an independent agency created for that purpose could hope to supervise the filing of reports and make them fully adequate for the purposes intended.

6

Eavesdropping without Court Order

The protest against government eavesdropping without court order has been loud and agitated. A grant of power to invade privacy free of judicial control is, critics say, more appropriate to a totalitarian than a democratic society and opens the door to official abuse. Congress has been accused of trying to circumvent and subvert the constitutional requirements of freedom of speech and association under the First Amendment, as well as the Fourth Amendment restrictions against unreasonable search and seizure. Senator Sam J. Ervin, Jr. (Democrat of North Carolina), who consistently opposed electronic surveillance without court order in domestic security cases, expressed the nature and purpose of governmental intrusions in this way:

> These [government surveillance activities] are predicated on the theory that if government officials can only acquire sufficient information in advance on individuals, then they can predict and control behavior. So they seek to learn about how they think, how they behave in their personal lives; how they cut their hair; how they [read]; what their conduct and attitudes are in sexual matters; how they relate to their parents; what they dream about.[1]

The 1968 Federal law permits government eavesdropping without court order in two categories of cases:

1. Forty-eight-hour emergency, involving conspiratorial activity threatening national security or characteristic of organized crime.
2. Cases relating to national security, where eavesdropping is undertaken by authority of the President.

Each of these types of situations must be considered separately, for different problems have surfaced. The emergency power seems to have been used sparingly, if at all. Presidential authority in "national security" cases, on the contrary, was stretched by the Government beyond the limits acceptable to the public and now appears to have been curbed by the United States Supreme Court. In neither category of cases has the public been fully informed.

Forty-Eight-Hour Emergency Eavesdropping

Both Federal and State officials may carry on emergency eavesdropping for forty-eight hours without obtaining a court order. The Federal law permits it to be conducted by "any investigative or law enforcement officer" who may be specially designated by the Attorney General of the United States, or by the chief prosecuting attorney of any State or subdivision acting under a State statute [Sec. 2518(7)]. No standard is provided to limit the number of designees or to determine their qualifications. The United States Attorney General has named no one officially. On the State level, New Jersey appears to be the only one to have provided for emergency eavesdropping. The New Jersey law is more restrictive than Title III. Informal application may be made to a judge who may grant verbal approval without an order, to be followed within forty-eight hours by application for an order. It must relate to investigation of conspiratorial activities of organized crime. If no application is made, or if the application is denied, the taped recordings of conversations must be delivered to the court and sealed. Failure to do so is punishable as contempt of court.[2] The District of Columbia law also provides for emergency eavesdropping; application for an order must be initiated within twelve hours of the emergency and be completed within seventy-two hours.[3]

The Federal law describes emergency situations as those involving conspiratorial activity: (1) threatening national security, and (2) characteristic of organized crime. "National security" is not defined, nor does the law indicate what offenses are "characteristic of organized crime." In the debate to restrict an emergency situation to one involving imminent threat to human life, Senator Philip A. Hart (Democrat of Michigan) commented caustically on the vagueness of the word "emergency";

> If one is a good policeman everything is an emergency to him.[4]

The forty-eight-hour emergency provision has been dubbed an "invitation to misuse" that opens up great possibilities for "leads" and corroborative information rather than obtaining specific evidence of a particular crime. Former Supreme Court Justice Tom C. Clark maintains that it encourages a laxness reminiscent of *Berger* and is suspect on its face.[5]

Grave constitutional questions are raised by the forty-eight-hour emergency clause. The language of the Supreme Court in its 1967 decision in *Katz v. United States* would seem to indicate that surveillance without court order is unreasonable under the Fourth Amendment to the Constitution. *Katz* did not have to deal with the question of what is an emergency, but it did state that a court order *precedent* to surveillance was necessary. The Court's opinion in *Katz* terms search warrants without prior judicial authorization "per se unreasonable." Control of emergency eavesdropping under Title III comes *after* the invasion of privacy has occurred. Subsequent judicial approval, argue the critics, is not a neutral assessment of justification for search; it is doubtful if an emergency can ever justify dispensing with the court order. Allowing a search to proceed without judicial authorization, even for forty-eight hours, they maintain, seems to violate the Fourth Amendment and should be declared unconstitutional.

The forty-eight-hour emergency provision requires that all conditions necessary for issuance of an order under Title III be present before emergency surveillance begins. Skeptics say it would be unrealistic to assume that these conditions will always be satisfied. A law enforcement officer facing what he thinks is an emergency will have a rough time deciding whether the stringent, technical standards of "probable cause" and other requirements of the law exist. That is a job for a judge, not an investigator. Suppose that after forty-eight hours of listening in, a judge to whom an application is made decides that the necessary conditions did *not* exist and denies the application. The evidence obtained may still be used outside of court. Or, if after forty-eight hours of eavesdropping a law enforcement officer decides not to apply for an order, the invasion of privacy may never become known to anyone but himself. All that the law provides is that if the application is denied or no order is issued, the interceptions are treated as having been obtained in violation of the law and notice must be served "on the person named in the application."

A wide variety of situations fall under the emergency power, including many where lack of time to get an order or risk of losing evidence may be cited to justify it. It is possible that time is not the real reason for eavesdropping first and getting a court order later. Officials questioned admitted frankly that in case of an emergency, a court order could always be obtained without delay. Very few of those interviewed could see any need for the forty-eight-hour emergency provision except, perhaps, in extreme cases such as kidnapping where the life of an individual might be in danger. Court orders are not very useful in kidnapping cases. No court orders were reported to have been obtained in 1972 in kidnapping cases. In 1971, only one court order was obtained in such an investigation; in 1970 none; in 1969 only two, and in 1968 only one. Consent of the individual whose telephone is tapped in such cases is generally obtainable, and no court order is required.

The weaknesses of emergency eavesdropping are so patent that little use has been made of this technique, at least as far as can be known. Title III does not require any report to be made of forty-eight-hour emergency eavesdropping and no such reports have been filed. One expert suggests restricting emergency wiretapping to cases involving a threat to actual or potential attack by a foreign power, collection of foreign intelligence information, or investigation of espionage activity.[6] Imminent threat to life might be added to this list. In no other cases does power with such potential for abuse seem justified.

"National Security" Eavesdropping

No section of Title III has created greater public turmoil than the "brief and nebulous paragraph" allowing wiretapping and electronic surveillance *without court order* to protect "national security" under authority of the President. The Attorney General, John N. Mitchell, as head of the Department of Justice and in the name of the President, claimed that "national security" included threats from domestic political dissidents as well as from foreign powers, and that the Government had power to eavesdrop on persons and organizations that it regarded as subversive without first obtaining court approval. This broad claim of power by the Executive was asserted publicly for the first time in the prosecution of antiwar activists.

In a thirty-two-page document filed with the United States District Court on June 13, 1969 in the trial of the "Chicago 7" charged with inciting riots at the Democratic National Convention in August 1968, the Justice Department contended that no court order was required to eavesdrop on groups that "use unlawful means to attack and subvert the existing structure of government." Admitting that the telephones of antiwar activists had been tapped, the brief stated:

> There can be no doubt that there are today in this country organizations which intend to use force and other illegal means to attack the existing forms of government. Faced with such a state of affairs any President who takes seriously his oath to "preserve, protect and defend the Constitution" will no doubt determine that it is not "unreasonable" to utilize electronic surveillance to gather intelligence concerning these organizations which are committed to the use of illegal methods to bring about changes in our form of government.[7]

The brief in the "Chicago 7" case was prepared by William H. Rehnquist, then an attorney in the Department of Justice, and now a Justice of the United States Supreme Court appointed by President Nixon.

Eavesdropping without court order was conducted by the Government in investigations of a wide assortment of dissidents. The Executive's claim of authority was upheld by the United States District Court in Illinois (the "Chicago 7" case) and in Kansas. It was rejected by the United States District Court in California and in Michigan. The Michigan case reached the Court of Appeals for the Sixth Circuit; in June 1971, the appellate court ruled that the Attorney General had no power to authorize wiretapping in internal security matters without judicial sanction. This judgment was affirmed by the United States Supreme Court on June 19, 1972.[8]

In an 8 to 0 decision that the press characterized as a "stunning defeat" for the Department of Justice, the Supreme Court decided that presidential authority to protect the nation does not give the Government power to tap without court order the wires of domestic radicals who have "no significant connection with a foreign power, its agents, or agencies." (*United States v. United States District Court*). The opinion of the Court was written by Justice Lewis F. Powell, Jr., who had defended the Government position prior to his appointment to the Supreme Court by President Nixon and had called the fierce opposition to warrantless eavesdropping a "tempest in a teapot." Justice Rehnquist did not participate in the consideration or decision of the case. Chief Justice Burger concurred in the result. Justices Douglas and White filed concurring opinions.

The unanimous decision of the highest Court, in which three of the four Nixon appointees joined, reflects the strength of public pressure to reject the Executive's claim to unchecked power. Justice Powell gave official recognition to the "deep-seated uneasiness and apprehension" of "law-abiding citizens" over the use of electronic surveillance by the Government and the desire of the Court to reassure the public:

> By no means of least importance will be the reassurance of the public generally that indiscriminate wiretapping and bugging of law-abiding citizens cannot occur.[9]

Resolution of the "delicate question" of the President's power was a "matter of national concern requiring sensitivity both to the Government's right to protect itself from unlawful subversion and attack and to the citizens' right to be secure in his privacy against unreasonable Government intrusion."

The facts in the Michigan case, as presented to the Supreme Court, reflected the ferment and violence of the times. Three young men, reportedly members of the "White Panthers," were charged with *conspiracy* to destroy government property in violation of a Federal law. One of them, "Pun" Plamondon, was also accused of the dynamite bombing of an office of the Central Intelligence Agency in Ann Arbor, Michigan. Before trial, defendants moved in the District Court to compel the Government to disclose all logs and records of electronic surveillance directed at the defendants or co-conspirators. They also asked for a hearing to determine if any of the evidence on which the grand jury indictment was based or which the Government intended to introduce at trial was "tainted" by illegal surveillance. The Government replied that it had no knowledge of any such surveillance, that a further inquiry was being conducted with the F.B.I., and that if evidence of electronic monitoring was discovered the Court would be advised.

Subsequently, an affidavit was filed, signed by the Attorney General, stating that he had authorized wiretapping. Plamondon was not the object of the surveillance, but his conversations had been overheard. The Government claimed that although no prior judicial aproval had been obtained the surveillance was lawful as a reasonable exercise of the President's power to protect the national security under Sec. 2511(3) of Title III which provides:

> Nothing . . . in this chapter . . . shall . . . limit the constitutional power of the President to take such measures as he deems necessary to protect the United States against the overthrow of the Government by force or other unlawful means, or against any other clear and present danger to the structure or existence of the Government.

The District Court ruled that the surveillance violated the Fourth Amendment and ordered the Government to make full disclosure to Plamondon of his overheard conversations. The Court of Appeals for the Sixth Circuit upheld the lower court. The Supreme Court, affirming the decision of the Court of Appeals, made it clear that the question decided was a limited and narrow one:

> Whether safeguards other than prior authorization by a magistrate would satisfy the Fourth Amendment in a situation involving the national security.[10]

This was the question left open by the Supreme Court in *Katz v. United States* in 1967, according to a footnote in that case by Justice Stewart. In reaching a decision in the Plamondon case, the Supreme Court did not consider any constitutional challenge to electronic surveillance as authorized by Title III. Nor was there "any question or doubt as to the necessity of obtaining a warrant in surveillance of crimes unrelated to the national security interest."[11] The Court made no judgment on the scope of the President's surveillance power with respect to the activities of foreign powers, within or without the United States. It addressed itself only to the *domestic* aspects of national security, not to activities of foreign powers or their agents. The holding of the Court, as expressed by Justice Powell, was that under the Fourth Amendment, prior judicial approval is required for the type of domestic security surveillance involved in the Plamondon case, and that such approval may be made in accordance with such reasonable standards as the Congress may prescribe.

> Fourth Amendment freedoms [against unreasonable searches and seizures] cannot properly be guaranteed if domestic surveillance

may be conducted solely within the discretion of the executive branch.

Congress was, in effect, invited to prescribe different protective standards for domestic security surveillance than in ordinary criminal investigations. Disclaiming any intent to delineate possible variations precisely, Justice Powell suggested that "probable cause" requirements might be different; application could be made to a member of a specially designated court such as the District Court or Court of Appeals for the District of Columbia; time and reporting requirements might be eased.

The Court looked at the language of Sec. 2511(3) in Title III and found it essentially "neutral." At most, it recognized that the President has certain powers under the Constitution in protecting the nation, but conferred no power on him. Congress left presidential powers where it found them and merely disclaimed any intention to "limit the constitutional power of the President." In support of this interpretation, the Court cited the colloquy between Senators Hart, Holland, and McClellan on the Senate floor when the bill was being debated. Senator Hart read Sec. 2511(3) and raised the question of what it meant.

> *Sen. Holland:* We are not affirmatively conferring any power upon the President. We are simply saying that nothing herein shall limit such power as the President has under the Constitution. . . . We certainly do not grant him a thing.
>
> *Sen. McClellan:* We make it understood that we are not trying to take anything away from him.
>
> *Sen. Holland:* The Senator is correct.
>
> *Sen. Hart:* There is no intention here to expand by this language a constitutional power. Clearly we could not do so.
>
> *Sen. McClellan:* Even though we intended, we could not do so.
>
> *Sen. Hart:* We are agreed that this language should not be regarded as intending to grant any authority, including authority to put a bug on, that the President does not have now. . . . I think our exchange makes clear, nothing in Section 2511(3) even attempts to define the limits of the President's national security power under present law, which I have always found extremely vague . . . Sec. 2511(3) merely says that if the President has such a power, then its exercise is in no way affected by Title III.[12]

Since the Court viewed Sec. 2511(3) as a Congressional disclaimer and expression of neutrality, it tested the constitutional powers of the President by the limitations of the Fourth Amendment and ruled that a court order was necessary. Two basic values were "balanced" by the Court: the duty of Government to protect the domestic security, and the potential danger posed by unreasonable surveillance to individual privacy and free expression. A warrant prior to surveillance was essential to protect the individual and would not frustrate the Government need for secrecy. The Court reasserted the role of the judiciary under the Fourth Amendment:

> This judicial role accords with our basic constitutional doctrine that individual freedoms will best be preserved through a separation of powers and division of functions among the different branches and levels of Government.[13]

It also defended the ability of the Court to evaluate internal security matters.

> Courts regularly deal with the most difficult issues of our society. . . . If the threat is too subtle or complex for our senior law enforcement officers to convey its significance to a court, one may question whether there is probable cause for surveillance.[14]

Any inconvenience in obtaining a court order, said Justice Powell, was justified in a free society. He rejected the suggestion that the court could review the action of the Attorney General *after* surveillance. Post-surveillance review would never reach those surveillances which failed to result in prosecutions.

Justice Powell did not confront directly the claim that electronic surveillance by the Government violates the First Amendment guarantee of freedom of speech. He did, however, recognize that national security cases often reflect a convergence of First and Fourth Amendment values. The investigative duty of the Executive may be stronger in such cases, but there is also a greater jeopardy to constitutionally protected speech.

> The danger to political dissent is acute where the Government attempts to act under so vague a concept as the power to protect "domestic security." . . . The price of lawful public dissent must not be a dread of subjection to an unchecked surveillance power. Nor must the fear of unauthorized official eavesdropping deter vigorous citizen dissent and discussion of Government action in private conversation. For private dissent, no less than open public discourse, is essential to our free society.[15]

The opinion of the Court reviewed the use of surveillance in internal security cases by Presidents and Attorneys General since July 1946. This was the date of a letter to President Truman by Attorney General Tom Clark (later a Justice of the Supreme Court and father of former Attorney General Ramsey Clark) that wiretapping was needed "in cases vitally affecting the domestic security." Clark quoted from a 1940 memorandum by President Franklin Delano Roosevelt to Attorney General Jackson authorizing such surveillance, but omitted Roosevelt's concluding sentence that wiretapping should be kept to a minimum and that it should be limited so far as possible to aliens. Justice Powell doubted that President Roosevelt meant to authorize surveillance to apply to solely domestic subversives, but he did not reject outright the idea that threats and acts of sabotage against the government justify eavesdropping. Electronic surveillance by the Government was an "unwelcome development" of the technological age, but it was needed as a matter of policy:

> It would be contrary to the public interest for the Government to deny to itself the prudent and lawful employment of those very techniques which are employed against the Government and its law-abiding citizens.[16]

The two concurring opinions, each about ten pages long, differed widely in tone and in content. Justice Douglas, who concurred in the opinion of the Court, delivered a fiery denunciation of the evils of official eavesdropping. Justice White, who concurred only in the judgment, expressed a low-keyed, wistful dissatisfaction with the breadth of the Court's decision—ignoring Justice Powell's claim that it was limited and narrow. Justice Douglas stressed the lengthy period of national security wiretaps and the huge number of irrelevant conversations overheard:

> We are told that one national security wiretap lasted for 14 months and monitored over 900 conversations. Senator Edward Kennedy found recently that "warrantless" devices accounted for an average of 78 to 209 days of listening per device, as compared with a 13-day per device average for those devices installed under court order.[17]

The Fourth Amendment, said Justice Douglas, was intended to check "the recurring desire of reigning officials to employ dragnet techniques to intimidate their critics." More than our privacy is threatened, he warned. Also at stake is the Government's power to intimidate its critics.

> We have as much or more to fear from the erosion of our sense of privacy and independence by the omnipresent electronic ear of the Government as we do from the likelihood that fomenters of domestic upheaval will modify our form of governing.[18]

Justice Douglas was convinced that we are currently in the throes of a "national seizure of paranoia," as in the McCarthy era of the 1950s, the Palmer Raids of the 1920s, and the Alien and Sedition Acts at the end of the eighteenth century. While he concurred in the Court's opinion, he reiterated in a footnote his belief that it would be very difficult to write a search warrant specifically naming the particular conversations to be seized.

While Justice Douglas intimated that the Court had not gone far enough in striking down warrantless eavesdropping, Justice White felt that the Court had gone too far. Justice White would have liked the Court to avoid entirely the constitutional issue of Fourth Amendment requirements. The surveillance by the Government in the Plamondon case was illegal under the requirements of Title III, according to Justice White, and so it was unnecessary and improper to consider or decide the constitutional questions reached "improvidently" by the District Court and the Court of Appeals. The affidavit of the Attorney General asserting that monitoring conversations was necessary to protect the nation was inadequate; there was no showing that the attempts of domestic organizations involved "force or other unlawful means" or any "clear and present danger" to the existence or structure of the Government.

The importance of this first case to reach the Supreme Court on warrantless eavesdropping in the interest of "national security" goes far beyond the facts or litigants. Many facets of the problem of eavesdropping without court order, some of which were not considered by the Supreme Court, are illuminated by the Michigan case as it moved through the lower courts. The forceful and sometimes impassioned opinions in the District Court and in the Court of Appeals received more public attention than is usually accorded to lower court pronouncements. The press treated the decision of the Supreme Court almost as a personal triumph for Judge Damon J. Keith of the United States District Court in Michigan. Rejecting the claim of the Government that the President has power to authorize eavesdropping in national security cases without judicial warrant and to determine unilaterally whether a given situation is within the scope of national security, Judge Keith declared:

> We are a country of laws and not of men . . . the President is still subject to the Constitutional limitations imposed upon him by the Constitution . . . the Constitution is the Supreme Law of the Land. . . . We are dealing . . . with the possible infringement of a fundamental freedom guaranteed to all American citizens.[19]

Judge Keith did not reach the issue, presented by the defendants, of whether the broad grant of authority to the President is an unlawful delegation of power by Congress. Nor did he rule on the claim that eavesdropping without court order violates the First Amendment because it has a "chilling effect" on freedom of speech and association. Like Justice Powell in the Supreme Court, Judge Keith relied on the constitutional limitations in the Fourth Amendment.

The District Court decision reached the Court of Appeals by way of a petition for writ of mandamus to compel Judge Keith to vacate his order directing disclosure of conversations overheard. The order, the Government complained, was an abuse of discretion by the judge that would force dismissal of the prosecution against "Pun" Plamondon. The petition was denied by a divided Court of Appeals.[20] Disclosure, observed the Court of Appeals, might be "the only effective protection against illegal wiretapping available to defend the Fourth Amendment rights of the American public."

The majority opinion of the Court of Appeals, written by Judge Edwards, characterized the sweep of assertion of presidential power as "breathtaking." The Court could find not one written phrase in the Constitution, statutes, or case law which exempts the President, the Attorney General, or Federal law enforcement from the restrictions of the Fourth Amendment. Judge Edwards viewed the Government claim as a challenge to constitutional freedom and reasserted the historic role of the judiciary to see that "in periods of crisis when the challenge to constitutional freedoms is the greatest, the Constitution . . . remains the supreme law of our land." Quoting Benjamin Franklin, he warned:

> They that can give up essential liberty to obtain a little temporary safety deserve neither liberty nor safety.[21]

The Court of Appeals saw the "national security" problem in the Plamondon case as the exact sort of situation anticipated by Congress in the section permitting forty-eight-hour emergency eavesdropping without court order. It is obvious, said the Court, that the Attorney General chose not to employ this emergency procedure.

A sharp dissenting opinion was written by Judge Weick of the Court of Appeals. He could see no reason why the powers of the President should be any different in dealing with either foreign or domestic subversives. Both are equally harmful and only the Executive can cope with such dangers. Judge Weick recalled the words of Chief Justice Vinson in *Dennis v. United States*, the 1951 case in which top Communist leaders were convicted during the McCarthy era for conspiracy to organize the Communist Party:

> If Government is aware that a group aiming at its overthrow is attempting to indoctrinate its members and to commit them to a course whereby they will strike when the leaders feel the circumstances permit, action by the Government is required.[22]

Surveillance of Plamondon without court order seemed entirely reasonable to Judge Weick. He concluded his dissent with Professor Wigmore's tart answer to Justice Holmes's much-quoted comment that wiretapping is "dirty business":

> But so is likely to be all apprehension of malefactors. Kicking a man in the stomach is "dirty business" normally viewed, but if a gunman assails you and you know enough of the French art of sa-

vatage [sic] to kick him in the stomach and thus save your life, is that dirty business for you?

After the Supreme Court decision in the Plamondon case in June 1972, the Department of Justice announced that it had directed termination of all electronic surveillance in cases involving national security that conflict with the Court's opinion. It then faced the choice of disclosing conversations overheard in domestic security cases without court order or dropping the prosecutions. Was this the "stunning defeat" for the Government proclaimed by the press? The unanimous decision of the Court was a surprise to many of the experts, but at least one crack was left open by the opinion of Justice Powell. The Department of Justice may still claim that some radicals whose phones have been tapped without court order do have "a significant connection with a foreign power, its agents, or agencies," thus removing them from Fourth Amendment protection. In discussing the difference between "internal security" and "domestic affairs," the *Senate Report* on Title III singled out the domestic Communist Party and its front groups as instruments of the foreign policy of a foreign power, although it did not consider what bearing the law might have on political dissenters other than Communists.[23]

What would happen if the Department of Justice should claim that the Communist Party had infiltrated into organizations such as the National Council of Churches, the peace movement, or civil rights groups? So much bitterness was stirred up by warrantless wiretapping on political dissidents before the Supreme Court decision of June 1972 that the Department of Justice is unlikely to engage in it in the future without the most careful consideration and except in the clearest of cases. One commentator likened the claim of executive power to eavesdrop without court sanction to seventeenth century autocracy:

> A staggering proposition . . . which, for sheer audacity in the assertion of executive power may well have been unsurpassed by anyone since the late Oliver Cromwell installed himself as the Protector of England in 1653.[24]

The suspicion of civil libertarians as to the real motive for enacting Title III was reinforced by eavesdropping on political dissenters without court order. Was the law really designed to combat organized crime as its proponents claimed, or was it intended from the beginning to be used for political purposes? Some thoughtful observers found eavesdropping without court order under the umbrella of Title III worse than past illegal wiretapping. A distinguished law professor and constitutional expert warned that if such eavesdropping became legitimized, it would be "next to impossible to reverse the trend in calmer days." There is a great difference, he said, between quietly tapping in violation of the law and obtaining the imprimatur of the courts.

The Supreme Court has taken the first step in outlawing Government eavesdropping without court order in domestic security cases. The warrantless interception circumvents the "probable cause" requirement, and no disclosure to a judge or anyone else need ever be made. There is no way for the public to know how much eavesdropping is going on if no court order is obtained. "Domestic security" is a vague concept and it may be difficult to determine if a threat is foreign or domestic without first tapping or bugging. Legal experts suggest that if adequate delineation is impossible, then the warrant procedure must be required in all cases and no "national security" exception to a court order exists.

In May 1973, almost a year after the decision of the Supreme Court declaring that the President had no power to authorize wiretapping without court order in domestic security cases, it was revealed that extensive warrantless eavesdropping of newsmen and White House aides had occurred between 1969 and 1971. Among the telephone conversations intercepted was one by Dr. Daniel Ellsberg while he was a guest at the home of Dr. Morton Halperin, assistant to Henry Kissinger. The White House claimed that they involved "national security" and were legal at that time.[25]

The records of the seventeen wiretaps were reported to have been found in the safe of John D. Ehrlichman, at the White House, about an hour after the criminal action against Ellsberg for espionage, theft of the Pentagon Papers, and conspiracy was dismissed in the United States District Court by Judge William M. Byrne, Jr. It was said that the files had been transferred from the office of the F.B.I. after threats by J. Edgar Hoover to disclose the wiretaps if an attempt was made to compel his retirement.[26] One commentator, acknowledging that the claim of authority to wiretap without warrant may have been legal at the time it was started, called it "a dirty and indefensible business." Another characterized it as "distasteful."[27] Now that the Supreme Court has decided in *United States* v. *United States District Court* that eavesdropping without court order in domestic security cases is illegal, could such wiretapping of newsmen and others occur again? Not legally, perhaps, without court order, but the decision of the Supreme Court has been criticized as having left a loophole:

> *United States* v. *United States District Court* made it easy to get authorization for such domestic security taps by suggesting that traditional warrant requirements were not "necessarily applicable" to domestic security cases.[28]

7

State Eavesdropping
in Practice

States have established their own daily routines in eavesdropping under Title III requirements. Uniformity of practice has not been achieved, or even attempted. Indeed, practice and procedure vary even among officials within a particular State. All officials are aware in varying degrees of the many problems presented by government eavesdropping, and are groping for solutions. Some are more highly trained, more skillful than others, and better equipped to meet the heavy burdens imposed upon them by the law. They know that the ultimate fate of eavesdropping as a tool of law enforcement depends on how it is used in practice, but guidelines at the State level are inadequate or nonexistent.

This chapter describes the procedures developed and used by various State officials (see Chapter 8 for Federal practice and procedure), in an attempt to evaluate the *practical operation* of Title III and State laws as distinguished from the legal requirements analyzed in the previous chapters. The material is based largely on answers to questions in personal interviews, and the replies are given verbatim. Since New York has had the most extensive experience with official eavesdropping and serves as a model for other States, most of the interviews were conducted in that State. Some written interrogatories were used, but eavesdropping is such a highly charged subject that they were not very productive. Questionnaires were prepared in advance merely as a reminder of topics to be broached whenever the talk seemed to be wandering too far afield.

Information on official eavesdropping is not revealed readily. The surreptitious nature of wiretapping and electronic surveillance makes law enforcement officers wary and secretive. Continued criticism of eavesdropping under law has produced great sensitivity and defensiveness in officials. They must be convinced that objective discussion is possible, and that frank disclosure of day-to-day practice is necessary to enlist public support if government eavesdropping under Title III and State statutes is to be preserved.

An interview to gather information about the practical workings of official eavesdropping is a delicate operation that must be tailored to the rank and personality of the particular official. Once the hurdle of suspicion has been leaped, however, the interviewer is amazed at the eagerness with which law enforcement officials discuss the work of preparing applications, getting orders signed by judges, monitoring recordings, sealing documents and tapes, filing reports, sending out notices, and prosecuting suspects. The only barrier to full exposure of current practices is, in most instances, the need to protect continuing investigations and pending cases. District Attorneys and their staffs are an articulate, friendly lot, even if harried and overworked. They are proud of their role in law enforcement and anxious for public approval and support. The topics discussed in the following pages reflect those aspects of government eavesdropping in practice that have been the subject of sharpest criticism and require closest examination.

Application for Court Orders

Who decides whether or not to apply for an order to wiretap or conduct electronic surveillance in a particular case? Critics complain that too many people can apply for orders under the law. Congress intended to narrow the number to prevent abuse through indiscriminate eavesdropping, but it is quite large. Authority is given to "the principal prosecuting attorney" of the State or political subdivision. In a small State like Georgia, applications are made by one man, the State Attorney General. In a large State with many political subdivisions, such as New York, dozens of persons may submit requests for orders. New York State has sixty-two counties, each with its own District Attorney. Any one of these may apply for a court order to wiretap or "bug."

How does "the principal prosecuting attorney" decide when an application for an order should be made? He must rely on the many investigating agents attached to or cooperating with his office. An order to eavesdrop originates from an investigation carried on by members of the District Attorney's staff or by employees of outside agencies. It may start through a grand jury investigation. Local police departments and other law enforcement bureaus assign agents to work with the local District Attorney.

Each District Attorney's office is set up differently. For example, in Suffolk County on Long Island, New York, half of the seventy-five or more detectives in the District Attorney's office come from the Suffolk County Police Department; the rest are employees of the District Attorney's office. In Westchester County, New York, the District Attorney has a staff of over a dozen investigators and works with agents from the Sheriff's office and from forty different police agencies. Any one of these investigating agents may come to the District Attorney and recommend that application for an eavesdrop order be made. If the District Attorney can be convinced that the agent has sufficient facts on which an application can be based and that the cost is warranted, the papers are prepared by an Assistant District Attorney in charge of the case and presented to a "judge of competent jurisdiction." Some agents are experienced enough to draft their own affidavits to accompany the application.

In a carefully prepared application for a court order to wiretap or conduct electronic surveillance, documents presented to a judge would normally consist of the following:

1. A detailed, sworn statement by the investigating agent giving all facts on which "probable cause" is based.
2. An affidavit of the District Attorney, which may merely be a summary of what the agent told him and his belief that an order is needed. An Assistant District Attorney may also submit a statement supplementing the facts.
3. A form of order authorizing the wiretap or electronic surveillance.

District Attorneys questioned as to documents presented to the judge invariably said that a sworn statement of the investigating agent was included, as well as that of an Assistant District Attorney. The investigating agent, they explained, was in a position to give first-hand information; the Assistant District Attorney could only set forth the facts told to him by the agent and his belief as to their accuracy. However, some of the applications examined were accompanied only by the sworn affidavit of an Assistant District Attorney outlining the course of the investigations; no affidavit of an agent was attached. This procedure opens the door to attack on the sufficiency of the facts on which the court order is based. One such case in Florida reached the United States Court of Appeals, but it was decided on other grounds.[1]

The judge may require an applicant to furnish additional testimony in support of the application. It is, therefore, common practice to have the agent appear in person before the judge, accompanied by the Assistant District Attorney in charge of the case. Some District Attorneys believe that a personal appearance before the judge by the investigating agent is mandatory under Title III, but the language of Sec. 2518(2) is ambiguous. District Attorneys claimed that the agent *always* appears before the judge so that he can be questioned under oath. Judges, too, emphasized the fact that they require police officers to appear before them as a condition of signing an order. This may be true as a general rule, but at least one judge's law clerk admitted that sometimes the police officer came in personally and sometimes not. "It's not always convenient," he explained almost apologetically.

Appointments are often made in advance with the judge to whom an application is to be presented, and statements accompanying the application may be signed and sworn to in the presence of the judge. The oral testimony of an agent may be recorded on tape or taken down by a stenographer. Some judges insist on this to protect themselves against subsequent criticism that the order was issued without adequate proof of "probable cause" and need for eavesdropping. Judges have discovered, to their great annoyance, that signing an order can give them lots of trouble. Defendants in criminal cases have alleged that the judge signed without knowing all the facts, abused his discretion, and made mistakes.

The judge may question the agent with respect to accuracy and sufficiency of the facts, and as to the existence and reliability of his informant. Wiretapping and bugging, like much of law enforcement, depend on the informant. He may be an undercover agent, but more often he is an individual who has been granted immunity from prosecution or more lenient treatment after arrest in return for divulgence of information against other suspects. Informants usually come out of the jails and their reliability is always open to doubt. Every court order is subject to attack as to the reliability of the informant. Reliability may be established by showing:

1. Record of past reliability.
2. Arrests and convictions that have resulted from information previously furnished.

Accuracy of an informant's statements may have to be checked by physical surveillance and independent investigation before application for an eavesdrop order is made. A District Attorney offered the following example of a typical narcotics case in which eavesdropping is being considered:

> An informant may say that he has been in the target's apartment, has purchased narcotics from him freely; that he uses the telephone regularly to make purchases; that the target makes phone calls to other States to his wholesaler to obtain additional narcotics. To check his reliability, the District Attorney has one of the Sheriff's undercover men introduced to the target as a user of narcotics, and the undercover agent will make purchases from him to make sure he is in the narcotics business.

An informant does not appear before the judge as a rule, and most judges do not even want to know his name. If disclosure of identity is demanded, the name may be "whispered in the judge's ear." One young Assistant District Attorney volunteered the information that he sometimes writes the informant's name on the inside flap of the folder containing the documents. His superior, who was present at the interview, was visibly annoyed that this risky practice had been revealed. The usefulness of an informant may be destroyed if he becomes known to more than one or two persons. Some District Attorneys would rather drop a case than disclose the name of the informant.

To establish the *existence* of an informant, he may occasionally be brought before a judge. This dispels any suspicion that an alleged informant may be fictitious and that the information presented may have been obtained by illegal wiretapping. The procedure was described by a cautious, conscientious District Attorney who made a practice of chamber conferences:

> I bring the informant in before the judge. I don't tell his name, but merely say: "We would like you to meet Mr. X, a person who has given us useful information and is known to the police. I would like the record to say that we produced the informant and that he is here to swear whether the allegations are true." The proceedings are recorded by a stenographer. If the judge asks for his name, we say there is no need to disclose his name . . . what difference does it make what label the man gives himself?

The record of the chamber conference may be used to disprove a contention, on motion to suppress the eavesdrop evidence, that the informant was fictitious.

Since secrecy is of the essence in eavesdropping, the number of copies made of the application and accompanying affidavits should be limited. Most offices prepare an original and three copies and if additional copies are needed they are duplicated later. Applications and orders must be sealed by the judge and the law provides that custody "shall be wherever the judge directs." No particular mode of sealing is specified in Title III and the usual practice is simply to put the documents in a folder, bind it with adhesive tape, and have the judge put his signature across the tape. The seal is rather a makeshift affair and most of those observed looked as if tampering would not be too difficult, even for an amateur. No formal seal was used in any office visited. As to custody, most judges are content to leave the original documents with the District Attorney and keep one copy in a confidential file.

Some District Attorneys who use court-ordered wiretapping extensively have had standard forms of orders printed up to save time in preparation. One busy office set up a form of affidavit as well, to be adapted in future cases. This timesaver is disdained by most law enforcement officials who say that each set of facts in an affidavit is unique and cannot be standardized. Practically every District Attorney keeps a checklist of the numerous items that must be covered in the supporting documents to comply with Title III and State requirements.

Showing of Probable Cause

The job of the person who applies for a court order is to convince a judge that probable cause exists as to commission of the offense and the likelihood of overhearing conversations about it. (For the legal problems raised by the probable cause requirement see Chapter 5.) In a practical sense, probable cause means something that would satisfy a reasonable man; it is a 51 percent probability that tapping a particular telephone will produce a particular type of conversation, relating to the particular offense. How is any applicant to satisfy this slippery requirement? Several law enforcement officials voiced vehement objection to the probable cause provision and said flatly that it imposed a burden of proof that was impossible to meet. One suggested that the requirement to show probable cause should be altered in the case of organized crime:

> We may have to take a more liberal view of the requirement for probable cause in organized crime activity. If underworld figures are known to be consorting with other criminals, and spend no time on any legitimate pursuit that would be a source of income, that should be sufficient to raise the presumption that they are engaged in organized criminal conspiracy, and eavesdrop orders should be issued without requiring the specificity of facts now required to establish probable cause.

This is an extreme view that would raise even more practical and constitutional problems. Probable cause must be shown within the four corners of the affidavit, or in a personal appearance before the judge, under oath. It is not enough for the investigating agent or police officer to say that an informant told him thus and so; he must show why it is reasonable to believe the informant, and he must set forth the sources of the informant's statements. Reliability of the informant is a factor in establishing probable cause. A District Attorney may even be willing to disclose his identity if necessary. One affidavit of a District Attorney in a narcotics case stated:

> The identity of the confidential informant cannot be disclosed in this application without endangering his life. However, if required, his identity will be disclosed orally to the Court. [Subject] told the confidential informant that he is using a telephone instrument bearing number_____ . The confidential informant telephoned [Subject] in my presence to discuss the price of heroin. The informant has in the past purchased narcotics from [Subject].

Every District Attorney interviewed claimed that all the facts were always stated in detail in the affidavits accompanying the application for an order, in order to spell out probable cause. Careful drafting of supporting affidavits is to the District Attorney's own best interests:

I am more zealous in setting forth all the required facts and details than perhaps even a judge. He does not want to be reversed a a matter of pride. I do not want to be reversed because I may have to try the case over again. I am the one who is going to have trouble if an eavesdrop order is not right.

Some of the documents submitted for examination were indeed models of skilled draftsmanship, covering many pages detailing actual en counters and transactions with the target of the order and facts supporting ground for belief in the statements of the informant. Others were more sketchy. It was apparent from the documents inspected that affidavits are drawn up with much unevenness, even in the same office, and that some District Attorneys are more adept than others. (An interviewer, especially one without subpoena power, cannot hope to see every application and must be grateful for those that are opened to an outsider.) Not all the affidavits met the highest standards. Some could qualify as candidates for re jection by a judge.

On application for extension of an order, *new probable cause* must be shown. This is done by relating what has happened since obtaining the order and what conversations were overheard to show that the wiretap is producing results. Some District Attorneys attach a copy of the log or transcript of part of the intercepted conversations as proof that useful ma terial is coming across the wires. The wisdom of this practice is doubtful One official who attached the log in asking for an extension vowed he would never do it again; on a motion to suppress evidence the suspect and his at torney would automatically see the log as part of the application and order and know which of his conversations were overheard.

Inadequacy of Normal Investigative Procedures

Affidavits attached to an application for a court order to eavesdrop must show that "normal investigative procedures" have been tried and found wanting, or that they may be too dangerous. This is almost as tough a requirement to fulfill as probable cause. Mere assertion of the fact is not enough; the circumstances must be set forth in full. Usually the detailed affidavit of the investigating agent recites what has been done up to the time of application and the improbability of obtaining further evidence without an order. This is corroborated in the affidavit of the prosecuting official.

Some District Attorneys complain bitterly that the requirement with respect to "normal investigative procedures" is unrealistic and unnecessary that it is almost impossible to show that wiretapping is being sought as a last resort, and that it limits the effectiveness of the eavesdropping technique "If normal procedures were adequate," said a District Attorney, "we would not be asking for a wiretap order." Normal techniques of investigation con sist of physical surveillance and use of informants and undercover agents. It is argued that the chronological order in which various investigative measures should take place cannot be determined in advance and that they should be permitted to be used simultaneously.

> While you are trying other means and holding off on the wiretapping, the evidence may go down the drain . . . it may be too late, or it may be used less advantageously.

One disgruntled District Attorney characterized the requirement as meaningless. "It makes us sound foolish." When one is dealing with bookies, he said, it is obvious that there is no way of getting information about particular betting transactions except through wiretapping.

Not all District Attorneys resent the "normal investigative procedures" clause. Many feel that it is possible to enumerate facts justifying a wiretap order, depending on the type of case. One reason offered in many affidavits is that it is dangerous to follow a particular person in a moving vehicle.

> [He] is extremely tail-conscious and drives in a reckless and dangerous manner, jumping red lights and dashing over crossings. He stops suddenly to see if he is being followed. [Informant] says that [Subject] does business only over the telephone and rarely meets his contacts, that his associates are constantly looking about, checking each person passing in the area on foot and in automobiles.

Some descriptions of the driving habits of suspects trying to give investigators the slip are more vivid and read like a scenario for "The French Connection":

> He will slow down to five miles an hour as he approaches a red light, and then jump the light at 50 miles an hour. He will dive down the wrong way on a one-way street, and if you follow him he will know he is being tailed. He stops suddenly, gets on a thruway, gets off at an exit and then dashes right back.

In narcotics cases, some affidavits state that dealers hop in and out of five or six automobiles before they bring heroin to a "factory" to be diluted and packaged, making it impossible to follow them. Physical surveillance by car or foot is ineffective in certain areas; lookouts are posted, a stranger is spotted instantly, and a signal may be broadcast by a simple gesture like removing a hat or lighting a cigarette.

One affidavit directed against a Cuban gambling operation said that the individuals conspiring to promote gambling dealt only with Cuban nationals, that they would not even do business with Puerto Ricans except at the lower echelon; that they knew each other by face, although sometimes they did not know one another's name; that use of undercover police officers for surveillance would be fruitless.

A typical reason offered to justify wiretapping is the danger to which an undercover agent is being exposed by normal investigative techniques. A District Attorney's office had a police officer infiltrating an organized crime operation. The affidavit stated that his identity was unknown and he was in a position to give information on what he had observed. But the more the District Attorney made him disclose, the more exposed the undercover agent was to detection by members of the organized crime group and to possible physical harm. The agent could continue his observations, but it was important to hear the conversations of other participants while he was not present, otherwise the District Attorney would have to expose the agent in building up a case.

Some affidavits on which court orders to wiretap have been obtained give facts showing inadequacy of normal techniques in a very general way:

> Since the subjects are wary of police interest in their activities, a physical surveillance of the subject would reasonably appear to be unlikely of success. Other investigative techniques have been employed but they have failed to establish affirmatively any links between . . . and other co-conspirators, their source of supply, the people to whom they ordinarily sell narcotics, the present location of narcotics, particularly cocaine, marijuana, and heroin, and their distribution outlets.

This seems to state conclusions rather than persuasive facts, but it was accepted by the judge and a wiretap order was issued. So far as could be ascertained, no judge ever turned down an application for an order on the ground that it failed to show that "normal investigative techniques" had been tried and found wanting or that they would be dangerous. The judge has to rely on the experts as to what various methods can or cannot accomplish. But even the experts admit that the very need to show that normal techniques are inadequate tends to prevent a hasty conclusion that wiretapping is necessary.

The Time Period

The policy problems and constitutional questions raised by permitting eavesdrop orders to remain in effect for as long a period as thirty days, with an unlimited number of extensions, each up to thirty days, have been discussed in Chapter 5. Most District Attorneys feel that the time is not too long. One thought it was not enough; even fifty days did not seem excessive to him. Another who used the full thirty-day time in most cases said he would not be averse to limiting it to ten days:

If you can't get it [the conversation sought] in ten days, your sources are not so great. Sometimes you will get it in two or three days. You can always reapply for an order if you think some conversations are forthcoming.

According to the reports to Congress, the length of time authorized for conducting an intercept during 1972 varied from a low of 6 hours to a high of 180 days (including 5 extensions), and in 1971 from 5 hours to 300 days. In New York State, out of a total of 294 orders, the vast majority authorized interception for an original period of 30 days. Most District Attorneys are aware that a wiretap should be terminated as soon as the conversations sought have been obtained and they insist that although temptations are tantalizing there is not much abuse of the period allowed:

> By and large the time period is not abused, for District Attorneys know that if it is, the wiretap may be held invalid. If an arrest is made before the time period has expired, the wiretap is terminated, although sometimes it is tempting to try to get additional incriminating information. If the wiretap continues, the conviction may be upset.

It is also claimed that there is little abuse as to the number of hours during which wires are tapped in the course of a twenty-four-hour period.

> It must be shown in the affidavits that the telephone is used at all hours, otherwise wiretapping may be done only during the hours fixed. If an affidavit sets forth facts showing that a bookmaker is only on the phone during daylight hours and does not use the telephone at night, the order would provide for tapping only during the day.

Nighttime interceptions have been upheld by at least one United States District Court in a case where a court order to tap a private telephone line contained no restriction as to hours of interception.[2]

Extensions of wiretap orders have been granted in many cases, according to the *Report to Congress*. District Attorneys admitted, without any sense of wrongdoing, that extensions were often requested not only because continuation of the wiretap appeared necessary to intercept relevant communications, but in order to delay giving the required notice to a suspect in the face of a continuing investigation. To obtain an extension, new probable cause would have to be shown. Preparation of affidavits is a time-consuming job and some District Attorneys have been using a shortcut; the police officer appears personally before the judge who signed the original eavesdrop order. One District Attorney described the "conference procedure" to cut down on paperwork involved in obtaining an extension:

> We go to the judge who signed the eavesdrop order with the stuff that is coming off the wires and say: "Here is what the subject is saying." A stenographer takes down our comments. We indicate that we would like the record to state that the detective was here at the conference with the tape. We ask him: "Do you swear that this is the tape covered by the eavesdrop order entered _____,19_____? Do you recognize the voice on the tape as the voice of [subject]? Will you play the record for the judge?

The judge indicates that he is ready to listen to the playback. The stenographer notes that the judge heard the tape and indicated that probable cause exists for the extension order. The District Attorney and the detective swear to the truth of their allegations, and then the judge says:

> Let the record show that I am now signing an extension of the eavesdrop order of   ,19   , and that I am giving the original extension order to District Attorney. . . .

The record of the conversation before the judge is sealed, and the sealed record is kept in the possession of the court stenographer.

Did the law contemplate any such shortcut method to obtain extension of an eavesdrop order? It seems unlikely. What judge could give the matter of extension his most careful consideration under such circumstances and resist pressure to grant an extension? Section 2518(5) of Title III says extensions may be granted only on application in accordance with subsection (1)—the same procedure by written application as is provided for the original order. It may be significant that few applications for extensions have been denied. In 1969, only two were turned down; in 1970, none were denied; in 1971, none. The report for 1972 makes no mention of whether any applications for extension were denied, and it can be assumed that none were reported for that year. If judges are not rubber-stamping extension applications, they are relying heavily on the applicant's assertion that the extension is needed. Experience with eavesdrop orders may prove to parallel the ordinary search warrant:

> With crowded court calendars, the notion that most judges have the time to weigh carefully the merits of a request for a warrant is naive.[3]

The Judge in Court-Ordered Eavesdropping

The concept of a detached, impartial magistrate protecting privacy is the basis of the Fourth Amendment to the Constitution, to which eavesdropping has been declared subject. Privacy must ultimately depend on the judge. Competent, alert, and aggressive judges are the key to maintaining the safeguards provided by law (see Chapter 5). Judicial control is interposed at various stages of the proceeding: in signing orders and extensions, fixing custody of documents and recordings, deciding who shall be notified and what interceptions shall be revealed. The judge to whom an application for an order is presented must be satisfied that probable cause is shown in the affidavits and that the normal investigative procedures would be inadequate; neither of these is easy to judge. If District Attorneys can shop around for a compliant and undemanding judge, the dangers of abuse of privacy through eavesdropping may be greatly increased. Wide latitude is offered by the Federal law in defining which State judges may sign orders. It includes "a judge of any court of criminal jurisdiction" authorized by State law. This may qualify a large number of judges in a large State.

In counties of metropolitan New York, some District Attorneys said that they were required to present applications to whichever judge was sitting in a special "Part." It is customary to rotate assignments to this Part on a monthly basis. Outside of metropolitan New York, an application could be presented to any qualified judge. After some probing, there was ample reason to conclude that an unwilling judge, hostile to eavesdropping, could always be avoided. At the worst, one could postpone presenting an application and wait until another judge was assigned to the special Part. The question was put bluntly to one judge and answered unequivocally:

> *Question:* Is it possible to avoid presenting an application to a judge who is believed to oppose wiretapping on philosophical or other grounds?

> *Answer:* Yes, it is possible. The District Attorney can wait until some other judge is assigned to the special Part.

District Attorneys and their assistants can and do go to judges who know them. "A judge relies on us," one District Attorney explained. "He knows we won't give him papers that are inadequate and may embarrass him later." Another said:

> We go to the judges who have had experience with court-ordered eavesdropping. Those who are unfamiliar with the law are reluctant to sign orders, not so much because they are against wiretapping, but because they do not want to get involved in matters with which they are not familiar.

A judge's law clerk gave the following revealing explanation of why a particular judge may be selected:

> *Question:* How do you account for the fact that so many applications
> for eavesdrop orders have been presented to Judge X?
> *Answer:* He is popular because he is around the office at late hours.
> We are here at 4 P.M. and 5 P.M. when the applications are pre-
> sented. Besides he has the most criminal experience.
> *Question:* Doesn't an application have to be presented to the judge
> sitting in a special Part?
> *Answer:* No. It doesn't have to be brought to any special Part. . . .
> The District Attorney has confidence in Judge X. The Judge
> knows the Assistant District Attorneys. They do not like to bring
> applications to a new judge . . . they would have to explain. . . .
> It is a matter of convenience.

This account was corroborated by an Assistant District Attorney with
much experience in presenting applications under Title III. He stated
frankly that he presents his papers to a judge who knows him, who has
confidence in the accuracy and sufficiency of his information, and who is
willing to have papers presented to him at any hour, even at his home—one
who does not insist on their being left on his desk where they may be seen
by prying eyes.

A few State court judges have acquired a reputation for opposing
wiretapping and electronic surveillance. The late Judge Samuel Hofstadter
of New York made no secret of the fact that he would sign no eavesdrop orders. Some judges, it is reported, simply say: "Don't bother me." Others are
known to believe that gambling and other so-called "moral" offenses that
are frequent targets of eavesdrop orders should not be classified as serious
crimes. One State judge who had signed a few orders but was reputed to be
cool to the idea of wiretapping and electronic surveillance discussed the
problem of the unwilling judge freely in an interview:

> *Question:* Is it possible that word has been spread that you do not
> favor wiretap orders and that this may account for the fact that
> so few applications have been presented to you?
> *Answer:* It is very possible. I have expressed myself as being opposed
> in general to wiretapping.

Pressed as to the basis for his opposition to eavesdropping, this judge offered
the following mixture of philosophical and practical grounds:

> Some of it [opposition] is based on liberal thinking . . . pro-
> tection of rights of individuals against invasion of privacy. Some of it is
> based on experience. I was a lawyer in East Harlem. I actually saw
> police beat up people in the police station. A policeman does not
> change his character when he suggests a wiretap order. Suppose a
> young policeman makes an arrest because an individual has a policy

slip in his possession . . . the case is thrown out for insufficient evidence . . . after the eighth time he comes into court with insufficient evidence he learns what that evidence should be . . . if he can't get it he manufactures it. It is the same with wiretap orders. You learn what facts are needed to make a showing of "probable cause."

The question of probable cause was a very important one, in the opinion of this judge, and he said that he had refused to sign orders several times when he felt that the facts set forth in the affidavits were inadequate. Despite his aversion to wiretapping, he conceded that there were certain types of crimes where wiretapping might be indispensable, if a crime is serious as in a homicide case. The judge was candid in discussing his suspicion that police officers were wiretapping illegally to get leads prior to making an application for a court order:

Question: Do you interrogate the police officer who makes the affidavit?

Answer: Yes, the officer is questioned by me very closely. I read the affidavit . . . then ask a few questions. All I see is an affidavit and an officer who tries to justify the fact that he has some information that could lead to an arrest. The officer is under oath. Sometimes I ask him: "How long have you been wiretapping before this [illegally]?" The answer always is: "Not at all."

Question: What do you say to him then?

Answer: I sometimes say, "You are full of baloney."

Question: Do you refuse to sign an order where you suspect the police officer may have been tapping illegally before making the application?

Answer: I have no way of proving that he did so. If the wiretap is needed in this case and would have been needed whether he tapped beforehand or not, I would grant the order.

In none of the cases in which a wiretap order had been signed by this judge had an extension been granted. When asked to explain this in view of the fact that so many extensions had been granted on orders signed by other judges, he said, "I give them a hard time on extensions."

A study of the background and experience of judges who have signed many wiretap orders may throw some light on why some favor eavesdropping while others oppose it. A psychoanalytical study might be even more revealing. No such analyses were attempted, but general inquiry produced some interesting facts. Several of the judges to whom applications were frequently presented were former District Attorneys. Others reputed to be hostile to eavesdropping spent their earlier years as counsel for defendants in criminal cases. This may prove nothing more than the fact that judges are human beings influenced by their past experience, but it does seem to indicate that attitudes toward eavesdropping may have deep psychological and emotional roots and do not change with time. An inquiry regarding a District Attorney who did not favor eavesdropping, although he used it as a tool in law enforcement, elicited the interesting fact that he had spent almost two decades as counsel for defendants in criminal cases.

Several years ago, before Title III was enacted, a critic of State eavesdropping noted:

> Judges, being human, vary in their responses to requests for wiretap orders. Some grant them readily, without much regard for the victim's privacy, others are hard-nosed about it. It may be safely assumed that police officers, also being human, keep track of judges' attitudes and rely most on the easygoing ones.[4]

Judges do not have a large office staff and most of them are not inclined to keep detailed records. Some State judges, however, have signed so many wiretap orders that they have been forced to devise a system for following up expiration dates, extensions, and filing of reports. An example of a record book for eavesdrop orders, suggested to a judge by a District Attorney is shown in Figure 1. Note that provision is made in the record for *three* extensions!

Date signed	Asst. D.A.	Starts	Expires	Ren.	Ren.	Ren.	Tapes sealed	Report (State)	Report (Wash.D.C.)

Figure 1. Form of Record Book for Eavesdrop Orders

A judge signing many orders is also faced with the problem of storing the documents in a safe place. When an order is signed, a complete set of the papers, including the affidavits conformed to the original, is left with the judge who keeps them in a confidential file. Judges say that the files are kept under lock and key, and this is probably so for the most part. One judge's law clerk complained that the papers were piling up so high that soon there would not be enough room in the judge's safe. Another actually departed for lunch, leaving on his desk a sorely tempting pile of eavesdropping documents on which he had been working!

The place of custody for tape recordings is left by law to the judge's discretion, but almost invariably the District Attorney or the police agency keeps physical possession. The original tapes are placed in a box, tied up and fastened with adhesive tape; the judge puts his initials across the tape. After a transcript of the recordings has been made, a copy of the transcript may be placed in the judge's file on the case.

One of the serious weaknesses of State practice is the failure of judges to require *progress reports*. (The purpose and importance of these reports are indicated in Chapter 5.) State judges have not required progress reports because it adds to their burden. Some judges say they are kept advised informally as to developments under a wiretap order, and a report may be made to the judge on termination of the wiretap. At least one Federal court has ruled that the use of oral reports does not constitute error, although it would be better practice to submit written reports.[5]

Judges have also found it too much trouble to prepare the report required to be filed with the Administrative Office of the United States Courts within thirty days after expiration of an order or extension. The judge's report is often prepared by the District Attorney's office, presented to him for signature, and then mailed to Washington, D.C. by the judge's law clerk. "Making the report," said one judge, "is a nuisance." One District Attorney prepares the judge's report in triplicate and sends it up to the judge's office with an addressed envelope. The judge's law clerk checks off the report to make sure the details are correct, has the judge sign it, mails it out to Washington, and then notes the date of mailing in his record book. The report contains no identifying name of the person whose wire is being tapped and no telephone number.

The annual report of prosecuting officials is checked against judges' reports on particular orders by the Administrative Office of the United States Courts in Washington, D.C. The purpose of this dual reporting system would appear to be frustrated, to some extent at least, by the practice of having District Attorneys fill out judges' forms and present them for perfunctory signing. The reporting job is obviously distasteful to the judges, and prosecuting officials anxious to create good will are willing to take it off their hands.

The requirement of reports by State judges to the Administrative Office was criticized as unconstitutional at the Senate hearings on the eavesdropping bill:

> Such a provision establishes an administrative relationship between the Federal and State judicial establishments which is inconsistent with the spirit and rationale of the Supreme Court's holding ... and incompatible with the constitutional scheme which constitutes the State judiciary a coordinate judicial apparatus of equal standing and dignity.[6]

The report by State judges is, however, merely statistical in character, and no attempt has been made by the Administrative Office of the United States Courts to exercise any control over the State judiciary or hold it to account.

A more serious practical problem of jurisdiction is presented by the requirement of Title III that an eavesdrop order may authorize interception of communications only "within the territorial jurisdiction of the court in which the judge is sitting" [Sec. 2518(3)]. Had the drafters of Title III foreseen how this provision would work out in actual practice, the statute might have been worded differently. As it stands, a matter may originate in New York County but the District Attorney in that County may have to apply to a judge in Bronx County for an order to tap a Bronx telephone. District Attorneys claim that a security problem may arise if they have to go to a judge in another county simply because the installation is to be made in that other county. New York's eavesdropping statute does permit a judge of the Appellate Division to sign an order covering phones or premises in his department, and this department may include more than one county. But District Attorneys have presented few applications to Appellate Division judges, perhaps because they made it clear that they do not want to be bothered with applications.

The risks involved in going into another county for evidence under an eavesdrop order were elaborated by the Appeals Bureau of a District Attorney's office:

> Suppose a narcotics case starts in X County but it is necessary to go into another county for a wiretap order. The execution of the order is left to the police, and the police in the other jurisdiction may be less supervised. X County has a large narcotics staff and a good rackets squad; it has a police contingent trained for narcotics investigation, and execution of the eavesdrop order in X County would be supervised by an Assistant District who gets daily reports from trained detectives. Other counties may not be as well equipped.

A jurisdictional question involving several counties was presented in an actual case, and no answer could be found in Title III.

> There was probable cause to believe that a criminal conversation would occur in an automobile and that this conversation would occur within a certain period, that it was very imminent. However, from past experience it appeared that this car would travel within various counties. The question arose: Would an order issued in one county be valid in another county across a bridge where the car was likely to go?

Would the District Attorney of one county be obliged to apply to a judge in the county where the conversation actually took place? A District Attorney would probably forego application for a wiretap order rather than risk having it declared invalid later.

No applications for eavesdrop orders were denied by State judges in 1970 or in 1971, according to the annual report to Congress. In 1972, only four applications were denied, all by Connecticut State judges, and one application to a Federal judge was withdrawn. This does not mean that judges have been indiscriminate in signing orders. If a judge feels that supporting affidavits presented and personal testimony adduced are inadequate, additional facts may be obtained and the papers resubmitted to the judge. State judges know that their orders may be attacked on motions to suppress eavesdrop evidence and in the appellate courts. The most disquieting aspect of the reliance placed by Title III on the judicial process is the low opinion that some law enforcement officials expressed of the judiciary. A knowledgeable and experienced Assistant District Attorney volunteered the following harsh judgment:

> The caliber of State judges is uneven and leaves much to be desired. Federal judges are generally considered to be of higher caliber than their equivalent in the State system. The prospects for selection of better State judges are not particularly bright.

The Telephone Company and Wiretapping

Cooperation of the telephone company in government wiretapping was optional until 1970. The company could help officials or not, just as it pleased. In 1970 the Federal law was amended to provide that if an applicant requests it, an order for eavesdropping must direct "a communication common carrier" or other person to furnish necessary information and assistance.[7] This change in legislative policy was the outcome, according to some observers, of refusal of a telephone company in Nevada to help carry out a court order to wiretap. The company had decided not to cooperate because it considered the 1968 law ambiguous and feared that it might be declared unconstitutional. A 6 million dollar lawsuit had been brought against the Nevada company in 1964 for helping the F.B.I. and this time it was taking no chances.[8]

While the telephone company must now cooperate if the court order so provides, its aid in installing a wiretap is not always needed. Police and investigative agents often have ample expertise to do the job themselves and prefer to do it that way to insure secrecy. The telephone company, on its part, is happy to be let off the hook. An official of the Bell System in New York City stated the telephone company's position frankly:

> We try to minimize our role to the greatest extent. The less we know the better, from the standpoint of law enforcement. The

primary interest of the Bell System is the preservation of secrecy of communications to the maximum extent compatible with the public interest. Whether or not law enforcement officers should wiretap is a question for Congress to determine on a balancing of interests. Since Congress has passed Title III authorizing court-ordered eavesdropping, the Telephone Company accepts the law and assumes that it is constitutional.

The spokesman for the Bell System said it was always believed to be to the best interests of the company to cooperate in order to avoid irreparable damage that may be done to its property. Law enforcement officers have a right to enter under the order to make the installation, and if they do not have the right information they may "come on the grounds and thrash around." The telephone company considers itself the watchdog. "We police our facilities as well as we can."

A routine has been established by the Bell System in New York City for handling eavesdrop orders. The telephone company requires that an order be served on it before it will release any information as to "cable and pair numbers." Asked whether the telephone company is always served with a copy of the order, the official said:

> We do not always get a copy of the order. Agents may have sufficient expertise to instal a wiretap without telephone company aid. In New York City many police and investigative agents have considerable experience and don't need to come to the Telephone Company.

Law enforcement agents need to know the cable and pair numbers in order to effectuate a tap on a particular telephone line—the *cable* in which the suspect's telephone line is located and the particular *pair* in the cable. Once the agent has the cable and pair information, he can usually tap a wire without further assistance from the telephone company.

Executives of the Bell System say they do not know what proportion of wiretaps are installed without their aid, and they claim not to know how many are brought to their attention through orders. The company does not keep track of wiretapping in general, other than accepting orders served and keeping them for ten years.

Before 1968, some District Attorneys who had established friendly relations with the telephone company could get information over the phone. Today they know that if they need information, a copy of the court order will have to be served. District Attorneys do not complain about this requirement, for the needed information is furnished promptly. A District Attorney in a county outside the New York City area described the procedure that he follows:

I telephone an investigator in the Security Supervisor's office of the _____ Telephone Company . . . and tell him an order has been signed. I give him the number and the name of the subscriber. Then I send an investigator . . . down to his office with the order. On the phone I ask him to have the information ready. When the order is delivered the data is released at once.

In some cases information other than cable and pair numbers may be needed about a subscriber. According to an official of the Bell System in New York City, State law enforcement officers in several States sought background information about a subscriber from the company's business records to check on identity. A subpoena was served compelling disclosure of the records, and the company complied.

The procedure established in New York City for handling wiretap orders served on the telephone company was described as follows:

Each order served is reviewed by the proper person in our organization to determine whether it is valid *on its face*. We see only the order, not the accompanying affidavits. We check to see whether . . . Sec. 2516 (authorization for interception) and Sec. 2518 (procedure) have been complied with. We keep a checklist of: (1) offenses covered by Title III; (2) jurisdiction of the Court issuing the order and the judge who signed it; (3) persons who may apply for an order; and (4) findings required to be set forth in the order.

The order is served on a person in the telephone company designated for that purpose, either a security marshal or an attorney. Only certain people are authorized to receive the order, and law enforcement officials know who they are. The telephone company generally has close contact with law enforcement officers, and will inform a District Attorney upon inquiry whom to call when he expects to serve a wiretap order so that the information will be ready.

According to officials of the Bell System, only the appropriate employee sees a wiretap order. Each company in the Bell System has its Security Department. This department calls certain personnel for cable and pair number information. Since such information could be sought for a dozen routine reasons, the employee furnishing the details would not know why it was required.

Question: Is it not possible for Telephone Company employees to hand out information without authorization?

Answer: Former employees can, of course, trade information, and there are always a few bad apples in the lot. As to current employees, we try to prevent widespread dissemination of information. The Security Department calls only key members of lower management.

Police investigators and District Attorneys have generally preferred to by-pass the telephone company, if possible, in order to eliminate the possibility of "leaks" through telephone company employees.[9] Unwarranted intrusions on customers' phone conversations by company employees were revealed in hearings on invasion of privacy held in 1967 by the Senate Subcommittee on Administrative Practice and Procedure. A vice president of the American Telephone and Telegraph Company at that time testified that the Bell System favored a ban on all eavesdropping except in national security cases:

> Privacy of communications is a basic concept in our business. We believe the public has an inherent right to feel that they can use the telephone with confidence, just as they talk face to face. Any undermining of this confidence would seriously impair the usefulness and value of telephone communications.[10]

Employees of the telephone company, it was claimed, were trained and supervised to minimize intrusions, and were subject to discharge for violation of rules of secrecy of communications and records. However, service observing and random monitoring by the telephone company in the name of efficiency offered wide opportunity for invasion of privacy; Title III sought to close this loophole.[6]

Section 2511(2)(a) of the 1968 Act exempts from the prohibition against private eavesdropping employees or agents of "communications common carriers" in the normal course of employment, but such carriers are forbidden to use service observing or random monitoring except for service quality control checks. The effectiveness of this interdiction depends on the vigilance of the telephone company. Executives of the Bell System claim that every effort is being made to protect the privacy of subscribers. The public can only hope that the effort is successful.

Live Monitoring and Automatic Recording

Tapping wires, setting up electronic devices, and listening in on conversations are details usually assigned to the investigating agency that initiates an eavesdrop order. If agents or police officers do not have enough experience to instal equipment, they enlist the aid of experts. The court order to eavesdrop authorizes entry into such portion of the premises or telephone lines as will permit interception. A receiving station is then set up at some other place, either a central office of the agency or a rented location where the intercepted conversations are recorded on tape. Most of the wiretapping and recording equipment used in eavesdropping appears to be owned by the investigating agencies.

Opinion is divided as to whether the law requires live monitoring and prohibits automatic recording. In live monitoring (also called "manual recording") police officers or agents sit continuously at the receiving station, listening to the recordings and making notes of relevant conversations on a typewriter or in longhand. The recorder can be shut off when innocent, irrelevant, or privileged conversations are taking place, if they can be recognized as such. In automatic recording, the conversations are recorded on tapes without listeners and are later played back at intervals, the frequency depending on the circumstances and on the practice established in a particular office. The automatic device records *all* conversations.

Live monitoring for a twenty-four-hour period each day requires at least six men, two for each eight-hour shift, a costly expenditure of manpower. One man stays at the receiving set; the other may have to dash out and act on some "hot" information that comes across the wires. These men report periodically to the Assistant District Attorney in charge of the case, either at the end of each day or more often if the wiretap is producing good results. Several extra men may be needed to cover absences for sickness, days off, vacations and other assignments.

Before 1968, in States where court-ordered eavesdropping was permitted, it was common practice to use automatic monitoring and play back the record at twenty-four-hour intervals. Title III of the Omnibus Act of 1968, however, requires that a wiretap cease when the conversation sought has been obtained, and that the interception be conducted in such a way as to minimize interception of communications not covered by the court order. If automatic recording is used, interception may continue beyond the point authorized by the order. An official in a District Attorney's office, expert on the law governing eavesdropping, states emphatically:

> There is no excuse for automatic monitoring. It is illegal, unconstitutional. If wiretapping is properly monitored, it is self-limiting.

This view is shared by eminent authorities who feel that intelligent monitoring is essential if the surveillance is to be sustained by the courts and not considered an "indiscriminate dragnet." Each District Attorney interviewed was asked whether he used live monitoring or automatic recording. Those convinced that live monitoring is required by the 1968 law invariably said they always use it. Following is a typical answer of this group:

> We use live monitoring. Legally it is wrong to use automatic recording, for you might have an obligation to pull the wire out immediately after you have obtained the conversation sought. You can't pull it out if it is being monitored automatically.

Those law enforcement officers who were unaware or uncertain of the need for live monitoring under Title III furnished a variety of answers indicating that automatic recording is still used, at least to some extent. For example:

> We are getting away from automatic monitoring.

> We no longer have automatic recording with checking at twenty-four-hour intervals. There are, however, occasions when for personnel reasons, or if we do not see the need to sit there all the time, the men may come back every few hours.

> For the most part we use live monitoring, but on some occasions for lack of manpower, when some emergency arises, we may leave the recorder in a particular location.

> It depends on the nature of the case, on the circumstances, on manpower available.

> Sometimes a man might be left on to monitor it manually, at least for the first two days.

> Live monitoring has not been the rule. In one or two cases we had it monitored because we had to act on information that minute . . . looking for a fugitive.

Mailed questionnaires which asked whether automatic recording was used produced the answer "sometimes."

A police officer monitoring a recording keeps a "log" of the telephone conversations intercepted (Figure 2). Logs may be handwritten or typed on a sheet that has printed on it various hours of the day. The sheet indicates every phone call that took place. The telephone calls intercepted are numbered consecutively on the log, so that when the annual report is filed by the District Attorney with the Administrative Office of the United States Courts, the total number of telephone calls intercepted is known without adding them up and can be indicated on the report. Each number called when the tapped wire is in use is indicated by an electronic device called a "pen register" or "penwriter." On old standard telephones, the pen register notes the number by dashes. On modern dial phones, an instrument known as a Touch Tone Recorder is used that types out the numbers.

The log may list a call simply by stating the number called, by whom and to whom the call was made, with a note that the conversation was not relevant (marked "n/r"). Where a conversation appears to be significant, the police officer notes the gist of the conversation opposite the hour that it occurred. The form of the log indicates the type of machine on which the recording was made, so that it can be played back on the same type of ma-

Plant No...   Date...
Case No...   Tape No...
Telephone No...   On...
Subscriber..   Off..
                                                            Machine...

Stop	Time	Call No.	In	Out	Number Called	Subjects	Summary

Figure 2. Form of Log for Intercepted Conversations

chine. Stops are indicated by number on the machine. Various makes of instruments are used.

At the end of the day or the following morning the log is brought to the Assistant District Attorney in charge of the case or to the District Attorney himself, and the record is put on a machine so that the significant portion can be played back. A grand jury stenographer may be called in to type out the portion of the conversation verbatim on a steno machine. Sometimes large portions of the tape are transcribed in this way. Eventually a full transcript of the tape recording is typed up. A District Attorney described the reason for this dual process of selective and complete transcription:

> For prosecution purposes, we transcribe selectively the conversations that are relevant, as determined by the Assistant District Attorney in charge. These transcripts are used in the presentation to the grand jury . . . it is easier to organize the material from the transcripts than to play back the record. But ultimately the defendant and his counsel will be entitled to the entire tape and may insist on a transcript, so the whole tape must be transcribed.

District Attorneys generally insist on listening to the taped recordings and will not rely on transcripts. As one explained:

> I want to hear the voices. . . . Not that I don't trust a detective to make an accurate transcript. But sometimes the interpretation of a word has legal consequences that I can foresee and the detective cannot.

Although the law requires minimization of interception of conversations not covered by the court order, it does not say how overhearing of innocent, irrelevant, or privileged conversations is to be avoided. This problem is aggravated by the fact that monitoring is done by agents or police officers whose judgment and integrity cover a wide range. Conscientious District Attorneys are painfully aware of the dilemma:

> We try to have the recording device turned off when a non-criminal conversation is taking place. It is, however, difficult because you are leaving it to policemen to determine whether it is an innocent or a criminal conversation. The District Attorney hopes they are honest, hardworking policemen, but he knows that a policeman may be corrupted, may try to line his own pockets.

What is a non-criminal conversation? What is a relevant conversation? What is "innocent" or non-incriminating? In dealing with organized crime, a conversation coming over the wires may be between the wife of a target and a girlfriend of a suspected criminal. Is the agent to shut this off because it will probably yield nothing but chitchat? Some District Attorneys advise police officers to listen to such conversations:

> They may talk about the people they were out with and where, and about matters that lead to incriminating evidence. Wives talk to one another and sometimes tell where their husbands are going and why.

Most District Attorneys insist that police officers are not interested in listening to irrelevant conversations, that it is a dreadful bore involving a constant struggle to keep awake. Police stop listening, they claim, when the conversation is irrelevant.

> It is sheer fantasy to believe that detectives listen to irrelevant conversations and that some do it with ulterior motives.

Former Congressman Emanuel Celler (Democrat of New York), a consistent foe of eavesdropping, counters this with a rhetorical question and a pointed answer that seems irrefutable:

> How can police stop listening when the conversation is irrelevant? They don't know whether or not it is irrelevant unless they listen, and it may be irrelevant one moment and relevant the next. They *must* continue to listen, because the next moment something pertinent may be said. If they shut it off they may miss something they want to hear.

A disproportionate number of innocent conversations seems to have been overheard in some cases; in one case reported to the Administrative

Office of the United States Courts, 400 telephone calls were intercepted to get one incriminating conversation; in another over 1,000 for 20. In a third case 1,342 intercepts were reported to have been made, not a single one of which was incriminating. How is this to be avoided? Even if police officers are instructed not to listen to non-incriminating conversations, no guidelines are available to determine whether a conversation is "criminal" or not. One District Attorney maintains there is no such thing as a non-incriminating conversation:

> You have to spell incrimination out of a conversation. Many telephone calls may be made between conspirators. Some of the conversations may not appear to be incriminating . . . that doesn't mean that in fact they were not incriminating . . . it simply means it gave us no information.

Another pointed out that a wide difference between the total number of intercepts and incriminating calls did not necessarily mean that a great many conversations of innocent people were overheard. It was suggested that what was important was not the number of incriminating intercepts in proportion to the total number, but whether the wiretap resulted in an arrest.

Over 70 percent of wiretaps were installed in private homes, apartments, and multiple dwellings, as distinguished from business establishments, in 1971, 1970, and 1969, according to the annual reports to Congress. In 1972, the figure reached 78 percent. Wiretapping residences involves greater risk of intercepting conversations of innocent persons. This, of course, cannot be the concern of the prosecuting official if organized criminals carry on their enterprises from their homes. Few wiretap orders covered public phones. This is where there is real danger of overhearing innocent conversations; precautions can be taken but not without risk of discovery. In one case, narcotics agents hid in a packing case near an airport public telephone and signaled to the monitoring agent when the target of the eavesdrop order entered the booth, so that the wiretap could be shut off at all other times. A United States attorney revealed the comic aspects of this serious operation; maintenance employees at the airport, unaware of the presence of the agents, tried to move the packing case into a warehouse!

The police officer manning the electronic device decides when to stop listening to a particular conversation, but the District Attorney determines when the eavesdropping is to terminate. He makes an assessment based on the facts:

> We have to decide whether we are getting the information we want . . . whether we should spend any more time and money on it . . . whether we should try to apprehend the suspect now or delay arrest

while we seek additional evidence . . . whether we should turn it over to some other agency who might apprehend a confederate elsewhere.

Some wiretaps are terminated before expiration of the period allowed by the order; however, this seems to be the exception. Section 2518(1)(d) provides:

"If the nature of the investigation is such that the authorization for interception should not automatically terminate when the described type of communication has been first obtained," the application must set forth "a particular description of facts establishing probable cause to believe that additional communications of the same type will occur thereafter."

Section 2518(4) requires that each order shall include "a statement as to whether or not the interception shall automatically terminate when the communication has been first obtained."

One District Attorney who believes that Title III is *too* restrictive claims it is often difficult to show that termination on first attainment of the authorized objective should not be required. Termination on first attainment of the conversation sought, he says, decreases the ability of law enforcement officials to deal with organized crime; initial conversations do not reveal organized crime enterprises. Another District Attorney who can find no fault with Title III believes that prosecuting officials are not obligated to terminate immediately on hearing one conversation of the type specified in the order. "Generally, it is a continuing operation."

No criteria are furnished by the law to aid in determining whether or not a particular conversation intercepted is that specified in the order, and formulation of guidelines may have to be undertaken by the courts. The difficulty of the problem is most clearly exemplified in a conversation that conforms in part with the subject matter described in the order. It may be so close to the description of the type of conversation in the order that the wiretap must terminate, even if it is not enough to prove the offense. A series of conversations may be needed to spell out the crime, but each conversation may be couched in such guarded language that it is impossible to see its significance in advance.[11]

A high quality of recording is essential if intercepted conversations are to be used as evidence. This is one of the reasons why most eavesdrop orders under Title III have been for wiretapping and not electronic surveillance. Wiretapping generally produces clearer recordings, with less difficulty in installation and at lower cost. In any case use of eavesdrop evidence can open up a Pandora's box of troubles even if the equipment was good and the operator capable. There are problems of voice identification, audibility, and intelligibility of conversations.[12] Much of the language of organized crime is in code, and groups have their own terminology. Narcotics agents may have discovered that "tea" means marijuana, "strawberries" are L.S.D., cocaine is "Charley," and heroin is "Henrietta." They may catch on that a "suit" is a pound, "pants" an ounce, and that "shirts" and "ties" are not always articles of clothing. But organized criminals are ingenious in developing new language to confound the eavesdropper and to make it difficult for law enforcement officers to use intercepted communications as proof of crime.

The fact that a wiretap order has been obtained and information gathered does not mean that intercepted communications will be used in evidence at a trial even if there is an arrest and indictment. In one case where seven extensions of a wiretap order were obtained, the District Attorney said that "none of the information in the wiretaps is going to be used in prosecution because we have independent evidence."

> *Question:* Then of what use was the wiretap?
> *Answer:* We did not know at the beginning of the investigation that we would not have to use the wiretap information.

The difference between eavesdropping for "strategic intelligence" as distinct from gathering evidence of a specific offense has been discussed in Chapter 5. Each District Attorney interviewed was asked point-blank:

> Do you ever seek information under Title III merely for intelligence purposes?

Some District Attorneys answered that they do not; that Title III may not be used to gather strategic intelligence:

> No . . . it's not permitted . . . the law provides that you can't do that.

Several of these admitted, however, that one could get *leads* without seeking them, and that they would not be turned down.

1. You try to get evidence of gambling and it may lead you to evidence of some other crime, maybe murder. You would have to amend your wiretap order to include it.
2. It's not unusual to have a wiretap that results in no incriminating statements but some information is overheard that is useful in obtaining evidence later.

A few District Attorneys were frank in saying that eavesdropping was more helpful from an investigative standpoint than for actual evidence.

> Suppose in a policy case our man is accepting bets. We want to know whom he is working for. We get the information over the telephone . . . he is discussing layoffs and talking about other people

doing the same thing. We have no evidence to establish proof against
his boss. We may find out who his boss is and yet not be able to prove
it. We might find out the number of people involved, the periods
when they make reports . . . it is "intelligence" . . . it may have future
value.

The gathering of "strategic intelligence" seems to be extensive. Since
this practice is constitutionally doubtful and the law is obviously ambiguous, clarification of this point is urgent.

Does Title III permit eavesdropping to *apprehend* a suspected
criminal? There is a difference of opinion among State officers. Some admit
that they use court-ordered eavesdropping to apprehend a suspect, and they
defend the practice:

> It can be used to gain information as to a crime or information which
> would disclose the whereabouts of a person. We have used wiretap-
> ping here in cases where we were looking for a desperado at large and
> we had reason to believe that he might telephone a certain person and
> disclose his location.

Other officials disagree; while it might have been reasonable to cover
apprehension of a criminal for serious crimes such as murder or where a vital
public interest was involved, the law has not done so, they maintain. Suppose a suspected murderer calls his mother and says: "Send me money."
That is not evidence of a crime as called for by Title III, nor does it relate
necessarily to a crime.

Notice and Disclosure

Mixed feelings prevail among District Attorneys with respect to the
requirement that notice must be given within ninety days after termination
of the time period specified in the eavesdrop order. Some of them say they
"can live with it." Others object vehemently:

> Suppose in a homicide case there is justification for an order. But
> the man is not talking on the telephone. You now have to serve notice
> on him. He will get the order . . . and he will know what evidence you
> have at that time that can be used against him.

An extreme view is that the notice requirement sounds the death knell of
eavesdropping:

> The notice requirement has proved and will continue to prove
> harmful to the whole purpose of wiretapping. It puts the suspected
> person on the alert . . . puts him on guard. He then avoids the

telephone. I believe this requirement will mean the end of wiretapping as a useful tool in law enforcement.

It has been suggested that notice should be required only if an indictment has been handed down and the subject arrested for the crime which was the subject matter of the wiretap order. Where an investigation is still open, all the notice does is to inform the suspect that he is a target and make him doubly careful. An eavesdrop order is different from a search warrant, it is claimed.

> Where a search warrant is executed, the man knows he has been a target. If he is indicted, arrested, nothing is lost by serving him with notice. When notice is given under an eavesdrop order, the informant is endangered. It becomes possible for the target to identify the informant.

The danger to the informant by the giving of notice was elaborated on by another District Attorney:

> When the papers on which the wiretap order was procured are made available to the attorney, his client can tell from the statement of facts who the informant is—by narrowing down the possible informants. If an affidavit states that your confidential, reliable informant observed the subject speaking on the telephone and overheard him discussing the future sale of a shipment of narcotics totaling over $35,000 on a particular date at a particular place, the person whose wire is tapped can figure out who that person is. You place your informant's life in danger, and it makes it difficult to get additional informants.

Some District Attorneys have circumvented the effects of the notice requirement, or at least postponed it, by asking for an extension of the eavesdrop order. This can protract the time period of the order over a considerable period since the number of extensions permissible is not restricted by law; all that is required is that the applicant show new probable cause why the wiretap should be continued. This does not seem to be too difficult to do.

Judges have generally refused to extend the time for giving the ninety-day notice beyond an additional ninety days. Asked whether he would under some circumstances grant a longer extension, a State judge said:

> I might if it was necessary. But if more time was needed the District Attorney would probably apply for an extension before the wiretap was terminated.

The following excerpt from an affidavit of an Assistant District Attorney accompanying an application for postponement of time to give notice illustrates a typical reason offered for requesting additional time:

> This investigation is still continuing. The Hon. _____ signed other eavesdrop orders pertaining to [Subject] and many of these orders are presently in effect.
>
> To notify [Subject] that he has been under electronic surveillance by this office would alert him and his associates, make them wary of electronic eavesdropping, and thwart this continuing investigation.

An affidavit of the District Attorney accompanying the application corroborated the statements of his assistant:

> That he has read the affidavit of Assistant District Attorney _____; that based on the affidavit he believes that the disclosure to [Subject] of the existence of the eavesdrop order would seriously hamper the investigation into the crimes of promoting gambling and criminal usury and would make successful prosecution of the crime impossible.
>
> That he believes that there are set forth in the affidavit of _____ sufficient facts to warrant postponing notice to [Subject] of the fact that these conversations were the subject of an eavesdrop order.

The order of the judge granting postponement of notice merely stated:

> It appearing from the affidavits that there is sufficient cause to believe that notice to [Subject] that he was the subject of the above mentioned eavesdrop order would seriously hinder the investigation of this matter,
>
> It is ordered that such notice to _____ be postponed for a period not to exceed ninety days to _____, 19__.

The notice requirement has its defenders as well as its critics. A District Attorney with extensive experience in court-ordered eavesdropping said:

> Notice does hurt the investigation . . . but it has a restraining influence on the best of us to know that some day the basis of the order will be analyzed by the subject. If the prosecution is abusing its authority, getting orders on a speculative rather than factual basis, if the judge was not so alert, the public should know about it.

Without notice, if no arrest resulted from the wiretap order, an abuse of authority or improper order would probably never come to light. Several prosecuting officials agreed that the notice requirement made them extremely careful to have the application and supporting papers conform to statutory requirements in every detail. When a set of documents is drafted, the District Attorney is conscious of the fact that eventually the papers will be examined by someone who is hunting for flaws.

Report by Prosecuting Officials

State law enforcement officials are instructed to use the standard form of report supplied by the Administrative Office of the United States Courts, Washington, D.C. According to regulations issued by the Administrative Office, an additional supply of forms may be reproduced locally by the electrostatic process or other suitable means of reproduction, if preferred. Few, if any, State officials are impressed with the importance of the reports that they must file annually, and some find it extremely irksome. A harried District Attorney complained:

> When I saw the form I was simply annoyed to be forced to fill in so many details . . . just more and more paperwork for which we are understaffed. I now work 14 hours a day and it took one and a half hours of my time answering those questions. We object to it because of lack of time.

Lack of space on the form to fill in information requested was another source of irritation. The item at the bottom of the form, asking for an assessment of the importance of the interception in obtaining a conviction, seemed particularly objectionable. "It's superfluous," several District Attorneys maintained, since the form also asks whether the wiretap resulted in an arrest or conviction. Many of the reports examined personally in the files of the Administrative Office of the United States Courts in Washington, D.C., simply ignored the item and left it blank. Others disposed of it in a brief sentence:

> *Example 1.* Arrest of defendant and seizure of dangerous drugs would not be possible without wiretap.
> *Example 2.* Gambling arrests resulting would not be possible without wiretaps, inasmuch as this activity occurs primarily by telephone.

One report said the wiretap revealed the *innocence* of the suspects, not guilt:

> *Example 3.* State police, acting under my direction, became fully satisfied by reason of the intercepted communications that the two suspects were not involved in the homicide under investigation. Without the interceptions, the suspects would have remained under police suspicion and would not have been cleared of such suspicion.

Another said the wiretap was not necessary to obtain the conviction that was ultimately effected:

> *Example 4.* Subject of wiretap subsequently arrested and indicted for narcotics violations. However, conversations which may have served as basis for arrest or search warrant not necessary to obtain conviction.

District Attorneys could not be convinced that the annual report to the Administrative Office serves an important function as a research tool in evaluation of court-ordered eavesdropping under Title III. One tart comment illustrates the generally unfavorable view of the report:

> I don't see what they can prove since the items required to be reported are largely ambiguous. Some of them are meaningless.

Pressed to identify the items on the report lacking in clarity, the following six were enumerated:

Average frequency of intercept, per day: How is this to be computed? Should one take the total number of days of interception and the total number of interceptions and average them up? Suppose in one day there is one interception; on another day there are twenty-three interceptions. Would the average frequency of interceptions for the two days be twelve? Suppose during a thirty-day period no interceptions occurred except on the last day when there were thirty interceptions. Is the average frequency one? How could such an average be of any significance?

Number of persons whose communications were intercepted. Does this mean the number of people involved in the offense designated, or the number of people using that particular phone or calling that number, whether or not their conversations were relevant?

Number of communications intercepted. Does this mean the number of completed calls? Does it include attempted calls that were not completed, incoming or outgoing? Suppose calls are made but nobody picks up the telephone, as often happens. Is the telephone number called not to be counted as an interception?

Number of incriminating communications intercepted. What is an "incriminating" conversation? X telephones Y and says: "I will meet you in ten minutes." Is this incriminating? It takes an expert to interpret telephone conversations. If you want to reinforce the statute, show that many incriminating statements are overheard, prove that court-ordered eavesdropping is effective, you can include many calls in the category of "incriminating." Someone else may find that these conversations were *not* incriminating but innocent, and demonstrate that the wiretap was not very productive.

Convictions. A conviction may be obtained in a case subject to a wiretap order, but this does not mean that the conviction resulted from the order. The wiretap may have nothing to do with the evidence presented.

Cost. The annual report of prosecuting officials, as revised in 1969, must include a separate estimate of (1) manpower, and (2) other resources. How is cost of manpower to be computed? If you use a senior investigator on a case who is paid much more than a regular agent, do you include the exact amount paid to him? Is cost calculated on the basis of average wage or exact amount paid to each man involved in the wiretap? Regulations issued by the Administrative Office of the United States Courts on December 13, 1972 tried to clarify the question of reporting on cost by the following definitions:

> "Manpower" costs should include the cost of the time spent by officers or employees both in installing and in monitoring the equipment and time spent in preparing transcripts. "Resource" costs should include the costs of installation where the installation is done on a contractual basis; rental, lease, or amortization of equipment; and the cost of supplies including magnetic tapes and discs.

Cost of equipment is apparently to be included, but is the receiving plant considered an element of cost? Suppose that in order to avoid detection or for some other reason it is necessary to set up a "cheese box" and monitor the calls in the District Attorney's office. (A "cheese box" is an electronic device for relaying intercepted communications to another wire in some other location so that the telephone call cannot be traced.[13]) What location expenses could be considered part of cost?

Several District Attorneys interviewed could see no point whatsoever to including the item of "Cost" in the report of prosecuting officials, and some actually leave the item blank in protest.

> Is a wiretap to be evaluated in dollars and cents? Does it make any difference whether a wiretap costs $100 or $1,000? A prosecuting officer is open to criticism if he measures the cost of bringing a criminal to justice. Cost doesn't mean anything. What is important is *effectiveness* of the eavesdrop . . . that is what the Administrative Office should want to know.

The only District Attorney who conceded the importance of knowing how much it costs to wiretap was one who was *not* enthusiastic about eavesdropping under Title III. He said:

> Suppose we spend hundreds of thousands of dollars in wiretapping and get one conviction for a misdemeanor. That shows it isn't productive enough for the manpower spent.

Manpower is obviously the chief item of cost in eavesdropping and, properly conducted with live monitoring, it can be a strain on personnel. Some "plants" may have as many as twelve men listening to recordings at the same time. The salary of these men is generally paid by the police agency carrying on the investigation, but the District Attorney must decide whether the services of agents assigned to him would be most effectively employed in wiretap monitoring or some other form of investigation. District Attorneys who are strong supporters of eavesdropping are less troubled than others by the necessity of making a choice. "It takes manpower to get evidence regardless of the technique used."

The method of computing manpower cost to be reported annually is not uniform; some estimates are rougher than others. In one office, an estimate is made of the number of men on the job and whether they had any other assignments or spent full time on the wiretap. If a tap was conducted for thirty days and the police officer earns $1,500 a month, then $1,500 of his salary is charged to the cost of the wiretap. A more accurate computation may be made:

> We take the total number of detectives on the wire and estimate the total numbers of hours they spend on the wire and the time it takes them to transcribe the recording. Multiply this by the amount they get paid, computed on an hourly basis. This gives us the cost of manpower. Manpower cost on an hourly basis may be $10 an hour, per man.

As to *other resources* as an element of "Cost," prosecuting officials generally agreed that it was insignificant. "It doesn't amount to much and doesn't mean much." It may include:

1. Cost of the tapes, at most $100 or $200, depending on how long the wiretap runs.
2. Cost of machines, valued at $400 to $700, with a life expectancy of about five years.
3. Rent for setting up the recording and listening device location.

Cost is rarely decisive in determining whether or not to apply for a wiretap order, although it may be taken into account. Some county budgets include provision for eavesdropping expenses, and efforts have been made to get funds for eavesdropping from the Law Enforcement Assistance Administration under Title I of the Omnibus Crime Control and Safe Streets Act of 1968. The Annual Report to Congress by the Administrative Office of the United States Courts, summarizing reports of prosecuting officials and judges, comments on "Cost of Intercepts" for the year 1972 as follows:

The reported cost of a single intercept installed (in terms of manpower, equipment and other costs) ranged from a low of $5.00 to a high of $82,628. The average cost for the 805 intercept orders for which a cost was reported was $5,435.

A table of comparison showing average cost per order in each jurisdiction *where the cost was reported* was also furnished to Congress. There would seem to be some justification for the criticism of prosecuting officials that no evaluative purpose can be served by statistics indicating that some intercepts cost $5.00 and others $82,628 without relating cost to the results of the intercepts.

More serious objections to the forms have been voiced by the American Civil Liberties Union in Washington, D.C. The A.C.L.U. claims that the reporting provisions of Title III are incomplete, and characterizes them as a fraud. No information is included with respect to the forty-eight-hour emergency taps without court order or warrantless eavesdropping in so-called "national security" cases. Neither the A.C.L.U. nor the District Attorneys would concede that the annual report to the Administrative Office by State law enforcement officials may serve as a subtle deterrent to excessive use of wiretapping and misuse of this investigative technique.

Combating Organized Crime

The offenses covered by an eavesdrop order must be set forth in the report of State prosecuting officials and judges to the Administrative Office of the United States Courts in Washington, D.C. These are generally listed simply as "Gambling," or "Narcotics," or some other offense, without indication of the seriousness of the charge. A gambling offense may involve the head of a national or international operation, payoff man, bookmaker, or small-time runner. Narcotics offenses may range from smuggling enormous quantities of heroin into the United States to peddling a few marijuana cigarettes on the street. Every prosecuting official interviewed was asked whether court orders applied for by him were directed against organized crime, and whether they involved top, middle, or low echelon members. The answers indicate that State officials pursue whatever suspected criminals they can, regardless of affiliations or position in the hierarchy. They were surprisingly candid:

1. I would hesitate to use the wiretap technique against the average person. But if the "big money" of organized crime comes from gambling, then the bookmaker is bad and should be the target of a wiretap even if he is not high echelon. We have to assume that he is involved with the Mafia. But my nightmare is: Suppose I wake up some day and find there is no Mafia!

2. We get what we can. We don't always get to the top, but we know that if we get to lower echelon, it is a harassment for the top men and it has a salutary effect.

3. It is true that eavesdropping orders may be directed to lower echelon members of organized crime—bookies, runners—but this is useful because it makes organized crime expensive . . . the lower echelon pay tribute to the higher-ups . . . criminal prosecutions are an expense of operation.

4. We have used it in gambling cases which are linked to organized crime . . . local gambling. Bookies lay off bets with people in other counties and ultimately the money goes to organized crime. We are unlikely to get a high echelon member. Even if you get captains—you will never get the top men. The lieutenants would rather die than testify against them.

5. Generally we know something about the subjects of the eavesdrop order. Their names are known and we believe they are at the upper level, but they may not be top men.

6. The majority of criminal cases that come to the attention of the District Attorney deals with lower echelon. It is difficult even in narcotics to get to the top. For that you need a lucky break. Someone will have to call up a person in the upper echelon. Their code is: "Don't use the telephone." But eventually they must use the telephone if only to warn somebody.

7. We would like to get to the upper echelon, but we have to start further down. In a policy racket we may begin by keeping the "controller" under observation. In gambling, we may start out with a bookmaker who calls a consolidated wire room which we know is connected with another big operation with which the top men may communicate.

One District Attorney who found Title III so restrictive that he used it very sparingly said:

> Others may obtain wiretaps on any type of gambling activity. We will only make an eavesdrop on gambling if we have reasonable grounds to believe that it is operated by organized crime and if it is a large enough operation.

Some law enforcement officials expressed doubt that Title III was intended only for organized crime or serious crime. One pointed out that under New York law enacted to conform to Title III, even "misdemeanor gambling" was a covered offense. Another claimed his office was "selective," it went only after members of organized crime, "people who are carried on the records of the Police Department Special Investigation Bureau as major violators and on records of the Federal Bureau of Narcotics and Dangerous Drugs."

There is much current interest in narcotics cases, and some law enforcement officials use wiretapping almost exclusively for this offense. They admit that middle and upper level members of organized crime do not touch narcotics, and that Blacks and Spanish-speaking people predominate in lower echelons. Nevertheless, they say, the drive against narcotics violators is an attack on organized crime.

> Top organized crime skims off the top of narcotics first and uses the funds in other enterprises.

In one county with many "factories," where people are employed to mix heroin with sugar and place the diluted powder in glassine bags for retail sale, wiretapping is used to reach these factory workers even if they merely handle narcotics as wage laborers. In other counties where few "mix" and dilute, wiretapping is reported to be used only against those who participate in smuggling loads and half loads into the United States for storing in a plant in the county; those who merely handle heroin in smaller quantities are not the subjects of eavesdrop orders.

Few law enforcement officials will admit that concentration on narcotics cases may have political implications and reflect the ease with which a record of arrests can be established in this area, but their comments seem to indicate that this is at least part of the reason for the present emphasis on narcotics eavesdropping:

> The District Attorney can be more effective in this area. In narcotics cases you can get the most information . . . a junkie seller has to make a buy somewhere, and most victims tell where they got it. Penalties for possession or sale to minors may be severe, so the man on narcotics or in the business of selling drugs will talk to lower the penalties. A core of informers can be developed—the best source of information on narcotics.

District Attorneys were asked: "Why not conduct a drive against loan sharking, the offense that generates violence and may even result in murder?" The answer is obvious. "In the usury area you don't get the information. The man who lends you money is doing something for you; he is a friend in need, and the borrower is not likely to squeal on him."

Cooperation and Conflict among Competing Agencies

Each State official interviewed was asked: "Do you get cooperation from other State law enforcement agencies and from Federal bureaus? Has cooperation increased or decreased since enactment of Title III in 1968? Is there competition?" One District Attorney replied without hesitation:

There is competition. Everybody wants to get a big narcotics ring for political purposes. The District Attorney runs for office.

Cooperation has not increased under Title III, it was generally agreed. Some said law enforcement was more competitive now than heretofore. One official who found "unsettling" the spurt of interest in crime, "law and order," and law enforcement explained how State and Federal agencies come into conflict.

If I find the F.B.I. talking to the same witnesses that I am talking to, the same informants, I ask: "Why? Are they here to make a shot in the dark, a big splash?" If our County Police Department is working on a case, and the State Police have an interest in the same matter, and the Governor comes down with his superpolice, and we also have a State Crime Commission, then law enforcement is competitive.

Despite the conflict, this official insisted that he was in constant touch with F.B.I. agents, State and County police, and that they were in and out of his office. "You have to get along personally with people," he said.

As a matter of security, if for no better reason, not all information can be shared. Cooperation among State officials takes place where some personal relation has previously been established. The National Association of District Attorneys has been a strong force in promoting contacts and developing good faith among its members. Reasons for conflict and conditions for cooperation were summed up by one official:

There is a natural reluctance of any agency to give information to another agency. This reluctance is dissipated only by building up confidence and trust. There is not going to be free and open disclosure, but there can be cooperation. It depends on personalities ... how well they know one another. If a District Attorney whom I know well telephones me for information I give it to him; if I don't know him well, I don't.

Some law enforcement officials admit frankly that they work at "winning friends":

You can get help from a friend. I do not think that Title III has done it. We simply have developed a healthy relationship with other local and Federal people through personal contact. The cooperation is there when we need it.

Cooperation is compelled sometimes by jurisdictional limitations. A wiretap order in a gambling case may be obtained in one jurisdiction and an arrest made in another, making it necessary to turn over the evidence obtained. In intercounty crimes, law enforcement officials often work together.

As to cooperation with Federal agencies, State officials complained that Federal agencies did not share information readily, particularly the F.B.I. "Federal agencies do not trust local prosecutors," was the common observation. Few State officials had had any contact with the Strike Forces of the United States Department of Justice scattered throughout the country and designed to promote cooperation among law enforcement agencies in order to move more effectively against organized crime.

L.E.A.A., Organized Crime, and State Eavesdropping

The Law Enforcement Assistance Administration (L.E.A.A.) can have great impact on State eavesdropping to combat organized crime. This agency was established within the Department of Justice by Title I of the Omnibus Crime Control and Safe Streets Act of 1968; no mention of it appears in Title III, the eavesdropping section. The purpose of L.E.A.A. is to promote improvement in State and local criminal justice systems through Federal grants-in-aid. Generous funds have been made available for planning, action programs, research, and technical assistance.[14] A special section of L.E.A.A. deals with organized crime.

States may obtain funds from L.E.A.A. in two ways: (1) block grants, and (2) discretionary grants. *Block grants* are based on a policy formula. Each State and territory receives a certain amount depending on population, after submitting a comprehensive plan to L.E.A.A. The plan under a block grant must relate to the needs of the State criminal justice system, and be approved by L.E.A.A. A special condition may be fixed by L.E.A.A.—that the money be used in conformity with State and Federal law and constitutional interpretations. This is true whether the funds are to be used to purchase electronics devices for eavesdropping or equipment for other purposes.

Discretionary grants are subject to complete control by L.E.A.A. A State that does not have statutory provision authorizing court-ordered eavesdropping in conformity with Title III will not be permitted by L.E.A.A. to use funds to buy electronic devices that could be used only in violation of Federal law. States may, however, purchase equipment to be used in "consent eavesdropping" for which no court order is required under Title III. Proposals for discretionary grants are made by L.E.A.A., and it is reported that these have been "light on equipment." L.E.A.A. is interested primarily in building capability, training people. Where purchase of electronic devices has been funded, it has been in conjunction with a larger project. In a discretionary grant, L.E.A.A. knows whether or not any funds were used to buy electronic devices for eavesdropping. Reports as to operation must be submitted to L.E.A.A. by the States.

L.E.A.A. has run a number of training programs in reference to organized crime, and these have included sessions on electronic surveillance, the law involved in its use, and live monitoring. An official for the organized crime section of L.E.A.A. said:

> We try to inculcate in law enforcement officials, prosecutors, and judges the understanding that use of this equipment is a tool supporting a lot of hard work, and that they should live within the law. It is a highly sophisticated tool, and the help of a specialist is needed. It requires a well-trained, experienced person, and sufficient control procedures on use of the equipment and personnel.

Of particular concern to L.E.A.A. is the dissemination of information about acceptable practices and procedures to State and local officials. It conducts conferences that bring together law enforcement people, that is, police, prosecutors, judges, criminal justice planners. Representatives are invited from various State agencies. The purpose of the conferences is to discuss problems relating to organized crime and help States to develop programs. With respect to wiretapping and electronic surveillance, two types of problems have developed:

1. *Technical.* There can be poor reception, inaudibility. Intercepted conversations may be rejected as evidence because of lack of clarity, unintelligibility, or lack of control procedures. Without experienced operators, the desired results may not be obtained.
2. *Legal.* There must be compliance with the law. Interpretation of the law requires study and discussion, and L.E.A.A. is concerned with promoting more uniformity in State practice and procedure in carrying out the law.

L.E.A.A. is also concerned with the problem of getting caught doing the eavesdropping. If that happens, a good investigation can go down the drain. Leaks are always possible. Wiretap and recording equipment must be set up. Entry into a basement may be necessary. A superintendent of the building can go out to get a drink and tell the bartender all about it! It has happened.

Illegal eavesdropping is another delicate subject that L.E.A.A. has raised at conferences, realizing that the temptations are great:

> We try to make law enforcement officials understand that if they violate the law they will ruin it for everybody else. When the law enforcement officer takes the stand, defendant's counsel will ask him whether there has been any illegal eavesdropping. He will have to answer honestly or face the possibility of a charge of perjury.

L.E.A.A. has tried to promote cooperation among State and local law enforcement officials, but so far the results are not promising:

There are 40,000 police departments in the States. There are conflicts between Sheriffs and Chief of Police. The States should be consolidating police services. There are other State and local law enforcement problems that make cooperation difficult. People on the staff of prosecutors are either Democrats or Republicans. With whom will they cooperate? In the State of _____, 55 prosecutors were elected. Most of them had never been prosecutors before; five had not passed the Bar, and one had flunked the Bar examination!

L.E.A.A. officials were asked whether they planned to evaluate the *effectiveness* of the law enforcement effort with respect to organized crime, including use of electronic surveillance. They believed this would be done by the National Institute of Law Enforcement and Criminal Justice, the research arm of the law enforcement assistance program. Electronic surveillance, in their opinion, was only a small part of the effort against crime, and whether it was successful depended on how one measured "effectiveness."

If all that law enforcement is doing after X dollars have been spent is to arrest three people, and the criminal operation continues, it means electronic surveillance is not very good and that other tools of law enforcement are not very good. Electronic surveillance has made a lot of cases, but this does not mean that it has been effective in law enforcement or in dealing with organized crime . . . we first have to define organized crime. Do you call security manipulations organized crime? It may have more of an impact economically than a gambling enterprise.

Criticism of L.E.A.A. has not been lacking.[15] In the House of Representatives, a Congressman from Ohio complained that while L.E.A.A. has been generously funded, its program has not worked; the pipeline was clogged with red tape so that the money remained at State capitals and did not reach the urban centers of high crime. States forced cities into regional bureaucracies that failed to give priority to citizens' needs. A 1970 amendment to the Omnibus Act of 1968 gave urban areas a greater proportion of the funds granted to the States, but it is claimed that this has been ineffective and that the cities are still not getting their fair share. In the first three years, Congress provided more than ¾ billion dollars for L.E.A.A. For the fiscal year 1972, the agency was awarded almost 700 million dollars, the full amount requested. This is a lot of money by anybody's standards, and the public should show greater interest in what it has produced than it has so far expressed.

National Institute of Law Enforcement and Criminal Justice

The research arm of L.E.A.A., known as the unpronounceable N.I.L.E.C.J., was created by Title I of the Omnibus Act of 1968 to encourage research and development to improve law enforcement. It has sponsored projects measuring various aspects of organized crime. Results have been mixed, and on the whole inconclusive and disappointing. A pilot study attempted to gauge the actual amount of money involved in gambling. Ordinary citizens were questioned in telephone interviews. The researchers found that few people were candid in revealing their gambling habits. Another study of the overall impact of organized crime in an inner city urban community—social, political, and economic—likewise produced scant dependable data. The chief sources of information were police seizures and confidential investigative records, and no provable generalizations could be drawn from the information obtained. A third project to investigate ways of measuring the effectiveness of organized crime control efforts produced more promising results. This study attempted to trace relative changes over a period of time, rather than ascertain absolute amounts. The greatest hurdle encountered by N.I.L.E.C.J. in its research was how to define "organized crime" before a study was begun. As one official of N.I.L.E.C.J. put it: "Who can tell the difference between a crooked pension plan and one managed by inept administrators?"

Attention thus far has been focused on the internal structure of organized crime and the hierarchy of boss, captain, lieutenant, soldiers, and so on. The Institute believes that attention should be redirected to the interaction of individuals within this supposed monolith. It is possible that the entire setup of organized crime, if considered as a running business, is unprofitable because of the large number of unproductive people whom organized crime keeps "on welfare." The Institute is convinced of the need for more accurate data on organized crime:

> We have been making decisions on too little information. We have been accepting hearsay for so long that we accept statements at face value. It is time we started looking a bit more closely.

A dearth of information on the economic aspects of organized crime and its business practices was pointed out in the L.E.A.A. Summary of Requirements submitted to the Subcommittee of the House Committee on Appropriations in 1970. In hearings of the Subcommittee, the members of the House of Representatives were also informed of the need for increased research efforts into possible unauthorized use of electronic surveillance devices.[16] These are important areas of research that N.I.L.E.C.J. should be urged to explore.

Court Decisions on State Eavesdropping

Challenges in the courts to interception of wire or oral communications by State officials have been made on various grounds: that Title III is unconstitutional in whole or in part; that certain provisions of State eavesdropping laws conflict with the Federal Act; that State officials or monitoring agents failed to comply with State or Federal law; that a particular court order was defective; that officials did not execute the order properly or give notice as required. Attacks on eavesdropping have been made in motions to suppress evidence or in appeals from convictions for crimes under State law. The wide range of problems in eavesdropping by State officials is apparent from the following brief summary of decisions on some novel and knotty questions.

Offenses Covered

Georgia statute lists the offenses for which a court order to eavesdrop may be obtained, as provided by Federal law [Title III, Sec. 2516(2)]. An order was issued by a State judge to obtain evidence regarding the offense of "improperly influencing legislative action." Based on the information secured under the order, an Alderman of the City of Atlanta and his abettor were convicted of soliciting $30,000 for an agreement to procure passage of zoning legislation. Defendants moved to suppress the evidence on the ground that the offense described in the eavesdrop order was not "bribery" as the word is used in State and Federal eavesdropping laws. The Court of Appeals of Georgia ruled that the offense described in the order was a species of bribery and was a covered offense within the meaning of the law. The motion to suppress the evidence was denied (*Ansley v. State*).[17]

Defendants were indicted in Colorado for illegal drug traffic and possession of marijuana. They moved to suppress evidence obtained through wiretapping on the grounds that the Colorado eavesdropping was invalid because it may be used for a misdemeanor punishable by imprisonment for less than a year, in conflict with Federal law [Title III, Sec. 2516(2)]. The Supreme Court of Colorado decided that defendants had no "standing" to object to the evidence. The crime for which they were charged carried a minimum penalty of from two to ten years. Even if at some future time it is held that lesser crimes were not intended to be covered, it would not render the entire Colorado statute invalid (*People v. Martin*).[18]

Procedure to Obtain Court Order

The practice and procedures followed in the busy office of New York County's District Attorney have been considered at length by a United

States District Court. Since New York County has had extensive experience with court orders for eavesdropping and the judge who signed the order in the particular case granted many applications, the decision of the Federal Court furnishes an excellent opportunity to scrutinize day-to-day procedures in obtaining wiretap orders from State judges, and to improve practices in the future. While the Federal Court concluded in this case that the requirements of Title III and New York State law had been satisfied and refused to vacate the eavesdrop warrant, the facts indicate that other procedures might have been preferable (*United States v. Tortorello*).[19]

The Tortorello case involved prosecution for violation of the antifraud provisions of securities laws. The court order to wiretap was signed by Justice Schweitzer of the New York Supreme Court on application of the District Attorney of New York County, Frank S. Hogan. The District Attorney never appeared personally before the Justice. Applications were prepared by a young Assistant District Attorney, Lawrence Hochheiser. They were reviewed by the Chief of the Rackets Bureau, Alfred J. Scotti, "especially where it was an original, rather than a renewal order." According to the testimony, the Assistant presented the papers to the District Attorney himself, and the latter gave each application his personal attention "with one exception." Two affidavits were prepared, one to be signed by the Assistant, and the other by the District Attorney. Factual grounds for obtaining an order appeared in the affidavit of the Assistant. The District Attorney's affidavit said:

> Based upon the facts set forth in Mr. X's affidavit I respectfully submit to the Court that there are reasonable grounds to believe that the essential evidence of crime may be obtained by the interception of wire and oral communications described.

The District Attorney was the named applicant; his affidavit authorized the application and gave his opinion that no practical alternative means of acquiring comparable evidence or information existed. Both the District Attorney and the Assistant swore to their respective affidavits before an office notary public. After this, the affidavits were presented to Justice Schweitzer who examined them with Hochheiser present. The young Assistant did not recall swearing to his affidavit a second time before the judge.

The defendant Tortorello attacked the eavesdrop order on the ground that the affidavits should have been sworn to in the presence of the judge, and that in the absence of the District Attorney, the judge was provided no opportunity to inquire into probable cause. The Federal Court ruled that nothing in the Fourth Amendment to the United States Constitution required prosecuting attorneys to swear to the contents of their affidavits in the presence of the judge, and that in this case the District Attorney's absence was not material since his affidavit did not supply the facts showing probable cause.

The decision did not openly criticize the procedure followed, but obviously the personal appearance of the prosecuting official named as applicant and swearing to affidavits in the judge's presence would constitute stricter compliance with statutory requirements and intent of the law and render the order less vulnerable to attack.

Defective Order—Month and Year Omitted

A court order to wiretap showed the date of issuance as "17," but through an inadvertence, failed to indicate the month or year. It was later amended to correct the error. The Supreme Court of Georgia upheld the validity of the order despite the omission, and the motion to suppress evidence obtained under it was denied (*Dudley v. State*).[20] Carelessness in preparing orders can create a great deal of trouble, even if the court ultimately rules that the error is not serious enough to invalidate the order.

New Crime: Unnamed Persons

A court order was obtained under the law of New York State to intercept conversations relating to promotion of gambling. Conversations of a person not named in the order were overheard implicating him in the crime of usury. Some time later the order was amended to include the new crime. The New York Supreme Court in Rockland County ruled that interception of conversations relating to the new crime of usury was unlawful because the eavesdrop warrant was not *immediately* amended to include this crime. Surveillance could be continued only after such immediate amendment and judicial determination of probable cause that the new crime was being committed. However, the conversation of a person not named, which relates to the crime set forth in the order, may be intercepted without a new determination of probable cause; amendment to include the new person's conversations is a ministerial act that can be carried out at a subsequent time (*People v. DiLorenzo*).[21]

A similar ruling with respect to persons not named in the court order was made by the Colorado Supreme Court. The Colorado eavesdropping statute required that application be made *as soon as practicable* after interception of information as to an offense other than those specified in the order. A defendant who was not named in the order, but whose conversations with the subject of the order were overheard, contended that application should have been made *immediately* after he was a party to the conversations. The Colorado Court ruled that the State law refers to offenses different from those named in the order, not to persons other than those named (*People v. Martin*).[18]

Both *DiLorenzo* and *Martin* implied that an amendment was necessary if the conversations of the unnamed person were to be used against him. The highest court in New York State, however, seems to have arrived at a different conclusion. In June 1972 the New York Court of Appeals ruled that the conversation of the outside party, not named in the order, could be used against him even if the order was never amended. Amendment is required only where different crimes are disclosed (*People v. Gnozzo; People v. Zorn*).[22] The New York Court cited cases in the Federal courts in which a similar conclusion was reached.

Probable Cause

A common objection to evidence obtained through wiretapping is that the affidavits on which the court order was based failed to show probable cause. The New York Court of Appeals, in a typical gambling case, found that the following facts, taken together, established probable cause (*People v. Zorn*):

> The named inside person . . . was a known and convicted gambler . . . had been under observation . . . when the eavesdropping warrant was issued. He had been seen conversing with other known gamblers, and . . . overheard talking about losses, relaying bets, and obtaining "lines" on future sporting events. He had been observed in the public telephone booth in question on four occasions . . . was overheard mentioning losses on a professional basketball game.[23]

A judge "may take additional testimony" on application for a court order both under Title III [Sec. 2518(2)] and under the Colorado law which is modeled on the Federal Act. This permits the taking of oral testimony. The Colorado Constitution, however, requires that proof of probable cause be reduced to writing. The Supreme Court of Colorado ruled that the State statute meets the constitutional mandate. The Court reasoned that if the Federal scheme is valid, so is the Colorado law (*People v. Martin*).[18]

Thirty-Day Period of Interception

Constitutionality of the lengthy period (thirty days) allowed for interception of conversations under Federal and most State laws has come under frequent attack. The New York Court of Appeals has upheld the thirty-day period, noting that it has been repeatedly sanctioned by lower Federal courts (citing *United States v. Leta, United States v. Sklaroff, United States v. King*).[24] The New York Court considered the time not excessive in view of the extent and nature of the activities under surveillance in the case before it: promoting large-scale gambling, betting on sports events, and placing or "laying-off" of bets (*People v. Zorn*).[23]

A New Jersey Court, upholding the constitutionality of the State eavesdropping statute, ruled that the thirty-day period provided in the New

Jersey law was not to be construed as blanket authorization for a continuous, unremitting surveillance of that duration. In all cases, duration of an intrusion was limited to that shown to be "necessary under the circumstances." If an initial communication was cryptic or equivocal, or did not identify or inculpate all participants or disclose the full extent of a criminal operation, the wiretap could be authorized beyond interception of an initial conversation (*State v. Christy*).[25]

In an earlier New York case involving illegal wagering, a court order to wiretap was held invalid because it was not sufficiently precise and discriminate in fixing the time for interception of conversations; the order authorized twenty-four-hour surveillance for more than two weeks, to terminate at such time as the conversations sought were recorded. The New York District Court in Nassau County decided that this was termination at the pleasure of the police officers. The police, in fact, continued their wiretapping for two weeks after they had intercepted criminal conversations (*People v. Botta*).[26]

Nighttime Interceptions

In a case involving a gambling offense under New York law, defendants contended that the order should have limited interception of conversations to daylight hours. The order made no restriction as to day or night. The New York Court of Appeals rejected this view (*People v. Zorn*).[23] It quoted from *United States v. Becker* decided by a United States District Court in the Southern District of New York:

> It is a matter of common knowledge that the activities of [a gambling] enterprise . . . are not limited to such specific hours that an interception order can . . . define precisely and limit the period during which interception can be conducted.[27]

Mandatory Provisions: Prompt Execution, Minimization, Termination

A wiretap order obtained under Maryland law was declared invalid because it failed to provide that it be executed as soon as practicable, or that the interception "shall be conducted in such a way as to minimize the interception of communications not otherwise subject to interception." Also, the order did not include a statement "as to whether or not the interception shall automatically terminate when the described communication has been obtained or on attainment of the authorized objective." The Court of Special Sessions of Maryland ruled that these provisions are mandatory under Federal law [Title III, Sec. 2518(4)(3) and Sec. 2518(5)]. Merely limiting the period of surveillance is not enough. State procedures may be more restrictive than Federal requirements, but Federal law must be followed if State law fails to require the court order to include the provisions indicated (*State v. Siegel*).[28]

Irrelevant Conversations

The United States District Court that examined the procedure for obtaining court orders in New York County also considered the matter of intercepting irrelevant conversations (*United States v. Tortorello*).[19] The District Court ruled that it was sufficient if genuine and accepted safeguards and efforts were made to minimize interception of nonpertinent conversations.

Under the procedure adopted by the District Attorney in New York County, daily records or "line sheets" of the detectives who monitored the interceptions indicated the time a conversation deemed pertinent commenced and ended, and the nature of that conversation. They also contained entries noting the time nonpertinent calls or conversations were initiated. The detectives testified that they monitored only when they were also recording; this reduced or eliminated the opportunity for an improper eavesdrop which would not be recorded.

The Court conceded that some nonpertinent items crept in because they were recorded before relevancy could be determined. Other irrelevant items were included because they appeared in conversations containing some pertinent material. Still others represented the monitoring agents' determination of pertinency with which the Court might disagree. Overall, said the Court, the nonpertinent items intercepted were kept to a minimum.

Tape Recordings: Custody, Audibility, and Use in Evidence

Maryland law made no provision for disposition of tape recordings of wiretapped conversations. A State judge ordered tapes, logs, and transcripts to be delivered to counsel for the defendant, to be preserved under seal in a fireproof safe, and not to be opened without order of the judge. The Court of Special Appeals of Maryland ruled that this disposition was proper under Federal law and that Federal law prevails where State law is repugnant to it (or in the absence of State law) (*State v. Siegel*).[29]

Georgia law allowed tape recordings to be delivered within thirty days to the judge who issued the eavesdrop order. However, Federal law [Title III, Sec. 2518(8)(a)] requires that recordings of communications intercepted shall be made available to the judge *immediately* on expiration of the order and sealed under his direction. The Court of Appeals of Georgia decided that evidence obtained under the wiretap order was admissible despite failure to give the judge immediate custody of recordings. Penalty for noncompliance, said a majority of the Court, is limited to punishment for conempt under Title III, Sec. 2518(10). The majority of the Court also rejected the contention that the recordings were so inaudible and indistinct in many portions that a jury would have to speculate as to what was said (*Ansley v. State*).[17] A strong dissenting opinion was handed down in this case. The dissenting judge enumerated the elements to be established before recordings can be introduced in evidence:

1. That the mechanical transcript device was capable of taking the testimony.
2. That the operator of the device was competent to operate it.
3. That the recordings are authentic and correct.
4. That changes, additions, or deletions have not been made.
5. That the recordings have been properly preserved; manner of preservation must be shown.
6. Identification of the speakers in the conversations recorded.
7. That testimony elicited was freely and voluntarily made, without duress.

The dissenting judge argued that there was no evidence in this case as to competency of the operator of the mechanical device, nor was it shown that changes had not been made; in fact there was testimony to show that the tapes had been altered!

Consent to Eavesdropping—Jail Phone Extensions

Three boys were convicted in Michigan of breaking into a grocery store and taking a case of beer. The mother of one of them offered an alibi; she testified at the trial that at 4 A.M. on the morning in question she heard a record player going and told her son to go to bed. To destroy credibility, the prosecutor introduced testimony of an undersheriff. He had listened in on an extension to a telephone conversation in jail between the defendant and his mother. The mother asked her son if he was mixed up in the affair. According to the undersheriff's testimony, the defendant, speaking over the jail telephone, said:

We have got it all set. They are going to say I wasn't there.

The Court of Appeals in Michigan ruled that neither party to the conversation had consented to the listening in, and that it was error to admit evidence of the conversation. Use of a telephone with an extension is not necessarily consent to an interception under Sec. 2511(2)(c) of Title III. The conviction was reversed and the case remanded for a new trial (*People v. Tebo*).[30]

A similar ruling was handed down by a California Court. It was held that tape recordings by police of incriminating conversations between spouses from a telephone located in a jail are inadmissible in a subsequent prosecution of the spouses (*Halpin v. Superior Court of San Bernardino County*).[31]

Constitutionality of Title III

The final word on whether the Federal law authorizing official eavesdropping is valid rests with the United States Supreme Court, but some State courts have considered the question and declared that it is constitutional. The Court of Special Appeals of Maryland has stated that lawfulness of interception of communications is to be tested only under the Fourth Amendment of the United States Constitution; that fear of surveillance is not a denial of free speech under the First Amendment, if Fourth Amendment standards are met; nor is the Fifth Amendment violated merely because of seizure of incriminating testimonial statements (*State v. Siegel*).[29]

In *Dudley v. State*, the Supreme Court of Georgia ruled that Title III was not subject to constitutional attack either under the First, Fourth, or Fifth Amendments. In answer to a defendant's claim that the statute violated the right to free speech guaranteed by the First Amendment, the Court said (citing *United States v. Escandar*):

> Fear of electronic surveillance is not a direct limitation of free speech . . . some restriction on the right of free speech is necessary in community living.[32]

Title III was recognized as a valid exercise of Congressional power in *Halpin v. Superior Court of San Bernardino County*. The California Court rejected the People's contention that the Federal law was unconstitutional as applied because it infringed on the *police power* of the State, reserved to it by the Tenth Amendment.[31] The Court suppressed as evidence a tape recording of conversations overheard on an extension of a jail telephone. California law required that a telephone call from jail be made in the presence of an officer. Title III, said the Court, preempted particular fields of wiretapping and electronic surveillance. Since the interception was not authorized as required by Title III, the conversation was inadmissible as evidence.

8

Federal Eavesdropping
in Practice

A high degree of centralization in the Department of Justice under the
Attorney General has characterized eavesdropping at the national level.
Uniformity of Federal procedures and control of applications for court orders contrast sharply with the varied practice and dispersed authority prevailing in the States. Power to authorize applications to a Federal judge is
limited to "the Attorney General, or any Assistant Attorney General specially designated by the Attorney General." A hierarchical line of com-
mand, moving through several levels, is reported to have been established
in the Justice Department to fix policy on wiretapping and electronic surveillance and to use authority granted by Title III.[1]

The procedure as described by a member of the Department of Justice
is as follows:

> Application for a court order is generally initiated by the investi-
> gative agency having jurisdiction of the offense, such as the Federal
> Bureau of Investigation (F.B.I.), the Bureau of Narcotics and Dan-
> gerous Drugs (B.N.D.D.), or the Bureau of Customs. After a
> preliminary review of the application and affidavits by United States
> Attorneys in the field, the documents are sent to Washington, D.C., to
> the Organized Crime and Racketeering Bureau, a section of the De-
> partment of Justice. A staff of attorneys in this Bureau reviews the
> form and substance of applications "with particular emphasis on
> assuring strict adherence to the required statutory standards." When
> the papers have been approved by this staff, they are submitted for
> review to the Deputy Chief of the Organized Crime and Racketeering
> Bureau, then to an Assistant Attorney General, and finally, to the At-
> torney General himself.

The question of whether the authorization procedure established by
the Justice Department complies with the intent of the law to place

responsibility on the Attorney General himself has been litigated in several cases that have reached the Court of Appeals (see Court Decisions on Federal Eavesdropping at the end of this chapter).

Manual for Conduct of Electronic Surveillance

In an effort to achieve uniformity of procedure, the Department of Justice has prepared a *Manual* for Conduct of Electronic Surveillance under Title III. This has been described as a set of guidelines for Federal agents, attorneys, and other Federal officials involved in court-ordered eavesdropping, reflecting the policy of the Department of Justice. An aura of secrecy has surrounded the *Manual* which one United States Attorney sought to justify in this way:

> We do not want our internal policies made any more public than they have been made already. We do not want to walk into Court and have someone say: "This is the Department's policy—A, B, and C— but they did not do B." We would have to justify our standards which are stricter than the statute's standards. We do not want the Department of Justice charged with acting like "Big Brother" and using the statute indiscriminately.

Another United States Attorney said:

> Maybe it was a wrong decision to keep it secret. But a defense attorney might pick up the *Manual* and say, "You did not comply with your own *Manual*." Or the *Manual* may spell out a certain procedure when we could have formulated a better procedure. We might want to make changes.

Despite lack of public disclosure of the *Manual*, its contents are known and at least one court has criticized it (*United States v. King*).[2] The *Manual* is divided into twelve sections. Step by step, the procedure for court-ordered eavesdropping outlined in Title III of the Omnibus Act of 1968 is discussed, with warnings of weaknesses in the law and how best to overcome them. Eavesdropping *without* court order is not covered. The *Manual* indicates that the Attorney General has reserved to himself the right to make ultimate decision as to use of forty-eight-hour emergency eavesdropping, and "national security" cases are not dealt with in the *Manual*. An official who called the *Manual* "probably the most closely held document in the Department of Justice" (prior to Watergate) nevertheless described it in detail:

> The Manual begins by describing the scope of the statute—what situations require a court order and what do not. It tries to analyze the

legislative history, together with the statute, which is extremely confused. . . . Part of our effort was to straighten out those areas which seemed unclear and to put restrictions on that part which looked troublesome.

The opening section is followed by procedural matters—to whom requests for applications are to be made, who is to clear them, who has final authority to approve or disapprove an application. The *Manual* indicates who is to make the application in the field, the relationship between the investigative agency and the attorney who is supervising the application, what information must be supplied to the Department of Justice to make a judgment as to whether the application should be approved, and the kind of situations in which approval will be granted.

It includes a discussion of the contents of the application, and admonishment that every effort should be made to include as much information as possible (not to follow the time-honored search warrant procedure of putting in an affidavit just as little as is needed) . . . to make sure the application meets the requirements of "probable cause."

To show why "normal investigative procedures" are inadequate and unlikely to succeed, the *Manual* advises setting forth all the investigations that have previously been conducted. The *Manual* outlines the form of the order, line by line, states that it is to be presented to a United States District Court judge, and tells how to make presentation and ask for sealing of documents. It recommends limitation of the period of the order, and states that provision should be included in the order requiring periodic *progress reports* to the judge.

Conduct of the interception is discussed—what kind of agents ought to be assigned to the job, the need for skilled and intelligent personnel to monitor interceptions, make transcripts of tapes, when live monitoring should be used, what to do if a tape recorder breaks down, how to protect oneself by memorandum if the interception is fouled up, whether to get off the line under certain circumstances. The *Manual* tells what to do with the tapes and with the transcripts when they are completed; tapes are to be kept by the investigating agency that initiated the order and conducted the monitoring. It also explains:

. . . how to handle the problem of disclosure of information among the various investigative agencies. Congress intended that there should be *cooperation* among the agencies. We point out situations where disclosure may or may not be made. There are controls for dissemination of all the information picked up.

The *Manual* advises agents and attorneys to lay a foundation in advance for dealing with the telephone company by ascertaining the name of the company's chief security officer, the telephone company's requirements, and the official who must be informed of entry of a court order to wiretap. It discusses what to do when conversations are overheard that appear to be privileged communications, as for example between husband and wife, or lawyer and client. When the *Manual* was first issued, it contained instructions to cut recording off when a privileged conversation began. This is reported to have been changed because sometimes incriminating statements are made in what at first appears to be privileged communication, such as a lawyer purchasing narcotics from the client whose wire is being tapped! Under current practice duplicate tape recordings are made. One tape records everything, including privileged communications. The other, it is reported, is selective, and privileged communications are not transcribed.

The Justice Department's *Manual* has not been circulated among the States, although Federal experts are aware that flaws in State applications may imperil all of court-ordered eavesdropping under Title III. A Justice Department attorney said:

> I have seen some papers in the State of _____. If I were a judge I would throw them out. Title III can go down the drain if people do not take enough care as to what they put into applications. Title III papers are drafted for the appellate courts where ultimate controls lie.

If the Federal government furnished guidelines for the States, it might be accused of encroaching on State powers. Besides, guidelines are subject to change; they are not hard and fast rules and may not be suitable for all States. Each Federal official interviewed was asked whether cooperation between Federal and State law enforcement officials had increased since enactment of Title III. The following reply reflected the consensus of opinion that cooperation was spotty:

> Title III has not made any difference. The Department of Justice recognizes the need for cooperation and there has been cooperation. It is a sensitive area and one in which there has been a great deal of mutual distrust . . . it is a very serious problem. The States scream that the Federal agencies do not give them assistance or information.

"Strike Forces" against Organized Crime

The Department of Justice has organized "Strike Forces" throughout the United States on which it relies heavily in its effort to combat organized crime. The eighteenth Force was set up to focus on infiltration of organized crime into finance. Some Forces have a number of field offices. A Strike Force is a team of Federal prosecutors who cooperate with investigators from key Federal agencies and with State and local enforcement divisions in a particular region. Ideally, there is pooling of intelligence-gathering and of investigative and prosecutorial resources. Headquarters are maintained in major cities. Each Strike Force is headed by an attorney selected in Washington, D.C. to act as coordinator. The Strike Forces are part of the Organized Crime and Racketeering Bureau of the Justice Department. The concept of a Strike Force was initiated by former Attorney General Ramsey Clark, but it was expanded by the Nixon Administration.[3]

Since the primary purpose of Strike Forces is to fight organized crime and as eavesdropping is reported to have been used for this purpose, coordinators interviewed were asked, "Do you use court-ordered eavesdropping only in cases involving organized crime?" The answers, of which the following is typical, mirrored the uncertainty of all law enforcement officials as to what is or is not organized crime:

> Technically we deal only with organized crime. But organized crime is subject to interpretation. Anything which involves a criminal ring, a syndicate, is considered organized crime, whether it is a ring for importation of narcotics from South America or a gambling ring in the United States.

If a case involved one sale of narcotics by a distributor on the street, one not involving a large conspiracy, or if it involved taking orders over a telephone that could result in the arrest of only one individual, the Strike Force would, according to one coordinator, turn it over to the United States Attorney in the District. "We do try to get to top echelon."

A Justice Department attorney admitted that some eavesdropping by Strike Forces may have involved unimportant and unfortunate individuals rather than leading organized crime figures:

> The Detroit raid was a small numbers racket. . . . A lot of the people involved were homebody people, not breaking heads, just taking bets on the side. We have to decide whether we should proceed against these minor people when we know they are just caught up in this way of life. There are a lot of blacks involved and poor whites, especially in numbers games . . . five and ten cent games. Some of the people in gambling are leaders in their own community.

He was talking about the big gambling raids following eavesdropping under Title III carried on by the Detroit Strike Force, in which the F.B.I. was reported to have cooperated fully.

The Strike Forces have used wiretap orders, but not as extensively in some areas as might have been expected. When pressed to explain why this tool of law enforcement had not been employed more often, a Strike Force coordinator explained:

> It has not often been applicable. We have been able to make a case without it and we have had more indictments and convictions than any Strike Force in the country.

Strike Forces have developed new techniques to encourage informants either before or after eavesdropping. A witness, or an informant whose identity has become known, may be relocated with his entire family, given a new home, new job, new identity, and in some cases even plastic surgery. A story is told of "Mama," a Newark "banker" (known as a "sitter") for a numbers racket allegedly controlled by a "Mafia" chieftain. Mama netted about $150 a week for recording bets in certain areas of New Jersey and New York, until she became ill and had to get a replacement. Her son was later jailed on a narcotics charge, and Mama hit on a plan for his speedy release. She turned over to the F.B.I. a telephone book containing code names and numbers of her former customers, and that of her replacement. A court order was then obtained to tap the telephones of people on Mama's list.

A member of the Strike Force arranged to ship Mama and her whole family to a new home, but she refused to leave Newark unless her dog went along. Since government regulations made no provision for relocating pets, the Strike Force member had to pay for the dog's transportation out of his own pocket. But that wasn't the end of the story. Every now and then Mama got nervous and telephoned her Strike Force benefactor. She heard "sounds" in her backyard. "They are coming to get me," she cried one day over the telephone. It was her son shooting a BB gun.

Procedure in Eavesdropping by Strike Forces

Applications for court orders to eavesdrop made by Strike Forces in the field are subject to strict supervision in Washington, D.C. The Federal *Manual* is followed as a guide by Strike Forces. All applications must be submitted to the Department of Justice in Washington. Heads of Strike Forces interviewed did not seem to find this strict control burdensome, nor did they believe that such centralized authority delayed issuance of orders.

> Where it is necessary, the Washington people will put other things aside and give the matter immediate attention. In Washington they are not caught up in the fervor of the particular investigation, so they can consider each case objectively.

One Strike Force coordinator called it a "systematic, cautious approach, regimented and controlled." He believed it was a good method "if you have competent people to review it."

Some Strike Force headquarters have streamlined the procedure for obtaining court orders, and can get one through within two days or less, including approval from Washington. A magnafax machine reproduces the application and affidavits and automatically transmits the documents to Washington. Each typewritten sheet is inserted in the machine, and an exact copy is pulled from a similar machine in Washington. Technology has helped in getting wiretap orders, as well as in carrying them out.

According to heads of Strike Forces, the Justice Department in Washington bends over backwards to see that facts showing probable cause are spelled out clearly, sometimes to the annoyance of the investigative agencies. Agents are reluctant to divulge information for fear that the identity of an informant may be revealed; they want to limit the facts in an affidavit to the minimum. Sometimes Strike Force attorneys have to compromise and omit details that may pinpoint a particular individual as the informant. The *Manual* advises that probable cause be updated every few days when progress reports are made to the judge. If Strike Force attorneys feel that there is insufficient information on which to base probable cause, they will tell the agent to get additional information. Where authorities in Washington find facts inadequate to show probable cause, the Strike Force accepts that judgment.

Strike Force coordinators confirmed the fact that Federal applications generally ask for an order terminating in fifteen days, although Title III allows up to thirty days. The following explanation of this practice was offered:

> If you can go to the Court in 5 days and show that you are getting something on a 15-day order, you strengthen your case on a motion to suppress. If you are not getting anything after the 5-day period, we would consider dropping the wiretap. We ask for 15-day orders; it can always be extended if it is productive. . . . If we are more conservative than the law requires, it places us in a better position to sustain the wiretap.

Progress reports are made about every five days, either orally or in writing, to the judge who issued the order. Some judges demand detailed reports of what has been overheard; others are satisfied with a summary. Periodic reports of intercepted conversations are also made to the head of the Strike Force by the agency monitoring the wiretap, either orally or by typewritten summary.

Since control of eavesdropping by an impartial judiciary is crucial to the safeguards to privacy sought to be provided by Title III, each Strike

Force member interviewed was asked how the judge is selected to whom a Federal application is presented. The reply invariably was, in essence:

> Applications are presented to the judge sitting in the Motion Part in the United States District Court . . . whoever happens to be sitting. If we could not get him for some reason, we would go to the Chief Judge.

Federal, like State law enforcement officials, all claimed they did not shop around for a compliant judge but presented the application to whichever judge was sitting that month in a "Part" that handles procedural matters.

> At 10:30 every morning and in his chambers in the afternoon, this judge handles arraignments, passes sentences out to defendants who plead guilty, assigns cases out to trial parts, receives ex parte applications. Federal judges all take their turn in handling criminal matters, unlike State judges, some of whom are unfamiliar with the criminal branch of the law.

The head of a Strike Force outlined the office procedure followed. An original and three or four copies of the application and accompanying affidavits are prepared. The original is sealed and filed with the Clerk of the United States District Court. The conformed copies are kept in the Strike Force office in a safe. One copy of the order is served on the telephone company.

Monitoring of conversations is handled by the investigative agents. The agencies use their own equipment; sometimes they share one another's electronic devices. A Strike Force does not have any electronic surveillance equipment of its own. When asked whether automatic or live monitoring was used, the answers seemed evasive:

> It depends on the form of the order. It is the responsibility of the head of the Strike Force to see that agents do not cross the bounds and record conversations other than those authorized to be intercepted by the order.

In order to protect innocent persons, said one Strike Force head, the order will be explicit as to when the wiretap shall go on and off, and when conversations shall not be recorded. For example, if a wiretap is placed on a public telephone, the order may provide that the conversation shall be recorded only when the person under surveillance is at the particular place where the wiretapped phone is located and only if the voice speaking can be recognized as belonging to the subject of the wiretap. An agent listening to the recording makes a log of the conversation—a summary of conversations that the agent considers relevant. Later, a transcript is made of the conversations recorded. The head of the Strike Force looks at the logs personally, but he does not work directly with the agents once the wiretap is on. That task is assigned to a staff attorney.

Reports by prosecuting officials, required under the law, are prepared in Washington, D.C. The Strike Force merely sends a letter or memorandum to the Organized Crime and Racketeering Bureau of the Justice Department, indicating what action was taken under each court order.

Cooperation and Competition in Strike Forces

The key to success of the Strike Forces against organized crime is cooperation, and this depends to a considerable extent on how a Strike Force is set up and the personality of its members. The composition of each Strike Force varies. The Detroit Strike Force has full-time representatives from eight Federal investigative agencies and three State agencies, as well as a Canadian Royal Mounted Police representative. It also has on its staff several United States Attorneys from the Department of Justice. The F.B.I. does not maintain a full-time representative but makes available to the Detroit Strike Force its reports on organized crime activities.

One of the most active of the Strike Forces is the Joint Strike Force in the Southern District of New York. This unit operates under a written agreement with State and local agencies. It covers New York County, Bronx County, and an area extending north to Albany. The District Attorneys of New York County and Bronx County participate in the Joint Strike Force. Local agencies have representatives on various committees of the Force, including a committee on Gambling, Labor Racketeering, Bars and Restaurants, Hijacking, Pornography, and Securities Frauds. Narcotics cases are handled by a separate Narcotics Strike Force consisting of representatives from the United States Bureau of Narcotics and Dangerous Drugs (B.N.D.D.), the New York City Police Department Narcotics Division, and the State police. District Attorneys do not participate in the Narcotics Strike Force.

In the Eastern District of New York, the area of the Strike Force includes Brooklyn, Queens, Staten Island, Suffolk County, and Nassau County. This Force, with headquarters in Brooklyn, does not meet with local agencies; it works with representatives of Federal Bureaus, including B.N.D.D., Bureau of Customs, Internal Revenue Service, Secret Service, and the Department of Labor. There may be some cooperation with local agencies. For example, if the Brooklyn Strike Force carries on a Federal grand jury investigation, local investigators may participate.

Although the F.B.I. does not assign a special agent to the Strike Forces, some coordinators work closely with F.B.I. agents investigating organized crime, and see them daily. Both the Southern and Eastern District

Strike Forces in New York have an F.B.I. "liaison man" who can be called upon when needed. The F.B.I. has a special department investigating organized crime, and it is reported that an F.B.I. coordinator is assigned to each of the five families of "La Cosa Nostra" in the New York Metropolitan area. The Strike Force coordinator in Brooklyn explained his connection with the F.B.I.:

> I have a personal relationship with each of these F.B.I. coordinators. They come to me if they want a grand jury investigation, if they want a subpoena, if they are planning an investigation, if they want legal advice.

Emphasis is placed on pooling of criminal intelligence data. Representatives of the agencies working with the Strike Force are charged with the duty of keeping the Force informed as to investigations being conducted by the agency. Justice Department attorneys on the Strike Force staff have the responsibility of determining whether an offense has been committed that may be the subject of prosecution, and whether eavesdropping should be considered to further an investigation. Ideally, a continuous dialogue is supposed to take place between agents and Strike Force attorneys, and between the coordinator of the Strike Force and the United States Attorney in the district.

Much effort is exerted by the Strike Force to indoctrinate its staff as to activities of organized crime, the most effective methods for developing evidence, including eavesdropping, and the effect of United States Supreme Court decisions. There is frequent contact and communication among coordinators, and between coordinators and the Organized Crime and Racketeering Bureau in Washington, D.C. Section meetings are held periodically, and occasionally there is a meeting of the full staff.

While success of a Strike Force depends on how well it works with other agencies, cooperation has not yet been fully achieved, as a Justice Department admitted ruefully:

> In an area where a State District Attorney has been firmly entrenched for years and free of political influence, it is difficult for him to accept any interference from Federal authorities, particularly where his previous experiences with men from Washington have not always been happy ones.

The degree of cooperation with both State officials and Federal agencies varies. The question was asked repeatedly: "Is it true that the F.B.I. is reluctant to share information with other groups, including the Strike Forces?" The answer of a Justice Department attorney reflected the general opinion.

When the Strike Forces were first organized, the F.B.I. seemed reluctant to share information. It is an old organization, a very professional one . . . conservative in . . . new law enforcement techniques . . . cooperation of the F.B.I. is getting better.

Competition among Federal agencies and between these agencies and Strike Forces creates added difficulties in operation of the Strike Force against organized crime. In one case the Bureau of Customs got word that the Strike Force was talking to certain individuals whom the Bureau had been investigating for three years. The Bureau considered this a gross interference with its work. In another instance, the Bureau of Narcotics and Dangerous Drugs and the Bureau of Customs came into conflict when it was discovered that both were working on the same narcotics smuggling investigation. The coordinator of the Strike Force is supposed to straighten out such conflicts as part of his job. How this is done was explained by one coordinator:

I invite the agents to come in and talk the matter over. The Strike Force may have some information that could be helpful to a ruffled agent. The competing agencies may have different information that they can share. I convince them that one agency is not trying to steal information from the other.

The head of a Strike Force has no authority to direct an agency not to pursue a particular investigation. In an impasse between agencies, the matter is referred to Washington, D.C. A coordinator declared that it "never reaches that stage," but another United States Attorney admitted:

We settle the problem quickly, but sometimes by that time the damage has been done to the likelihood of making a case.

Insufficient coordination seems to be the chief weakness of the Strike Forces, as one member of the House of Representatives noted in the *Congressional Record:*

A great deal more needs to be done to coordinate Federal activities in the fight against organized crime . . . there are ten separate government agencies responsible for the Forces . . . unfortunately relations among the ten . . . have often been characterized by petty bureaucratic jealousies, lack of communication and general confusion.[5]

Comic incidents with near-tragic consequences may occur from lack of cooperation and coordination among agencies. The following true story was reported in a national magazine: An agent from the Treasury Department's Bureau of Customs and an agent from the Justice Department's Bureau of Narcotics and Dangerous Drugs were each, independently, assigned to tail a narcotics smuggler from the Mexican border to a large city where a pickup was supposed to take place. Neither agent knew that the other had been assigned to the case. When they spotted each other at the pickup area, they both started firing. Neither one was killed, but it was a close shave that must have left even these tough investigators shaken.[6]

United States Attorneys and Eavesdropping

The Department of Justice has almost a hundred United States Attorneys scattered in various districts throughout the United States. Most of them are political appointees, subject to removal when a new administration comes into office. Use of Strike Forces to combat organized crime has created some practical problems in the division of labor between the United States Attorney in a district and Strike Force staff in the area. Theoretically, cooperation to the fullest extent should exist, in order to deal effectively with organized crime.

A skilful coordinator of a Strike Force can establish cordial relations with the United States Attorney in the district, provided they are both of the same political party and accept control by officials in Washington. The conflict between former United States Attorney Robert M. Morgenthau, a holdover Democrat in the Southern District of New York, and the Joint Strike Force, was a matter of common knowledge.[7] After appointment of Whitney North Seymour, Jr., a Republican, a more amicable allocation of functions was apparently established. The division of responsibility was described as follows:

> The United States Attorney for the Southern District is responsible in terms of prosecutions for everything the Joint Strike Force does. He signs their indictments and sees that they are in proper form to be filed. The United States Attorney in the District also agrees to Strike Force applications under Title III in terms of form, but does not follow them up.

The major role of the United States Attorney's office in relation to the Strike Force is "to make an effort to help with manpower." In the Southern District of New York, the United States Attorney has a staff of forty or fifty attorneys in the Criminal Division alone. The Joint Strike Force has only a few attorneys. They work together on investigations where the Strike Force does not have sufficient manpower. After approving the form of an application for an eavesdrop order, the United States Attorney has nothing further to do with the order unless it results in an indictment. It then becomes his responsibility to get the case ready for trial.

Many Federal agencies work with the United States Attorney, including the Immigration and Naturalization Service, the Secret Service, and the Internal Revenue Service. The bulk of the United States Attorney's contact, however, is with the F.B.I. and the Bureau of Narcotics and Dangerous Drugs. The agencies do not assign specific individuals to the United States Attorney's office; agents are assigned to *cases*. When an investigation is going on, the agent works with an Assistant United States Attorney in charge of the case. The Attorney may, in the course of the investigation, suggest use of a wiretap, but the matter would be discussed at a meeting of the Strike Force.

Regular meetings of the Strike Force are attended by the United States Attorney, accompanied by members of his staff working on specific cases who are brought up to date on pending matters. A Chief Assistant United States Attorney expressed satisfaction with the relationship established with the Strike Force, with qualifications:

> We do not have quite the same feeling of . . . interest . . . as we do with our own people.

In the District of Columbia, a special United States Attorney handles what is known as "major crime unit" matters, that is, cases dealing with organized crime. Initiation of eavesdropping parallels State practice in a general way, but it is subject to centralized control in the Department of Justice as outlined in the Federal *Manual*. An attorney in the "major crime unit" described the preliminaries:

> An agent of the F.B.I. might come into my office with information about narcotics traffic. We discuss whether we should tap . . . whether there is any other way to approach the problem. Is the person involved important enough . . . is it worth while wiretapping. The agent gives me a rough draft of all the information he has and we put it in final form here in the United States Attorney's office. I draw up the application, affidavits, and order.

United States Attorneys in the District of Columbia rely heavily on the information furnished to them by agents of the F.B.I., for they are considered to be of high caliber. Office procedure with respect to eavesdrop orders resembles that of the States. Generally, an original and three copies of the papers are drawn, one for the District Court, one for the agency that initiated the application, one for the Organized Crime and Racketeering Bureau of the Department of Justice, and one for the United States Attorney himself. The original documents are placed in a box, sealed by the court, and left in the custody of the United States Attorney's office.

Interception of conversations is recorded in accordance with instructions in the *Manual*. The reason for making two tape recordings was given as follows:

> We feel that this way it meets any claim that the tape has been tampered with. . . . One tape plays continuously . . . you can tell the exact time a call was made, since the tape is put on at a certain time and it plays at a certain speed; this is designated as the original and is left intact. The other is the working copy. If one machine malfunctions, the other can take over.

United States Attorneys in the District of Columbia insist that eavesdropping is not used for intelligence gathering by them; that it is employed to get specific evidence of a designated offense. However, where a wiretap for one offense leads to information as to other crimes and additional offenders, a subsequent application can be made to a judge to approve the interception under Sec. 2517(5) of Title III. This provision was upheld by the Supreme Court in 1972 (*Cox v. United States*) discussed in Chapter 5.[8]

The problem of deciding who shall be served with an "inventory" within ninety days after termination of interception troubles the United States Attorneys in the District of Columbia.

> Much is left to the judge's discretion. But the judge really relies on the United States Attorney handling the case. Where the recordings are voluminous, it is impossible for a judge to review all the material in order to decide who shall receive notice of eavesdropping.

The attorneys are fully aware of the ambiguities in the notice requirements of Title III, as pointed out in Chapter 5.

Federal Eavesdropping on Trial

The Government knows that as soon as it gives notice of wiretapping and overhearing of conversations, as the law requires it to do, a motion to suppress the evidence can be expected. Targets of eavesdropping attack the validity of the court order, the manner in which it was carried out, and the constitutionality of Title III as a whole and in part. Litigation has brought to light many of the practical problems of eavesdropping, as well as constitutional questions. Some novel solutions were arrived at in a narcotics case on which the Federal government has spent a vast amount of money and manpower (*United States v. Tantillo*).[9] Wires were tapped continuously for thirty-eight days, seven days a week, twenty-four hours a day. Between 6,000 and 7,000 conversations were overheard and recorded on 105 reels of tape. About 300 hours were required to play all the recordings! This may not sound like a typical situation contemplated by Title III, but the Justice

Department has treated it as a test case on court-ordered eavesdropping. It is discussed in detail in the following pages to illustrate the practical application of eavesdropping under Title III. Attendance at the trial and examination of the documents filed with the Court furnished a unique opportunity to study official wiretapping and electronic surveillance at close range.

The investigation in this case was initiated by the Bureau of Narcotics and Dangerous Drugs (B.N.D.D.), an agency formerly part of the Treasury Department, but now in the Department of Justice. Application for a wiretap order was prepared by a special Assistant United States Attorney in charge of "major crime unit" matters in the District of Columbia. This is the unit that deals with organized crime. An affidavit accompanied the application, sworn to by an agent of B.N.D.D., setting forth facts based on information obtained by overhearing conversations between an informant and one "Lawrence Jackson." A radio transmission device was concealed on the informant, and in overheard conversations Jackson allegedly made two sales of heroin, one a half ounce and the other a full ounce.

The order was signed by a United States District Court judge authorizing wiretapping for a thirty-day period. It was the first wiretap under Title III installed in the District of Columbia and was believed to involve one of the largest distributors of heroin and other drugs in the District. The judge required a progress report at specific intervals. The application, supporting affidavits, and order were duly sealed. The Court was to retain custody of the documents during interception and then transfer them to the Clerk of the United States District Court, to be kept for ten years from the date the order was signed. Disclosure of the documents was prohibited to all except those showing good cause to the judge, or in his absence, some other "judge of competent jurisdiction." About a month later, the Government sought antecedent justification for interception of communications at a related telephone. The interception was authorized by the same judge and an extension granted.

Interception of conversations continued day and night without interruption for thirty-eight days, thirty under the original order, plus the eight-day extension. Of the thousands of telephone calls intercepted, a high percentage, the Government claimed, was related to the purpose of the wiretap. The agency monitoring the recordings, B.N.D.D., rented an office about a mile away from the tapped telephones for listening to the recordings. The judge received ninety-one reels of tape of conversations intercepted on one telephone and fourteen reels on the other. These were sealed and transmitted to the Clerk of the United States District Court, to be kept by him for ten years. The following day the judge entered an order authorizing a deputy clerk to transmit the reels of tape from one of the phones to law enforcement officials to have a duplicate made. Duplicates of the tapes on the other phone had been made contemporaneously with the interceptions. An expert assigned by the Justice Department transcribed all the intercepted conversations, covering a total of over 15,000 pages.

After the wiretapping, over fifty defendants were charged in five separate cases with conspiracy for illegal distribution of narcotics. The first case involved seven defendants reputed to be "major domos," that is, high echelon members of organized crime; two of them were reported to be members of the "Mafia." The second case included seventeen "lieutenants," persons who perform major functions in a crime syndicate; the third, fourth, and fifth cases each involved ten lower-echelon defendants charged with buying narcotics from the organization for resale.

The first case of top echelon defendants received a great deal of publicity in the newspapers of Washington, D.C. and elsewhere. After the indictments, Senator McClellan made the following comment:

> When one series of wiretaps can bring to book two members of La Cosa Nostra, a major wholesaler, a crooked policeman and an assorted group of other criminals, never again should anyone doubt that wiretapping is necessary to break the back of organized crime's exploitation of our people.

A defense counsel expressed indignation at this public pronouncement. To him the Senator's statement seemed extravagant, premature, and prejudicial; obtaining an indictment in one narcotics case in the District of Columbia, he said, is not proof of need for or effectiveness of eavesdropping in "breaking the back of organized crime."

Eavesdropping Evidence before Trial

After the case was filed with the Clerk of the United States District Court, a judge was assigned to hear it. He was black. Three of the defendants were white; four were black. The judge issued a "protective order" removing all papers from the Clerk's office into his chambers and directing that all future documents be filed with the judge. Tape recordings and related materials were unsealed by the Court for the limited purpose of pretrial preparation. Recordings to be played for the parties were to stay under court control as the court deemed necessary. Contents of materials were not to be disclosed to anyone but those connected in good faith with the prosecution or defense of the case.

Several important questions regarding court-ordered eavesdropping surfaced at this preliminary stage:

1. Should defendants have access to the *entire* recording and to the entire transcript?

2. Should such access be given *before* formal motion to suppress is made?
3. If full disclosure is made of tapes and transcripts, how can the privacy of individuals whose conversations are overheard be protected?

Pretrial conferences were held and a schedule set up to handle the difficult and contested procedural problems. A date was fixed for formal filing of the motion to suppress eavesdrop evidence, after giving defendants and their attorneys sixty days in which to listen to the tapes and additional time to read the complete transcripts. The Government was given a month to respond. Defendants were represented by various well-known New York and Washington criminal lawyers, some white, some black. The "major crime unit" assigned four United States Attorneys to devote full time to preparation of the case.

All the tapes were played for defendants' counsel; portions were replayed for further study. In an attempt to balance the needs of defendants for disclosure and the rights of innocent persons overheard on the tapes, only two copies of the transcripts were made available to seven defendants. The Government also furnished a transcript of parts of the recordings that it believed were particularly relevant to the charges; this was in addition to the chronological transcription of all the recordings. A spokesman for the United States Attorneys handling the case said that the Government had gone out of its way to give defendants every opportunity to prepare their case fully, not out of goodness of heart but because:

> This is a key case on wiretapping and one in which *all* of Title III may be at stake.

The Government claimed it was doing everything possible to minimize invasion of privacy:

> There is great concern on the part of the United States Government for the rights of the people whose voices are recorded on the tapes, and a tremendous effort is being made to see that they do not suffer any greater invasion of privacy than is absolutely necessary. That is the only way the statute [Title III] can be held constitutional. If the United States Supreme Court finds the Government has been "sloppy" about protecting the privacy of individuals, all of Title III may fall!

Defendant's counsel saw it with different eyes—the Government had trampled on constitutional rights of privacy. Narcotics agents, said one of the attorneys, listened to the recording with "manic enjoyment" while problems of birth, life, sex, and death passed over the wires indiscriminately.

If you wiretap for such a long period [38 days] you get a great number of people who talk on the phone—incoming or outgoing calls. A husband and wife, or a guy and his girlfriend, may talk for a couple of hours. It exposes the most intimate facts of their lives, often pathetic facts. The Government seems to believe nothing is privileged, that they do not have to select. It thinks that if the people they are listening to are suspected of crime and the phone is believed to be a business phone, they can listen to everything and don't have to stop.

Hearings on the motion to suppress eavesdrop evidence continued for six consecutive weeks, with the press excluded. Much time was devoted to the issue of whether or not the statements in the agent's affidavit were correct or reasonably thought to be correct. The judge then deliberated for a week and wrote a draft opinion upholding the wiretap and finding it in all respects constitutionally in conformance with Title III. The opinion was delivered orally from the bench.

Eavesdropping Evidence at the Trial

Mechanical problems in presentation of intercepted conversations were anticipated by both sides. A defense counsel said before the trial began:

You would be amazed at how much of it is inaudible and unintelligible. In wiretapping a face may be too close or too far from the phone to get a clear recording. The conversation recorded may take place in a bedroom where a television set or radio is going full blast. The listener sometimes is not sure whether he is hearing the phone conversationalist or the broadcaster. Musical background may interfere with the sound. The equipment itself sometimes breaks down entirely.

Voice identification was also foreseen as presenting difficulties. Substantial disagreement could develop as to who is who on the telephone, particularly in the case of lengthy tapes on which numerous people appear and reappear.

You have to listen a long time to know the various names they go by. A voice says: "This is Bobby." This does not mean that it is Bobby. Five people call and say it is Bobby. The same voice can change. A speaker can be high, drunk, mad, giddy; he sounds different at 10 A.M., midnight, and 4 A.M., and depending on whether or not he is alone. There is the problem of white people identifying black voices . . . to whites, blacks tend to sound alike.

Serious dispute was expected with respect to "incriminating statements." If selection must be made of portions of the tape to be played in
presenting evidence, when is a call "incriminating"?

> A voice says: "Did you meet R. and give her that thing?" What
> does it mean? In one second a conversation may include what
> someone may consider an incriminating phrase, and then the parties
> go on and talk about something personal.

The trial began before a predominantly black jury, not an extraordinary occurrence in Washington, D.C. with a 70 percent black population.
Women predominated on the jury. The first few days of the trial were taken
up with testimony as to installation of the wiretap and monitoring device.
The Government then placed on the stand the informant who had furnished
the Narcotics Bureau with the facts on which the wiretap order had been
based. This was unusual, since an informant's usefulness is generally ended
if his identity becomes known. Defendants had attacked both identity and
reliability of the informant in the motion to suppress. Cross-examination of
the informant revealed that he had been arrested twice in New York on narcotics charges without advising the Department of Justice, although he had
collected payments during that time from the Justice Department for
alleged services. He claimed that when he had testified several days before,
the arrests had not "come into his mind." A slight titter ran through the
audience, but the jurors maintained a correct, stony silence.

The Government now faced the tactical, logistical problem of how to
present the wiretap evidence to the jury. Defense counsel had indicated the
questions that would have to be met in a pretrial interview:

> Can they simultaneously present the recording of a telephone
> call and their explanation of what it means? How long should the
> Court permit a tape to be played? Will the Judge stop the playing of a
> tape whenever he thinks the conversation is not incriminating? In the
> ordinary case, when a witness testifies the Judge can control the ques-
> tioning and stop it when it is irrelevant.

Government representatives had spent months weighing the alternatives. "A totally new problem is presented every step of the way, and no one
knows the right move from the wrong," said one of the United States Attorneys. Should there be amplifiers in the courtroom if the recordings are
not sufficiently audible? Should the tapes be played to the jury through
earphones? Is a reading of the transcript to the jury enough without playing
any of the tapes? What is the status of the transcript?

The Government claimed that the law permitted introduction of the
transcript as testimony to avoid repetitive replays. It offered the transcript
as a guide to the jury. The defense contended that the jury should be barred

from viewing the transcript since it was merely the Government's "hypothesis" as to the meaning of the recordings; that the jury should be permitted to listen to the tapes without being influenced by the Government's version of the conversations. After extensive conferences at the bench and in the Judge's chambers, the Court established the following procedure:

1. The transcript was withheld from the jury. Selected conversations from the tapes were to be replayed to the jury.
2. The Government placed two amplifiers in the courtroom, directly facing the jury.
3. The Government set up a chart, about five by seven feet, showing the meaning of words, phrases, and code terms used in the intercepted conversations, subject to objection by defense counsel.
4. The Judge listened to a tape recording in his chambers, in the presence of counsel on both sides, and ruled as to each conversation— whether it was relevant, incriminating, and admissible in whole or part. Only admissible conversations or parts were to be replayed.
5. Any juror could ask for a replay of a conversation that he found inaudible or unintelligible.

The presiding Judge delivered an explanation to the jury:

> With respect to the recording you are about to hear, the Court has already determined their admissibility . . . you are to consider these along with other evidence . . . on some you will hear a completed telephone call; on other telephone conversations you will hear parts, maybe the first part of the intercept and a later part and maybe not that in between. With respect to every recording . . . any individual member of the jury may indicate if [you] desire it to be repeated. . . . It will require your close attention.

He also warned the audience that a high degree of cooperation would be required, that no one would be permitted to enter or leave the courtroom during the playing of any one recording. The courtroom had suddenly become packed with tourists, law students, and lawyers as word spread through the building that wiretap testimony was about to begin.

A special agent of the Bureau of Narcotics and Dangerous Drugs took the stand and qualified as a voice expert. He testified that he had been assigned to review the tape recordings taken from intercepts in the case. For a total of 550 hours over a period of five months he had listened to all the conversations, noted the voices, made transcriptions. Over a period of three months he had listened for an additional seventy-five hours to the tapes selectively, made notes of parts of conversations, and had done the same subsequently for another seventy-five hours.

Question by Government Counsel: Are you prepared to play some of
the calls from the original tapes?

Answer: Yes.

Question: How did you arrange to play the tapes?

Answer: I will announce the date and time of the call, whether it was
incoming or outgoing. My associate, Mr. _____ will play it.

The voice expert then explained the procedures he had used to become familiar with the various voices on the tape. As he played the recordings, he said, he became familiar with the voices so that he recognized
them. If he could not recognize a voice, he replayed the tape. Two
recorders were used to help identify the voices; first one recorder would be
played and then the other. The witness gave the date, time of the first
telephone call to be played, an incoming call on telephone number _____
and the playing of the recordings began.

Question by Government Counsel: How many voices do you recognize?

Answer: Two voices. The first calls himself Bob.

Question: The one who called himself Bob, are you familiar with that
voice?

Answer: Yes.

Question: Are there other conversations with the person "Bob."

Answer: Yes. Bob and Bobby are different.

The next telephone call was then identified in a similar way as to date
and time, an incoming call on a designated phone number, and it was
played to the jury.

Question: How many voices do you recognize?

Answer: Two voices. The first person—that was the caller. The other
person was "Lawrence."

Question: Will that name appear in the conversations to be played?

Answer: Yes, many times.

The jury continued to listen to the conversations, one after the other.
The voice of "Lawrence" was identified in many of them. Not a single juror
requested a replay. When Court adjourned after the first day of playing the
recordings to the jury, the attorneys for the Government and for the defendants were asked privately whether they believed the jury had understood the conversations. To the press and spectators sitting in the front row,
a few feet away from the jury box, the tapes were largely unintelligible. Occasionally a few phrases came through the amplifiers with reasonable
clarity:

Say, who dat? How be ya? Hey, hello. What's up? I tell ya what.
Whozis? O.K. G'bye.

Bob, are you asleep? What did ya call for? Did ya call Lawrence? Did he come? Did ya really make it? What ya want me to do? Where d'ya get it? Ha wanna be here. Be here. I say 300. O.K. If you can get down. Awright.

Counsel on both sides believed the conversations were clear to the jurors sitting directly in front of the two large amplifiers and familiar with Washington "dialect." Selected conversations were played to the jury for more than a week. Other witnesses appeared for the prosecution to corroborate the eavesdrop evidence. The defendants did not take the stand, nor did any witnesses testify in their behalf. Defense counsel rested on the insufficiency and illegality of the eavesdropping and other evidence submitted by the Government. After a trial that lasted two months, the jury brought in a verdict of guilty for all seven defendants, three Italians and four blacks, one of them a woman.

Release of Documents on Motion to Suppress

During the trial, the Court permitted various documents to be released from the protective order of secrecy and remain on file in the office of the Chief Clerk of the United States District Court in Washington, D.C. Among these were the papers on the motion to suppress eavesdrop evidence. The reason given for the release was that defendants in later cases resulting from the same wiretap should be allowed to examine the documents in preparation for trial. The application, affidavits, and order for the wiretap were not among them. Asked for an explanation as to why these documents continued to remain secret when their contents were discussed fully in other instruments released, a defense counsel said:

> We are in complete confusion as to what is secret and what is not. We have put the burden on the Judge and he is in agony.

The Government had objected to release of *any* document; secrecy of all records was urged to avoid the charge that the privacy of innocent persons was unduly violated. Memoranda in support of and in opposition to the motion to suppress, examined in the Chief Clerk's office, presented practically every argument that counsel on both sides could muster in a case involving eavesdropping. In support of the motion to suppress eavesdrop evidence defense counsel contended:

1. That eavesdropping is per se a violation of a constitutional right.
2. That even if a statute could be drafted that satisfied constitutional requirements, Title III had failed to do so; that it contravenes the Third, Fourth, Fifth, Sixth, and Ninth Amendments to the Constitution.

3. That the wiretap order and affidavit on which it was based did not comply with the requirements of Title III; that the application was defective, insufficient, false, and erroneous.
4. That the interception was not conducted so as to minimize improper, unauthorized, unwarranted intrusions as required by Sec. 2518(5) of Title III.
5. That there were or may have been intercepts of wire or oral communications *without* judicial sanction in violation of Title III.

As to the first two items listed above, the defense relied heavily on an article in the University of Pennsylvania Law Review.[10] The thirty-day period of interception, with an unlimited number of extensions as permitted by Sec. 2518(5), was claimed to contravene *Berger* and *Katz*. The provision of Sec. 2518(4) requiring the order to specify the *type* of communication sought violated the particularity requirement of Supreme Court decisions. Power of the Court to postpone indefinitely the ninety-day notice to aggrieved persons under Sec. 2518(8)(d) was said to be unreasonable.

As to item (3) listed above, the affidavit and order were attacked for failure to show *probable cause*, lack of facts to prove that *normal investigative procedures* were inadequate, and absence of *particularity* as to conversations to be intercepted. The defense claimed that the affidavit was neither factual nor truthful; that it misled the judge who signed the order. The affidavit alleged that the telephone to be tapped was used for criminal activities from Mexico to Laredo, Texas, to Washington, D.C., but no such transactions occurred in the intercepted conversations. The claim that "normal investigative techniques" would not succeed was contradicted by the extensive surveillance carried on in the investigation and the fact that, without wiretapping, the Government's informant effected two narcotics sales transactions carrying heavy penalties. As to particularity, the application merely stated that there would be a conversation in violation of some narcotics law; it did not describe the particular communication sought, nor the class or nature of the conversation. In fact, argued the defense, it is impossible to describe a telephone conversation sought with particularity.

In conclusion, the interceptions were declared by the defense to be "a massive set of intrusions run continuously" which allowed the monitoring agents to hear everything that came over the wires.

The Government submitted a 150-page memorandum in opposition to the motion to suppress eavesdrop evidence. It sought to prove, first theoretically and then empirically by the facts in the case, that court-ordered eavesdropping is constitutionally permissible and that adequate safeguards are provided by Title III to satisfy constitutional requirements.

Justification for the scope and length of interceptions—thirty-eight days, seven days a week, twenty-four hours a day—was the Government's chief worry, for such continuous and extended eavesdropping opened the door wide to attack on the ground that privacy had been unduly invaded.

The Government wanted to show that it elicited conversations related to the purpose of the wiretap. An intricate statistical analysis of intercepted conversations was constructed to demonstrate that narcotics-related calls were spread continuously throughout the entire twenty-four-hour period every day of the week. Some of the 7,000 conversations intercepted were admittedly non-incriminating. Instead of classifying them as incriminating or non-incriminating, as is done in the annual report to Congress, the Government grouped the conversations in seven categories, three relating to narcotics distribution, three unrelated, and one ambiguous, as follows:

1. The substance of which reasonably concerned the illicit narcotics distribution scheme.
2. A *part* of which reasonably concerned the illicit narcotics distribution scheme, utilizing the tapped telephone network.
3. No reference to the trafficking operation, but of particularly crucial evidentiary value—identification of name, telephone number, etc.
4. Might relate to trafficking, but vague, ambiguous.
5. No part relates to trafficking enterprise utilizing the tapped phones. Contains communications which in themselves constitute criminality of another sort or refers to other criminality.
6. Weather recordings, time recordings, telephone company recordings.
7. Communications no part of which reasonably related to the trafficking operation or to other criminality.

In five tables the Government showed how many conversations dealing with narcotics occurred each day, and how many took place during each six-hour period of the day. Table I presented a breakdown of the seven categories with totals for each of the thirty-eight days of interceptions. It showed that on an average day, 129 calls were received, one every twelve minutes. For only six of the thirty-seven full days of intercepts were fewer than 100 calls made and received over the telephone network. The daily number of communications was considered important in assessing the degree to which the telephone was in continuous use. Tables II, III, IV, and V were identical with Table I, except that they covered four 6-hour periods: 12:01 A.M. to 6 A.M.; 6 A.M. to noon; noon to 6 P.M.; 6 P.M. to 12:01 A.M. These tables showed the content of communications for each of the 152 six-hour periods during the entire intercept. The Government analyzed the conversations statistically to show how many conversations relating to narcotics activity actually occurred each day, and also during each six-hour period. The particular call served as the basic unit of content, regardless of length of the conversation. Hundreds of calls were non-communicative, the caller hanging up after the answerer said "Hello." Summarizing the tables, the Government found that of the calls intercepted, 4,910 were sufficiently communicative to permit content analysis. Of these:

1,999 (41%) related in substance to the trafficking operation.

  310 (6%) related in part to the trafficking operation.

    46 (1%) were of mere evidence value.

1,792 (36%) were ambiguous.

  143 (3%) were unrelated to the trafficking operation, but referred to other criminality.

More than 100 purchasers, the Government claimed, negotiated thousands of narcotics transactions, revealing the characteristics of a vigorous commercial enterprise, and constituting a continuing offense that justified continuous wiretapping. If a planned narcotics activity was carried on day and night by sophisticated operators who were skilful in employing counter-investigative techniques, then eavesdropping without interruption over an extended period of time, said the Government, was not overreaching under the rulings of the United States Supreme Court.

The Government's memorandum described the counter-investigative techniques used by the suspects. They were concerned about police surveillance, tried to locate police through binoculars, to identify their license numbers, and became circumspect. In an intercepted conversation, one said:

Ain't nobody making money ain't being observed some kind of way.

It was claimed that suspects used the device of changing automobiles, decoyed surveilling vehicles, avoided daylight deliveries of customers' orders, had a warning system and were confident of neighborhood support. They avoided dealing with individuals on probation and checked arrest warrant lists. Drugs were kept at a "stash," not at headquarters, and when too many people knew the location it was moved to a new place. The Government charged that suspects also had weapon protection and anticipated the existence of the wiretap. One said in an intercepted conversation: "Mine is tapped. I know that."

Sometimes they spoke directly to the monitoring agents: "Hey, excuse me, Mr. Fed." Despite the strong suspicion of wiretapping, the telephone continued to be used to effect narcotics transactions. Overt reference to drugs, however, was avoided and code words were used. The Government concluded that Title III on its face comported in all respects with the demands of the Fourth Amendment; that it adhered rigidly to the judicial process, met the requirements of *Katz* and *Berger*, and that the Government conformed its conduct to the demands of the statute.

Balancing the Need to Search against Privacy

The Government admitted that "value predispositions and pure subjectivity" could easily find their way into its analysis, but assured the Court that a determined effort had been made to eliminate these factors. All Fourth Amendment questions involved a *balancing* of interests and reasoned "accommodation of competing values," the need to search as against the invasion of privacy which the search entails. In wiretapping in this particular case, argued the Government, this balance had been achieved.

Denial of the motion to suppress eavesdrop evidence resulted in a trial that lasted two months, involving tremendous expense and postponement of appeal by the defendants until after trial. Would the balancing process have been better served if the motion to suppress had been granted? The Government could then have taken an appeal and the Supreme Court might have decided the issues raised by Title III at once. A Government representative in Washington, D.C. aptly termed the question of choice open to the United States District Court judge as one of "functional judicial management." The Judge simply decided to give the defendants their day in court. Why did the Federal government not arrest Lawrence Jackson as soon as it had evidence of conversations effecting two illegal sales to its informant? The Government's answer is that with the tool of court-ordered eavesdropping it was possible to reach the narcotics suppliers, as well as the wholesale dealer. Defense counsel claims this is in violation of Title III.

The ultimate fate of Title III, and of the defendants, will hang in the balance while this test case and others make their way to the Supreme Court. The Government believes that if the conviction of the seven defendants is sustained, the District of Columbia will be a better place in which to live and work. It sees the defendants as leaders of organized crime. Defense counsel retort that the "community has as great a concern with the erosion of personal freedom, privacy, and dignity by arbitrary police practices as it does with vigorous law enforcement." The defendants are little people, they say, poor, low-echelon victims of narcotics traffic whom frustrated Government agents want to see in jail rather than face the social problems of drugs and poverty.

A social interpreter is needed, says a defense attorney, to sort out the racial overtones of this case; there are racial implications in the Government's assertion that normal investigative procedures are inadequate in a ghetto area and that wiretapping is needed. Even among defense counsel, all of whom oppose wiretapping, a difference of attitude is said to exist, depending on whether the attorney is white or black. White civil libertarians argue the constitutional issues and practical problems of Title III on an intellectual level. Black attorneys in Washington, D.C., it is said, consider wiretapping an aspect of discriminatory law enforcement practices and sense racial and ethnic undercurrents in the vigor with which the Government is prosecuting its "test case."

Court Decisions on Federal Eavesdropping

Some of the problems that surfaced at the trial in the District of Columbia described above have been considered by Federal courts in various parts of the country. Other troubling questions involving Title III have been presented and decisions rendered, not all of them consistent. Conflicting opinions of United States District Courts have reached the Court of Appeals in several circuits, and the Supreme Court has settled a few serious disputes among the Circuit Courts. The following summary highlights the ingenuity of the judiciary in deciding novel questions in the absence of clear guidelines. Federal courts have faced the facts of official eavesdropping realistically on the whole, and sought practical solutions.

Authorization of Application for Court Order

Litigation has been extensive over the procedure of the Department of Justice in authorizing applications to obtain wiretap orders. Section 2516(1) of Title III requires that an application be authorized by the Attorney General or by an Assistant Attorney General specially designated by the Attorney General. Individuals whose conversations were intercepted complained that the Justice Department did not conform strictly to the technical language of the law. In some cases a memorandum of authorization carried the initials of the Attorney General (John N. Mitchell, who resigned in 1972), but it appeared that the initials were actually affixed by his Executive Assistant, Sol Lindenbaum (*United States v. Cihal*).[11] In other cases, a letter of authorization purportedly signed by the Assistant Attorney General (Will Wilson, who later resigned under fire for conflict of interest) was actually signed by the Deputy Assistant Attorney General (*United States v. La Gorga*).[12]

The United States Court of Appeals for the Second Circuit considered the matter at great length and concluded that authorization was acceptable where the Attorney General affixed the initials himself and approved the request for authorization (*United States v. Pisacano*).[13] Three authorizations were at issue in this case: one was approved by the Attorney General's initialing a memorandum himself; another was approved by telephone authorization to his Executive Assistant; the third was approved even more informally—the Executive Assistant affixed the Attorney General's initials "on the basis of his conclusions, stemming from his knowledge of the Attorney General's actions on previous cases that he would approve the request if submitted to him."

All three authorizations were declared to be valid by the Court of Appeals for the Second Circuit. It was conceded that perhaps the procedures adopted by the Justice Department were not the best, but the responsible official was "reasonably identifiable." The intent of Congress was to establish "a unitary policy in the use of the awesome power conferred in Title III, and the Attorney General assumed full responsibility for what was done even if he did not act himself in every case." The Court of Appeals ruling in *Pisacano* has been followed by some Federal District Courts (*United States v. Consiglio; United States v. Doolittle*). A contrary opinion was reached by the Court of Appeals for the Fifth Circuit (*United States v. Robinson*)[14] and in the Fourth Circuit (*United States v. Giordano*).[15] The Court in the Fourth Circuit in Richmond, Virginia, said:

> When government consistently tramples upon those parts of the law that do not suit its momentary purpose and seeks to justify its conduct by sophistic argumentation, neither respect for law nor societal order is promoted.[16]

In March 1973 the United States Supreme Court agreed to decide whether wiretap evidence obtained under orders that had not been authorized strictly according to Title III could be used. It had been informed that the issue had been raised in more than one hundred cases in the lower Federal courts.

Probable Cause

The claim that no probable cause existed for issuance of a wiretap order is raised in many cases. A common point of attack is the reliability of the information on which supporting affidavits are based. In the Second Circuit, the Court of Appeals ruled that where the affiant relied on information furnished by an unnamed informant and swore that the informant had given correct information on about fifty prior occasions, a claim that no probable cause existed must be rejected (*United States v. Fantuzzi*).[17] In the Eighth Circuit, the Court of Appeals, deciding that the affidavit considered as a whole provided probable cause, held that an affidavit may rest on hearsay as long as it sufficiently presents to the judge the underlying facts and circumstances, both (1) from which the informant drew his conclusions, and (2) from which the affiant concluded that the informant was credible and that his information was reliable (*United States v. Kleve*).[18]

Length of Period of Interception

The argument that Title III is unconstitutional because it does not provide safeguards against lengthy, unnecessary, and prolonged surveillance was rejected by the United States District Court in southern Florida. The Court noted that Sec. 2518(5) requires that the order be executed as soon as practicable, that it be conducted to minimize interceptions, and that it terminate on attainment of the authorized objective. A further safeguard is provided in Sec. 2518(6) authorizing the judge who issued the order to require progress reports so that he can control duration of the interceptions (*United States v. Sklaroff*).[19] A contrary conclusion was reached by a United States District Court in Pennsylvania. The Court decided that Title III violated the Fourth Amendment to the Constitution because the law allowed continuous interceptions for too long a period (*United States v. Whitaker*).[20]

The Court of Appeals in the Sixth Circuit has ruled that absence of a date on a court order to wiretap made its duration unlimited, authorized wiretapping for an unreasonable length of time, and rendered the order invalid. Subsequent amendment of the order was deemed insufficient to correct the error. However, invalidity of the order did not require reversal of conviction for possession and sale of counterfeit reserve notes. The trial court had instructed the jury to disregard the testimony resulting from the wiretaps, and the Court of Appeals concluded that the wiretap evidence had played no part in the conviction (*United States v. Lamonge*).[21]

Nighttime Interceptions

Where a court order covering private telephone lines contained no specific time during which a wiretap could be maintained, but the affidavits established that the phones were used in an extremely active gambling enterprise, the United States District Court in the Southern District of New York decided that it was of no relevance that nighttime interceptions were not prohibited under the order. As a practical matter, said the Court, the order cannot define precisely the period during which interception can be conducted, since activities of such an enterprise are not limited to specific hours (*United States v. Becker*).[22] This decision was followed and cited by the New York Court of Appeals (*People v. Zorn*).[23]

Conversations in Public Places

A Court order to wiretap signed by a Federal judge in Pennsylvania provided that no conversations at a designated Health Club, a public location, were to be monitored unless either of two named persons participated. Federal agents intercepted conversations between two other persons at the location indicated. The United States District Court in Pennsylvania ruled that the interception violated the order, and evidence as to that conversation must be suppressed (*United States v. La Gorga*).[12]

A conviction for illegal gambling activity was reversed by the United States Court of Appeals, Sixth Circuit, where conversations were intercepted "in utter disregard of the provisions of the order of the District Court." The order provided that interceptions shall be conducted only when surveillance by special agents of the F.B.I. indicate that either of two named persons are within the described premises, and shall be continued only when it is determined by voice recognition that these two are using the phone. No copy of the order was furnished to the officer monitoring the calls. The protective limitations of the order, said the Court, were completely defeated (*United States v. George*).[24]

Particularity—Type of Conversation

The United States District Court in the Southern District of Florida held that an applicant for a wiretap order need not describe the specific content of an anticipated conversation. He cannot predict in advance the exact language of a conversation which has not yet occurred. It is sufficient for the order to show a finding of probable cause that conversations will be overheard implicating the suspect in a specific *pattern* of criminal conduct (*United States v. Sklaroff*).[19]

In particularizing the type of wire communications which customs agents were authorized to intercept in a narcotics smuggling investigation, a United States District Court in California decided in *United States v. King*[2] that an order was valid if the communications were described as those concerning:

1. Date, time, and place of loading marijuana by a named vessel in Mexican waters.
2. Date, time, and place of arrival of that vessel with marijuana in the United States.
3. Identities of confederates of the named subject of the order.

Identity—Persons Not Named in Order

Section 2518(4)(a) of Title III requires that the court order to eavesdrop specify the identity of the person, if known, whose communications are to be intercepted." Suppose conversations of unknown parties, not named in the order, are intercepted. May the conversations be used as evidence? A United States District Court in Florida ruled that if a lawful court order to intercept communications of named persons has been issued, and conversations between the named persons and others not named in the order are intercepted, the conversations of the unnamed persons and the evidence derived therefrom are admissible in evidence in a criminal trial against the unnamed persons, if otherwise relevant and material (*United States v. Sklaroff*).[19]

A similar decision was made by a United States District Court in California. The Court upheld interception of conversations of persons not named in the order where the wiretap was instituted to uncover the whereabouts of contraband marijuana and to ascertain the identity of confederates of the target named in the order (*United States v. King*).[2]

The New York Court of Appeals, in a case decided in June 1972, noted that the Federal courts have consistently held that intercepted conversations are usable against persons not named in the warrants (*People v. Zorn*).[23]

Progress Reports to Judges

A Federal court order to wiretap required written reports to be made to the issuing judge on the fifth and tenth day of interception. No written reports were, in fact, submitted, but the special United States Attorney in charge of the case orally advised the judge that the objectives of the wiretap had not yet been achieved. The attorney did not enumerate the specific number of calls intercepted. A United States District Court in Pennsylvania decided that, while it would be better practice to submit written progress reports, Title III does not insist that they be in writing or specifically require any reports at all; it is discretionary with the judge. Use of oral reports did not constitute error, although the *Manual* of the Justice Department urges written reports as a matter of policy (*United States v. La Gorga*).[12]

Minimizing Interceptions

Federal courts have been perturbed by the large volume of innocent, irrelevant, and private conversations intercepted in eavesdropping under law. Failure to minimize interceptions as required by Title III has led some courts to suppress all the evidence obtained (*United States v. Scott*).[25] In *Scott*, all the conversations were monitored, although 60 percent were irrelevant. The District Court in the District of Columbia concluded that this was the kind of surveillance proscribed by *Katz* and *Berger*.[26]

Some Federal courts have excluded only the irrelevant conversations (*United States v. La Gorga*).[27] The United States District Court in Pennsylvania noted in this case that it is often impossible to determine irrelevancy until a conversation has terminated. The Court said:

Monitoring agents are not gifted with prescience and cannot be expected to know in advance what direction the conversation will take.

In the early stages of surveillance, agents must familiarize themselves with voices. In *La Gorga* they were instructed to cut off conversations that were not pertinent "where it was possible to do so." The special United States Attorney assigned to the case testified:

> I instructed the agents, where possible, to terminate calls that weren't relevant. However, there were problems and I left it to their discretion. I certainly understood that it wasn't possible to terminate some conversations because they didn't know whether the phone would be turned over to another individual in gambling life or a particular conversation, personal at one point, may involve gambling a moment later.

The Court in *La Gorga* followed the decision of the United States District Court in California in *United States v. King* involving a huge marijuana smuggling operation. Prosecution was based on conversations over the telephone of King in his apartment, intercepted under court order.[2] Over 10,000 pounds of marijuana were seized aboard a vessel off the northern California coast, and another vessel was taken in San Francisco Bay. In suppressing some of the conversations intercepted and admitting others, the Court in *King*, while rejecting the conclusions in *Scott*, quoted from the Scott opinion:

> The statute does not require the order to state how the agents are to minimize receipt of communications "not otherwise subject to interception"; nor does the 4th Amendment prescribe such a requirement. It is sufficient for the Order to state the requirement and direct the officer to carry out the mandate of that Order.[28]

The wiretap on King's telephone was in effect for 45 days, 24 hours a day, producing 1,556 pages of transcript. Every communication over the tapped wire was recorded, regardless of who the parties were or the nature of the conversation; about 90 percent of the phone calls were monitored. An agent testified that he was instructed to record every conversation except those between attorney and client concerning a pending criminal case.

The District Court in California questioned the Government's adherence to minimization requirements. A conversation between King and an unidentified female named Phyllis ran for forty-four pages in the transcript; it was totally irrelevant except for two pages in the middle. A phone call between a female named Barbara and her mother, which made no reference to the smuggling conspiracy, took up fourteen pages. The

Court termed as "suspect" an analysis of percentage of irrelevant conversations (14 percent) made by the Government five months later, after minimization had become an issue; the analysis appeared to contradict progress reports which showed a high percentage (75 percent) of irrelevant conversations during some intervals.

The Court in the King case criticized the Justice Department's *Manual* for Conduct of Electronic Surveillance under Title III as incorrect with regard to instructions for conduct of wiretaps by agents. If, as the *Manual* asserted, interception under Title III is to be considered an investigative tool of last resort, the Government need not wiretap with the idea of gleaning every conceivable shred of relevant conversation from every phone call.

> The requirements of the Fourth Amendment cannot be met by intercepts executed in blanket fashion with the hope that the passage of time may invest them with a relevance not immediately apparent.

While the entire wiretap was not excluded, a warning for the future was sounded. "Total suppression may well prove to be the only feasible solution," said the Court, if the Government fails voluntarily to adhere to limitations of the statute.[2]

Not all courts have been so critical of Government practice. In one of the first litigated cases arising under Title III, the United States District Court in southern Florida ruled that interceptions were conducted in such a way as to minimize interceptions. A total of 324 calls were overheard over pay telephones relating to gambling. The Court rejected the contention that the wiretap should have been terminated earlier. Testimony showed that until the last day of interception, information was being received about new matters, different numbers were coming up on different days. The pattern of the gambling operation did not emerge until the end of six days of interception (*United States v. Sklaroff*).[19]

In 1972, the United States Court of Appeals for the Eighth Circuit considered the question of minimizing interceptions and came to the conclusion that it must be considered on a case by case basis. There was no failure to minimize, said the Court, merely because a substantial portion of the intercepted conversations were found to have no evidentiary value (*United States v. Cox*).[29]

Attorney-Client Privilege

Must an agent stop listening the minute he hears an attorney talking to his client? Apparently not. In *United States v. King*, the marijuana smuggling case mentioned above, one of the defendants whose conversation was overheard was an attorney who was later indicted as a member of the alleged conspiracy. The United States District Court in California ruled that the conversation could be used as evidence; the privilege inhering in the attorney-client relationship was not violated. The privilege is for the protection of the client, not the attorney; it does not protect illegal activities.[2]

Background Conversation

In the *King* case discussed above, surveillance equipment used to tap King's telephone could pick up not only communications coming from the telephone, but any conversations in the room within hearing distance of the defendant when the receiver was off the hook. These background conversations were relevant to the conspiracy and were recorded by monitoring agents. Since they were not specifically described in the court order to wiretap, the United States District Court in California decided that interception of the background conversations was an unreasonable search and seizure in violation of the Fourth Amendment and the conversations were not admissible as evidence.

Pen Register

A court order authorized use of a pen register so that destination of outgoing telephone calls could be determined. Defendants claimed that use of the pen register was unlawful under Sec. 605 of the Federal Communications Act and that it violated the Fourth Amendment as a general and exploratory search. The United States District Court in California held that the pen register did not aid in actual interception of verbal communications; that its use is not governed by Title III, nor is it prohibited by Sec. 605 (*United States v. King*).[2]

A motion for discovery of telephone numbers, if any, obtained by the Government through use of a pen register or other device on telephones used by defendants, was denied by the United States District Court in the Southern District of Florida (*United States v. Sklaroff*).[19]

Notice of Interception

A Federal court order to wiretap concluded with a statement that notice to the subject of the order "is hereby expressly waived." The judge never caused notice to be served within ninety days after termination of interception as required by Sec. 2518(8)(d) of Title III. Nor did he ever postpone service, as he might have done under that section. He intentionally eliminated service of notice. This vitiated the wiretap and precluded use of the evidence derived from it (*United States v. Eastman*). Service of notice is a necessary link in the chain of protective measures built into the statute.

The provision for . . . notice within ninety days eliminates, insofar as practicable, the possibility of completely secret electronic eavesdropping and grants to the person involved an opportunity to seek redress for abusive interception either by civil action for damages or by a suppression of the evidence in a criminal case.[30]

In another case (*United States v. La Gorga*), delay in filing the notice or "inventory" was deemed not to be prejudicial conduct of such dimension as to require the Court to suppress the evidence. The judge had granted two 90-day extensions within which to give notice, and there was some confusion as to the due date. The purpose of the notice, said the United States District Court in Pennsylvania, is to prevent Government abuse and continuing secrecy.[31]

Pre-indictment Motion to Suppress

An order denying a motion to suppress wiretap evidence made before indictment is not a final decision, and is therefore not appealable. The United States Court of Appeals for the Fifth Circuit dismissed such an appeal for lack of jurisdiction (*Application of United States*).[32] The appellants contended that if pre-indictment motion to suppress were not allowed, there would be no remedy for individuals whose communications were intercepted but who were not subsequently indicted. The Court of Appeals was impressed with the argument, but based its decision on the facts of the particular case:

> The argument is an interesting one . . . but in this case the appellants were indicted.

Constitutionality of Title III

In attacking the constitutionality of Title III as a whole or in part, it has been urged that safeguards are inadequate, that eavesdropping is an invasion of privacy and an unreasonable search and seizure in violation of the Fourth Amendment; that it has a "chilling effect" on freedom of speech in violation of the First Amendment, and that it also violates the Fifth Amendment protection against self-incrimination. Courts have noted that many of the arguments are concerned with policy and undesirability of the practice of eavesdropping (*United States v. La Gorga*).[12] Claims of unconstitutionality have been rejected by various United States District Courts. A sweeping declaration upholding Title III appears in *United States v. King* mentioned above;[33] the Court said that the provisions of Sec. 2518 of Title III "meet the requirements of specificity, narrowness, particularity, and judicial supervision, set out in *Berger, Katz,* and *Osborn*" and represent no invasion of Fourth Amendment rights.[34]

Despite Federal court decisions upholding the constitutionality of Title III, a United States District Court in Philadelphia ruled that Title III was unconstitutional on its face as a violation of the Fourth Amendment because of the lengthy period of eavesdropping permitted (*United States v. Whitaker*).[20]

The United States Supreme Court has not yet considered constitutionality of Title III as a whole. It has inferentially admitted constitutionality of some sections of the law. In *Cox v. United States*, the Supreme Court declined to review a decision of the Court of Appeals for the Tenth Circuit upholding Sec. 2517(5) which permits interception and use of a communication relating to an offense other than that specified in the court order if the judge finds, on subsequent application, that the conversations were intercepted as provided by Title III.[8] This case is discussed at length in Chapter 5. The Supreme Court has also acknowledged the validity of Title III indirectly by interpreting some of its provisions (*United States v. United States District Court; Gelbard v. United States*).[35] The first case involved warrantless eavesdropping on political dissidents in so-called "national security" cases discussed in Chapter 6. The Gelbard case was concerned with refusal of witnesses to testify before a grand jury on the ground of illegal eavesdropping.

Grand Jury Witnesses—Illegal Eavesdropping

Civil contempt proceedings were brought in several cases against witnesses who refused to testify before Federal grand juries on the ground that interrogation was based on illegal eavesdropping. May such a recalcitrant witness invoke the evidentiary prohibition of Sec. 2515 as a defense to the contempt charges? Conflicting opinions in various Circuits of the Court of Appeals have been considered by the United States Supreme Court and a decision was handed down at the end of June, 1972 (*Gelbard v. United States*). In a 5 to 4 opinion, the Supreme Court upheld the right of witnesses to invoke Sec. 2515 of Title III as a defense to contempt charges.[36]

In the Ninth Circuit, the Court of Appeals had decided that witnesses were *not* entitled to refuse to testify (*United States v. Gelbard; Bacon v. United States*).[37] The Court of Appeals in the Third Circuit came to a contrary conclusion, holding that they could refuse (*In re Egan*).[38] In the District of Columbia Circuit, the Court of Appeals reversed the District Court which had held the witnesses in contempt; the Court of Appeals referred to the *Egan* case in the Third Circuit as offering "the only sensitive and penetrating analysis" of the law (*In re Evans*).[39]

The majority opinion of the Supreme Court in *Gelbard* was written by Justice Brennan. Concurring opinions were presented by Justices Douglas and White. A sharp dissenting opinion by Justice Rehnquist was joined in by

ustices Burger, Blackmun, and Powell, thus presenting a solid front by the
our Nixon appointees. Justice Brennan noted that protection of privacy was
n overriding Congressional concern in enacting Title III; the prohibition
gainst use of evidence obtained through illegal eavesdropping was to
nforce limits imposed on wiretapping and electronic surveillance. It is
entral to the legislative scheme, observed Justice Brennan, and its im-
ortance as a protection for "the victims of an unlawful invasion of privacy"
ould not be made more clear. Section 2515 not only serves to protect the
rivacy of communications, but also to insure that the courts do not become
artners to illegal conduct.

Justice Douglas used even stronger language in his concurring
opinion. He reiterated his opposition to *all* wiretapping and bugging:

> I would hold that Title III of the Omnibus Crime Control and
> Safe Streets Act of 1968 offends the Fourth Amendment, as does all
> wiretapping and bugging, for reasons which I have often expressed
> elsewhere.[40]

The case under consideration by the Court was compared by Justice
Douglas with a Supreme Court decision handed down more than half a
century ago (*Silverthorne Lumber Co. v. United States*) in which Justice
Holmes wrote the opinion barring the Government "from reaping any fruit
from its forbidden act."[41] Justice Douglas urged that petitioners in *Gelbard*
be given an opportunity to prove their allegations of illegal eavesdropping
and, if successful, to withhold from the Government "any further rewards
of its 'dirty business' ". It degrades the integrity of the judicial system, he
argued, when a court assists the Government in extracting fruits from the
victims of its lawless searches. Justice Douglas seemed convinced that
illegal eavesdropping had occurred:

> We are told that police are often tempted to make illegal
> searches during the investigations of a large conspiracy. Once the
> police have established that several individuals are involved, they may
> deem it worthwhile to violate the constitutional rights of one member
> of the conspiracy (particularly a minor member) in order to obtain evi-
> dence for use against others.[42]

Justice White took a milder stand in his concurring opinion. He would
have preferred to distinguish between cases in which the Government
produced a court order and those involving warrantless eavesdropping.
This issue was left open by the Court's decision. Justice White stressed that
if the Government officially denied electronic surveillance of the witness,
the matter was at an end and the witness would have to answer. A stay of
sentence for civil contempt was, in fact, denied in another case by Justice

Douglas as Circuit Judge, where the Government represented to the District Court that no wiretap had been used and the applicant presented no evidence or indicated probable cause to believe that his privacy had been invaded by wiretapping (*Russo v. United States*).[43]

The dissenting opinion of Justice Rehnquist in *Gelbard* boldly accused the majority of "utter disregard for the relevant legislative history" of Title III, and flatly stated that the decision of the Court was "wrong." While conceding that two pertinent sections of the 1968 Act conflict [Sec. 2515 and Sec. 2518(10)(a)], Justice Rehnquist offered a different construction which he believed was "at least equally plausible." He accused the majority of attributing to the drafters of the *Senate Report* on Title III "a lower level of understanding of the subject matter with which they were dealing than I believe is justified." The Court, he said, "has at least figuratively stood on its head both the language and the legislative history" of this provision of Title III.[44]

The political overtones of the cases involving recalcitrant witnesses before the grand jury and their charge of illegal eavesdropping by the Federal government seem to be reflected in the opinions of the Justices of the Supreme Court in *Gelbard*. At stake was the fate of grand jury witnesses in the *Egan* case (Third Circuit) and in *Evans* (District of Columbia). In the Third Circuit, Sister Joques Egan, a member of the Order of Sacred Heart, was called to testify before the grand jury as to an alleged plot to kidnap Henry Kissinger, adviser to President Nixon, and other offenses. She refused to answer on grounds of conscience, and also because the information which prompted the questions propounded flowed from illegal wiretapping and electronic surveillance. The Government did not deny wiretapping or claim that it had obtained authorization by court order. In the District of Columbia, the questions which the witnesses refused to answer related to their connection with peace movements. Carol Evans refused to answer the following questions on the ground that they were the fruit of an unlawful wiretap:

1. Have you now or ever had any connection with the People's Coalition for Peace and Justice?
2. What is the May Day Collective and have you ever been a member of that Collective, or had any connection with the Collective?
3. Have you ever traveled for, or on behalf of, the People's Coalition for Peace and Justice?
4. Have you ever attended any meetings with members of the May Day Collective in which May Day activities were discussed?

In *Evans*, the District of Columbia Court noted that there was far more at stake than just the smooth functioning of grand jury investigations. Circuit Court Judge J. Skelly Wright, in a concurring opinion, called it a "fantastic absurdity" to claim that the civil contempt judgment of the lower court should be affirmed on the ground that the witness had no "standing" to raise the issue:

> For a Court, on petition of the executive department, to sentence a witness, who is herself the victim of the illegal wiretap, to jail for refusal to participate in the exploitation of that crime in violation of the explicit command of Section 2515 is to stand our whole system of criminal justice on its head.[45]

Justice Rehnquist believes that the majority of the Supreme Court, by its decision in *Gelbard v. United States*, has "stood on its head" the language and legislative intent of Title III. Judge Wright of the Court of Appeals seems equally certain that if the view of the dissenters in *Gelbard* had prevailed, the whole system of criminal justice would have been "stood on its head"![46]

Federal Eavesdropping in States Banning Interceptions

What happens when State law prohibits eavesdropping, but Federal agents intercept conversations in the State under court order authorized by Title III of the Omnibus Act of 1968? Should a Federal court sitting in that State refuse to admit the conversation in evidence? If a State official participated in the eavesdropping, would the Federal government be barred from using the intercepted communications? This is a problem in Federal-State relations that may ultimately have to be decided by the United States Supreme Court, unless all the States enact laws permitting eavesdropping in conformity with Title III. The question has been considered by at least one court, the United States District Court in California (*United States v. King*).[2]

In the King case, defendant contended that since California law prohibited wiretapping, a Federal court in that State should not admit any information so obtained, even without participation by a State official. The District Court rejected this view on the basis of the "supremacy clause" of the United States Constitution, Article VI, clause 2, which provides:

> This Constitution, and the Laws of the United States which shall be made in Pursuance thereof . . . shall be the supreme Law of the Land . . . any Thing in the Constitution or Laws of any State to the Contrary notwithstanding.

The testimony in *King* showed that a San Diego County Deputy Sheriff was present at the surveillance site on one occasion during wiretapping by Federal agents. The District Court ruled that his participation was minimal and that the wiretap evidence was admissible.

9

Evaluation of Eavesdropping

Balancing Liberty against "Law and Order"

Eavesdropping under law can be justified, its supporters say, through a balancing process. The individual's right to privacy and freedom guaranteed by the Constitution must be weighed against society's need for "law and order." In a scheme of "ordered liberty" such as the American system of government, the scale is in equilibrium when wiretapping and electronic surveillance are allowed, with adequate safeguards to protect privacy.

The balance approach to the problem of government intrusions into private lives appeals to common sense, but it is difficult to apply. To strike a balance between competing interests, the elements on both sides should be measurable and capable of being weighed in similar terms. The right to privacy and freedom, however, does not lend itself to accurate measurement.

> If a measure in the long run restricts freedom, who can say whether freedom has been reduced, and by how much?[1]

It is also almost impossible to assess either need or effectiveness of eavesdropping in achieving "order." Senator Philip A. Hart (Democrat of Michigan), a strong opponent of eavesdropping, doubts that "balancing" can ever work:

> I did not buy the idea that we could balance out these competing principles, society's interest, the individual's rights, in the fashion that they proposed it without doing more damage than good. I still have terrible difficulty convincing myself that there is a way.

> How you can balance these things, I don't know, and I envy the editorial writers who think they do.[2]

The same skepticism as to "balancing" was expressed by Ramsey Clark in his testimony before the Senate Subcommittee on Administrative Practice and Procedure in 1967:

I really do not subscribe to the balance theory. In my judgment we have the potential to enlarge simultaneously the public safety and the right of privacy. I do not think it is a matter of balance . . . it is a matter of devotion of adequate resources to secure the public safety. . . . Manpower . . . devoted to wiretapping and electronic eavesdropping . . . might be more beneficially used for purposes of public safety in other ways.[3]

Clark rejected the idea that a conflict exists between the rights of the individual and the safety of society:

There is no contest between liberty and safety. We have the means of enlarging both. Unless we do, we will lose both, because neither freedom nor security can long endure without the other . . . nothing can so weaken security as the loss of liberty.[4]

There may be logic in the argument against balancing liberty against public safety, but so far as wiretapping and electronic surveillance are concerned, the balancing process cannot be avoided. Eavesdropping under law is an accomplished fact, and in order to evaluate it in practice, the significant elements on each side of the scale must be identified and weighed as accurately as possible. Selection of factors to be pitted against each other can obviously distort the conclusions. Suppose, for example, one weighs the rights of the individual against the "survival of society," as Senator Hruska did in the debate on the eavesdropping law:

Sen. Percy: Does the Senator from Nebraska feel that the pendulum of our system of criminal justice has swung too far away from the public's right to protection from the criminal element?

Sen. Hruska: There has been a loss of balance . . . between the rights of the individual on the one hand and the rights of survival of society on the other.[5]

The conclusion from this dialogue is that whatever is needed for the survival of society must outweigh the rights of the individual. But is it the survival of society that is at stake in balancing liberty against "law and order"? Crime is bad and dangerous, but it is not the atom bomb. The right of privacy and freedom in a democratic society has to be balanced, not with survival, but against the needs of law enforcement and the effectiveness of eavesdropping.

As to the *right of privacy,* one must ask whether intrusions against innocent persons have been minimized by the safeguards provided by the law and have been carried out in practice. Some weight must also be given to the potential for abuse inherent in eavesdropping and whether Title III has reduced illegal eavesdropping. As to law enforcement *needs* and *effec-*

tiveness of eavesdropping, it must be determined whether public security has been strengthened by use of Title III against organized crime and serious offenses. Has the law been used against the targets intended, and has it resulted in convictions of top echelon offenders? The sensitivity of the public in a society that places a high value on "freedom" must also be considered in weighing the right of privacy against law enforcement needs, and this depends on who are the subjects of surveillance and for what purpose wires have been tapped.

The American Civil Liberties Union claims that the safeguards of Title III are a fraud and that eavesdropping is an indiscriminate dragnet. This is an extreme view and can be questioned in an objective appraisal of Title III. Examination of the law in operation, however, reveals that overhearing a vast number of innocent conversations is unavoidable where interceptions are continued over a long period of time. In *United States v. Tantillo*, the case described in Chapter 8, many conversations intercepted during almost a thousand hours of wiretapping had no relation to the offense covered by the court order. Invasions of privacy can be minimized only by limiting the duration of orders to a short period, restricting them to serious cases where less intrusive tools of law enforcement are clearly not serviceable, and supervising monitoring of conversations closely. Court orders have authorized eavesdropping for periods that appear excessive; they have been used extensively against individuals in all levels of gambling and narcotics; and supervision of monitoring agents has not been very stringent, particularly at the State level. Even in Federal eavesdropping, instructions to monitoring agents have been criticized by the courts.

The most careful scrutiny by an impartial judge of applications for orders and continued judicial concern throughout the period of the order are essential if safeguards are to be meaningful and invasion of privacy is to be kept to a minimum. The ease with which it is possible to go to a friendly judge who will sign an order for whatever period a prosecuting officer asks, and the failure of State judges to require written progress reports, leave the door open to unjustified invasions of privacy.

The conclusion is inescapable that to the extent that safeguards provided by Title III are ambiguous, the statute as enacted is inadequate in protecting privacy. Insofar as the ideal of continuing scrutiny by an impartial magistrate has not been realized in practice, the safeguards against undue invasion of privacy have not been fully applied. In balance, privacy has been weakened.

After several years of operation under Title III, Senator McClellan who sponsored the eavesdropping statute declared that "there has not been reported a single instance of abuse or misuse of the authority and the power that the Act confers." [6] This may, of course, be pure rhetoric to attest to the success of the law. There really is no way of knowing how much illegal eavesdropping has been going on. The temptations are so great, the opportunities so wide, and the risk of detection so slight that it would be naive to believe that Title III has eliminated all illegal eavesdropping. Senator McClellan is not naive, and it is not unlikely that his confidence has been shaken since disclosures in the Watergate case.

Each person interviewed in obtaining data for this study was asked whether he or she believed that investigating agents were eavesdropping illegally despite Title III which now makes legal wiretapping and electronic surveillance available. Some said illegal eavesdropping was possible, others said it was probable, and a few were sure that conversations not covered by court orders were being intercepted. Former Congressman Emanuel Celler, long a foe of eavesdropping, is certain that illegal wiretapping occurs all the time:

> Once you give them the tool, you can't stop it. The police with wiretapping equipment listen to everything, if only out of curiosity.

A member of the staff of the Subcommittee on Administrative Practice and Procedure, headed by Senator Edward M. Kennedy (Democrat of Massachusetts), who has expressed doubts as to the wisdom of official eavesdropping, declared unequivocally that illegal eavesdropping continues:

> Proponents of Title III said this was going to stop illegal eavesdropping, but it hasn't. If the police get a certain amount of authorization, they are going to say they do wiretapping with authorization. . . . If they met constitutional standards, there would hardly be any eavesdropping. The court order gives them a piece of paper and they use it to justify listening to everything.

Those who favor eavesdropping under Title III are inclined to minimize the potential for abuse; those who oppose it are sure that illegal eavesdropping is extensive. There is nothing to indicate that Title III has made any appreciable difference either in increasing or reducing illegal eavesdropping.

Since early 1971, the Federal government has discontinued its past policy of making voluntary disclosure to criminal defendants of illegal electronic surveillance. A man convicted of planting a bomb on an airliner argued, on petition to the United States Supreme Court for a writ of certiorari, that the Government must disclose whether there had been electronic surveillance, and that he was entitled to a judicial determination of the existence and legality of any eavesdropping. The Government had refused to reveal whether he had been the object of indirect eavesdropping. The Supreme Court by a vote of 7 to 2 denied the petition for appeal and let the conviction stand. The Court refused to consider the issue of the Government's burden to disclose any type of illegal eavesdropping evidence (*Cook v. United States*).[7]

Justice Douglas, joined by Justice Brennan, protested vehemently in dissent that the appeal should have been granted. "Electronic surveillance is today common and pervasive," said Justice Douglas, "as we know from reports filed pursuant to Sec. 2519(3) of the Act [Title III] and from various Senate and House investigations, including the one by Senator Ervin." The Government's refusal to make disclosure raised new and important questions involving "high matters of policy" affecting many cases. Said Justice Douglas:

> It is appropriate that we reach the questions here and now so that the procedures to be used in protecting the rights of the citizen and confining the prosecution within constitutional bounds be resolved. . . . The procedure . . . is not relevant only to criminals. . . . These invasions of privacy apparently touch not only criminals but also reputable people whose only offense is political, social, or ideological non-conformity.

Even if the Government admits to eavesdropping, the right of a defendant to examine the transcript is not clearly established. In the case of the secret study on the Vietnam War, known as the "Pentagon Papers" (discussed in Chapter 5), the trial of Dr. Daniel Ellsberg and Anthony J. Russo, Jr. was postponed temporarily while the question was being litigated, but the Supreme Court eventually dissolved the stay.[8] The Government could have decided to disclose the details of the wiretap and proceeded at once with the trial. However, if the eavesdrop was conducted on a foreign embassy or other sensitive area, this revelation would have been even more objectionable than delay in the trial.

In some cases the Justice Department has dropped prosecutions to avoid answering defendant's motion to disclose details of electronic surveillance. The indictment against Leslie Bacon for perjury before a grand jury in connection with bombing the United States Capitol in the Spring of 1971 was dismissed with permission of the Federal District Court in August 1972.[9] The Justice Department was unwilling to reveal either the nature of the surveillance or the persons involved. The Government also asked for dismissal of contempt charges against Bobby Seale, Black Panther leader, to avoid permitting him or his attorneys to examine transcripts of electronic surveillance recordings introduced at the conspiracy trial of the "Chicago 7."[10]

Opinion is divided on the *need* for eavesdropping in law enforcement. Before enactment of Title III in 1968, many police chiefs, prosecutors, and other law enforcement spokesmen testified before the Senate Subcommittee on Criminal Laws and Procedures that eavesdropping was an indispensable tool in dealing with organized crime. Opponents of eavesdropping, including some prosecuting officials, claimed it was a costly, wasteful, lazy-man's weapon, a threat to innocent persons, and useless against top echelon criminals. A decade of hearings in Congress produced nothing but conflicting expert opinion on the question of need for eavesdropping. No one ever succeeded in proving need, or even in defining it clearly; nor was it ever settled who should bear the burden of proving need. How, then, is need to be weighed in a balancing process? As a start, alternatives to eavesdropping would have to be analyzed, and time and cost factors compared. Would the same resources devoted to normal types of surveillance produce equal or better results, or no results at all? If Title III has not been used effectively against organized crime or limited to serious offenses, the need for eavesdropping to promote public safety is weakened in balancing it against invasion of privacy.

Operation of Title III since 1968 has demonstrated neither need nor lack of need for eavesdropping. Nor does the information required to be furnished in reports under Title III further the examination and analysis of need. Cost of each wiretap order must be reported, but the basis of cost is ambiguous and the relation between cost and results of interception is unclear.

Has Title III been *effective*? If it has not, then the balance is tipped in favor of the right of privacy and against eavesdropping in law enforcement. "Effectiveness" is a vague concept. One factor that Congress seems to have considered significant in "effectiveness" is the number of arrests and convictions that result from eavesdropping, since this item of information must be included in official reports. Commenting on the number of arrests and indictments shown in the annual report to Congress, Senator McClellan said:

> The effectiveness of this statute in the war on organized crime is now firmly established.[11]

But former Attorney General Ramsey Clark insists that many of the persons whose wires were tapped might have been arrested and convicted without eavesdropping.[12] Those who favored eavesdropping before the law was passed now claim it is effective. Those who opposed it question the adequacy of the statistics to show effectiveness and deny that any meaningful relationship exists between wiretapping and arrests or convictions.

A leading academic spokesman for foes of eavesdropping, reporting on its costs and benefits in December 1971, noted that eavesdropping in 1970 involved 10,260 people, conversations overheard totaled 147,780, and only forty-eight convictions were produced. In the twenty-one non-gambling and non-drug cases reported for 1970, no convictions resulted. According to his interpretation of the figures, eavesdropping under law is ineffective—and expensive!

The report to Congress by the Administrative Office of the United States Courts gives the average number of persons involved "per order where installed." For 1972 the average number of persons involved per order was reported to be fifty-one. Since 855 orders were issued in 1972, it is simple to calculate that the number of persons involved were 43,605 (855 × 51)—more than four times the number in 1970. The report, however, does not present this statistic. As to number of conversations overheard, the report to Congress for 1972 states that the average number of conversations overheard was 600, and that at least one half of the intercepts produced incriminating evidence. For 1971 it was reported that six out of ten intercepts were incriminating.

The report for 1972 notes that "there was only a 5 per cent increase in wiretap applications filed in 1972 over 1971." It acknowledges, however, that the number of authorizations increased 184 percent from 1969, the first complete calendar year the statute was in effect. Senator John L. McLellan, who observed publicly that court-ordered wiretapping rose 43 percent from 1970 to 1972, relies on the high cost of eavesdropping to prevent excessive use.[13] For 1972 the reported cost of a single intercept installed (in terms of manpower, equipment, and other costs) ranged from a low of $5 to a high of $82,628. The average cost reported was $5,435, but the average cost of a Federal order was considerably higher—$9,795. Cost must, of course, be weighed against result. Title III of the Omnibus Act of 1968 requires supplementary reports to be filed by prosecuting officials concerning court activity arising out of intercepts previously reported. The annual report to Congress for 1972 contained a table of arrests and convictions as a result of intercept orders installed during the calendar years 1969–1972. The annual report contained the totals shown in Table 3.

Law enforcement officials say that arrests and convictions could not have been obtained without wiretapping. Critics of eavesdropping, however, can always cite important investigations in which it proved to be of insignificant or no value, compared with normal techniques. It can be conceded that eavesdropping has been effective in some cases in obtaining arrests and convictions. This does not prove that other methods of surveillance would not have been equally productive. Nor, in determining effectiveness of Title III, can the quality of an arrest or conviction be ignored. If, as critics claim, Title III has been successful in apprehending

Table 3. Arrests and Convictions Resulting from
Intercept Orders for 1969–1972

Year of report	Arrests	Convictions
1969	965	381
1970	2,493	989
1971	3,452	1,030
1972	2,861	402

only small-time offenders and has failed to reach leaders of organized crime, then court-ordered eavesdropping has missed its mark. Nothing in Title III restricts use of eavesdropping to important cases. The offenses for which a Federal order may be obtained cover a wide range as the listing in Chapter 5 shows, and the types of crimes for which State orders may be obtained are practically unlimited.

Criminologists go further in denying "effectiveness"; they say that the efforts of law enforcement in offenses such as gambling, narcotics, and loan sharking which involve willing participants rather than victims can have only limited effectiveness no matter what tools are used. So long as the public wants the services provided and the demand is not satisfied through lawful channels, the illegal activities will continue. Sociologists are inclined to agree; they deplore the refusal of forces favoring wiretapping to acknowledge the relationship between crime and slums, racism, poverty. The approach of both Congress and the Executive to crime has been criticized as *political* and in large part misguided.[14]

The Government admits that while some organized crime figures have been convicted, none of the major "Cosa Nostra families" have been destroyed. Speaking of the overall impact on organized crime, the Attorney General said:

> I won't say we have them on the floor yet, but I will say they're taking a terrific pounding.[15]

Others take a dimmer view of what eavesdropping has accomplished in the battle against organized crime:

> What's being done is a hard punch on a bag of canvas packed full of water.[16]

The Nixon Administration has kept its promise to use eavesdropping extensively, and no one knows how much of it has been going on without court order in forty-eight-hour emergency and in so-called "national security" cases. It was mere chance and dogged persistence that brought to light the seventeen wiretaps on newsmen and others in the name of national security (discussed in Chapter 6).

Has all this eavesdropping been effective in establishing "law and order" and in combating organized crime? Assuming that "effectiveness" can be measured by the statistics, the answer, unfortunately, depends on how one reads the figures. It is like the F.B.I. statistics on crime. In the report on crime during 1971, the Director of the F.B.I. said that crime was rising; reading the same figures, the Attorney General said the rate of crime was decreasing. Art Buchwald, the humorist, explained the contradiction this way:

> Percentagewise crime has gone down . . . crimewise it has gone up.

In despair over slippery statistics, Buchwald decided to consult his friend, "Professor Heinrich Applebaum, the great Justice Department statistician whose definitive book *Do Decimal Points Have a Sex Life?* is used in every math class in the country." [17] Crime is no laughing matter, but an impartial observer is forced to admit that the statistics in the reports filed under Title III are not very helpful in determining whether eavesdropping has been effective in law enforcement. [18]

Since *need* and *effectiveness* are such elusive elements and defy measurement, some other factors must be found if the balancing process is used in evaluating eavesdropping. It is suggested that instead of attempting to balance the right of privacy and liberty against law enforcement needs and effectiveness of eavesdropping, one should weigh competing *values*. Is the apprehension of some criminal suspects worth the risks to privacy and personal freedom inherent in eavesdropping? If eavesdropping is permitted under a law that is ambiguous, and if it is carried on without clear standards and uniform guidelines by a large number of officials in a wide variety of cases without adequate control, the risks may be too great.

Congress and the Executive have endorsed eavesdropping by law enforcement officials under Title III, and the courts are now considering its constitutionality in theory and in practice. Has the public accepted it? Until recently, most individuals objected to wiretapping and electronic surveillance only when their own conversations or those of a group with which they identify were intercepted. In a public opinion poll conducted by a national periodical in 1969, the count was heavily in favor of eavesdropping. People in the West seemed to favor wiretapping and electronic surveillance as much as those in the East, South, or North. Many said they did not find it objectionable so long as it was restricted to organized crime or espionage. The response from big cities was no different from that of small-town residents. Public outcry against eavesdropping under Title III developed only among those who perceived themselves as special targets—Italian-Americans, political dissidents, and blacks prosecuted for gambling and narcotics offenses. [19]

Today there is popular concern about wiretapping. Revelations of surveillance by Army intelligence agents of political figures has heightened awareness of the public to governmental intrusions on the right of privacy. [20] Senator Sam J. Ervin, Jr. has charged that computerized files compiled by Federal agencies are leading the country toward a police state. Some of the information in these files was obtained through eavesdropping. Four weeks of hearings before the Subcommittee on Constitutional Rights revealed that most of the surveillance was carried on in the name of "national security." The alleged involvement of high government officials in illegal private bugging at Watergate has created wide public concern with the problem of *all* eavesdropping.

Unless eavesdropping is limited to persons suspected of serious crime, and is conducted with circumspection and restraint, public disapproval may increase and pressure may be exerted on Congress, the Executive, and the Courts to tip the scale in favor of the right of privacy. The balance between competing values of privacy and law enforcement is constantly shifting and requires periodic reexamination. Today the fear of crime is so great, that the public may still be willing to accept eavesdropping—or at least is ambivalent about it. Tomorrow it may protest vigorously against governmental intrusions if the powers under Title III are not exercised with adequate care.

National Commission for Review of Title III

Eavesdropping by law enforcement officials was authorized as an experiment, a tentative procedure on trial. Congress recognized this by providing for a fifteen-member National Commission for the Review of Federal and State Laws Relating to Wiretapping and Electronic Surveillance (called the "Commission") to come into existence six years from 1968. After pressure to bring the Commission into action at once, Congress reduced this to five years. The Commission is to file a report within two years after its formation and then go out of existence.[21]

The function of the Commission, as stated in Title III of the 1968 Act is "to conduct a comprehensive study and review of the operation of the provisions" of the law in order to determine its "effectiveness." It is not clear whether "operation" refers only to procedures and practice without consideration of ambiguities and other flaws in the law, nor does the statute indicate what is meant by "effectiveness." Is effectiveness to be determined by the impact of wiretapping and electronic surveillance on organized crime? On serious crime? As pointed out in Chapter 4, "organized crime" has been defined vaguely, and the reports do not show the seriousness of the offense for which an eavesdrop order was obtained. Is the Commission to measure "effectiveness" by the number of arrests and convictions produced? Arrests are not convictions, and convictions reported as a result of interceptions installed may have been achieved through other investigative techniques.

Is the Commission to assume that a significant relationship exists between man-hours and dollars spent and number of incriminating conversations overheard? There is dispute as to what is "incriminating" and the most effective eavesdropping in terms of number and type of conversations intercepted may entail the greatest invasion of privacy. The scope of the Commission's function does not seem to include the extent of governmental intrusion and whether eavesdropping has been excessive. The "need" for eavesdropping seems to be assumed; the Commission is only instructed to deal with "effectiveness."

According to Title III, the report of the Commission due within two years after it comes into existence is to be based on "statistical data, reports, and other information deemed necessary by the Commission to perform its function." These must be furnished by "each department, agency, and instrumentality of the executive branch, including independent agencies." How is the Commission to enforce this requirement? Subpoena power has been provided under an amendment to the 1968 Act contained in the Omnibus Crime Control Act of 1970, but even if it is available, executive agencies determined to withhold information can find ways to do so. The data to which the Commission will surely have access and on which it must rely, at least in part, consists of:

1. Reports by prosecuting officials and judges to the Administrative Office of the United States Courts.
2. Annual Reports to Congress by the Administrative Office.

According to the *Senate Report* on Title III, these were "intended to form the basis for a public evaluation" of the operation of Title III. These statistical compilations are, however, inadequate. As is abundantly clear from the data presented here, the press is justified in saying that:

> Only an independent inquiry which goes beyond the statistics can provide full light on this difficult issue of crime control and the right of privacy.[22]

The study on which this book is based is an independent inquiry that tries to show how an evaluation of official eavesdropping and a balancing of liberty and "law and order" can go beyond the statistics. An official Commission, generously funded, may be able to delve more deeply into the daily practices of law enforcement officials and perform an invaluable public service. A meaningful evaluation by the Commission must deal with the fact that ambiguities in Title III, lack of clear standards, and failure to establish and follow uniform guidelines may create threats to privacy and liberty that are intolerable in a free society. An impartial review of Title III must analyze all available data in an effort to determine whether the protections offered by the law are adequate, whether they have been weakened in practice, and in what respect modifications are needed in both law and procedure. It is hoped that the Commission will be free of political partisanship. Its fifteen member composition is fixed by Sec. 804a of Title III:

> Four appointed by the President of the Senate from Members of the Senate.
>
> Four appointed by the Speaker of the House of Representatives from Members of the House.

Seven appointed by the President of the United States from all segments of life in the United States, including lawyers, teachers, artists,
businessmen, newspapermen, jurists, policemen, and community
leaders, none of whom shall be officers of the executive branch of the
Government.

The public has an enormous stake in government eavesdropping to
combat crime. It must be alert on the one hand to the dangers of organized
crime and the difficulties in dealing with it, and on the other hand to the
gravity of the threat to privacy presented by excessive and unwarranted
eavesdropping. If liberty is to be balanced against "law and order," the
public must stand at the center of the scale and keep a watchful eye on both
sides.

10
Proposals and
Predictions

Government eavesdropping under law has involved a tremendous and costly effort in law enforcement. It has produced many arrests and some convictions, a large number of them in gambling and narcotics cases, that law enforcement officials insist would not have been possible without eavesdropping. No one claims that it has been a panacea in detecting or deterring crime. Comparatively few of the 5,000 alleged members of the "Mafia" appear to have been convicted on evidence obtained through court-ordered eavesdropping. Fear of crime has not abated.

Proposals to combat organized crime by legalizing gambling and narcotics distribution and undercutting its profits have been discussed in Chapter 4. They are gaining support, but not enough to threaten the monopoly of the crime syndicates. Analysis of the economics of loan sharking has also been suggested; financial policies of respectable lending institutions may be driving the poor, the gambler, and the ordinary businessman into the arms of the loan sharks. The most drastic remedy urged by the sociologists is a concerted effort to eliminate the slums and ghettos in which organized crime is believed to breed. Sociologists are convinced that our approach to the problem is at fault; eavesdropping permits us to do what we have been doing since the Prohibition days of the 1920s—ferreting out individual criminals who are replaced by others as soon as they are incarcerated. We must change our values and not our tools of law enforcement, give up our myths and stop being a nation of "overnight fortune hunters." Lack of success in curbing crime is a sociological and political failure, not a reflection of police inadequacy.

Long-range proposals of sociologists, criminologists, civil libertarians, and others deserve the most careful consideration, but more immediate action is needed to deal with organized crime and serious offenses. Congress has provided eavesdropping as a law enforcement tool, and Americans must live with it, at least until Congress repeals it, the Supreme Court declares it unconstitutional, or the Executive orders its agencies not to use it. Since none of these events is likely in the foreseeable future, public attention must be directed to minimizing invasion of privacy and maximizing meaningful law enforcement by correcting weaknesses in eavesdropping law and practice. The following steps are urgent if liberty is to hold its own against "law and order":

1. Clarify ambiguous provisions of Title III of the Omnibus Crime Control and Safe Streets Act of 1968.
2. Limit eavesdropping to organized crime and serious offenses.
3. Establish uniform procedures and standards for State and Federal officials.
4. Improve reporting requirements.
5. Check Federal and State practices periodically.

Clarify Ambiguous Provisions

Flaws in the law permitting court-ordered eavesdropping have been pinpointed in Chapter 5. The complex provisions outlining the procedure to be followed leave some large questions open to conflicting interpretation. Who is entitled to notice that eavesdropping has taken place? When may a motion to suppress eavesdrop evidence be made? What conversations are "incriminating"? Is it possible to satisfy the requirement that the "type" of communication be set forth in the application and order? Is gathering of "strategic intelligence" permissible?

Who Is Entitled to Notice of Eavesdropping?

Notice that eavesdropping has taken place is made mandatory by the law only with respect to the person named in the order. Others whose conversations are overheard may be notified within the discretion of the judge. Some individuals whose privacy has been invaded may never learn about it, or discover it too late to protect their rights. Of what use, then, is the provision including such persons within the definition of an "aggrieved person" who may move to suppress the eavesdrop evidence at any trial, hearing, or proceeding? Without notice of interception, the right to suppress may be meaningless. Judges recognizing the ambiguity in the law may require that notice be given to persons whose conversations were overheard, but since not all judges will do so, Congress should be urged to clarify the requirement. One United States District Court in Philadelphia ruled in June 1972 that Title III is unconstitutional on its face because it does not require subjects of secret surveillance to be promptly notified when surveillance is completed (*United States v. Whitaker*).[1]

When May Motion to Suppress Evidence Be Made?

An aggrieved person may make a motion to suppress evidence obtained by eavesdropping "before the trial, hearing, or proceeding," unless there was no opportunity to do it or the person was not aware of the grounds of the motion. The ambiguity of this provision in the law has been exposed in various cases in the courts. One case involving a motion to suppress made before arrest or indictment reached the Court of Appeals, but the result was inconclusive since the Court refused to hear the appeal.[2] In the Federal narcotics case discussed in Chapter 8 (*United States v. Tantillo*), the Court devoted six weeks to hearings on the motion to suppress and disposed of it prior to trial. In the trial of the "Chicago 7" however, the judge refused to consider or rule on such a motion until the trial was completed.[3] The question of when motions to suppress may be made and when they must be heard will ultimately reach the Supreme Court. The Court may, of course, decline to hear the question and leave clarification to Congress.

What Conversations Are Incriminating?

The frequency of intercepting "incriminating" conversations is a matter which Congress seems to have considered highly significant. It must be included in the annual report of prosecuting officials. The inference to be drawn is that if the number of incriminating conversations in relation to total number overheard is large, then the eavesdropping has been effective and interception of innocent conversations has been minimal. No attempt was made by Congress to define "incriminating." In actual practice, prosecuting officials have a hard time deciding what is incriminating, as the comments in Chapter 7 show. In the Federal government's test case discussed in Chapter 8, the Justice Department acknowledged that no two-way distinction could be made, such as incriminating or non-incriminating. Even a seven-category grouping did not insure 100 percent accuracy in describing the conversations. Some guidelines are sorely needed to help law enforcement officials determine whether or not a conversation is "incriminating." Judges may bar introduction of conversations which they consider irrelevant and juries may ignore conversations admitted as evidence which they believe are non-incriminating, but this is scant comfort for innocent persons whose conversations are intercepted. Further, the statistical figures in the reports, showing the number of intercepted conversations that were "incriminating," can carry no weight without some basis for judging accuracy. Perhaps the courts will accept the suggestion of one law enforcement official that if a conversation furthers investigation of the crime, it is incriminating. Senator McClellan who sponsored Title III says:

With more experience. . . it seems apparent that the intercepts are becoming more discriminating, a development that works well both for privacy and justice. In 1969, 39% were incriminating; in 1970, 45% were incriminating.[4]

Opponents of eavesdropping read the same figures differently: in 1969, 61 percent of conversations intercepted were *not* incriminating; in 1970, the percentage of innocent conversations intercepted was reduced by only 6 percent![5] The 1971 annual report to Congress notes that "at least six out of every ten conversational intercepts produced incriminating evidence." It appears to have arrived at the 60 percent result in this way:

Average number of intercepts per order 643

Average number of incriminating intercepts per order 399

$$\frac{399}{643} = 60\%$$

Statistics are tricky! How one reads them depends on where one believes the emphasis should be placed. The report to Congress for 1972 states that "approximately one-half of the conversational intercepts produced incriminating evidence." The report stresses averages; only a close look at each listing would reveal that in one Federal case only 10 out of 500 intercepts were incriminating (2 percent), and in another case 3 out of 191 intercepts (.015 percent), and in a third none out of 1,342 (0 percent).

What Does "Type of Communication" Mean?

A description of the type of communication sought to be intercepted must be included in the application for a court order. The order itself must indicate the type of communication. If all that is necessary is a statement of the nature of the offense to which the conversation is to relate, then the provision is meaningless, for details of the particular offense have already been set forth in the application and stated in the order. If it means a particular description of a particular conversation, then compliance may in many cases be impossible. The meaning of "type of communication" takes on added importance by the requirement that interception must end automatically when the described type of communication has first been obtained, unless the application shows probable cause to believe that additional communications of the same type will occur later.

In *Berger v. New York* the Supreme Court made it clear that the order must particularly describe the communication, conversation, or discussion to be seized, in order to discourage indiscriminate prying.[6] *Katz v. United States* did not mention this requirement.[7] The variation in wording of Title III which requires description only of the *type* and not the particular communication may be justified by practical necessity. In offenses of a continuing nature, it would be difficult if not impossible to describe a particular conversation sought. Even if a conversation could be described exactly, it is unlikely that this would inhibit intrusions where eavesdropping continued over a prolonged period. To comply fully with *Berger*, the particularity requirement would have to be narrowly construed, and strict enforcement would make Title III unusable in organized crime cases. In litigation attacking the constitutionality of Title III, the argument is almost invariably made that the particularity requirement of what is to be seized, laid down in *Berger*, is impossible to fulfill, and that therefore no warrant to permit eavesdropping can be valid. This is a question that will have to be dealt with by the Supreme Court.

May Strategic Intelligence Be Sought by Eavesdropping?

Doubt as to whether gathering strategic intelligence is allowed by the law strikes at the heart of government eavesdropping. If Title III's purpose is to combat organized crime and if top level members can be identified and reached only through wiretapping, then gathering of strategic intelligence must be allowed, or its definition clarified and procedural requirements changed. In *United States v. Tantillo* discussed in Chapter 8, a court order directed against a suspected wholesaler in narcotics yielded the name of an alleged supplier. The Government claims this is what Title III was intended to accomplish. The defense contends that the wiretap was a broad-ranging fishing expedition barred by the statute and by constitutional requirements; that the law permits eavesdropping only to obtain evidence of a particular offense by a particular person. Until the question is settled, law enforcement officials should exercise restraint and seek orders to obtain evidence of a specified offense by an identified suspect. It cannot be assumed that court-ordered eavesdropping is available for "leads." Under the present language of Title III, the Supreme Court is unlikely to sustain an order whose objective is clearly to gather information indirectly. Where, however, a wiretap incidentally discloses information as to identity of higher-ups or as to some other crime, subsequent authorization appears to be permissible under the Cox case discussed in Chapter 5.

Limit Eavesdropping to Organized Crime and Serious Offenses

Prosecuting officials admit that the vast majority of court orders obtained under the law were not directed at top echelon members of organized crime, since leaders are isolated securely from actual commission of specific offenses. Most State prosecutors acknowledged freely that they were not even sure that targets were syndicate members. Their only concern was to use the tool of court-ordered eavesdropping where investigation showed it might be useful in obtaining evidence, and to reach as high up in any criminal hierarchy as possible. If the crime revealed by an investigation was an offense covered by Title III and seemed to justify the cost, application for an order was made and generally granted. A New York law enforcement officer with long experience in court-ordered eavesdropping summed up the matter of targeting since 1968 in this way:

> There has been an increase in indictments and convictions; there is much more activity. A lot appears to cover low-ranking members of criminal groups. Some claim there is no intent to indict or convict top racketeers.

One judge voiced with startling frankness and cynicism an opinion that had been intimated by others:

> Law enforcement officials do not care whether it is organized crime or not. Once a statute is on the books it is going to be used to its utmost. Local police have wiretaps on people in the policy game. Most. . . know there is no "Mafia" in the policy game any more. . . there is not enough money in it because the payoffs to the police are too great.

As to serious crime, the annual reports to Congress show that the largest number of court orders were issued in gambling cases, with narcotics in second place. Since the annual reports do not indicate the level of the offense, it is possible that many of the targets were small-time gamblers and narcotics peddlers. One critic of wiretapping asserted flatly that official eavesdropping has not been limited to serious offenses:

> It is simply not true that electronic eavesdropping has been most often used in serious crime. In New York where it has been used most extensively, it was . . . for minor gambling and vice offenses.

Invasion of privacy of some innocent persons is inevitable in eavesdropping. It may be justified in cases of organized crime and serious offenses where other investigative techniques are inadequate, but not in ordinary cases. If prosecuting officials continue to use this powerful tool indiscriminately, they may lose it altogether. Congress may be pressed to take another look at the offenses for which a court order may be obtained. Meanwhile some self-regulation and self-restraint on the part of prosecutors seem to be in order.

Establish Uniform Procedures and Standards

Federal and State officials try to comply with the procedures in Title III to the best of their ability and follow the safeguards prescribed, as they understand them. They know that the validity of every eavesdrop order depends on such compliance, and that proper practice is as important to survival of court-ordered eavesdropping as the law itself. Irresponsibility in carrying out the procedural scheme can result in establishment of more rigid requirements by the Supreme Court, a development that could spell the end of eavesdropping as a practical law enforcement tool. Some requirements of Title III, however, offer wide opportunity for exercise of discretion, and these have been met with varying judgment and skill. The deepest pitfalls relate to: (1) contents of the application; (2) time period of the order; (3) method of monitoring; and (4) termination of interception.

Applications by State officials differ widely in meeting "probable cause" requirements and in showing inadequacy of "normal investigative techniques." Each applicant has to depend on his own competence, experience, and ingenuity. Some simply lack the training, skill, and sophistication needed to prepare applications that can survive attack in the appellate courts. Training programs and standards of draftsmanship are needed. Federal applicants are aided by centralized control in Washington, but even Federal documents vary in quality.

State officials have asked for the maximum period of thirty days in many cases. The *period fixed for interception of communications* in Federal orders has generally been limited to fifteen days. Extensions have been granted freely, and the full period has often been used. Requests for orders covering a longer period than is necessary frustrate the specific requirements of the law. State and Federal officials claim that an extended period is needed where the offense is a continuing one, but some admitted frankly that extensions are sometimes asked to postpone giving notice of the interceptions. The American Civil Liberties Union (A.C.L.U.) in Washington, D.C. says the thirty-day period does not square with *Katz v. United States* in which the Supreme Court expressed approval of interception of specific, not continuous, conversations. As to renewals, A.C.L.U. would like to see them eliminated entirely. A spokesman for the organization said in an interview:

> The moment you extend a wiretap you are engaging in intelligence surveillance and not really trying to get some specific evidence.

Even those who accept the validity of the thirty-day provision on its face favor restricting the period to less time if possible. The conservative section of the American Bar Association (A.B.A.) recommended an initial period of fifteen days in its 1971 "Standards Relating to Electronic Surveillance." The more liberal Criminal Law Council of the A.B.A. had proposed a drastic reduction to five days:

> Surveillance should be limited in all cases to an initial period of 5 days and to one extension of 5 days.[8]

Some automatic *monitoring* is still going on, at least by State officials. This defeats the requirement for minimization of interception of innocent conversations. Federal attempts at protection of innocent, privileged, and irrelevant conversations also seem to be ineffective. If monitoring is not conducted with intelligence and restraint and innocent conversations are intercepted indiscriminately, the Supreme Court may hold that the invasion of privacy outweighs the legitimate needs of law enforcement. No test has been offered to decide at what point interception is "indiscriminate." It is asking a great deal, perhaps too much, of monitoring agents to determine without guidelines when permissible limits have been reached. What is a monitoring agent to do when privileged communications are overheard unexpectedly? Often it requires legal judgment and knowledge as to the law of the jurisdiction, which the agent probably lacks. He can stop listening and recording, and risk loss of a golden opportunity to get valuable information! More often, the agent accepts the dilemma philosophically and acts accordingly. As former Congressman Celler said:

> Until one listens to a conversation it is impossible to know whether it is innocent.

Another practical problem is raised by the requirement that *interception* must cease on attainment of the authorized objective. The agent who monitors a wiretap has initial responsibility to decide when the communication sought has been overheard and to end eavesdropping at once. He must exercise on-the-spot judgment. But it is very difficult to know whether a particular conversation overheard is the one specified, and whether it will be sufficient evidence in a criminal proceeding. The tendency seems to be to continue the interception for the full period in the hope that more stuff will come across the wires to reinforce the evidence. This is surely not what Congress intended. Agents need guidance and close supervision to help them comply with the law. So far, they seem to have been left much on their own.

Administrative regulations are needed to control the agents who man the monitoring devices. Recommendations of the American Bar Association for such regulations reflect the potential and actual abuses resulting from ambiguities in the law and from lack of uniform standards, procedures, and sanctions:

1. Limit the number of agents authorized to employ the techniques.
2. Specify the circumstances under which the techniques may be used, giving preference to those which invade privacy least.
3. Set out the manner in which techniques must be used to assure authenticity.
4. Provide for close supervision of agents authorized to use the techniques.

5. Circumscribe acquisition and custody of, and access to electronic equipment by agents.
6. Restrict transcription and custody of, and access to overheard or recorded communications by agents.
7. Incorporate into training programs the materials on administrative regulation of agents employing techniques of eavesdropping.[8]

Theoretically, eavesdropping is subject to *supervision* by an impartial, wise judge. Judges, like prosecuting officials, try to comply with the required procedures. Practical necessity, however, forces them to rely on the integrity and competence of prosecutors and agents. The gap between what a judge is supposed to do and what he can do makes him vulnerable and extremely sensitive to criticism. Orders signed in good faith have been attacked in court cases, making judges very reluctant to discuss their role in eavesdropping. A friendly Federal judge in Washington, D.C. defended the secretiveness of his colleagues:

> Remember that people come to Washington . . . when they go back they write an article to blast you . . . that is what people have discovered in Washington . . . a lot of people have gotten gun-shy.

Few, if any, judges, prosecuting officials, or agents deserve to be "blasted." They make a valiant effort to comply with the complex procedures outlined in the law. Full compliance may not always be achieved, for guidelines are insufficient or non-existent, and eavesdropping presents an almost intractable problem in minimizing invasion of privacy.

Improve Reporting Requirements

The system set up in Title III for filing reports was designed to keep Congress and the public informed as to the extent of eavesdropping, offenses for which it was used, manner in which surveillance was conducted, and identity of prosecuting officials who applied for orders and judges who signed them. It was also to serve as a basis for evaluation by the fifteen-member Commission scheduled to come into being after the law had been in operation for a few years. All three reports required are statistical—the report by prosecuting officials, the report by judges, and the annual report to Congress by the Administrative Office of the United States Courts. They do not reveal any confidential information.

The standard form of report in current use by all prosecuting officials and judges was prepared by the Administrative Office with which it must be filed. Each State prosecuting official makes his own report in January of each year on each application for an order or extension during the preceding year. Federal reports are prepared by United States Attorneys, subject to final execution by the Department of Justice in Washington. Each judge who signs or denies a court order also, theoretically, makes his own report within thirty days after expiration of the order or its denial. Section 2519(2) of Title III requires prosecuting officials to report on all the items listed for judges' reports and some additional facts. In practice, the information is divided between the two types of reports. The annual report to Congress in April collates the information in the reports of prosecuting officials and judges submitted to it.

The importance of the reports has been stressed over and over again by sponsors of Title III. Senator McClellan said:

> Public accounting is essential to any system of the limited use of electronic surveillance techniques. Public support for the exercise of the power to wiretap and bug—even under court order—can only be obtained where the public is responsibly informed of the extent and character of its use.[9]

Law enforcement officials, however, do not seem to take the reports very seriously. They are a source of irritation. It takes time to fill in the forms and mail them to Washington, and why, they ask, waste precious hours answering questions that are ambiguous and furnishing information that is meaningless. State prosecuting officials are more openly critical of the reports than Federal officers. The items in the report of prosecutors that are considered vague and objectionable have been identified in Chapter 7 describing State practice in eavesdropping:

1. Average frequency of intercept.
2. Number of persons whose communications were intercepted.
3. Number of communications intercepted.
4. Number of incriminating communications intercepted.
5. Number of convictions.
6. Cost.

Disgruntlement of prosecutors is not unjustified. "Average frequency of intercepts" appears to furnish no significant information, as they contend. Taking an extreme example, if a wiretap order authorizing interception for thirty days produces nothing until the thirtieth day when fifteen conversations are overheard, a statement that the average frequency was one-half per day is meaningless. This item in the report might be improved to require a statement of the total number of days in which interceptions actually occurred out of the total number of days authorized.

"Number of communications intercepted" should include attempted as well as completed calls, for numbers calling or called can serve to identify persons connected with the suspect. Any information concerning such individuals, revealed without their consent, is an invasion of privacy that should be reflected in the report.

"Number of incriminating communications intercepted" is ambiguous, for it is not clear when a statement is "incriminating." Interpretation by the courts may be needed. Meanwhile, prosecuting officials should exercise restraint and avoid the temptation to exaggerate the number in order to justify the intrusion.

"Number of convictions" may be a misleading bit of information. It has been the source of much dispute between those who attest to the success of court-ordered eavesdropping and those who denigrate it. Officials should be required to indicate whether the conversations intercepted were used as evidence in obtaining a conviction, whether in their opinion these intercepted communications contributed substantially to conviction, and whether evidence was obtained by other investigative techniques and used.

"Cost" should require a statement of the exact amount paid to each investigator and all other individuals who spent time on the particular eavesdrop. It should include cost of equipment, plant, and any other items of expense involved in intercepting conversations, recording, and making logs and transcripts. Dollars and cents cost of a wiretap or "bug" may not be an accurate estimate of the value of bringing a criminal to justice, as some prosecuting officials argue, but it does furnish a yardstick for comparing cost by eavesdropping with cost by other methods of investigation.

The judge's report furnishes some information that does not appear in the report of the prosecuting official: the offense specified in the application, the original period authorized, the number of extensions, the period in operation, the total number of days intercepts were authorized, and the place under surveillance such as residence, business, or apartment. The offense is listed as "gambling," "narcotics," "usury," without any indication of the seriousness of the offense.

Weaknesses in reports of prosecuting officials and judges are reflected in the annual report to Congress by the Administrative Office of the United States Courts. The report to Congress summarizes the information filed with the Administrative Office by prosecuting officials and judges. Some critics claim that the annual report to Congress serves no purpose at all. They point with derision to the item averaging the cost of eavesdropping and indicating the wide range of cost, without any attempt to relate cost to results. It is true that the annual report to Congress is purely statistical, but it does fulfill an important function; the report receives a great deal of publicity in the press and brings to public attention the fact that government eavesdropping has been going on, the extent of wiretapping and electronic surveillance, and the types of offenses for which it has been used. The public is reminded that "eavesdropping under law" is a reality, and is at least given the opportunity to consider whether it has been worth the cost in invasion of privacy.

Friends of government eavesdropping believe the figures in the reports vindicate the use of this tool in law enforcement. Senator McClellan is happy with the results:

> It is seldom that an individual is privileged to see successful results mature so quickly from his efforts to strengthen the hand of law enforcement in dealing with the forces of crime and corruption.[10]

Foes of government eavesdropping feel that the results are meager and the cost in invasion of privacy too high. A spokesman for opponents of eavesdropping asks:

> Since . . . gambling and drugs cannot either be stamped out or freed from criminal entanglement merely by law enforcement techniques, is it worth allowing such a gross invasion of privacy?

He also ventures the opinion that many costs of eavesdropping are "grossly understated" in the reports. The figures show "an enormous amount of surveillance, affecting many people, at great expense, and with uncertain to meager results."[11]

Value predispositions seem to affect conclusions as to how much invasion of privacy has occurred and how far "law and order" has been furthered by government eavesdropping. The Commission that is to evaluate "effectiveness" of Title III and State statutes authorizing eavesdropping should be forewarned of the limitations of statistics in the reports, and make an independent, impartial, objective, and thorough investigation of the operation of eavesdropping under law. Only a full-scale review of this technique, in practice as well as under law, can reassure Americans that their privacy and liberty are not threatened in the effort to control crime. Without such reassurance, government eavesdropping may lose public support.

Check Federal and State Practice Regularly

Responsibility for overseeing practice and procedure under Title III and State statutes has been assumed by the Subcommittee on Criminal Laws and Procedures, headed by Senator McClellan who sponsored the law in 1968. This is standard practice in the Senate, a tradition like "senatorial courtesy" in Federal appointments and "seniority" in the committee system. No written rule prevents the Subcommittee on Administrative Practice and Procedure, chaired by Senator Edward Kennedy, or any member of Congress who doubts the wisdom of legalized eavesdropping, from checking on operation of the law. It simply has not been done. Pressure of other business is the stated reason, protocol probably a greater barrier.

The sponsoring committee with "oversight" privilege made an effort in 1969 to ascertain what law enforcement officials were doing under Title III and State statutes. Public hearings on law and practice were reported to be planned for 1972, but they were postponed. Some minor criticisms emerged from the investigation of 1969. Since then, satisfaction has been expressed with the results of eavesdropping under law. Investigation and conclusions as to practice in carrying out the law were undoubtedly made in good faith, but a watchdog with no vested interest in the success of government eavesdropping might have greater credibility and be less subject to accusation of partisanship. Some attempt to improve practices in official eavesdropping has been made by the Law Enforcement Assistance Administration (L.E.A.A.) through conferences, as discussed in Chapter 7, but L.E.A.A. has no way of forcing acceptance of its suggestions.

Congress should be urged to consider creation of an impartial, non-political agency on a continuing basis to oversee government eavesdropping under law. The Commission provided for by Title III has a limited existence for a narrow and rather ambiguous purpose, and its composition makes it vulnerable to political pressure. The Commission on Individual Rights created by the Organized Crime Control Act of 1970 has so broad a function that the problems of wiretapping and electronic surveillance are likely to be submerged. Its composition is also politically oriented. Politics should play no part in "law and order" or in eavesdropping.

Tentative Predictions

Who is to clarify ambiguous terms and clauses in the law and decide what practices are acceptable in government eavesdropping? The provisions of Title III were frozen by Congress, at least for a number of years, by creation of the Commission to review operation in the future. Members of the House of Representatives who opposed official eavesdropping and still find it distasteful estimated in 1972 that not more than forty Congressmen could be induced to consider any amendment to Title III. In the Senate, those who were and still are uneasy about government wiretapping and electronic surveillance turned their attention to other matters and left the sponsors of Title III to oversee its operation. Watergate may make a difference!

Interpretation of clauses in Title III and terms of doubtful meaning will have to come from the United States Supreme Court. Challenged practices will also be subject to judicial review. Forecasting Supreme Court action is always hazardous since so much depends on conflicting pressures, personal attitudes of the Justices, and the circumstances surrounding presentation of an issue for decision. It is particularly risky today when a change in direction of the Court can be discerned but the arrows are not all pointing the same way. Of the present members of the Court, only Justices

Brennan and Douglas have expressed open hostility toward eavesdropping. While they joined the majority in *Katz. v. United States* in 1967, thus indirectly sanctioning eavesdropping under limited conditions, their comments during oral argument in *Berger v. New York* invalidating the old New York eavesdropping law were revealing. Justice Brennan called eavesdropping legalized burglary—like having a policeman hide in a closet, and Justice Douglas in his inimitable way commented that one might as well put a policeman under the bed! In June 1972, in the decision of the Supreme Court banning eavesdropping without court order in domestic security cases, Justice Douglas was still calling electronic surveillance a dragnet device and doubting that any wiretap order could satisfy the Fourth Amendment requirements.

Justice Thurgood Marshall did not participate in *Katz*. As Solicitor General of the United States he had the distinctly unpleasant task of disclosing to the Supreme Court that the Department of Justice had installed eavesdropping devices in the hotel suite of Fred B. Black, Jr., former business associate of Robert G. Baker, for a period of three months while Mr. Black was under indictment for income tax evasion. The Solicitor General later announced that the Department of Justice would review all past and pending cases in which evidence might have been obtained by illegal eavesdropping. Justice White dissented in *Berger;* Justice Stewart, while concurring in the result reached by the majority, agreed with the dissenters that the New York law was entirely constitutional. In *Katz*, Justices White and Stewart joined in holding that electronic listening and recording constituted a search and seizure within the meaning of the Fourth Amendment. In the Plamondon case relating to domestic security discussed in Chapter 6 (*United States v. United States District Court*), Justice White's concurring opinion indicated that he favored deciding eavesdropping cases on as narrow an issue as possible and avoiding constitutional questions.

The four newest members of the Supreme Court, all Nixon appointees, are committed to the doctrine of "judicial restraint." All of them, Chief Justice Warren E. Burger, Justices Harry A. Blackmun, Lewis F. Powell, Jr., and William H. Rehnquist, are avowed "law and order" men, anxious to project a "tough-on-criminals" image. Yet three of them joined in the unanimous decision of the court holding, 8 to 0, that the Federal government may not wiretap without court approval in domestic security cases.

It is reasonably safe to predict that the Supreme Court will not declare the whole of Title III unconstitutional within the foreseeable future. There are powerful political and practical reasons why it is unlikely to do so. Regardless of the composition of the Court and its "hands off" policy on legislation, the Court would expose itself to bitter attack if this tool of law enforcement were withdrawn at a time when "fear of crime" still grips the nation. The Court will surely limit its decisions to the specific facts of the cases that come before it. Precedent is strong for deciding constitutional issues on as narrow a basis as possible, and in the present climate of "strict construction" the Court will go no further than is necessary.

If law enforcement officials make a reasonable effort to comply with the safeguards provided by the law, the Court can be expected to uphold the general scheme of court-ordered eavesdropping. Applications for court orders will be scrutinized closely by the Court, and strict compliance with the protections provided by Title III will be required. The spirit of the present Court may lead it to narrow the rights of the accused in criminal cases, but law enforcement officials should not expect that constitutional liberties will be sacrificed lightly. Chief Justice Burger has warned:

> In periods of stress there are always some voices raised urging that we suspend fundamental guarantees and take short-cuts as a matter of self-protection . . . we often found, in retrospect, that we have overreacted when basic guarantees of the individual have been denied.[12]

As cases reach the Supreme Court, it will pass on the validity of some specific provisions of Title III and the procedures followed by Federal and State officials. The Court must wait until cases are presented to it for consideration, but immediate improvements in eavesdropping practices can be effected by law enforcement officials who apply for orders, by judges who sign them, and by agents who monitor recordings. In the long run the durability of Title III will depend, not only on how the Court is inclined to interpret it, but on the pressures exerted by the public on Congress, the Executive, and even the Courts. If the power of surveillance is diverted to unintended purposes, or if it is used indiscriminately for minor offenses against selected groups, eavesdropping as a tool of law enforcement can be completely lost. Banning government eavesdropping may not have present appeal, but the pendulum may swing the other way if extended interception of innocent conversations and misuse of power are revealed.

Almost half a century ago, Justice Louis D. Brandeis called the right of privacy "the most comprehensive of rights and the right most valued by civilized men."[13] Those to whom power is entrusted to invade privacy must use it with the greatest circumspection. Senator McClellan who champions Title III has cautioned government officials of their great responsibility:

> This is an invaluable and powerful tool that must not be subjected to abuse. Those who violate the standards can and must . . . be punished and if they cannot learn to follow the law they must face loss of this law enforcement tool.[14]

Clarity in the law, promulgation of uniform standards and guidelines, strictest conformity by officials with all available safeguards, and constant vigilance by the public and the Courts are imperative if the right of privacy and eavesdropping in law enforcement are both to survive. A good measure of the right to privacy and freedom that Justices Holmes and Brandeis defended in 1928 in the Olmstead case still exists. Orwell's *1984* with its frightening picture of pervasive and inescapable surveillance continues to be an imaginative work and not a prophecy fulfilled. But unless ambiguities in Title III are clarified, procedures carefully formulated, and practice more closely supervised, eavesdropping in the name of "law and order" can erode and even destroy liberty as Americans have known it for almost 200 years.

Background Notes

1 Conflict and Controversy in Eavesdropping

1. Berger v. New York, 388 U.S. 41, at p. 71 (1967).
2. Commentaries, Ch. 13, quoted in Dash, Schwartz, and Knowlton, *The Eavesdroppers*, p. 426; Westin, *Privacy and Freedom*, p. 178.
3. Quotation is from Carroll, *The Third Listener*, p. 89. Copyright © 1969 by John A. Carroll, published by E. P. Dutton & Co., Inc., and revised with their permission. For technology of eavesdropping, see Carroll, Ch. 6; Westin, *Privacy and Freedom;* Brown, *The Electronic Invasion*, p. 30; Long, *The Intruders*, p. 65; Dash, Schwartz, and Knowlton, *The Eavesdroppers*, p. 305; "Crime and Justice in America," *Cong. Quarterly Service*, Aug. 1967, pp. 11–12.
4. U.S. v. White, 401 U.S. 745, at p. 756 (1971).
5. Lopez v. U.S., 373 U.S. 427, at p. 466 (1963).
6. Cable-tapping is discussed in *Cong. Record*, Feb. 8, 1972, H 861.
7. Commerce clause, U.S. Constitution, Art. 1, Sec. 8, Subd. 3.
8. As to Federal control, see *Senate Report* on Title III (No. 1097), p. 92; Vernon, *Syracuse Law Review*, Spring 1969, p. 615.
9. Greenawalt, *New York Law Journal*, June 15, 1970, p. 4, col. 1.
10. *New York Times*, Nov. 3, 1971, p. 47, col. 1.
11. U.S. v. U.S.D.C., 407 U.S. 297, 92 S.Ct. 2125, 32 L.Ed.2d 752 (1972).
12. Definitions of privacy are from Westin, *Privacy and Freedom*, p. 32; Fried, "Privacy," *Yale Law Journal*, Jan. 1968, p. 483; *Hearings*, Subcommittee on Criminal Laws and Procedures, Senate, July 11, 1967, p. 12.
13. Dershowitz, "The First Ten in Jeopardy," *New York Times*, June 25, 1972, Sec. E, p. 14, col. 4.
14. Quoted in Salerno and Tompkins, *The Crime Confederation*, p. 303.
15. *Task Force Report: Organized Crime*, p. 1.
16. Cressey, *Theft of the Nation*, p. 319.
17. Beck, *Canada Bar Review* (1968) p. 643.

2 Four Decades of Indecision: 1928–1968

1. For list of Congressional hearings, see *American Bar Association*, Standards Relating to Electronic Surveillance," June 1968, App. E, p. 237; *Hearings*, Subcommittee on Administrative Practice and Procedure, Senate, March 20, 1967, p. 4.

2. For legislative history, see *Hearings*, Subcommittee on Criminal Laws and Procedures, Senate, July 11, 1967, pp. 909–910; Subcommittee on Administrative Practice and Procedure, Senate, Part 2, April 20, 1967, p. 381*n*.1.
3. Cook, *The Secret Rulers*, p. 18.
4. For Congressional hearings on organized crime, see *Cong. Record*, Senate, June 29, 1967, p. 1; Cook, *The Secret Rulers*, p. 103; *Cong. Quarterly Service*, Aug. 1967, p. 2.
5. A.C.L.U. Report, *Hearings*, Subcommittee on Administrative Practice and Procedure, Senate, April 20, 1967, p. 381. See also *Cong. Quarterly Service* Aug. 1967, p. 6.
6. The late Sen. Long summarized his findings in *The Intruders*.
7. President Johnson's message is quoted in *Hearings*, Subcommittee on Criminal Laws and Procedures, Senate, July 11, 1967, p. 984, from *New York Times*, Jan. 30, 1967, p. 1, col. 1.
8. See note 7, *Hearings, p. 978.*
9. Berger v. New York, 388 U.S. 41, 87 S.Ct. 1873, 18 L.Ed.2d 1040 (1967).
10. *Task Force Report: Organized Crime* (1967) p. 19.
11. 388 U.S. at p. 113.
12. Katz v. U.S., 389 U.S. 347, 88 S.Ct. 507, 19 L.Ed.2d 576 (1967).
13. Sec. 605: 48 Stat. 1103 (1934) as amended; 47 U.S.C.A., Sec. 605 (Supp. 1969).
14. Olmstead v. U.S., 277 U.S. 438, 48 S.Ct. 564, 72 L.Ed. 944 (1928). For an analysis of this case, see Murphy, *Wiretapping on Trial.*
15. 277 U.S. at p. 464.
16. 277 U.S. at p. 478.
17. 277 U.S. at p. 470.
18. For discussion of Sec. 605, see *Cong. Digest*, Vol. 46 (1967), p. 195; *Duke Law Journal*, Oct. 1968, p. 1011; Scoular, *St. Louis University Law Journal*, Summer 1968, p. 539.
19. Nardone v. U.S., 302 U.S. 379, 58 S.Ct. 275, 82 L.Ed. 314 (1937).
20. Nardone v. U.S., 308 U.S. 388, 60 S.Ct. 266, 84 L.Ed. 307 (1939).
21. Weiss v. U.S., 308 U.S. 321, 60 S.Ct. 269, 84 L.Ed. 298 (1939).
22. Schwartz v. Texas, 344 U.S. 199, 73 S.Ct. 232, 97 L.Ed. 231 (1952).
23. Lee v. Florida, 392 U.S. 378, 88 S.Ct. 2096, 20 L.Ed.2d 1166 (1968).
24. Fuller v. Alaska, 393 U.S. 80, 89 S.Ct. 61, 21 L.Ed.2d 212 (1968).
25. Benanti v. U.S., 355 U.S. 96, 78 S.Ct. 155, 2 L.Ed.2d 126 (1957).
26. Goldman v. U.S., 316 U.S. 129, 62 S.Ct. 993, 86 L.Ed. 1322 (1942).
27. Silverman v. U.S., 365 U.S. 505, 81 S.Ct. 679, 5 L.Ed.2d 734 (1961).
28. Berger v. New York, 388 U.S. 41, 87 S.Ct. 1873, 18 L.Ed.2d 1040 (1967); Katz v. United States, 389 U.S. 347, 88 S.Ct. 507, 19 L.Ed.2d 576 (1967).
29. 388 U.S. at p. 44.
30. For details of Berger investigation, see A.B.A., "Standards Relating to Electronic Surveillance," June 1968, pp. 58–70.
31. 388 U.S. at pp. 60, 63–64.
32. 388 U.S. at pp. 64, 67.
33. 388 U.S. at pp. 68–70.
34. 388 U.S. at pp. 71, 77.
35. 388 U.S. at pp. 89, 96, 101.
36. 388 U.S. at pp. 111–112.
37. *Hearings*, Subcommittee on Criminal Laws and Procedures, Senate, July 11, 1967, pp. 933, 957; *Cong. Digest*, Vol. 46 (1967), p. 195.
38. Katz v. U.S., 389 U.S. 347, 88 S.Ct. 507, 19 L.Ed.2d 576 (1967). For analysis of

Katz see Kitch, *Supreme Court Review*, 1968, p. 133; Greenawalt, *New York ,Law Journal*, June 15, 1970, p. 4, col. 1, June 17, 1970, p. 4, col. 1; *N.Y.U. Law Review*, Nov. 1968, p. 968; Schwartz, *Criminal Law Bulletin*, Jan.–Feb. 1968, p. 85; Scoular, *St. Louis University Law Review*, Summer 1968, p. 513.

39. 389 U.S. at pp. 350n.5, 351.
40. 389 U.S. at p. 353.
41. 389 U.S. at p. 359.
42. 389 U.S. at p. 361.
43. 389 U.S. at pp. 365, 372, 373.
44. Desist v. U.S., 394 U.S. 244, 89 S.Ct. 1030, 22 L.Ed.2d 248 (1969).
45. Wolf v. Colorado, 338 U.S. 25, 69 S.Ct. 1359, 93 L.Ed. 1782 (1949). For analysis of search and seizure decisions before *Wolf*, see Landynski, *Search and Seizure and the Supreme Court.*
46. Elkins v. U.S., 364 U.S. 206, 80 S.Ct. 437, 4 L.Ed.2d 1669 (1960).
47. Mapp v. Ohio, 367 U.S. 643, 81 S.Ct. 1684, 6 L.Ed.2d 1081 (1961).
48. On Lee v. U.S., 343 U.S. 747, 72 S.Ct. 967, 96 L.Ed. 1270 (1952).
49. Rathbun v. U.S., 355 U.S. 107, 78 S.Ct. 161, 2 L.Ed.2d 134 (1957).
50. Lopez v. U.S., 373 U.S. 427, 83 S.Ct. 1381, 10 L.Ed.2d 462 (1963).
51. Osborn v. U.S., 385 U.S. 323, 87 S.Ct. 427, 17 L.Ed.2d 394 (1966).
52. U.S. v. White, 401 U.S. 745, 91 S.Ct. 1122, 28 L.Ed.2d 453 (1971). See also Williamson v. U.S., 405 U.S. 1026, 92 S.Ct. 1323, 31 L.Ed.2d 486 (1972), in which the Supreme Court denied certiorari on appeal from a judgment of the Court of Appeals for the 5th Circuit upholding introduction in evidence of recordings of conversations of an undercover agent of the Treasury Department without a warrant, indicating that the defendant maintained an illicit whiskey still. U.S. v. White has been cited and followed in both State and Federal cases. See State v. Wigley (Supreme Court of Kansas, 1972), 502 F.2d 819 and U.S. v. Bishton, 463 F.2d 887 (Ct. of Appeals, D. of C., 1972). See also Markham v. Markham, S.Ct. of Florida, 270 So.2d 813 (1973) holding that the statute does *not* permit a husband-subscriber to tap his own telephone and record his wife's conversations with the recipient of her affections; consent of one of the *parties to the conversation* is necessary.
53. 401 U.S. at p. 749.
54. Lewin, *The New Republic*, April 17, 1971, pp. 12–17.
55. Westin, *Privacy and Freedom*, p. 131.
56. 401 U.S. at p. 786.
57. 401 U.S. at p. 790.
58. 401 U.S. at p. 762.
59. *Harvard Law Review*, Vol. IV, No. 5, pp. 193–220, at pp. 193, 198.
60. Galella v. Onassis, U.S. District Court, S.Dist. N.Y., 335 F.Supp. 196 (1972). Judge Irving Ben Cooper cited Nader v. General Motors Corp., 25 N.Y.2d 560, 307 N.Y.Supp.2d 647 (1970) in which the court upheld plaintiff Nader's right of privacy under District of Columbia law; defendant's activities consisted of surveillance, shadowing, and eavesdropping. The Court in Galella v. Onassis also cited Griswold v. Connecticut, 381 U.S. 479 (1965) in support of a constitutional right of privacy. See also *New York Times*, July 6, 1972, p. 1, col. 2. For development of the law relating to privacy, see Arthur R. Miller, *The Assault on Privacy.*
61. N.A.A.C.P. v. Alabama, 357 U.S. 449, at p. 460, 78 S.Ct. 1163, 2 L.Ed.2d 1488 (1958). Citing this case, the right of associational privacy was reaffirmed by the Court of Appeals, 9th Circuit, in Bursey v. U.S., 466 F.2d 1059 (1972). The

Court in *Bursey* upheld the refusal of grand jury witnesses to answer inquiries about the identity of associates on the newspaper, *The Black Panther*, and in the Black Panther Party; the questions infringed the right of associational privacy.

62. Watkins v. U.S., 354 U.S. 178, 77 S.Ct. 1173, 1 L.Ed.2d 1273 (1957). See also Talley v. California, 362 U.S. 60, 80 S.Ct. 536, 4 L.Ed.2d 559 (1960); Time, Inc. v. Hill, 385 U.S. 374, 87 S.Ct. 534, 17 L.Ed.2d 456 (1967); Westin, *Privacy and Freedom*, p. 331; *Columbia Law Review*, May 1967, pp. 926–952.
63. Justice Joseph Story, "Commentaries" (1883), quoted in Westin, *Privacy and Freedom*, p. 331.
64. Miranda v. Arizona, 384 U.S. 436, 460, 86 S.Ct. 1602, 16 L.Ed.2d 694 (1966).
65. Tehan v. U.S. *ex rel.* Shott, 382 U.S. 406, 86 S.Ct. 459, 15 L.Ed.2d 453 (1966).
66. Griswold v. Connecticut, 381 U.S. 479, 85 S.Ct. 1678, 14 L.Ed.2d 510 (1965).
67. 381 U.S. at p. 484.
68. 381 U.S. at pp. 488, 493, 496, 500, 502.
69. 381 U.S. at pp. 508–509, 511, 521, 523, 527, 529.
70. 381 U.S. at pp. 510–512, 521.
71. Griswold v. Connecticut was cited with approval by the Supreme Court in Eisenstadt v. Baird, 405 U.S. 438, 92 S.Ct. 1029, 31 L.Ed.2d 349 (1972), holding unconstitutional a Massachusetts law prohibiting distribution of contraceptives to single persons. In Roe v. Wade, 409 U.S. 817, 93 S.Ct. 705, 35 L.Ed.2d 147 (1973), the court recognized the existence under the Constitution of "a right of personal privacy, or a guarantee of certain areas or zones of privacy, as developed in a long series of decisions." By a vote of 7 to 2, the Court struck down several provisions of the Georgia abortion law and ruled that a State may not prohibit a voluntary abortion during the first three months of pregnancy. The majority opinion was written by Justice Blackmun; the dissenters were Justices White and Rehnquist. Justice Blackmun made it clear that he preferred to base this right of privacy on the "Fourteenth Amendment concept of personal liberty and restrictions upon state action," and not on the Ninth Amendment's reservation of rights to the people as the U.S. District Court had maintained. In a companion case (Doe v. Bolton), the Supreme Court invalidated entirely the Texas abortion law. Justice Stewart, who had dissented in Griswold v. Connecticut in 1965, joined the majority in the abortion cases of 1973.

3 Politics of "Law and Order"

1. The Australian is Sir Reginald Sholl, former Justice of the Supreme Court of Victoria, Australia. See *Cong. Record*, Jan. 26, 1972, S 509.
2. As to group pressure to enact Omnibus Act of 1968, see Heinz, Gettleman, and Seeskin, *Northwestern University Law Review*, July–Aug. 1969, pp. 277–358, at p. 350.
3. For criticism of how Omnibus Act of 1968 moved through Congress, see Harris, *The Fear of Crime;* Schur, *Our Criminal Society*, p. 236. Comments on "law and order" by foes of eavesdropping appear in *The New Republic*, June 29, 1968, pp. 5–6; Harris, *Justice*, pp. 36, 39; Carroll, *The Third Listener*, p. 35. See also *New York Times*, Edit., May 3, 1970, Sec. E, p. 14, col. 1; Clark, *Crime in America*, p. 345.
4. *Cong. Record*, Nov. 4, 1971, S 17608.
5. Miranda v. Arizona, 384 U.S. 436, 88 S.Ct. 1602, 16 L.Ed.2d 694 (1966); Mallory v. U.S., 354 U.S. 449, 77 S.Ct. 1356, 1 L.Ed.2d 1479 (1957); U.S. v. Wade, 388 U.S. 218, 87 S.Ct. 1926, 18 L.Ed.2d 1149 (1967).

6. *New York Times*, June 20, 1968, p. 1, col. 1; "Law and Order," *The New Republic*, June 29, 1968, Vol. 155, No. 2, pp. 5–6; *Rutgers Law Review*, Winter 1969, Vol. 23, No. 1, p. 319ff.
7. See note 3 to this chapter.
8. Nixon Administration action is discussed in *New York Times*, Feb. 12, 1969, p. 1, col. 3; Sec. E, p. 12, col. 3. See also Department of Justice, *Attorney General's Report*, Jan. 19, 1971.
9. As to politicization of Justice Department, see Dershowitz, "Crimes of Degree," *New York Times*, Feb. 21, 1971, Sec 7-Part II, p. 4; Bickel, "Crime, the Courts and the Old Nixon," *The New Republic*, June 15, 1970; *New York Times*, April 26, 1970, p. 12, col. 1; March 15, 1970, p. 16, col. 3; Jan. 18, 1970, Sec. L, p. 24, col. 4; Fly, *The Nation*, June 2, 1969, p. 698; McWilliams review of Harris, *Justice*, in *New York Times Book Review*, March 22, 1970, p. 7; Navasky, "A Famous Prosecutor Talks about Crime," *New York Times Magazine*, Feb. 15, 1970, p. 32, at p. 100.
10. *Senate Report* No. 1097, pp. 94, 95. For private eavesdropping, see Brown, *The Electronics Invasion*, pp. 26–27; Carroll, *The Third Listener*, pp. 14, 15; Brenton, *The Privacy Invaders*, pp. 158, 168; Long, *The Intruders*, p. 185; Vernon, *Syracuse Law Review*, Spring 1969, p. 622.
11. Monitoring duties of the F.C.C. are preserved by Sec. 2511(2)(b). In 1953, the F.C.C. agreed with the Justice Dept. that complaints of Sec. 605 violations would be referred to the Justice Dept. for investigation and action. No change in policy has occurred since amendment of Sec. 605 by Title III. A special investigations subcommittee of the House Commerce Committee reported to Congress that officials of the F.C.C. illegally monitored office telephones of the Commission's employees during a five-week period in 1970. *New York Times*, Jan. 7, 1973, p. 61, col. 1.
12. Carroll, *The Third Listener*, pp. 163–164. Conviction for unlawful interception of wire communications was affirmed by the U.S. Court of Appeals, 5th Circuit, in U.S. v. McCann, 465 F.2d 147 (1972). But see U.S. v. Bast, 348 F.Supp. 1202 (1972) and U.S. v. Carroll, 337 F.Supp. 1260 (1971). In *Bast*, the U.S. District Court in the District of Columbia stated that advertising of a recorder to be "worn in your shirt pocket" did not mean that it was intended for "surreptitious" use. In U.S. v. Carroll, the same Court dismissed an indictment for eavesdropping where defendant recorded conversations of a business competitor's "vulgar salesman" in an adjoining hotel suite. Since defendant could and did hear the conversations (much of it consisting of incoherent jokes) through the door with the naked ear and from an uncontrived position, the circumstances did not justify an expectation of privacy.
13. Maurice H. Stans, former Secretary of Commerce, instituted two countersuits against O'Brien, one a libel action for $5 million and the other for alleged abuse of judicial process for political purposes. Stans was indicted May 1973 for conspiracy to defraud the United States and to obstruct justice, along with John N. Mitchell, in connection with the Vesco campaign contribution. Four former White House aides were ordered by a Federal judge to give depositions to attorneys for the Democratic National Committee in the $6.4 million civil suit against the Committee for the Re-election of the President in connection with the Watergate bugging. *New York Times*, May 19, 1973, p. 18, col. 1.
14. *New York Times*, May 1, 1973, p. 1, col. 7; May 13, 1973, p. 1, col. 5; May 17, 1973, p. 36, col. 5.
15. *New York Times*, May 18, 1973, p. 18, col. 1. In the fall of 1972, before creation

of the Select Committee by Senate Resolution 60, a study of the Watergate affair had been begun by the Subcommittee on Administrative Practice and Procedure, Senate Committee on the Judiciary, under the chairmanship of Senator Edward M. Kennedy. The Senate appropriated $500,000 for a year's investigation.

16. Michael, *Loyola University Law Journal* (Chicago), Winter 1970, p. 33.
17. Biddle, *Pacific Law Journal*, Jan. 1970, p. 97. See also Karabian, *Pacific Law Journal*, June 1970, p. 133; *Montana Law Review*, Summer 1971, p. 265.

4   Organized Crime—Target of Title III

1. *Cong. Record*, Senate, Vol. 115, Part 17, Aug. 11, 1969, p. 23238; *Senate Report* No. 1097, p. 70.
2. *Senate Report* No. 1097, pp. 70–74.
3. *Hearings*, Subcommittee on Criminal Laws and Procedures, Senate, July 12, 1967, pp. 1090, 1094, 1095.
4. *Cong. Record*, May 10, 1971, S 6476.
5. *Hearings*, Subcommittee on Criminal Laws and Procedures, Senate, July 11, 1967, p. 962.
6. See note 5, *Hearings*, July 12, 1967, p. 1092.
7. For Mitchell's statements, see *New York Times*, Oct. 11, 1970, Sec. E, p. 9, col. 4; *Cong. Record*, Oct. 26, 1971, S 16784.
8. *New York Times*, July 28, 1971, p. 32, col. 1.
9. *New York Times*, April 13, 1972, p. 1, col. 5. See also Nicholas Gage, "But It Helps to Be a Hood," *New York Times*, Oct. 1, 1972, p. 8, col. 6.
10. For role of organized crime, see Schur, *Our Criminal Society*, p. 112; Tyler, *Organized Crime in America*; Dorman, *Payoff*; Bell, "Crime as an American Way of Life," *Antioch Review*, June 1953, pp. 131–154; Hills, "Combating Organized Crime in America," *Federal Probation*, March 1969, pp. 23–28. See also Ianni, *A Family Business*.
11. Bell, *Antioch Review*, June 1953.
12. Hills, *Federal Probation*, March 1969.
13. Cressey, *Theft of the Nation*; Salerno and Tompkins, *The Crime Confederation*; Pileggi, "The Story of T—To Be a Mafia Boss—It's Better than Being President of the United States," *New York Times Magazine*, March 29, 1970, p. 12. See also *New York Times*, Sept. 14, 1970, p. 15, col. 1.
14. For a discussion of the 1957 Apalachin meeting, see Cressey, "The Functions and Structure of Criminal Syndicates;" *Task Force Report: Organized Crime*, App. A, 1967, pp. 32–33.
15. *The Challenge of Crime in a Free Society*, U.S. Government Printing Office, Washington, D.C., Feb. 1967, pp. 192, 198–200. See also Clark, *Crime in America*, pp. 68, 83; Talese, *Honor Thy Father*, p. xiv.
16. For criticism of Department of Justice, see Harris, *Justice*, p. 162.
17. For protests of Italian-American Civil Rights League, see *New York Times*, July 5, 1970, Sec. E, p. 2, col. 7; July 14, 1970, p. 75, col. 4; July 19, 1970, Sec. L, p. 57, col. 1; July 31, 1970, p. 27, col. 3.
18. As to gangland murders, see *New York Times*, Aug. 17, 1972, p. 1, col. 7; Dec. 14, 1972, p. 56, col. 4; Jan. 18, 1973, p. 73, col. 3.
19. *Challenge of Crime in a Free Society*, p. 191.
20. *New York Times*, July 27, 1972, p. 35, col. 5.
21. For corruption in New York and naming of special state prosecutor on recommendations of the Knapp Commission, see *New York Times*, Aug. 7, 1972, p. 1,

col. 6; Sept. 20, 1972, p. 1, col. 5; Sept. 24, 1972, Sec. E, p. 9, col. 1; Sept. 25, 1972, p. 1, col. 4; Sept. 26, 1972, p. 31, col. 3; Dec. 16, 1972, p. 1, col. 6; Dec. 23, 1972, p. 26, col. 5. Connection between organized crime and corruption is treated in Dorman, *Payoff;* Turkus and Feder, *Murder, Inc.*, pp. 492–493; Cook, *A Two-Dollar Bet Means Murder*, p. 63; Allen, *Merchants of Menace*, p. 173; Cressey, *Theft of the Nation*, p. 249; Burnham, *New York Magazine*, Sept. 21, 1970, pp. 30–37; *New York Times*, June 8, 1970, p. 28, col. 1; May 10, 1972, p. 33, col. 3; Cook, *The Corrupted Land*, pp. 73, 255, 331, 335. For scope of police corruption, see *Cong. Record*, Dec. 2, 1971, E 12873.

22. *Police Times*, Jan.–Feb. 1972, p. 19. For discard of "rotten-apple" theory, see *New York Times*, Edit., Aug. 8, 1972, p. 32, col. 1.
23. William V. Shannon, "The Unhappy Police," *New York Times*, Sec. E, Oct. 24, 1971, p. 15, col. 1.
24. For gambling history, see King, *Gambling and Organized Crime*, p. 23; lotteries, pp. 72–74.
25. Numbers betting is discussed in *Hearings*, Subcommittee on Criminal Laws and Procedures, Senate, July 11, 1967, p. 90. See also, Cressey, *Theft of the Nation*, p. 134; *New York Times*, Edit., Dec. 13, 1972, p. 34, col. 1.
26. *New York Times*, May 13, 1970, p. 45, col. 1. See also *Commentary*, Jan. 1972.
27. *Hearings*, Subcommittee on Criminal Laws and Procedures, Senate, April 19, 1967, p. 510.
28. Public Law 91-452, 91st Congress, S 30, Oct. 15, 1970, Title VIII, Sec. 801–803. Constitutionality of the 1970 Act was upheld by the U.S. Court of Appeals, 8th Circuit, U.S. v. Wolk, 466 F.2d 1143 (1972).
29. A discussion of legalized gambling appears in *New York Times*, April 10, 1972, p. 28, col. 1; Nov. 26, 1972, p. 1, col. 5. See also *Cong. Record*, May 1, 1971, H 3827.
30. *New York Times*, July 28, 1972, p. 32, col. 2.
31. *New York Times*, July 27, 1972, p. 35, col. 4; Dec. 16, 1972, p. 1, col. 8.
32. For movement of narcotics, see Cressey, *Theft of the Nation*, pp. 93–94; *Forbes*, April 1, 1970, p. 19; *New York Times*, July 30, 1970, p. 14, col. 3; April 6, 1971, p. 1, col. 7; April 7, 1971, p. 29, col. 1; Oct. 24, 1971, Sec. L, p. 14, col. 1; Nov. 23, 1971, p. 45, col. 8; Aug. 6, 1972, Sec. E, p. 4, col. 4.
33. *Cong. Record*, June 9, 1971, S 8694.
34. "World Opium Survey, 1972" is discussed in *New York Times*, Aug. 17, 1972, p. 1, col. 8. See McCoy, *The Politics of Heroin in Southeast Asia;* Nelson Gross, "The Thai Effort," *New York Times*, July 29, 1972, p. 25, col. 7; Seymour M. Hersh, *New York Times*, July 28, 1972, p. 3, col. 5. For role of Laos on transshipment of opium, see *New York Times*, Dec. 23, 1972, p. 26, col. 3. As to the "Brazilian Connection," see *New York Times*, Nov. 2, 1972, p. 6, col. 1; the "Paraguan Connection," Dec. 6, 1972, p. 48, col. 1; Dec. 9, 1972, p. 72, col. 4; Dec. 13, 1972, p. 30, col. 1; the "Argentine Connection," Dec. 13, 1972, p. 55, col. 5; Dec. 15, 1972, p. 30, col. 3; Dec. 16, 1972, p. 1, col. 6. The story behind the "French Connection" appears in *New York Times*, Dec. 15, 1972, p. 30, col. 6; Dec. 16, 1972, p. 1, col. 6.
35. The deLouette-Fournier affair is discussed in *New York Times*, March 11, 1972, p. 26, col. 3; *Cong. Record*, Nov. 29, 1971, E 12694. For extradition from Paraguay of Joseph Ricord, charged with conspiracy to violate U.S. drug laws, see *New York Times*, Sept. 5, 1972, p. 34; Dec. 6, 1972, p. 48, col. 1; Dec. 9, 1972, p. 72, col. 4; Dec. 13, 1972, p. 30, col. 1.
36. For defense of the French, see *New York Times*, April 6, 1972, p. 10, col. 4.
37. For criticism of handling the drug crisis, see Finkelstein, *New York Law Journal*,

July 6, 1971, reprinted in *New York Times*, Oct. 24, 1971, p. 5, col. 2. A report to Congress by the General Acounting Office characterized the attempt of customs inspectors to intercept heroin at the borders as an effort "to find a needle in a haystack;" see *New York Times*, Dec. 13, 1972, p. 31, col. 1. It attributed some of the problems to jurisdictional disputes among Federal agencies; see *New York Times*, Dec. 9, 1972, p. 22, col. 3.

38. Salerno and Tompkins, *The Crime Confederation*, p. 229; Cressey, *Theft of the Nation*, pp. 77, 296. A rate of 134 percent a year was reported in *New York Times*, Oct. 26, 1972, p. 11, col. 1. Rates between 250 percent to 500 percent a year were reported in *New York Times*, Dec. 9, 1972, p. 38, col. 1.

39. Perez v. U.S., 402 U.S. at p. 149.

40. 114 *Cong. Record*, Senate, Part 11, May 22, 1968, p. 14490.

41. Perez v. U.S., 402 U.S. 146, 91 S.Ct. 1357, 28 L.Ed.2d 686 (1971).

42. 402 U.S. at p. 156.

43. 402 U.S. at p. 148.

44. 402 U.S. at p. 157.

45. For the story of the Brooklyn baker, see *New York Times*, Feb. 24, 1972, p. 35, col. 1.

46. For similarities, see Cressey, *Theft of the Nation*, pp. 7, 291; Cook, *The Secret Rulers*, p. 163. For differences, see Salerno and Tompkins, *The Crime Confederation*, pp. 203–204.

47. Hills, "Combating Organized Crime in America," *Federal Probation*, March 1969, p. 23.

48. *Task Force Report: Organized Crime*, App. D, 1967, p. 116.

49. *The Challenge of Crime in a Free Society*, p. 209.

50. "Manual on the Mafia," *Newsweek*, June 23, 1969, pp. 37–38.

51. Joseph Epstein, "Browsing in Gangland," *Commentary*, Jan. 1972, Vol. 53, No. 1, p. 54.

52. For difficulty in dealing with consensual crimes, see note 48 to this chapter; Clark, *Crime in America*, pp. 68–69.

53. *New York Times*, July 23, 1972, Sec. E, p. 4, col. 1.

54. *Cong. Record*, Senate, June 29, 1967, Vol. 113, No. 104, p. 3.

55. *Cong. Record*, May 11, 1971, H 3827.

56. *New York Times*, Aug. 20, 1972, Sec. E, p. 3, col. 1.

57. See note 54 to this chapter.

58. Thomas G. Schelling, "Economic Analysis and Organized Crime," App. D, annexed to *Task Force Report: Organized Crime*, 1967, p. 123; *Cong. Record*, Senate, 90th Congress, 1st sess., June 29, 1967, Vol. 113, No. 104, p. 2.

59. Public Law 91-452, 91st Congress, S 30, Oct. 15, 1970; U.S. Code, Title 18, Ch. 96, Sec. 1962.

60. *New York Times*, July 23, 1972, Sec. E., p. 4, col. 4.

61. Life-style of members of organized crime is described in *Cong. Record*, Senate, June 29, 1967, Vol. 113, No. 104, p. 8.

62. *New York Times*, May 12, 1972, p. 1, col. 2. For press comments on Hoover's death, see *New York Times*, May 3, 1972, p. 1, col. 3; p. 52, col. 1, 5; p. 53, col. 1; May 4, 1972, p. 45, col. 1; p. 18, col. 3.

63. Tom Wicker, "What Have They Done Since They Shot Dillinger," *New York Times Magazine*, Dec. 28, 1969, p. 3.

64. 86 *Cong. Rec.* App. 1472, March 18, 1940, quoted in *Hearings*, Subcommittee on Administrative Practice and Procedure, Senate, Part 2, April 20, 1967, p. 406.

65. *Ramparts*, Jan. 25, 1969, pp. 47–51.

66. Intelligence reports of F.B.I. are discussed in Cressey, *Theft of the Nation,* p. 22.
67. Travel Act, U.S. Code, Title 18, Sec. 1952, Public Law 87-27, Sec. 1-A, eff. Sept. 13, 1961, as amended by Public Law 89-69, eff. July 7, 1965.
68. For bugging by the F.B.I., see *New York Times,* June 14, 1969, p. 1, col. 6; Jan. 11, 1970, p. 68, col. 2; Clark, *Crime in America,* p. 296. Excerpts of recordings appeared in *New York Times,* June 11, 1969, p. 1, col. 6. See also *New York Times,* June 22, 1969, Part IV, Sec. E, p. 16, col. 4.
69. Alderman v. U.S., 394 U.S. 165, 89 S.Ct. 961, 22 L.Ed.2d 176 (1969).
70. Comments on recorded conversations appear in *New York Times,* June 15, 1969, p. 52, col. 1; June 17, 1969, p. 34, col. 1.
71. Navasky, *Kennedy Justice,* p. 70ff., p. 88ff. For an account of alleged circulation by F.B.I. personnel of recorded conversations of Dr. Martin Luther King, Jr., see Navasky, pp. 35n., 137.
72. *New York Times,* Jan. 9, 1972, p. 17, col. 8.
73. "J. Edgar Hoover Speaks Out," *Cong. Record,* Jan. 19, 1972, H 139.
74. Cook, *The F.B.I. Nobody Knows,* pp. 5, 363, 404–411; *The Christian Century,* July 9, 1969, p. 917; *New York Times,* July 14, 1970, p. 7, col. 2.
75. *New York Times,* March 24, 1971, p. 24, col. 3; March 28, 1971, Sec. E, p. 9, col. 1; April 13, 1971, p. 23, col. 1. For defense of the F.B.I., see *Cong. Record,* Nov. 2, 1971, E 11679, S17391; Nov. 9, 1971, H10779; Oct. 28, 1971, H 10129.
76. *New York Times,* March 19, 1971, p. 37, col. 1.
77. Gray's authority had already been undermined by withdrawal of his name as nominee for the office of Director of the F.B.I. in the face of Senate opposition to his confirmation. See *New York Times,* April 28, 1973, p. 14, col. 1.
78. Ruckelshaus had no previous law enforcement experience, and it was reported that a telegram of complaint against naming an outsider was sent to the President by 13 Assistant Directors and 58 of the 59 agents heading field offices of the F.B.I. See *New York Times,* May 13, 1973, p. 48, col. 6.
79. Public apathy is commented on by Sen. Hruska in *Cong. Record,* Senate, June 29, 1967, Vol. 113, No. 104, p. 1. See also Tyler, *Organized Crime in America,* p. 7; Long, *The Intruders,* p. 60. But some question the good faith of those who blame organized crime on public apathy; see King, *Gambling and Organized Crime,* p. 117.
80. For "Wincanton" study, see *Task Force Report: Organized Crime,* App. B, 1967.
81. The motion picture *The Godfather* is based on the book of the same name by Mario Puzo.
82. Nicholas Gage, *New York Times,* March 19, 1972, p. 6, col. 3.
83. *New York Times,* Edit., April 10, 1972, p. 34, col. 2.

5 Flaws in Court-Ordered Eavesdropping

1. U.S. v. U.S.D.C., 407 U.S. 297, 92 S.Ct. 2125, 32 L.Ed.2d 752 (1972).
2. *Senate Report* No. 1097, p. 97.
3. *American Bar Association,* "Standards Relating to Electronic Surveillance," June 1968, p. 96. "Standards" of the A.B.A. recommended in Jan. 1971 affirm the desirability of electronic surveillance in law enforcement but do not mention organized crime.
4. *Hearings,* Subcommittee on Criminal Laws and Procedures, Senate, April 19, 1967, p. 517.

5. Commonwealth v. Hunt, 45 Mass. (4 Met.) 11, 12 (1842). See also *Task Force Report: Organized Crime*, App. C, 1967.

6. The eleven-week conspiracy trial of the "Harrisburg Seven" resulted in a hung jury in April 1972. Father Philip F. Berrigan and Sister Elizabeth McAlister were subsequently convicted of smuggling letters in and out of Lewisburg prison. They appealed on the ground that the case was "tainted" by illegal wiretapping. See *New York Times*, Aug. 29, 1972, p. 20, col. 2. In June 1973, the United States Court of Appeals for the Third Circuit reversed the conviction on all but one count of smuggling on the ground that the prison warden was aware that the letters were being sent and received.

7. The wide range of offenses is criticized in Schwartz, "The Legitimation of Electronic Eavesdropping," *Michigan Law Review*, Jan. 1969, pp. 455–510, at p. 482; Theoharis and Meyer, "The 'National Security' Justification for Electronic Eavesdropping," *Wayne Law Review*, Summer 1968, p. 771; *The New Republic*, May 18, 1968, p. 4.

8. *Senate Report* No. 1097, p. 47.

9. *Hearings*, Subcommittee on Criminal Laws and Procedures, Senate, July 11, 1967, p. 975.

10. For arguments against eavesdropping to obtain strategic intelligence, see Schwartz, *Michigan Law Review*, Jan. 1969, p. 411; Vernon, *Syracuse Law Review*, Spring 1969, p. 619; Greenawalt, *New York Law Journal*, June 17, 1970, p. 1, col. 4.

11. For arguments favoring investigative eavesdropping, see *Northwestern Law Review*, March/April 1969, pp. 71–75.

12. *Hearings*, Subcommittee on Criminal Laws and Procedures, Senate, July 11, 1967, pp. 957–958, 976.

13. *Hearings*, Subcommittee on Criminal Laws and Procedures, Senate, April 20, 1967, p. 617.

14. U.S. v. Cox, 449 F.2d 679 (1971).

15. Cox v. U.S., 405 U.S. 932, 92 S.Ct. 1783, 32 L.Ed.2d 136 (1972).

16. *Cong. Record*, Dec. 1, 1971, pp. S 20041–20042.

17. U.S. v. U.S.D.C., E. Dist., Mich., 407 U.S. 297, 92 S.Ct. 2125, 32 L.Ed.2d 752 (1972).

18. 407 U.S. at p. 333n.

19. As to probable cause requirement, see *Senate Report* No. 1097, p. 102.

20. Clark, *California Western Law Review*, Fall 1968, p. 1, p. 6; Greenawalt, *New York Law Journal*, June 15, 1970, p. 4, col. 1.

21. Berger v. New York, 388 U.S. at p. 55. The definition in *Berger* also appears in Carroll v. U.S., 267 U.S. 132, 162, 45 S.Ct. 280, 69 L.Ed. 543 (1925).

22. For Supreme Court decisions see Aguilar v. Texas, 378 U.S. 108, 84 S.Ct. 1509, 12 L.Ed.2d 723 (1964); McCray v. Illinois, 386 U.S. 300, 87 S.Ct. 1056, 18 L.Ed.2d 62 (1967); Spinelli v. U.S., 393 U.S. 410, 89 S.Ct. 584, 21 L.Ed.2d 637 (1969).

23. 388 U.S. at p. 69.

24. *Senate Report* No. 1097, p. 101. As to "normal investigative procedures," see Linzer, *The Journal of Criminal Law, Criminology and Police Science*, pp. 203–214 at p. 209; Comment: *Northwestern Law Review*, March/April 1969, pp. 63–85, at p. 65n. 12.

25. *Senate Report* No. 1097, p. 104.

26. *Hearings*, Subcommittee on Criminal Laws and Procedures, Senate, July 12, 1967, p. 1118.

27. See note 26, *Hearings,* pp. 1089, 1090.
28. *Hearings,* Subcommittee on Criminal Laws and Procedures, Senate, April 20, 1967, p. 606; March 9, 1967, pp. 299, 312, 358–359.
29. See note 26, *Hearings,* at p. 1180.
30. For discussion of *time period,* see Schwartz, *Michigan Law Review,* at p. 463; Beck, *Canada Bar Review,* p. 691; Linzer, *Journal of Criminal Law, Criminology and Police Science,* p. 210.
31. *Senate Report* No. 1097, p. 104.
32. U.S. v. Whitaker, 343 F.Supp. 358, at p. 363 (1972).
33. People v. Holder, 331 N.Y.Supp.2d 557 (1972).
34. U.S. v. Scott, 331 F.Supp. 233 (1971).
35. U.S. v. King, 335 F.Supp. 523 (1971).
36. Alderman v. U.S., 394 U.S. 165, 89 S.Ct. 961, 22 L.Ed.2d 176 (1969). But see Title VIII of Public Law 91-452 (Oct. 15, 1970) which attempts to set aside the result of *Alderman* by setting up an *in camera* disclosure proceeding. It has been held that a person who was not a party to any conversation seized under a wiretap order may not assert Fourth Amendment rights. U.S. v. Wright, 466 F.2d 1256 (Ct. of App., 2nd Cir., 1972). See to same effect, *In re* Womack, 466 F.2d 555 (Ct. of App., 7th Cir., 1972).
37. Giordano v. U.S., 394 U.S. 310, 89 S.Ct. 1164, 22 L.Ed.2d 297 (1969).
38. Russo v. Byrne, 409 U.S. 1219, 93 S.Ct. 21, 34 L.Ed.2d 30 (1972); cert. denied 409 U.S. 1013. See *New York Times,* Nov. 19, 1972, p. 12, col. 1. A mistrial was declared Dec. 11, 1972 because of the long lapse of time between selection of a jury and commencement of trial; *New York Times,* Dec. 12, 1972, p. 32, col. 3; Dec. 15, 1972, p. 26, col. 4. A new jury was seated Jan. 12, 1973; *New York Times,* Jan. 16, 1973, p. 15, col. 1. As to suit for damages, see *New York Times,* Sept. 20, 1972, p. 9, col. 1.
39. *New York Times,* May 11, 1973, p. 1, col. 6; May 12, 1973, p. 1, col. 3; May 13, 1973, Sec. 4, p. 1, col. 2; May 15, 1973, p. 1, col. 8.
40. For postponement of notice by judge, see Schwartz, *Michigan Law Review,* Jan. 1969, p. 484.
41. U.S. v. Eastman, 326 F.Supp. 1038 (1971). The U.S. Court of Appeals, 3rd Circuit, 465 F.2d 1057 (1972), affirmed the judgment of the District Court, M.D. of Pa., granting the motion to suppress.
42. Application of United States, 427 F.2d 1140 (1970). See also U.S. v. Liddy, U.S.D.C., D. of C., 354 F.Supp. 217 (1973) denying motion of "aggrieved persons" to suppress contents of illegally intercepted wire and oral communications, and evidence derived therefrom.
43. *Senate Report* No. 1097, p. 106.
44. *Senate Report* No. 1097, p. 107. For effect of reports on judges, see Parente and Muratori, "The Advocate," *Bronx County Bar Assn.,* Nov. 1969, p. 131.

6 Eavesdropping without Court Order

1. *Cong. Record,* July 6, 1971, Vol. 117, No. 103, E 7043.
2. N.J. Stat.Ann.2A:156-A, 1–26 (Supp. 1969); Notes: *Rutgers Law Review,* Winter 1969, p. 323*n.* 7.
3. District of Columbia Court Reform and Criminal Procedure Act of 1970, Subchapter III, Sec. 23-541 to 23-556; Public Law 91-358, eff. July 29, 1970. See *Cong. Quarterly,* Weekly Report June 5, 1970, p. 1497; *Cong. Record,* House of Rep., Jan. 2, 1971, H 12693; *New York Times,* July 23, 1970, p. 14, col. 2; July 24, 1970, p. 1, col. 8.

4. Sen. Hart's statement is quoted in *Rutgers Law Review*, Winter 1969, p. 362.
5. Clark, *California Western Law Review*, p. 5. For criticism of and comments on emergency eavesdropping without court order, see Linzer, *The Journal of Criminal Law, Criminology and Police Science*, p. 214; *Rutgers Law Review*, Winter 1969, pp. 334, 351, 366; Comment: *Northwestern Law Review*, March/April 1969, pp. 78, 84; *Valparaiso University Law Review*, Fall 1968, p. 100; Fly, *The Nation*, June 2, 1969, p. 698.
6. *Rutgers Law Review*, Winter 1969, pp. 359, 386.
7. U.S. v. Dellinger, Criminal No. 69–180 (N.D., Ill., Feb. 20, 1970), quoted in *New York Times*, June 14, 1969, p. 1, col. 5. For criticism of Justice Dept., see *Rutgers Law Review*, Winter 1969, pp. 319–388, at p. 387; Zion, *New York Times*, June 22, 1969, Sec. E, p. 16, col. 1; *The New Republic*, July 5, 1969, p. 6; *New York Times*, June 21, 1969, p. 26, col. 2; Theoharis, *The Nation*, June 14, 1971, p. 744.
8. U.S. v. U.S.D.C., 407 U.S. 297, 92 S.Ct. 2125, 32 L.Ed.2d 752 (1972).
9. 407 U.S. at p. 321.
10. 407 U.S. at p. 309, quoted from Katz v. U.S., at p. 358n.3.
11. 407 U.S. at p. 308.
12. 407 U.S. at pp. 306–307.
13. 407 U.S. at pp. 316–317.
14. 407 U.S. at p. 320.
15. 407 U.S. at p. 314.
16. 407 U.S. at p. 312.
17. 407 U.S. at p. 333.
18. 407 U.S. at p. 325.
19. U.S. v. Sinclair, 321 F.Supp. 1074 (1971).
20. U.S. v. U.S.D.C., E. Dist., Mich., 444 F.2d 651 (1971).
21. 447 F.2d at p. 664.
22. Dennis v. U.S., 341 U.S. 494, 71 S.Ct. 857, 95 L.Ed. 1137 (1951).
23. *Senate Report* No. 1097, p. 94.
24. See "Comments," *U.C.L.A. Law Review*, June 1970, pp. 1205, 1248.
25. For a discussion of the Ellsberg case, see Chapter 5. The wiretaps allegedly requested and obtained by Henry A. Kissinger were reported in *New York Times*, May 15, 1973, p. 22, col. 3; May 17, 1973, p. 1, col. 5; May 18, 1973, p. 36, col. 1.
26. *New York Times*, May 7, 1973, p. 46, col. 7; May 15, 1973, p. 22, cols. 3 and 4; May 16, 1973, p. 27, col. 3.
27. Tom Wicker, "A Dark Atmosphere," *New York Times*, May 18, 1973, p. 37, col. 7; Anthony Lewis, "The End of the Affair," *New York Times*, May 21, 1973, p. 33, col. 1.
28. Tom Wicker, "The Real Contempt," *New York Times*, May 15, 1973, p. 39, col. 1.

7 State Eavesdropping in Practice

1. Dudley v. State, 427 F.2d 1140 (Ct. of App., 5th Cir., 1970).
2. U.S. v. Becker, 334 F.Supp. 546 (1971); aff'd 461 F.2d 230 (1972).
3. Greenawalt, "Privacy in Home, Person," *New York Law Journal*, June 15, 1970, Vol. 163, No. 14, p. 4, col. 2.
4. Brenton, *The Privacy Invaders*, pp. 159–160.

5. United States v. La Gorga, 340 F.Supp. 1397 (1972).
6. *Hearings,* Subcommittee on Criminal Laws and Procedures, Senate, April 20, 1967, pp. 407, 597–598.
7. Public Law 91-358, Title II, Sec. 211(b), July 29, 1970, 84 Stat. 654.
8. For an account of the 1964 lawsuit growing out of the Fred Black and Bobby Baker cases, see *Ramparts,* Jan. 25, 1969, p. 51.
9. For "leaks" by telephone company employees, see Dash, Schwartz, Knowlton, *The Eavesdroppers,* p. 73. See People v. Sierra, S.Ct., N.Y. County, 343 N.Y. Supp.2d 196 (1973) in which the court ruled that a San Juan telephone operator, who reported to police a conversation regarding shipment of narcotics to New York City that she had inadvertently overheard while checking the connection, acted in the normal course of employment and within the exception to the statute prohibiting wiretapping.
10. *Hearings,* Subcommittee on Administrative Practice and Procedure, Senate, May 18, 1967, Part 2, p. 576.
11. The problem of terminating interceptions is discussed in Vernon, *Syracuse Law Review,* Spring 1969, p. 620.
12. As to voice identification, see 29 Amer. Jur.2d Sec. 383, 381, 368. For admissibility of sound recordings, see 58 ALR 2d 1027, Sec. 2; 17 Amer. Jur.POF, Tape Rec. Sec. 60 (Supp.).
13. For discussion of operation of a "cheese box," see note 6, *Hearings,* p. 628.
14. For discussion of L.E.A.A. program, see *Cong. Record,* April 5, 1971, S 4612; June 4, 1971, E 5479; Feb. 7, 1972, S 1263; Feb. 9, 1972, E 1164.
15. For criticism of L.E.A.A., see *Cong. Record,* Nov. 16, 1971, H 11138; *New York Times,* Jan. 9, 1970, p. 28, col. 4; Feb. 18, 1970, p. 16, col. 1; March 3, 1970, p. 30, col. 4; June 19, 1970, p. 15, col. 2; Dec. 28, 1970, p. 1, col. 5; July 23, 1971, p. 34, col. 1. On Aug. 6, 1973, the President signed a law extending L.E.A.A. for three years, with increased discretion on the part of the States as to use of funds.
16. *Hearings,* Subcommittee on Dept. of State, Justice, etc., House Committee on Appropriations, 1970, Part 1, pp. 218, 875.
17. Ansley v. State, Ct. of App., Ga., 185 S.E.2d 562 (1971).
18. People v. Martin, S.Ct., Colo., 490 P.2d 924 (1971).
19. U.S. v. Tortorello, 342 F.Supp. 1029 (1972). Authorization of application for a wiretap order by an *assistant* county attorney was held insufficient, requiring suppression of evidence in State v. Frink, S.Ct. of Minnesota, 206 N.W.2d 663 (1973). See to same effect State v. Cocuzza, Essex County Ct., N.J. 301 A.2d 204 (1973).
20. Dudley v. State, S.Ct., Ga., 186 S.E.2d 875 (1971).
21. People v. DiLorenzo, 330 N.Y.Supp.2d 720 (1971).
22. People v. Gnozzo; People v. Zorn, 31 N.Y.2d 134, 335 N.Y.Supp.2d 257, 286 N.E.2d 706 (1972).
23. See note 22, People v. Zorn.
24. U.S. v. Leta, M.D.Pa., 332 F.Supp. 1357 (1971); U.S. v. Sklaroff, 323 F.Supp. 296 (1971); U.S. v. King, 335 F.Supp. 523 (1971).
25. State v. Christy, 270 A.2d 306 (1970).
26. People v. Botta, 304 N.Y.Supp.2d 362 (1969).
27. U.S. v. Becker, 334 F.Supp. 546 (1971).
28. State v. Siegel, 285 A.2d 671 (1971). See to same effect, State v. Lee, 295 A.2d 812 (1972).
29. See note 28, State v. Siegel.
30. People v. Tebo, 194 N.W.2d 517 (1972).

31. Halpin v. Superior Court of San Bernardino County, 101 Cal. Reporter 375 (1972).

32. U.S. v. Escandar, 319 F.Supp. 295 (1970).

8 Federal Eavesdropping in Practice

1. Federal procedure in court-ordered eavesdropping is discussed in letter of Henry E. Peterson, Dep. Asst. Atty. Gen., to Sen. John L. McClellan, July 13, 1970; see *Cong. Record*, Senate, July 31, 1970, S 12549.

2. U.S. v. King, 335 F.Supp. 523 (1971).

3. For Ramsey Clark's role in Strike Force concept, see Harris, *Justice*. See also McKeon, "The Strike Force," *American Bar Association Journal*, May 1970, pp. 453–454.

4. Mama's story is told in *Cong. Record*, April 29, 1971, S 5896. It appeared in *Wall Street Journal*, April 27, 1971, as told by John Bartels.

5. *Cong. Record*, Nov. 2, 1971, Vol. 117, No. 164, H 10258.

6. The story of the competing agents appears in *Cong. Record*, Nov. 2, 1971, H 10258.

7. Navasky, "A Famous Prosecutor Talks About Crime," *New York Times Magazine*, March 29, 1970.

8. Cox v. U.S., 405 U.S. 932, 92 S.Ct. 1783, 32 L.Ed.2d 136 (1972).

9. U.S. v. Tantillo, U.S.D.C., D. of C., Misc. 71-69 and 72-69; Criminal Case No. 1912-69.

10. Spritzer, "Electronic Surveillance by Leave of the Magistrate: The Case in Opposition," *Univ. of Pennsylvania Law Review*, Dec. 1969, pp. 169–186.

11. U.S. v. Cihal, 336 F.Supp. 261 (1972).

12. U.S. v. La Gorga, 336 F.Supp. 190 (1971); 340 F.Supp. 1397 (1972). See also U.S. v. Ianelli, 339 F.Supp. 171 (1971), distinguishing *Cihal* and *La Gorga*.

13. U.S. v. Pisacano, 459 F.2d 259 (1972). To same effect, U.S. v. Fiorella, 468 F.2d 688 (1972); U.S. v. Ceraso, 467 F.2d 657 (1972).

14. U.S. v. Consiglio, 342 F.Supp. 556 (1972); U.S. v. Doolittle, 341 F.Supp. 163 (1972); U.S. v. Robinson, 468 F.2d 189 (1972). Subsequent approval by the Attorney General was held to be insufficient to cure the defect in U.S. v. Boone (U.S. Dist. Ct., E.D., Va.) 348 F.Supp. 168 (1972). See also U.S. v. Fox, 349 F.Supp. 1258 (1972) in which the U.S. District Court in the S.D. of Ill. ruled that where authorization procedure was not followed in obtaining extension of an order, evidence obtained under the extension was inadmissible. For suppression of wiretap evidence by Judge William Mehrtens of the U.S.D.C. in southern Florida in eleven Federal gambling, narcotics, and bribery cases because of lack of proper authorization by former Attorney General John N. Mitchell, see *New York Times*, June 2, 1973, p. 14, col. 1.

15. U.S. v. Giordano, 469 F.2d 522 (1972).

16. 469 F.2d at p. 531.

17. U.S. v. Fantuzzi, 463 F.2d 683 (1972).

18. U.S. v. Kleve, 465 F.2d 187 (1972).

19. U.S. v. Sklaroff, 323 F.Supp. 296 (1971).

20. U.S. v. Whitaker, 343 F.Supp. 358 (1972).

21. U.S. v. Lamonge, 458 F.2d 197 (1972).

22. U.S. v. Becker, 334 F.Supp. 546 (1971); affirmed 461 F.2d 230 (1972). See to same effect, People v. Huff, Onandaga County Court, 335 N.Y.Supp.2d 118 (1972).

23. People v. Zorn, 335 N.Y.Supp.2d 257 (1972).

24. U.S. v. George, 465 F.2d 772 (1972).
25. U.S. v. Scott, 331 F.Supp. 233 (1971).
26. Katz v. U.S., 389 U.S. 347, 88 S.Ct. 507, 19 L.Ed.2d 576 (1967); Berger v. New York, 388 U.S. 41, 87 St.C. 1873, 18 L.Ed.2d 1040 (1967).
27. See note 12, U.S. v. La Gorga.
28. U.S. v. King, 335 F.Supp. at p. 538.
29. U.S. v. Cox, 462 F.2d 1293 (1972).
30. U.S. v. Eastman, 326 F.Supp. 1038 (1971); affirmed 465 F.2d 1057 (1972). See, however, U.S. v. Ripka, 349 F.Supp. 539 (1972) in which the U.S. Dist. Ct., E.D., Penna., ruled that failure to serve notice on an "aggrieved person" was cured by Sec. 2518(9) which requires furnishing a copy of the order and application to defendant within ten days before trial.
31. See note 12 to this chapter. See also U.S. v. Wolk, 466 F.2d 1143 (1972) in which the Court of Appeals, 8th Circuit, ruled that failure to serve timely formal notice does not mean that wiretap evidence should have been suppressed, where there was substantial compliance with the notice requirements.
32. Application of United States (Dudley v. United States), 427 F.2d 1140 (1970). The Court of Appeals, 10th Circuit, ruled that an order of the District Court denying a motion to suppress was not appealable. U.S. v. Smith, 463 F.2d 710, (1972). See also U.S. v. Calandra, 465 F.2d 1218 (1972) in which the Court of Appeals, 6th Circuit, said that the status of an individual as an "aggrieved person" is determinative of his or her recourse to a motion to suppress, and not the intention of the U.S. Attorney to file an indictment against the individual.
33. See note 2 to this chapter. Constitutionality of the Omnibus Act of 1968 was upheld by the U.S. Court of Appeals, 8th Circuit, in U.S. v. Cox, 462 F.2d 1293 (1972). See also U.S. v. Askins, U.S.D.C., D. of Md., 351 F.Supp. 408 (1972) listing cases upholding constitutionality of Title III.
34. Berger v. New York, 388 U.S. 41, 87 S.Ct. 1873, 18 L.Ed.2d 1040 (1967); Katz v. United States, 389 U.S. 347, 88 S.Ct. 507, 19 L.Ed.2d 576 (1967); Osborn v. United States, 385 U.S. 323, 87 S.Ct. 429, 17 L.Ed.2d 394 (1966).
35. U.S. v. U.S.D.C., 407 U.S. 297, 92 S.Ct. 2125, 32 L.Ed.2d 752 (1972); Gelbard v. U.S., 408 U.S. 41, 92 S.Ct. 2357, 33 L.Ed.2d 179 (1972).
36. See note 35, Gelbard v. U.S.
37. U.S. v. Gelbard, 443 F.2d 837 (1971); Bacon v. U.S., 446 F.2d 667 (1971).
38. *In re* Egan, 450 F.2d 199 (1971).
39. *In re* Evans, 452 F.2d 1239 (1971).
40. 408 U.S. at p. 62.
41. Silverthorne Lumber Co. v. U.S., 251 U.S. 385, 40 S.Ct. 182, 64 L.Ed. 319 (1920).
42. See note 35, Gelbard v. U.S.
43. Russo v. U.S., 404 U.S. 1023, 92 S.Ct. 4, 30 L.Ed.2d 13 (1971); rehearing denied 405 U.S. 949.
44. 408 U.S. at pp. 71, 79, 82, 91.
45. 452 F.2d at p. 1252.
46. See note 35, Gelbard v. U.S. But see Cali v. U.S., 464 F.2d 475 (1972) in which the U.S. Court of Appeals, 1st Circuit, analyzed *Gelbard* and held that a motion to suppress contents of communications intercepted by the government is *not* available to a grand jury witness. See also Smilow v. U.S., 465 F.2d 802 (1972) in which the Court of Appeals, 2d Circuit, held that a grand jury witness may not refuse to answer on the ground that the government has illegally heard someone else's conversation on premises not owned or leased by the witness. In the 5th Circuit, the Court of Appeals rejected the claim of a grand jury witness

that government denial of electronic surveillance was inadequate because based on hearsay. The Department of Justice testified that it had checked with all agencies having anything to do with the investigation. *In re* Tierney, 465 F.2d 806 (1972).

9 Evaluation of Eavesdropping

1. Karabian, *Pacific Law Journal,* June 1970, p. 143.
2. *Hearings,* Subcommittee on Criminal Laws and Procedures, Senate, July 11, 1967, p. 904; Subcommittee on Administrative Practice and Procedure, Senate, April 4, 1967, p. 173.
3. *Hearings,* Subcommittee on Administrative Practice and Procedure, Senate, April 4, 1967, p. 56.
4. Clark, *Crime in America,* pp. 344–345.
5. *Cong. Record,* Senate, June 29, 1967, p. 6.
6. *Cong. Record,* Senate, July 31, 1970, S 12548.
7. Cook v. U.S., 401 U.S. 996, 91 S.Ct. 1224, 28 L.Ed.2d 535 (1971).
8. Russo v. Byrne, 409 U.S. 1219, 93 S.Ct. 21, 34 L.Ed.2d 30 (1972); cert. denied 409 U.S. 1013. See *New York Times,* Aug. 6, 1972, p. 1, col. 1; Sec. E, p. 8, col. 3. Ellsberg, Russo, and seventeen of their attorneys and consultants brought suit against Federal officials for illegal wiretapping, and asked for punitive as well as compensatory damages under Title III. See *New York Times,* Sept. 20, 1972, p. 9, col. 1.
9. The Bacon case is discussed in *New York Times,* Aug. 5, 1972, p. 1, col. 7.
10. *New York Times,* Sept. 18, 1972, p. 28, col. 4.
11. *Cong. Record,* Senate, July 31, 1970, S 12549.
12. For dispute as to effectiveness of eavesdropping, see *New York Times,* Oct. 11, 1970, Sec. E, p. 9, col. 4.
13. *New York Times,* May 6, 1973, p. 58, col. 4.
14. For criticism of approach to crime, see Bickel, *The New Republic,* June 15, 1970, p. 8.
15. *New York Times,* Oct. 18, 1970, Sec. E, p. 9, col. 1.
16. Comment of Ralph Salerno; see *Cong. Record,* Senate, Nov, 4, 1971, S 17608.
17. Buchwald's musings appear in *Cong. Record,* Vol. 117, No. 134, E 9694, and in *Washington Post,* Sept. 16, 1971.
18. For dispute on interpretation of F.B.I. crime statistics for 1972, see *New York Times,* Sept. 29, 1972, p. 30, col. 5.
19. For public opinion poll, see "Tapping a Vein of Controversy," *Nation's Business,* July 1969, p. 81.
20. As to Army surveillance, see *New York Times,* Dec. 27, 1970, p. 1, col. 7; Dec. 29, 1970, p. 13, col. 1; Jan. 19, 1971, p. 37, col. 1; April 2, 1971, p. 25, col. 3. See also Laird v. Tatum, 408 U.S. 1, 92 S.Ct. 2318, 33 L.Ed.2d 154 (1972) in which the U.S. Supreme Court held by a vote of 5 to 4 that a complaint of "chilling effect" on First Amendment rights by reason of Army's intelligence system was non-justiciable.
21. Public Law 91-644, 84 Stat. 1880 (Omnibus Crime Control Act of 1970, Title VI).
22. *New York Times,* Oct. 8, 1970, p. 46, col. 2.

10 Proposals and Predictions

1. U.S. v. Whitaker, 343 F.Supp. 358 (1972).
2. Dudley v. State, 427 F.2d 1140 (1970).

3. See also U.S. v. Hoffman, 334 F.Supp. 504 (1971), in which the U.S.D.C. in the District of Columbia held that a pretrial hearing was not necessary to determine whether the evidence to be presented at the trial was tainted.
4. *Cong. Record*, May 10, 1971, S 6477.
5. Herman Schwartz, *A Report on the Costs and Benefits of Electronic Surveillance*, prepared for the American Civil Liberties Union, Dec. 1971. See comment in *New York Times*, Dec. 15, 1971, Sec. L, p. 22, col. 1.
6. Berger v. New York, 388 U.S. 41, 87 S.Ct. 1873, 18 L.Ed.2d 1040 (1967).
7. Katz v. U.S. 389 U.S. 347, 88 S.Ct. 507, 19 L.Ed.2d 576 (1967).
8. *A.B.A. Standards Relating to Electronics Surveillance*, January 1971, pp. 2, 25.
9. *Cong. Record*, Senate, May 10, 1971, S 6476.
10. *Cong. Record*, Senate, Oct. 26, 1971, S 16784.
11. For criticism of government eavesdropping, see *New York Times*, Dec. 15, 1971, Sec. L, p. 22, col. 1.
12. *New York Times*, May 20, 1970, p. 1, col. 6.
13. Brandeis's statement appears in his dissent in Olmstead v. U.S., 277 U.S. 438, 48 S.Ct. 564, 72 L.Ed. 944 (1928).
14. *Cong. Record*, Senate, Aug. 11, 1969, Vol. 115, Part 17, at p. 23242.

Selected Bibliography

Books

Allen, Edward J., *Merchants of Menace: The Mafia: A Study of Organized Crime.* Springfield, Ill.: Charles C. Thomas, 1962.

Brenton, Myron, *The Privacy Invaders.* New York: Coward McCann, Inc., 1964.

Brown, Robert M., *The Electronic Invasion.* New York: John F. Rider Publisher, Inc., 1967.

Carroll, John A., *The Third Listener.* New York: E. P. Dutton & Co., Inc., 1969.

Clark, Ramsey, *Crime in America.* New York: Simon & Schuster, 1970.

Cook, Fred J., *The Corrupted Land: The Social Morality of Modern America.* New York: The Macmillan Co., 1966.

Cook, Fred J., *The F.B.I. Nobody Knows.* New York: The Macmillan Co., 1964.

Cook, Fred J., *The Secret Rulers: Criminal Syndicates and How They Control the U.S. Underworld.* New York: Meredith Press, 1966.

Cook, Fred J., *A Two-Dollar Bet Means Murder.* New York: Dial Press, 1961.

Cressey, Donald R., *Theft of the Nation: The Structure and Operations of Organized Crime in America.* New York: Harper & Row, 1969.

Dash, Samuel, with Richard F. Schwartz, and Robert E. Knowlton, *The Eavesdroppers.* New Brunswick, N.J.: Rutgers University Press, 1959.

Dorman, Norman, *Payoff: The Role of Organized Crime in American Politics.* New York: David McKay Co., Inc., 1972.

Harris, Richard, *The Fear of Crime.* New York: Frederick A. Praeger, 1968.

Harris, Richard, *Justice: The Crisis of Law, Order and Freedom in America.* New York: E. P. Dutton & Co., 1970.

Ianni, Francis, A. J., *A Family Business: Kinship and Social Control in Organized Crime.* New York: Basic Books, 1972.

King, Rufus, *Gambling and Organized Crime.* Washington, D.C.: Public Affairs Press, 1969.

Landynski, Jacob W., *Search and Seizure and the Supreme Court.* Baltimore, Md.: The Johns Hopkins Press, 1966.

Long, (former Senator) Edward V., *The Intruders: The Invasion of Privacy by Government and Industry.* New York: Frederick A. Praeger, 1967.

McCoy, Alfred W., *The Politics of Heroin in Southeast Asia.* New York: Harper & Row, 1972.

Miller, Arthur R., *The Assault on Privacy: Computers, Data Banks and Dossiers.* Ann Arbor: The University of Michigan Press, 1971.

Moore, Robin, *The French Connection.* Boston, Mass.: Little, Brown and Co., 1969.

Murphy, Walter F., *Wiretapping on Trial.* New York: Random House, Inc., 1965.

Navasky, Victor S., *Kennedy Justice.* New York: Atheneum, 1971.

Puzo, Mario, *The Godfather.* New York: G. B. Putnam's Sons, 1969.

Salerno, Ralph, and Tompkins, John S., *The Crime Confederation: Cosa Nostra and Allied Operations in Organized Crime.* Garden City, New York: Doubleday & Co., 1969.

Schur, Edwin M., *Our Criminal Society: The Social and Legal Sources of Crime in America.* Englewood Cliffs, N.J.: Prentice-Hall, Inc., 1969.

Talese, Guy, *Honor Thy Father.* New York: The World Publishing Co., 1971.

Turkus, Burton B., and Feder, Sid, *Murder, Inc.* New York: Farrar, Straus and Young, 1951.

Tyler, Gus, *Organized Crime in America.* Ann Arbor: The University of Michigan Press, 1962.

Westin, Alan F., *Privacy and Freedom.* New York: Atheneum, 1967.

Periodicals

Beck, Stanley M., "Electronic Surveillance and the Administration of Criminal Justice," *Canada Bar Review,* 1968, Vol. 46.

Bell, Daniel, "Crime as an American Way of Life," *The Antioch Review,* June 1953, Vol. XIII, No. 2.

Bickel, Alexander M., "Crime, the Courts and the Old Nixon," *The New Republic,* June 15, 1970, Vol. 158, No. 25.

Biddle, W. Craig, "Court-Supervised Electronic Searches: A Proposed Statute for California," *Pacific Law Journal,* Jan. 1970, Vol. 1.

Bisantz, Mary E., "Electronic Eavesdropping Under the Fourth Amendment—After Berger and Katz," *Buffalo Law Review*, Winter 1968, Vol. 17, No. 2.

Brandeis, Louis D., and Warren, Samuel D., "The Right of Privacy," *Harvard Law Review*, Vol. IV, No. 5 (1890).

Burnham, David, "How Corruption is Built Into the System—and a Few Ideas of What to Do About It," *New York Magazine*, Sept. 21, 1970, Vol. 3, No. 38.

Clark, Ramsey, "The Death of Privacy," *McCall's*, Feb. 1970, Vol. XCVII, No. 5.

Clark, Tom C., "Wiretapping and the Constitution," *California Western Law Review*, Fall 1968, Vol. 5, No. 1.

Cook, Fred J., "The People v. The Mob; Or, Who Rules New Jersey," *New York Times Magazine*, Feb. 1, 1970.

Fried, C., "Privacy," *Yale Law Journal*, Jan. 1968, Vol. 77, Part I, No. 3.

Fly, Sally, "The Orwell Law; New Taps on Freedom," *The Nation*, June 2, 1969.

Greenawalt, Kent, "The Consent Problem in Wiretapping and Eavesdropping: Surreptitious Monitoring with the Consent of a Participant in a Conversation," *Columbia Law Review*, Feb. 1968, Vol. 68, No. 2.

Heinz, John P., Gettleman, Robert W., and Seeskin, Morris A., "Legislative Politics and the Criminal Law," *Northwestern University Law Review*, July–Aug. 1969, Vol. 64, No. 3.

Hills, Stuart L., "Combating Organized Crime in America," *Federal Probation*, March 1969, Vol. XXXIII, No. 1.

Karabian, Walter, "The Case Against Wiretapping," *Pacific Law Journal*, June 1970, Vol. 1.

Kitch, Edmund W., "Katz v. United States: The Limits of the Fourth Amendment," *The Supreme Court Review*, 1968.

Lewin, Nathan, " 'White on White.' Privacy and the Third-Party Bug. Case of James White." *The New Republic*, April 17, 1971.

Linzer, Stephen, "Federal Procedure for Court-Ordered Electronic Surveillance: Does It Meet the Standards of Berger and Katz?" *The Journal of Criminal Law, Criminology and Police Science*, 1969, Vol. 60.

Mascolo, Edward G., "The Staleness of Probable Cause in Affidavits for Search Warrants: Resolving the Issue of Timeliness," *Connecticut Bar Journal*, June 1969, Vol. 43, No. 2.

McKeon, Thomas J., "The 'Strike Force,' How the Government Combats the National Organized Crime Problem," *American Bar Association Journal*, May 1970.

Michael, Richard A., "Electronic Surveillance in Illinois," *Loyola University Law Journal* (Chicago), Winter 1970, Vol. 1.

Moore, Philip W., "The 'Chicago Eight' Wire Tap: Disclosed or Leaked?," *The Nation*, Oct. 27, 1969, Vol. 209, No. 14.

Navasky, Victor S., "A Famous Prosecutor Talks About Crime," *New York Times Magazine*, Feb. 15, 1970.

Parente, C. Albert, and Muratori, Jack R., "The Advocate," *Bronx County Bar Association*, Nov. 1969, Vol. 14, No. 5.

Pileggi, Nicholas, "The Story of T—To Be a Mafia Boss—It's Better Than Being President of the United States," *New York Times Magazine*, March 29, 1970.

Salerno, Ralph F., "Organized Crime and Criminal Justice," *Federal Probation*, Vol. XXXIII, No. 2, June 1969.

Schwartz, Herman, "Electronic Eavesdropping—What the Supreme Court Did NOT Do," *Criminal Law Bulletin*, Jan.–Feb. 1968, Vol. 4, No.1.

Schwartz, Herman, "The Legitimation of Electronic Eavesdropping: The Politics of 'Law and Order,' " *Michigan Law Review*, Jan. 1969, Vol. 67, No. 3.

Scoular, Robert F., "Wiretapping and Eavesdropping, Constitutional Development from Olmstead to Katz," *St. Louis University Law Journal*, Summer 1968, Vol. 12.

Spritzer, Ralph F., "Electronic Surveillance by Leave of the Magistrate: The Case in Opposition," *University of Pennsylvania Law Review*, Dec. 1969, Vol. 118, No. 2.

Theoharis, Athan G., "Misleading the Presidents: Thirty Years of Wiretapping," *The Nation*, June 14, 1971.

Theoharis, Athan G., and Meyer, Elizabeth, "The 'National Security' Justification for Electronic Eavesdropping," *Wayne Law Review*, Summer 1968.

Vernon, Laurens M., "Eavesdropping in New York: 1968 Legislation," *Syracuse Law Review*, Spring 1969, Vol. 20, No. 3.

Wicker, Tom, "What Have They Done Since They Shot Dillinger," *New York Times Magazine*, December 28, 1969.

Additional Periodicals

Christian Century, July 9, 1969, Vol. LXXXVI, No. 28.

Columbia Law Review, May 1967.

Commentary, January 1972.

"Wiretapping and the Constitution," *California Western Law Review*, Fall 1968, Vol. 5, No. 1.

"Inadmissibility of Wiretap Evidence in State Courts," *Duke Law Journal,* October 1968.

Forbes, April 1, 1970.

Minnesota Law Review, June 1971.

Montana Law Review, Summer 1971.

"Tapping a Vein of Controversy," *Nation's Business,* July 1969.

The New Republic, May 18, 1968; June 29, 1968; July 5, 1969.

Newsweek, June 23, 1969.

Notes: "From Private Places to Personal Privacy: A Post-Katz Study of Fourth Amendment Protection, *New York University Law Review,* November 1968, Vol. 43.

Comment: "Electronic Surveillance by Law Enforcement Officers," *Northwestern Law Review,* March/April 1969, Vol. 64, No. 1.

Police Times, Jan.–Feb. 1972.

Ramparts, Jan. 25, 1969.

Notes: "Wiretapping and Electronic Surveillance—Title III of the Crime Control Act of 1968," *Rutgers Law Review,* Winter 1969, Vol. 23, No. 2.

U.C.L.A. Law Review, June 1970.

Valparaiso University Law Review, Fall 1968.

Official Documents

Attorney General's Report, Jan. 19, 1971. U.S. Department of Justice, Washington, D.C.

Congressional Digest, Volume 46 (1967).

Congressional Hearings:

House of Representatives: Subcommittee on Dept. of State, Justice, etc., Committee on Appropriations, 91st Cong., 2d sess., Part 1, March 9, 1970.

Senate: Subcommittee on Administrative Practice and Procedure, Committee on the Judiciary: March 20, 1967; April 4, 1967; April 20, 1967. Subcommittee on Criminal Laws and Procedures, Committee on the Judiciary: March 9, 1967; April 19, 20, 1967; July 11, 12, 1967; March 9, 1970.

Congressional Quarterly, Weekly Report, June 5, 1970.

Congressional Record: 1967: June 29, Vol. 113, No. 104, pp. 1, 2, 3, 6, 8; *1969:* Aug. 11, pp. 23238, 23242; *1970:* July 31, S 12548–12549; *1971:* Jan. 2, H 12693; April 5, S 4612; April 29, S 5895; May 10, S 6476; May 11, H 3827; June 4, E 5479; June 9, S 8694; July 6, E 7043; Oct. 26 S 16784; Oct. 28, H 10129; Nov. 2, H 10258, E 11679, S 17391;

Nov. 4, S 17608; Nov. 9, H10779; Nov. 14, S 17608; Nov. 16, H 11138; Nov. 29, E 12694; Dec. 2, E 12873; *1972:* Jan. 19, H 137; Jan. 26, S 509; Feb. 7, S 1263; Feb. 8, H 861; Feb. 9, E 1164.

Report to Congress by Administrative Office of U.S. Courts: June 19–Dec. 31, 1968, Jan. 1–Dec. 31, 1969, Jan. 1–Dec. 31, 1970, Jan. 1–Dec. 31, 1971, Jan. 1–Dec. 31, 1972.

Senate Document 26, 90th Cong., 1st sess., "Combating Crime in the United States" (1967).

Senate Report No. 1097, 90th Cong., 2d sess., April 29, 1968.

The President's Commission on Law Enforcement and Administration òf Justice: General Report, *The Challenge of Crime in a Free Society* (1967); *Task Force Report: Organized Crime* (1967).

Court Decisions

Aguilar v. Texas, 378 U.S. 108, 84 S.Ct. 1509, 12 L.Ed.2d 723 (1964).

Alderman v. United States, 394 U.S. 165, 89 S.Ct. 961, 22 L.Ed.2d 176 (1969).

Ansley v. State (Ct. of App., Georgia), 185 S.E.2d 562 (1972).

Application of United States (Ct. of App. 5th Cir.), 427 F.2d 1140 (1970).

Bacon v. United States (Ct. of App. 9th Cir.), 446 F.2d 667 (1971).

Benanti v. United States, 355 U.S. 96, 78 S.Ct. 155, 2 L.Ed.2d 126 (1957).

Berger v. New York, 388 U.S. 41, 87 S.Ct. 1873, 18 L.Ed.2d 1040 (1967).

Bursey v. United States (Ct. of App. 9th Cir.), 466 F.2d 1059 (1972).

Cali v. United States (Ct. of App. 1st Cir.), 464 F.2d 475 (1972).

Carroll v. United States, 267 U.S. 132, 45 S.Ct. 280, 69 L.Ed.2d 543 (1925).

Commonwealth v. Hunt, 45 Mass. (4 Met.) 11 (1842).

Cook v. United States, 401 U.S. 996, 91 S.Ct. 1224, 28 L.Ed.2d 535 (1971).

Cox v. United States, 405 U.S. 932, 92 S.Ct. 1783, 32 L.Ed.2d 136 (1972).

Dennis v. United States, 341 U.S. 494, 71 S.Ct. 857, 95 L.Ed. 1137 (1951).

Desist v. United States, 394 U.S. 244, 89 S.Ct. 1030, 22 L.Ed.2d 248 (1969).

Doe v. Bolton, 409 U.S., 909, 93 S.Ct. 739, 35 L.Ed.2d. 201 (1973).

Dudley v. State (S.Ct., Georgia), 186 S.E.2d 875 (1971).

Eisenstadt v. Baird, 405 U.S. 438, 92 S.Ct. 1029, 31 L.Ed.2d 349 (1972).

Elkins v. United States, 364 U.S. 206, 80 S.Ct. 437, 4 L.Ed.2d 1669 (1960).

Fuller v. Alaska, 393 U.S. 80, 89 S.Ct. 61, 21 L.Ed.2d 212 (1968).

Galella v. Onassis (U.S.D.C., S.D., New York), 335 F.Supp. 196 (1972).

Gelbard v. United States, 408 U.S. 41, 92 S.Ct. 2357, 33 L.Ed.2d 179 (1972).

Giordano v. United States, 394 U.S. 310, 89 S.Ct. 1164, 22 L.Ed.2d 297 (1969).

Goldman v. United States, 316 U.S. 129, 62 S.Ct. 993, 86 L.Ed.2d 1322 (1942).

Griswold v. Connecticut, 381 U.S. 479, 85 S.Ct. 1678, 14 L.Ed.2d 510 (1965).

Halpin v. Superior Court of San Bernardino Co., 101 Cal.Rep. 375 (1972).

In re Evans (Ct. of App., District of Columbia), 452 F.2d 1239 (1971).

In re Grand Jury Proceedings, Harrisburg, Pa. [Egan] (Ct. of App. 3rd Cir.), 450 F.2d 199 (1971).

In re Tierney (Ct. of App. 5th Cir.), 465 F.2d 806 (1972).

In re Womack (Ct. of App. 7th Cir.), 466 F.2d 555 (1972).

Katz v. United States, 389 U.S. 347, 88 S.Ct. 507, 19 L.Ed.2d 576 (1967).

Laird v. Tatum, 408 U.S. 1, 92 S.Ct. 2318, 33 L.Ed.2d 154 (1972).

Lee v. Florida, 392 U.S. 378, 88 S.Ct. 2096, 20 L.Ed.2d 1166 (1968).

Lopez v. United States, 373 U.S. 427, 83 S.Ct. 1381, 10 L.Ed.2d 462 (1963).

Mallory v. United States, 354 U.S. 449, 77 S.Ct. 1356, 1 L.Ed.2d 1479 (1957).

Mapp v. Ohio, 367 U.S. 643, 81 S.Ct. 1684, 6 L.Ed.2d 1081 (1961).

Markham v. Markham (S. Ct. of Florida) 270 So.2d 813 (1973).

McCray v. Illinois, 386 U.S. 300, 87 S.Ct. 1056, 18 L.Ed.2d 62 (1967).

Miranda v. Arizona, 384 U.S. 436, 86 S.Ct. 1602, 16 L.Ed.2d 694 (1966).

Nader v. General Motors Corp., 25 N.Y.2d 560, 307 N.Y.Supp.2d 647 (1970).

Nardone v. United States, 302 U.S. 379, 58 S.Ct. 275, 82 L.Ed.314 (1937).

Nardone v. United States, 308 U.S. 388, 60 S.Ct. 266, 84 L.Ed.307 (1939).

N.A.A.C.P. v. Alabama, 357 U.S. 449, 78 S.Ct. 1163, 2 L.Ed.2d 1488 (1958).

Olmstead v. United States, 277 U.S. 438, 48 S.Ct. 564, 72 L.Ed. 944 (1928).

On Lee v. United States, 343 U.S. 747, 72 S.Ct. 967, 96 L.Ed. 1270 (1952).

Osborn v. United States, 385 U.S. 323, 87 S.Ct. 429, 17 L.Ed.2d 394 (1966).

People v. Botta, (N.Y. Dist. Ct., Nassau Co.) 304 N.Y.Supp.2d 362 (1969).

People v. DiLorenzo, (N.Y. S. Ct., Rockland Co.) 330 N.Y.Supp.2d 720 (1971).

People v. Gnozzo, (N.Y. Ct. of App.) 335 N.Y.Supp.2d 257 (1972).

People v. Holder, (S. Ct., Nassau Co.) 331 N.Y.Supp.2d 557 (1972).

People v. Huff (Onandaga County Court) 335 N.Y. Supp.2d 118 (1973).

People v. Martin (S.Ct., Colorado), 49 F.2d 924 (1971).

People v. Sierra (S. Ct., N.Y. County) 343 N.Y. Supp.2d 196 (1972).

People v. Tebo (Ct. of App., Michigan), 194 N.W.2d 517 (1972).

People v. Zorn, (N.Y. Ct. of App.) 335 N.Y.Supp.2d 257 (1972).

United States v. Consiglio (U.S.D.C., D., Connecticut), 342 F.Supp. 556 (1972).

United States v. Cox (Ct. of App. 8th Cir.), 462 F.2d 1293 (1972).

United States v. Dellinger, (N.D., Illinois), Crim. No. 69–180, Feb. 20, 1970.

United States v. Doolittle (M.D., Georgia), 341 F.Supp. 163 (1972).

United States v. Eastman (Ct. of App. 3rd Cir.), 465 F.2d 1057 (1972).

United States v. Escandar (U.S.D.C., S.D., Florida), 319 F.Supp. 295 (1970).

United States v. Fantuzzi (Ct. of App. 2d Cir.), 463 F.2d 683 (1972).

United States v. Fiorella (Ct. of App. 2nd Cir.), 468 F.2d 688 (1972).

United States v. Fox (U.S.D.C., S.D., Illinois), 349 F.Supp. 1258 (1972).

United States v. Gelbard (Ct. of App. 9th Cir.), 443 F.2d 837 (1971); reversed 408 U.S. 41, 92 S.Ct. 2357, 33 L.Ed.2d 179 (1972).

United States v. George (Ct. of App. 6th Cir.), 465 F.2d 772 (1972).

United States v. Giordano (Ct. of App. 4th Cir.), 469 F.2d 522 (1972).

United States v. Hoffman (U.S.D.C., District of Columbia), 334 F.Supp. 504 (1971).

United States v. Ianelli (U.S.D.C., Pennsylvania), 339 F.Supp. 171 (1972).

United States v. King, (U.S.D.C., S.D. California) 335 F. Supp. 523 (1971).

United States v. Kleve (Ct. of App. 8th Cir.), 465 F.2d 187 (1972).

United States v. LaGorga (U.S.D.C., W.D. Pennsylvania), 340 F.Supp. 1397 (1972).

United States v. LaGorga (U.S.D.C., W.D. Pennsylvania) 336 F.Supp. 190 (1971).

United States v. Lamonge (Ct. of App. 6th Cir.), 458 F.2d 197 (1972).

United States v. Leta (U.S.D.C., M.D., Pennsylvania), 332 F.Supp. 1357 (1971).

United States v. Liddy (U.S.D.C., District of Columbia), Crim. Case No. 1827–72, 354 F.Supp. 217 (1973).

United States v. McCann (Ct. of App. 5th Cir.), 465 F.2d 147 (1972).

United States v. Pisacano (Ct. of App. 2nd Cir.), 459 F.2d 259 (1972).

United States v. Ripka (U.S.D.C., E.D., Pennsylvania), 349 F.Supp. 539 (1972).

United States v. Robinson (U.S.D.C., W.D., Missouri), 311 F.Supp. 1063 (1969).

United States v. Robinson (Ct. of App. 5th Cir.), 468 F.2d 189 (1972).

United States v. Scott (U.S.D.C., District of Columbia), 331 F.Supp. 233 (1971).

United States v. Sinclair (U.S.D.C., E.D., Michigan), 321 F.Supp. 1074 (1971).

United States v. Sklaroff (U.S.D.C., S.D., Florida), 323 F.Supp. 296 (1971).

United States v. Smith (Ct. of App. 10th Cir.), 463 F.2d 710 (1972).

United States v. Tantillo (U.S.D.C., District of Columbia), Misc. 71–69 and 72–69; Crim. Case No. 1912–69.

United States v. Tortorello (U.S.D.C., S.D., New York), 342 F.Supp. 1029 (1972).

United States v. United States District Court, 407 U.S. 297, 92 S.Ct. 2125, 32 L.Ed.2d 752 (1972); affg. 444 F.2d 651 (1971).

United States v. Wade, 388 U.S. 218, 87 S.Ct. 1926, 18 L.Ed.2d 1149 (1967).

United States v. Whitaker (U.S.D.C., E.D., Pennsylvania), 343 F.Supp. 358 (1972).

United States v. White, 401 U.S. 745, 91 S.Ct. 1122, 28 L.Ed.2d 453 (1971).

United States v. Wolk (Ct. of App. 8th Cir.), 466 F.2d 1143 (1972).

United States v. Wright (Ct. of App. 2nd Cir.), 466 F.2d 1256 (1972).

Watkins v. United States, 354 U.S. 178, 77 S.Ct. 1173, 1 L.Ed.2d 1273 (1957).

Williamson v. United States, 405 U.S. 1206, 92 S.Ct. 1323, 31 L.Ed.2d 486 (1972).

Wolf v. Colorado, 338 U.S. 25, 69 S.Ct. 1359, 93 L.Ed. 1782 (1949).

Public Law 90-351
90th Congress, H. R. 5037
June 19, 1968

An Act

To assist State and local governments in reducing the incidence of crime, to increase the effectiveness, fairness, and coordination of law enforcement and criminal justice systems at all levels of government, and for other purposes.

Be it enacted by the Senate and House of Representatives of the United States of America in Congress assembled, That this Act may be cited as the "Omnibus Crime Control and Safe Streets Act of 1968".

* * * * * * * *

TITLE III—WIRETAPPING AND ELECTRONIC SURVEILLANCE

FINDINGS

Sec. 801. On the basis of its own investigations and of published studies, the Congress makes the following findings:

(a) Wire communications are normally conducted through the use of facilities which form part of an interstate network. The same facilities are used for interstate and intrastate communications. There has been extensive wiretapping carried on without legal sanctions, and without the consent of any of the parties to the conversation. Electronic, mechanical, and other intercepting devices are being used to overhear oral conversations made in private, without the consent of any of the parties to such communications. The contents of these communications and evidence derived therefrom are being used by public and private parties as evidence in court and administrative proceedings, and by persons whose activities affect interstate commerce. The possession, manufacture, distribution, advertising, and use of these devices are facilitated by interstate commerce.

(b) In order to protect effectively the privacy of wire and oral communications, to protect the integrity of court and administrative proceedings, and to prevent the obstruction of interstate commerce, it is necessary for Congress to define on a uniform basis the circumstances and conditions under which the interception of wire and oral communications may be authorized, to prohibit any unauthorized interception of such communications, and the use of the contents thereof in evidence in courts and administrative proceedings.

(c) Organized criminals make extensive use of wire and oral communications in their criminal activities. The interception of such communications to obtain evidence of the commission of crimes or to prevent their commission is an indispensable aid to law enforcement and the administration of justice.

(d) To safeguard the privacy of innocent persons, the interception of wire or oral communications where none of the parties to the communication has consented to the interception should be allowed only when authorized by a court of competent jurisdiction and should remain under the control and supervision of the authorizing court. Interception of wire and oral communications should further be limited to certain major types of offenses and specific categories of

253

crime with assurances that the interception is justified and that the information obtained thereby will not be misused.

Sec. 802. Part I of title 18, United States Code, is amended by adding at the end the following new chapter:

"Chapter 119. WIRE INTERCEPTION AND INTERCEPTION OF ORAL COMMUNICATIONS

"§ 2510. Definitions

"As used in this chapter—

"(1) 'wire communication' means any communication made in whole or in part through the use of facilities for the transmission of communications by the aid of wire, cable, or other like connection between the point of origin and the point of reception furnished or operated by any person engaged as a common carrier in providing or operating such facilities for the transmission of interstate or foreign communications;

"(2) 'oral communication' means any oral communication uttered by a person exhibiting an expectation that such communication is not subject to interception under circumstances justifying such expectation;

"(3) 'State' means any State of the United States, the District of Columbia, the Commonwealth of Puerto Rico, and any territory or possession of the United States;

"(4) 'intercept' means the aural acquisition of the contents of any wire or oral communication through the use of any electronic, mechanical, or other device.

"(5) 'electronic, mechanical, or other device' means any device or apparatus which can be used to intercept a wire or oral communication other than—

"(a) any telephone or telegraph instrument, equipment or facility, or any component thereof, (i) furnished to the subscriber or user by a communications common carrier in the ordinary course of its business and being used by the subscriber or user in the ordinary course of its business; or (ii) being used by a communications common carrier in the ordinary course of its business, or by an investigative or law enforcement officer in the ordinary course of his duties;

"(b) a hearing aid or similar device being used to correct subnormal hearing to not better than normal;

"(6) 'person' means any employee, or agent of the United States or any State or political subdivision thereof, and any individual, partnership, association, joint stock company, trust, or corporation;

"(7) 'Investigative or law enforcement officer' means any officer of the United States or of a State or political subdivision thereof, who is empowered by law to conduct investigations of or to make arrests for offenses enumerated in this chapter, and any attorney

authorized by law to prosecute or participate in the prosecution
of such offenses;
"(8) 'contents', when used with respect to any wire or oral
communication, includes any information concerning the identity
of the parties to such communication or the existence, substance,
purport, or meaning of that communication;
"(9) 'Judge of competent jurisdiction' means—
"(a) a judge of a United States district court or a United
States court of appeals; and
"(b) a judge of any court of general criminal jurisdiction
of a State who is authorized by a statute of that State to
enter orders authorizing interceptions of wire or oral
communications;
"(10) 'communication common carrier' shall have the same
meaning which is given the term 'common carrier' by section
153(h) of title 47 of the United States Code; and
"(11) 'aggrieved person' means a person who was a party to
any intercepted wire or oral communication or a person against
whom the interception was directed.

"§ 2511. Interception and disclosure of wire or oral communications prohibited

"(1) Except as otherwise specifically provided in this chapter any
person who—
"(a) willfully intercepts, endeavors to intercept, or procures
any other person to intercept or endeavor to intercept, any wire or
oral communication;
"(b) willfully uses, endeavors to use, or procures any other person to use or endeavor to use any electronic, mechanical, or other
device to intercept any oral communication when—
"(i) such device is affixed to, or otherwise transmits a
signal through, a wire, cable, or other like connection used in
wire communication; or
"(ii) such device transmits communications by radio, or
interferes with the transmission of such communication; or
"(iii) such person knows, or has reason to know, that such
device or any component thereof has been sent through the
mail or transported in interstate or foreign commerce; or
"(iv) such use or endeavor to use (A) takes place on the
premises of any business or other commercial establishment
the operations of which affect interstate or foreign commerce;
or (B) obtains or is for the purpose of obtaining information
relating to the operations of any business or other commercial
establishment the operations of which affect interstate or
foreign commerce; or
"(v) such person acts in the District of Columbia, the
Commonwealth of Puerto Rico, or any territory or possession
of the United States;"
"(c) willfully discloses, or endeavors to disclose, to any other
person the contents of any wire or oral communication, knowing
or having reason to know that the information was obtained
through the interception of a wire or oral communication in
violation of this subsection; or
"(d) willfully uses, or endeavors to use, the contents of any
wire or oral communication, knowing or having reason to know
that the information was obtained through the interception of a
wire or oral communication in violation of this subsection;
shall be fined not more than $10,000 or imprisoned not more than five
years, or both.

Amended, see p. 267

"(2) (a) It shall not be unlawful under this chapter for an operator of a switchboard, or an officer, employee, or agent of any communication common carrier, whose facilities are used in the transmission of a wire communication, to intercept, disclose, or use that communication in the normal course of his employment while engaged in any activity which is a necessary incident to the rendition of his service or to the protection of the rights or property of the carrier of such communication: *Provided*, That said communication common carriers shall not utilize service observing or random monitoring except for mechanical or service quality control checks.

"(b) It shall not be unlawful under this chapter for an officer, employee, or agent of the Federal Communications Commission, in the normal course of his employment and in discharge of the monitoring responsibilities exercised by the Commission in the enforcement of chapter 5 of title 47 of the United States Code, to intercept a wire communication, or oral communication transmitted by radio, or to disclose or use the information thereby obtained.

"(c) It shall not be unlawful under this chapter for a person acting under color of law to intercept a wire or oral communication, where such person is a party to the communication or one of the parties to the communication has given prior consent to such interception.

"(d) It shall not be unlawful under this chapter for a person not acting under color of law to intercept a wire or oral communication where such person is a party to the communication or where one of the parties to the communication has given prior consent to such interception unless such communication is intercepted for the purpose of committing any criminal or tortious act in violation of the Constitution or laws of the United States or of any State or for the purpose of committing any other injurious act.

"(3) Nothing contained in this chapter or in section 605 of the Communications Act of 1934 (48 Stat. 1143; 47 U.S.C. 605) shall limit the constitutional power of the President to take such measures as he deems necessary to protect the Nation against actual or potential attack or other hostile acts of a foreign power, to obtain foreign intelligence information deemed essential to the security of the United States, or to protect national security information against foreign intelligence activities. Nor shall anything contained in this chapter be deemed to limit the constitutional power of the President to take such measures as he deems necessary to protect the United States against the overthrow of the Government by force or other unlawful means, or against any other clear and present danger to the structure or existence of the Government. The contents of any wire or oral communication intercepted by authority of the President in the exercise of the foregoing powers may be received in evidence in any trial hearing, or other proceeding only where such interception was reasonable, and shall not be otherwise used or disclosed except as is necessary to implement that power.

"§ 2512. Manufacture, distribution, possession, and advertising of wire or oral communication intercepting devices prohibited

"(1) Except as otherwise specifically provided in this chapter, any person who willfully—

"(a) sends through the mail, or sends or carries in interstate or foreign commerce, any electronic, mechanical, or other device, knowing or having reason to know that the design of such device renders it primarily useful for the purpose of the surreptitious interception of wire or oral communications;

"(b) manufactures, assembles, possesses, or sells any electronic, mechanical, or other device, knowing or having reason to know that the design of such device renders it primarily useful for the purpose of the surreptitious interception of wire or oral communications, and that such device or any component thereof has been or will be sent through the mail or transported in interstate or foreign commerce; or

"(c) places in any newspaper, magazine, handbill, or other publication any advertisement of—

"(i) any electronic, mechanical, or other device knowing or having reason to know that the design of such device renders it primarily useful for the purpose of the surreptitious interception of wire or oral communications; or

"(ii) any other electronic, mechanical, or other device, where such advertisement promotes the use of such device for the purpose of the surreptitious interception of wire or oral communications,

knowing or having reason to know that such advertisement will be sent through the mail or transported in interstate or foreign commerce,

shall be fined not more than $10,000 or imprisoned not more than five years, or both.

"(2) It shall not be unlawful under this section for—

"(a) a communications common carrier or an officer, agent, or employee of, or a person under contract with, a communications common carrier, in the normal course of the communications common carrier's business, or

"(b) an officer, agent, or employee of, or a person under contract with, the United States, a State, or a political subdivision thereof, in the normal course of the activities of the United States, a State, or a political subdivision thereof, to send through the mail, send or carry in interstate or foreign commerce, or manufacture, assemble, possess, or sell any electronic, mechanical, or other device knowing or having reason to know that the design of such device renders it primarily useful for the purpose of the surreptitious interception of wire or oral communications.

"§ 2513. Confiscation of wire or oral communication intercepting devices

"Any electronic, mechanical, or other device used, sent, carried, manufactured, assembled, possessed, sold, or advertised in violation of section 2511 or section 2512 of this chapter may be seized and forfeited to the United States. All provisions of law relating to (1) the seizure, summary and judicial forfeiture, and condemnation of vessels, vehicles, merchandise, and baggage for violations of the customs laws contained in title 19 of the United States Code, (2) the disposition of such vessels, vehicles, merchandise, and baggage or the proceeds from the sale thereof, (3) the remission or mitigation of such forfeiture, (4) the compromise of claims, and (5) the award of compensation to informers in respect of such forfeitures, shall apply to seizures and forfeitures incurred, or alleged to have been incurred, under the provisions of this section, insofar as applicable and not inconsistent with the provisions of this section; except that such duties as are imposed upon the collector of customs or any other person with respect to the seizure and forfeiture of vessels, vehicles, merchandise, and baggage under the provisions of the customs laws contained in title 19 of the United States Code shall be performed with respect to seizure and forfeiture of electronic, mechanical, or other intercepting devices under this section by such officers, agents, or other persons as may be authorized or designated for that purpose by the Attorney General.

Repealed, see p. 267

"§ 2514. Immunity of witnesses

"Whenever in the judgment of a United States attorney the testimony of any witness, or the production of books, papers, or other evidence by any witness, in any case or proceeding before any grand jury or court of the United States involving any violation of this chapter or any of the offenses enumerated in section 2516, or any conspiracy to violate this chapter or any of the offenses enumerated in section 2516 is necessary to the public interest, such United States attorney, upon the approval of the Attorney General, shall make application to the court that the witness shall be instructed to testify or produce evidence subject to the provisions of this section, and upon order of the court such witness shall not be excused from testifying or from producing books, papers, or other evidence on the ground that the testimony or evidence required of him may tend to incriminate him or subject him to a penalty or forfeiture. No such witness shall be prosecuted or subjected to any penalty or forfeiture for or on account of any transaction, matter or thing concerning which he is compelled, after having claimed his privilege against self-incrimination, to testify or produce evidence, nor shall testimony so compelled be used as evidence in any criminal proceeding (except in a proceeding described in the next sentence) against him in any court. No witness shall be exempt under this section from prosecution for perjury or contempt committed while giving testimony or producing evidence under compulsion as provided in this section.

"§ 2515. Prohibition of use as evidence of intercepted wire or oral communications

"Whenever any wire or oral communication has been intercepted, no part of the contents of such communication and no evidence derived therefrom may be received in evidence in any trial, hearing, or other proceeding in or before any court, grand jury, department, officer, agency, regulatory body, legislative committee, or other authority of the United States, a State, or a political subdivision thereof if the disclosure of that information would be in violation of this chapter.

"§ 2516. Authorization for interception of wire or oral communications

"(1) The Attorney General, or any Assistant Attorney General specially designated by the Attorney General, may authorize an application to a Federal judge of competent jurisdiction for, and such judge may grant in conformity with section 2518 of this chapter an order authorizing or approving the interception of wire or oral communications by the Federal Bureau of Investigation, or a Federal agency having responsibility for the investigation of the offense as to which the application is made, when such interception may provide or has provided evidence of—

"(a) any offense punishable by death or by imprisonment for more than one year under sections 2274 through 2277 of title 42 of the United States Code (relating to the enforcement of the Atomic Energy Act of 1954), or under the following chapters of this title: chapter 37 (relating to espionage), chapter 105 (relating to sabotage), chapter 115 (relating to treason), or chapter 102 (relating to riots);

"(b) a violation of section 186 or section 501(c) of title 29, United States Code (dealing with restrictions on payments and loans to labor organizations), or any offense which involves murder, kidnapping, robbery, or extortion, and which is punishable under this title;

"(c) any offense which is punishable under the following sec- Amended, see p. 268tions of this title: section 201 (bribery of public officials and witnesses), section 224 (bribery in sporting contests), section 1084 (transmission of wagering information), section 1503 (influencing or injuring an officer, juror, or witness generally), section 1510 (obstruction of criminal investigations), section 1751 (Presidential assassinations, kidnapping, and assault), section 1951 (interference with commerce by threats or violence), section 1952 (interstate and foreign travel or transportation in aid of racketeering enterprises), section 1954 (offer, acceptance, or solicitation to influence operations of employee benefit plan), section 659 (theft from interstate shipment), section 664 (embezzlement from pension and welfare funds), or sections 2314 and 2315 (interstate transportation of stolen property);

"(d) any offense involving counterfeiting punishable under section 471, 472, or 473 of this title;

"(e) any offense involving bankruptcy fraud or the manufacture, importation, receiving, concealment, buying, selling, or otherwise dealing in narcotic drugs, marihuana, or other dangerous drugs, punishable under any law of the United States;

"(f) any offense including extortionate credit transactions under sections 892, 893, or 894 of this title; or

"(g) any conspiracy to commit any of the foregoing offenses.

"(2) The principal prosecuting attorney of any State, or the principal prosecuting attorney of any political subdivision thereof, if such attorney is authorized by a statute of that State to make application to a State court judge of competent jurisdiction for an order authorizing or approving the interception of wire or oral communications, may apply to such judge for, and such judge may grant in conformity with section 2518 of this chapter and with the applicable State statute an order authorizing, or approving the interception of wire or oral communications by investigative or law enforcement officers having responsibility for the investigation of the offense as to which the application is made, when such interception may provide or has provided evidence of the commission of the offense of murder, kidnapping, gambling, robbery, bribery, extortion, or dealing in narcotic drugs, marihuana or other dangerous drugs, or other crime dangerous to life, limb, or property, and punishable by imprisonment for more than one year, designated in any applicable State statute authorizing such interception, or any conspiracy to commit any of the foregoing offenses.

"§ 2517. Authorization for disclosure and use of intercepted wire or oral communications

"(1) Any investigative or law enforcement officer who, by any means authorized by this chapter, has obtained knowledge of the contents of any wire or oral communication, or evidence derived therefrom, may disclose such contents to another investigative or law enforcement officer to the extent that such disclosure is appropriate to the proper performance of the official duties of the officer making or receiving the disclosure.

"(2) Any investigative or law enforcement officer who, by any means authorized by this chapter, has obtained knowledge of the contents of any wire or oral communication or evidence derived therefrom may use such contents to the extent such use is appropriate to the proper performance of his official duties.

"(3) Any person who has received, by any means authorized by Amended, see p. 268this chapter, any information concerning a wire or oral communica-

Amended,
see p. 268

tion, or evidence derived therefrom intercepted in accordance with the provisions of this chapter may disclose the contents of that communication or such derivative evidence while giving testimony under oath or affirmation in any criminal proceeding in any court of the United States or of any State or in any Federal or State grand jury proceeding.

"(4) No otherwise privileged wire or oral communication intercepted in accordance with, or in violation of, the provisions of this chapter shall lose its privileged character.

"(5) When an investigative or law enforcement officer, while engaged in intercepting wire or oral communications in the manner authorized herein, intercepts wire or oral communications relating to offenses other than those specified in the order of authorization or approval, the contents thereof, and evidence derived therefrom, may be disclosed or used as provided in subsections (1) and (2) of this section. Such contents and any evidence derived therefrom may be used under subsection (3) of this section when authorized or approved by a judge of competent jurisdiction where such judge finds on subsequent application that the contents were otherwise intercepted in accordance with the provisions of this chapter. Such application shall be made as soon as practicable.

"§ 2518. Procedure for interception of wire or oral communications

"(1) Each application for an order authorizing or approving the interception of a wire or oral communication shall be made in writing upon oath or affirmation to a judge of competent jurisdiction and shall state the applicant's authority to make such application. Each application shall include the following information:

"(a) the identity of the investigative or law enforcement officer making the application, and the officer authorizing the application;

"(b) a full and complete statement of the facts and circumstances relied upon by the applicant, to justify his belief that an order should be issued, including (i) details as to the particular offense that has been, is being, or is about to be committed, (ii) a particular description of the nature and location of the facilities from which or the place where the communication is to be intercepted, (iii) a particular description of the type of communications sought to be intercepted, (iv) the identity of the person, if known, committing the offense and whose communications are to be intercepted;

"(c) a full and complete statement as to whether or not other investigative procedures have been tried and failed or why they reasonably appear to be unlikely to succeed if tried or to be too dangerous;

"(d) a statement of the period of time for which the interception is required to be maintained. If the nature of the investigation is such that the authorization for interception should not automatically terminate when the described type of communication has been first obtained, a particular description of facts establishing probable cause to believe that additional communications of the same type will occur thereafter;

"(e) a full and complete statement of the facts concerning all previous applications known to the individual authorizing and making the application, made to any judge for authorization to intercept, or for approval of interceptions of, wire or oral communications involving any of the same persons, facilities or places specified in the application, and the action taken by the judge on each such application; and

"(f) where the application is for the extension of an order, a statement setting forth the results thus far obtained from the interception, or a reasonable explanation of the failure to obtain such results.

"(2) The judge may require the applicant to furnish additional testimony or documentary evidence in support of the application.

"(3) Upon such application the judge may enter an ex parte order, as requested or as modified, authorizing or approving interception of wire or oral communications within the territorial jurisdiction of the court in which the judge is sitting, if the judge determines on the basis of the facts submitted by the applicant that—

"(a) there is probable cause for belief that an individual is committing, has committed, or is about to commit a particular offense enumerated in section 2516 of this chapter;

"(b) there is probable cause for belief that particular communications concerning that offense will be obtained through such interception;

"(c) normal investigative procedures have been tried and have failed or reasonably appear to be unlikely to succeed if tried or to be too dangerous;

"(d) there is probable cause for belief that the facilities from which, or the place where, the wire or oral communications are to be intercepted are being used, or are about to be used, in connection with the commission of such offense, or are leased to, listed in the name of, or commonly used by such person.

"(4) Each order authorizing or approving the interception of any wire or oral communication shall specify— Amended, see p. 268

"(a) the identity of the person, if known, whose communications are to be intercepted;

"(b) the nature and location of the communications facilities as to which, or the place where, authority to intercept is granted;

"(c) a particular description of the type of communication sought to be intercepted, and a statement of the particular offense to which it relates;

"(d) the identity of the agency authorized to intercept the communications, and of the person authorizing the application; and

"(e) the period of time during which such interception is authorized, including a statement as to whether or not the interception shall automatically terminate when the described communication has been first obtained.

"(5) No order entered under this section may authorize or approve the interception of any wire or oral communication for any period longer than is necessary to achieve the objective of the authorization, nor in any event longer than thirty days. Extensions of an order may be granted, but only upon application for an extension made in accordance with subsection (1) of this section and the court making the findings required by subsection (3) of this section. The period of extension shall be no longer than the authorizing judge deems necessary to achieve the purposes for which it was granted and in no event for longer than thirty days. Every order and extension thereof shall contain a provision that the authorization to intercept shall be executed as soon as practicable, shall be conducted in such a way as to minimize the interception of communications not otherwise subject to interception under this chapter, and must terminate upon attainment of the authorized objective, or in any event in thirty days.

"(6) Whenever an order authorizing interception is entered pursuant to this chapter, the order may require reports to be made to the judge who issued the order showing what progress has been made toward achievement of the authorized objective and the need for continued interception. Such reports shall be made at such intervals as the judge may require.

"(7) Notwithstanding any other provision of this chapter, any investigative or law enforcement officer, specially designated by the Attorney General or by the principal prosecuting attorney of any State or subdivision thereof acting pursuant to a statute of that State, who reasonably determines that—

"(a) an emergency situation exists with respect to conspiratorial activities threatening the national security interest or to conspiratorial activities characteristic of organized crime that requires a wire or oral communication to be intercepted before an order authorizing such interception can with due diligence be obtained, and

"(b) there are grounds upon which an order could be entered under this chapter to authorize such interception,

may intercept such wire or oral communication if an application for an order approving the interception is made in accordance with this section within forty-eight hours after the interception has occurred, or begins to occur. In the absence of an order, such interception shall immediately terminate when the communication sought is obtained or when the application for the order is denied, whichever is earlier. In the event such application for approval is denied, or in any other case where the interception is terminated without an order having been issued, the contents of any wire or oral communication intercepted shall be treated as having been obtained in violation of this chapter, and an inventory shall be served as provided for in subsection (d) of this section on the person named in the application.

"(8) (a) The contents of any wire or oral communication intercepted by any means authorized by this chapter shall, if possible, be recorded on tape or wire or other comparable device. The recording of the contents of any wire or oral communication under this subsection shall be done in such way as will protect the recording from editing or other alterations. Immediately upon the expiration of the period of the order, or extensions thereof, such recordings shall be made available to the judge issuing such order and sealed under his directions. Custody of the recordings shall be wherever the judge orders. They shall not be destroyed except upon an order of the issuing or denying judge and in any event shall be kept for ten years. Duplicate recordings may be made for use or disclosure pursuant to the provisions of subsections (1) and (2) of section 2517 of this chapter for investigations. The presence of the seal provided for by this subsection, or a satisfactory explanation for the absence thereof, shall be a prerequisite for the use or disclosure of the contents of any wire or oral communication or evidence derived therefrom under subsection (3) of section 2517.

"(b) Applications made and orders granted under this chapter shall be sealed by the judge. Custody of the applications and orders shall be wherever the judge directs. Such applications and orders shall be disclosed only upon a showing of good cause before a judge of competent jurisdiction and shall not be destroyed except on order of the issuing or denying judge, and in any event shall be kept for ten years.

"(c) Any violation of the provisions of this subsection may be punished as contempt of the issuing or denying judge.

"(d) Within a reasonable time but not later than ninety days after the filing of an application for an order of approval under section

2518(7)(b) which is denied or the termination of the period of an order or extensions thereof, the issuing or denying judge shall cause to be served, on the persons named in the order or the application, and such other parties to intercepted communications as the judge may determine in his discretion that is in the interest of justice, an inventory which shall include notice of—

"(1) the fact of the entry of the order or the application;

"(2) the date of the entry and the period of authorized, approved or disapproved interception, or the denial of the application; and

"(3) the fact that during the period wire or oral communications were or were not intercepted.

The judge, upon the filing of a motion, may in his discretion make available to such person or his counsel for inspection such portions of the intercepted communications, applications and orders as the judge determines to be in the interest of justice. On an ex parte showing of good cause to a judge of competent jurisdiction the serving of the inventory required by this subsection may be postponed.

"(9) The contents of any intercepted wire or oral communication or evidence derived therefrom shall not be received in evidence or otherwise disclosed in any trial, hearing, or other proceeding in a Federal or State court unless each party, not less than ten days before the trial, hearing, or proceeding, has been furnished with a copy of the court order, and accompanying application, under which the interception was authorized or approved. This ten-day period may be waived by the judge if he finds that it was not possible to furnish the party with the above information ten days before the trial, hearing, or proceeding and that the party will not be prejudiced by the delay in receiving such information.

"(10)(a) Any aggrieved person in any trial, hearing, or proceeding in or before any court, department, officer, agency, regulatory body, or other authority of the United States, a State, or a political subdivision thereof, may move to suppress the contents of any intercepted wire or oral communication, or evidence derived therefrom, on the grounds that—

"(i) the communication was unlawfully intercepted;

"(ii) the order of authorization or approval under which it was intercepted is insufficient on its face; or

"(iii) the interception was not made in conformity with the order of authorization or approval.

Such motion shall be made before the trial, hearing, or proceeding unless there was no opportunity to make such motion or the person was not aware of the grounds of the motion. If the motion is granted, the contents of the intercepted wire or oral communication, or evidence derived therefrom, shall be treated as having been obtained in violation of this chapter. The judge, upon the filing of such motion by the aggrieved person, may in his discretion make available to the aggrieved person or his counsel for inspection such portions of the intercepted communication or evidence derived therefrom as the judge determines to be in the interests of justice.

"(b) In addition to any other right to appeal, the United States shall have the right to appeal from an order granting a motion to suppress made under paragraph (a) of this subsection, or the denial of an application for an order of approval, if the United States attorney shall certify to the judge or other official granting such motion or denying such application that the appeal is not taken for purposes of delay. Such appeal shall be taken within thirty days after the date the order was entered and shall be diligently prosecuted.

"§ 2519. Reports concerning intercepted wire or oral communications

"(1) Within thirty days after the expiration of an order (or each extension thereof) entered under section 2518, or the denial of an order approving an interception, the issuing or denying judge shall report to the Administrative Office of the United States Courts—

"(a) the fact that an order or extension was applied for;

"(b) the kind of order or extension applied for;

"(c) the fact that the order or extension was granted as applied for, was modified, or was denied;

"(d) the period of interceptions authorized by the order, and the number and duration of any extensions of the order;

"(e) the offense specified in the order or application, or extension of an order;

"(f) the identity of the applying investigative or law enforcement officer and agency making the application and the person authorizing the application; and

"(g) the nature of the facilities from which or the place where communications were to be intercepted.

"(2) In January of each year the Attorney General, an Assistant Attorney General specially designated by the Attorney General, or the principal prosecuting attorney of a State, or the principal prosecuting attorney for any political subdivision of a State, shall report to the Administrative Office of the United States Courts—

"(a) the information required by paragraphs (a) through (g) of subsection (1) of this section with respect to each application for an order or extension made during the preceding calendar year;

"(b) a general description of the interceptions made under such order or extension, including (i) the approximate nature and frequency of incriminating communications intercepted, (ii) the approximate nature and frequency of other communications intercepted, (iii) the approximate number of persons whose communications were intercepted, and (iv) the approximate nature, amount, and cost of the manpower and other resources used in the interceptions;

"(c) the number of arrests resulting from interceptions made under such order or extension, and the offenses for which arrests were made;

"(d) the number of trials resulting from such interceptions;

"(e) the number of motions to suppress made with respect to such interceptions, and the number granted or denied;

"(f) the number of convictions resulting from such interceptions and the offenses for which the convictions were obtained and a general assessment of the importance of the interceptions; and

"(g) the information required by paragraphs (b) through (f) of this subsection with respect to orders or extensions obtained in a preceding calendar year.

"(3) In April of each year the Director of the Administrative Office of the United States Courts shall transmit to the Congress a full and complete report concerning the number of applications for orders authorizing or approving the interception of wire or oral communications and the number of orders and extensions granted or denied during the preceding calendar year. Such report shall include a summary and analysis of the data required to be filed with the Administrative Office by subsections (1) and (2) of this section. The Director of the Administrative Office of the United States Courts is authorized to issue binding regulations dealing with the content and form of the reports required to be filed by subsections (1) and (2) of this section.

"§ 2520. Recovery of civil damages authorized

Amended, see p. 269

"Any person whose wire or oral communication is intercepted, disclosed, or used in violation of this chapter shall (1) have a civil cause of action against any person who intercepts, discloses, or uses, or procures any other person to intercept, disclose, or use such communications, and (2) be entitled to recover from any such person—

"(a) actual damages but not less than liquidated damages computed at the rate of $100 a day for each day of violation or $1,000, whichever is higher;

"(b) punitive damages; and

"(c) a reasonable attorney's fee and other litigation costs reasonably incurred.

A good faith reliance on a court order or on the provisions of section 2518(7) of this chapter shall constitute a complete defense to any civil or criminal action brought under this chapter."

Sec. 803. Section 605 of the Communications Act of 1934 (48 Stat. 1103; 47 U.S.C. 605) is amended to read as follows:

"UNAUTHORIZED PUBLICATION OF COMMUNICATIONS

"Sec. 605. Except as authorized by chapter 119, title 18, United States Code, no person receiving, assisting in receiving, transmitting, or assisting in transmitting, any interstate or foreign communication by wire or radio shall divulge or publish the existence, contents, substance, purport, effect, or meaning thereof, except through authorized channels of transmission or reception, (1) to any person other than the addressee, his agent, or attorney, (2) to a person employed or authorized to forward such communication to its destination, (3) to proper accounting or distributing officers of the various communicating centers over which the communication may be passed, (4) to the master of a ship under whom he is serving, (5) in response to a subpena issued by a court of competent jurisdiction, or (6) on demand of other lawful authority. No person not being authorized by the sender shall intercept any radio communication and divulge or publish the existence, contents, substance, purport, effect, or meaning of such intercepted communication to any person. No person not being entitled thereto shall receive or assist in receiving any interstate or foreign communication by radio and use such communication (or any information therein contained) for his own benefit or for the benefit of another not entitled thereto. No person having received any intercepted radio communication or having become acquainted with the contents, substance, purport, effect, or meaning of such communication (or any part thereof) knowing that such communication was intercepted, shall divulge or publish the existence, contents, substance, purport, effect, or meaning of such communication (or any part thereof) or use such communication (or any information therein contained) for his own benefit or for the benefit of another not entitled thereto. This section shall not apply to the receiving, divulging, publishing, or utilizing the contents of any radio communication which is broadcast or transmitted by amateurs or others for the use of the general public, or which relates to ships in distress."

Sec. 804. (a) There is hereby established a National Commission for the Review of Federal and State Laws Relating to Wiretapping and Electronic Surveillance (hereinafter in this section referred to as the "Commission").

(b) The Commission shall be composed of fifteen members appointed as follows:

(A) Four appointed by the President of the Senate from Members of the Senate;

(B) Four appointed by the Speaker of the House of Representatives from Members of the House of Representatives; and

(C) Seven appointed by the President of the United States from all segments of life in the United States, including lawyers, teachers, artists, businessmen, newspapermen, jurists, policemen, and community leaders, none of whom shall be officers of the executive branch of the Government.

(c) The President of the United States shall designate a Chairman from among the members of the Commission. Any vacancy in the Commission shall not affect its powers but shall be filled in the same manner in which the original appointment was made.

(d) It shall be the duty of the Commission to conduct a comprehensive study and review of the operation of the provisions of this title, in effect on the effective date of this section, to determine the effectiveness of such provisions during the six-year period immediately following the date of their enactment.

(e)(1) Subject to such rules and regulations as may be adopted by the Commission, the Chairman shall have the power to—

(A) appoint and fix the compensation of an Executive Director, and such additional staff personnel as he deems necessary, without regard to the provisions of title 5, United States Code, governing appointments in the competitive service, and without regard to the provisions of chapter 51 and subchapter III of chapter 53 of such title relating to classification and General Schedule pay rates, but at rates not in excess of the maximum rate for GS–18 of the General Schedule under section 5332 of such title; and

(B) procure temporary and intermittent services to the same extent as is authorized by section 3109 of title 5, United States Code, but at rates not to exceed $100 a day for individuals.

(2) In making appointments pursuant to paragraph (1) of this subsection, the Chairman shall include among his appointment individuals determined by the Chairman to be competent social scientists, lawyers, and law enforcement officers.

(f)(1) A member of the Commission who is a Member of Congress shall serve without additional compensation, but shall be reimbursed for travel, subsistence, and other necessary expenses incurred in the performance of duties vested in the Commission.

(2) A member of the Commission from private life shall receive $100 per diem when engaged in the actual performance of duties vested in the Commission, plus reimbursement for travel, subsistence, and other necessary expenses incurred in the performance of such duties.

Amended, see p. 269

(g) Each department, agency, and instrumentality of the executive branch of the Government, including independent agencies, is authorized and directed to furnish to the Commission, upon request made by the Chairman, such statistical data, reports, and other information as the Commission deems necessary to carry out its functions under this section. The Chairman is further authorized to call upon the departments, agencies, and other offices of the several States to furnish such statistical data, reports, and other information as the Commission deems necessary to carry out its functions under this section.

Amended, see p. 270

(h) The Commission shall make such interim reports as it deems advisable, and it shall make a final report of its findings and recommendations to the President of the United States and to the Congress within the one-year period following the effective date of this subsection. Sixty days after submission of its final report, the Commission shall cease to exist.

(i) (1) Except as provided in paragraph (2) of this subsection, any member of the Commission is exempted, with respect to his appointment, from the operation of sections 203, 205, 207, and 209 of title 18, United States Code.

(2) The exemption granted by paragraph (1) of this subsection shall not extend—

(A) to the receipt of payment of salary in connection with the appointee's Government service from any source other than the private employer of the appointee at the time of his appointment, or

(B) during the period of such appointment, to the prosecution, by any person so appointed, of any claim against the Government involving any matter with which such person, during such period, is or was directly connected by reason of such appointment.

(j) There is authorized to be appropriated such sum as may be necessary to carry out the provisions of this section.

(k) The foregoing provisions of this section shall take effect upon the expiration of the six-year period immediately following the date of the enactment of this Act.

Amended, see p. 270

AMENDMENTS TO TITLE III

§2511. Interception and disclosure of wire or oral communications prohibited

. . . .

(2) (a) (i) It shall not be unlawful under this chapter for an operator of a switchboard, or an officer, employee, or agent of any communication common carrier, whose facilities are used in the transmission of a wire communication, to intercept, disclose, or use that communication in the normal course of his employment while engaged in any activity which is a necessary incident to the rendition of his service or to the protection of the rights or property of the carrier of such communication: *Provided,* That said communication common carriers shall not utilize service observing or random monitoring except for mechanical or service quality control checks.

(ii) It shall not be unlawful under this chapter for an officer, employee, or agent of any communication common carrier to provide information, facilities, or technical assistance to an investigative or law enforcement officer who, pursuant to this chapter, is authorized to intercept a wire or oral communication.

As amended Pub.L. 91–358, Title II, §211(a), July 29, 1970, 84 Stat. 654.

. . . .

§2514. Immunity of witnesses

REPEAL

Pub.L. 91–452, Title II, §§227(a), 260, Oct. 15, 1970, 84 Stat. 930, 931, repealed this section effective four years following the sixtieth day after the date of the enactment of Pub.L. 91–452, which was approved Oct. 15, 1970, with such repeal not to affect any immunity to which any individual is entitled hereunder by reason of any testimony or other information given before such day. See section 260 of Pub.L. 91–452, set out as a note under section 6001 of this title.

§2516. Authorization for interception of wire or oral communications

(1) The Attorney General, or any Assistant Attorney General specially designated by the Attorney General, may authorize an application to a Federal judge of competent jurisdiction for, and such judge may grant in conformity with section 2518 of this chapter an order authorizing or approving the interception of wire or oral communications by the Federal Bureau of Investigation, or a Federal agency having responsibility for the investigation of the offense as to which the application is made, when such interception may provide or has provided evidence of—

* * * * * * * * * * *

(c) any offense which is punishable under the following sections of this title: section 201 (bribery of public officials and witnesses), section 224 (bribery in sporting contests), subsection (d), (e), (f), (g), (h) or (i) of section 844 (unlawful use of explosives), section 1084 (transmission of wagering information), section 1503 (influencing or injuring an officer, juror, or witness generally), section 1510 (obstruction of criminal investigations), section 1511 (obstruction of State or local law enforcement), section 1751 (Presidential assassinations, kidnapping, and assault), section 1951 (interference with commerce by threats or violence), section 1952 (interstate and foreign travel or transportation in aid of racketeering enterprises), section 1954 (offer, acceptance, or solicitation to influence operations of employee benefit plan), section 1955 (prohibition of business enterprises of gambling), section 659 (theft from interstate shipment), section 664 (embezzlement from pension and welfare funds), or section 2314 and 2315 (interstate transportation of stolen property), section 1963 (violations with respect to racketeer influenced and corrupt organizations), or section 351 (violations with respect to Congressional assassinations, kidnapping and assault).

As amended Pub.L. 91–452, Title VIII, §810, Title IX, §902(a), Title XI, §1103, Oct. 15, 1970, 84 Stat. 940, 947, 959, Pub.L. 91–644, Title IV, Jan. 2, 1971, 84 Stat. 1891.

* * * * * * * * * *

§2517. Authorization for disclosure and use of intercepted wire or oral communications

* * * * * * * * * *

(3) Any person who has received, by any means authorized by this chapter, any information concerning a wire or oral communication, or evidence derived therefrom intercepted in accordance with the provisions of this chapter may disclose the contents of that communication or such derivative evidence while giving testimony under oath or affirmation in any proceeding held under the authority of the United States or of any State or political subdivision thereof.

As amended Pub.L. 91–452, Title IX, §902(b) Oct. 15, 1970, 84 Stat. 947.

* * * * * * * * *

§2518. Procedure for interception of wire or oral communications

* * * * * * * *

(4) Each order authorizing or approving the interception of any wire or oral communication shall specify—

* * * * * * * *

An order authorizing the interception of a wire or oral communication shall, upon request of the applicant, direct that a communication common carrier, landlord, custodian or other person shall furnish the applicant forthwith all information, facilities, and technical assistance necessary to accomplish the interception unobtrusively and with a minimum of interference with the services that such carrier, landlord, custodian, or person is according the person whose communications are to be

intercepted. Any communication common carrier, landlord, custodian or other person furnishing such facilities or technical assistance shall be compensated therefor by the applicant at the prevailing rates.   •
As amended Pub.L. 91–358, Title II, § 211(b), July 29, 1970, 84 Stat. 654.

•   •   •   •   •   •   •   •   •   •

§2520. Recovery of civil damages authorized

Any person whose wire or oral communication is intercepted, disclosed, or used in violation of this chapter shall (1) have a civil cause of action against any person who intercepts, discloses, or uses, or procures any other person to intercept, disclose, or use such communications, and (2) be entitled to recover from any such person—

(a) actual damages but not less than liquidated damages computed at the rate of $100 a day for each day of violation or $1,000, whichever is higher;

(b) punitive damages; and

(c) a reasonable attorney's fee and other litigation costs reasonably incurred.

A good faith reliance on a court order or legislative authorization shall constitute a complete defense to any civil or criminal action brought under this chapter or under any other law.
As amended Pub.L. 91–358, Title II, §211(c), July 29, 1970, 84 Stat. 654.

Omnibus Crime Control Act of 1970
Pub.L. 91–644; 84 Stat. 880

TITLE VI—WIRETAP COMMISSION

Sec. 20. (a) Title III of the Omnibus Crime Control and Safe Streets Act of 1968 (82 Stat. 211) is amended by striking subsection (g) of section 804 and inserting the following:

"(g) (1) The Commission or any duly authorized subcommittee or member thereof may, for the purpose of carrying out the provisions of this title, hold such hearings, sit and act at such times and places, administer such oaths, and require by subpena or otherwise the attendance and testimony of such witnesses and the production of such books, records, correspondence, memorandums, papers and documents as the Commission or such subcommittee or member may deem advisable. Any member of the Commission may administer oaths or affirmations to witnesses appearing before the Commission or before such subcommittee or member. Subpenas may be issued under the signature of the Chairman or any duly designated member of the Commission, and may be served by any person designated by the Chairman or such member.

"(2) In the case of contumacy or refusal to obey a subpena issued under subsection (1) by any person who resides, is found, or transacts business within the jurisdiction of any district court of the United States, the district court, at the request of the Chairman of the Commission, shall have jurisdiction to issue to such person an order requiring such person to appear before the Commission or a subcommittee or member thereof, there to produce evidence if so ordered, or there to give testimony touching the matter under inquiry. Any failure of any such person to obey any such order of the court may be punished by the court as a contempt thereof.

"(3) The Commission shall be 'an agency of the United States' under subsection (1), section 6001, title 18, United States Code for the purpose of granting immunity to witnesses.

"(4) Each department, agency, and instrumentality of the executive branch of the Government, including independent agencies, is authorized and directed to furnish to the Commission, upon request made by the Chairman, on a reimbursable basis or otherwise, such statistical data, reports, and other information as the Commission deems necessary to carry out its functions under this title. The Chairman is further authorized to call upon the departments, agencies, and other offices of the several States, to furnish, on a reimbursable basis or otherwise, such statistical data, reports, and other information as the Commission deems necessary to carry out its functions under this title."

(b) Such title is further amended as follows:

(1) in subsection (h) of section 804, strike "one-year" and insert "two-year", and

(2) in subsection (k) of section 804, strike "six-year" and insert "fifth year".

(c) Section 1212 of the Organized Crime Control Act of 1970[16] is hereby repealed.

Approved January 2, 1971.

Index

Index

U.S. v. Ripka, 239
U.S. v. Robinson, 184, 238
U.S. v. Scott, 87, 187, 235, 239
U.S. v. Sinclair, 236
U.S. v. Sklaroff, 185, 186, 187, 189, 190, 237, 238
U.S. v. Smith, 239
U.S. v. Tantillo, 170, 210, 212, 238
U.S. v. Tortorello, 150, 154, 237
U.S. v. U.S. District Court, 225, 233, 234, 236, 239
  concurring opinions, 101, 221
  loophole in, 105
  opinion of Supreme Court, 97
  praise of Title III in, 72
  validity of Title III cited in, 192
U.S. v. Wade, 228
U.S. v. Whitaker, 86, 185, 192, 209, 235, 238, 240
U.S. v. White, 29–32, 225, 227
U.S. v. Wolk, 231, 239
U.S. v. Wright, 235

Valachi hearings, 12
Value predisposition in evaluation, 219
Vernon, Laurens M., 225, 229, 234
Victimless crimes, 203
Video tape, 4
Vietnam War. *See* Pentagon Papers case
Vinson, Chief Justice Fred M., 103
Voice expert, 177
Voice identification, 132, 174, 176, 237

Wagering offense, 73
  See also Gambling
Walsh, William F., 84
Warrantless eavesdropping
  on antiwar activists, 96
  categories of cases for, 93
  compared with 17th century autocracy, 104
  in domestic security cases
    comment of Justice Douglas, 221
    effect on free discussion, 34
    Nixon appointees' joinder in barring, 221
    opinion of Justice Douglas, 102
    outlawed by Supreme Court, 105
    Supreme Court decision, 97
  in emergencies, 6, 94–96
  in national security cases, 6, 7, 96–105
  on newsmen, 105
  Pentagon Papers case, 88

Warrantless eavesdropping (*continued*)
  protest against, 93, 235–236
  under *Katz v. U.S.*, 95
  White House aides, 105
Warren, Chief Justice Earl, 36, 39
Warren, Samuel D., 32
Watergate
  burglarizing files of Ellsberg's psychiatrist, 89
  civil suit for bugging, 229
  eavesdropping at, 44
  effect of, 45, 48, 204, 220
  "law and order" at, 41
  resignations in wake of, 69, 89
Watkins v. U.S., 34, 228
Weiss v. U.S., 18, 226
Westin, Professor Alan F., 31, 225, 227, 228
White, Justice Byron R.
  concurrence in *U.S. v. U.S. District Court*, 101, 102
  concurring opinion in *Gelbard v. U.S.*, 193
  Katz v. U.S., 25
  dissent in
    Berger v. New York, 23, 221
    Roe v. Wade, 228
  with majority in *Katz v. U.S.*, 221
  opinion in *Griswold v. Connecticut*, 36
White collar crime, 70
"White House horrors," 44
White Panthers, 97
Wicker, Tom, 68, 232, 236
Wigmore answer to "dirty business," 103, 104
Williamson v. U.S., 227
Wilson, Will, 183
Wincanton, U.S.A., 70
Wiretapping, 3
  cable and pair numbers, 124
  cooperation of telephone company in, 123
  culmination of law on, 15
  denounced by J. Edgar Hoover, 67
  Federal control of, 5
  homicide cases, 119
  importance of, against organized crime, 74
  narcotics cases, 60
  Supreme Court decisions, 16–18
  techniques, 4
  See also Eavesdropping; Electronic surveillance
Wolf v. Colorado, 27, 28, 227
World Opium Survey, 59

13 2